W0384422

Camden Town 4

Englisch für die Realschule
und verwandte Schulformen

Diesterweg

Camden Town 4

Englisch für die Realschule und verwandte Schulformen

Erarbeitet von Natalie Beer, Deborah Berger, Lorcan Flynn, Zoe Grigoriadou, Isabel Kombartzky, Barbara Shatliff, Andrea Windhausen
sowie Otfried Börner, Hannelore Debus, Ingrid Gebhard, Pat Jüngst, Phil Mothershaw-Rogalla, John Roberts, Christine Sturm und Jürgen Wrobel
Fachliche Beratung: Gabriela Patrzek, Barbara Suhr

Konzeptberatung:
Dr. phil. h.c. Christoph Edelhoff, StD a.D.,
Vorsitzender THE ENGLISH ACADEMY

Weitere Materialien zum Schülerbuch
- Workbook 4 mit Multimedia-Sprachtrainer und Audio-CD für Schüler (978-3-425-72304-4)
- Workbook 4 mit Multimedia-Sprachtrainer (978-3-425-72224-5)
- Workbook 4 mit Audio-CD für Schüler (978-3-425-72314-3)
- Workbook 4 (3-425-72214-6)
- Multimedia-Sprachtrainer 4 (978-3-425-72914-5)
- Audio-CD 4 für Schüler (978-3-425-72324-2)

Lehrer-Materialien
- Teacher's Manual 4 (978-3-425-72254-2)
- Lehrer-Software 4 (978-3-425-72274-0)
- Audio-CD 4 für Lehrer (978-3-425-72234-4)
- Copymasters 4 (978-3-425-72284-9)
- Folien 4 (978-3-425-72294-8)
- Lernerfolgskontrollen 4 mit CD-ROM (978-3-425-72264-1)

Dieses Werk folgt der reformierten Rechtschreibung und Zeichensetzung 2006. Ausnahmen bilden Texte, bei denen künstlerische, philosophische oder lizenzrechtliche Gründe einer Änderung entgegenstehen.

© 2007 Bildungshaus Schulbuchverlage
Westermann Schroedel Diesterweg
Schöningh Winklers GmbH, Braunschweig
www.diesterweg.de

Das Werk und seine Teile sind urheberrechtlich geschützt. Jede Nutzung in anderen als den gesetzlich zugelassenen Fällen bedarf der vorherigen schriftlichen Einwilligung des Verlages. Hinweis zu § 52 a UrhG: Weder das Werk noch seine Teile dürfen ohne eine solche Einwilligung gescannt und in ein Netzwerk eingestellt werden. Dies gilt auch für Intranets von Schulen und sonstigen Bildungseinrichtungen.
Auf verschiedenen Seiten dieses Buches finden sich Verweise (Links) auf Internet-Adressen. Haftungshinweis: Trotz sorgfältiger inhaltlicher Kontrolle wird die Haftung für die Inhalte der externen Seiten ausgeschlossen. Für den Inhalt dieser externen Seiten sind ausschließlich deren Betreiber verantwortlich. Sollten Sie bei dem angegebenen Inhalt des Anbieters dieser Seite auf kostenpflichtige, illegale oder anstößige Inhalte treffen, bedauern wir dies ausdrücklich und bitten Sie, uns umgehend per E-Mail davon in Kenntnis zu setzen, damit beim Nachdruck der Verweis gelöscht wird.

Druck A[1] / Jahr 2008
Alle Drucke der Serie A sind im Unterricht parallel verwendbar.

Redaktion: Demet Kömür, Daniel Shatwell und Henriette Vahle
Vokabelanhang: Dr. Wißner Verlag, Augsburg
(Redaktion: Andrea Ruf sowie Doris Bos, Hanau; Satz: Daniela Galle)
Herstellung: Harald Thumser, Frankfurt
Karten: Joachim Zwick, Gießen
Illustrationen: Christiane Hannecke, Rimpar; Ulf Marckwort, Kassel
Umschlaggestaltung: Blum Design & Kommunikation, Hamburg
Layout und Konzeption: Claudia Ehrlich, Jesse Konzept & Text GmbH, Hannover
Satz und Realisation: tiff.any GmbH, Berlin
Druck und Bindung: westermann druck GmbH, Braunschweig

ISBN 978-3-425-**72204**-7

12:00
18:00
N A D A
Albany
Moose
L. Nippigon
the
ESOTA
Lake Superior
MAINE
Augusta
Montpelier
Mohawk Reservation
NEW HAMPSHIRE
VER-MONT
Concord
MASSACHUSETTS
L. Ontario
Lake Huron
WISCONSIN
apolis
Mississippi
MICHIGAN
Lake Michigan
NEW YORK
Albany
Boston
Hartford
Providence
RHODE ISLAND
CONNECTICUT
Madison
Detroit
L. Erie
New York
NEW JERSEY
Chicago
Cleveland
PENNSYLVANIA
Trenton
Des Moines
Harrisburg
Philadelphia
INDIANA
OHIO
A M E R I C A
Dover
DELAWARE
Annapolis
Springfield
Indianapolis
Columbus
Washington D.C.
SOURI
ILLINOIS
Cincinnati
WEST VIRGINIA
MARYLAND
St. Louis
Frankfort
Richmond
Jefferson City
Ohio
VIRGINIA
KENTUCKY
Appalachian Mountains
ngfield
Raleigh
Nashville
Tennessee
NORTH CAROLINA
TENNESSEE
ARKANSAS
Memphis
SOUTH CAROLINA
Atlantic
Rock
Columbia
Mississippi
Atlanta
Ocean
MISSISSIPPI
ALABAMA
OUISIANA
Jackson
Montgomery
GEORGIA
Baton Rouge
Talahassee
Seminole Reservation
New Orleans
FLORIDA
Gulf of Mexico
ights in m
0 - 200
200 - 500
500 - 1000
1000 - 2000
> 2000
12:00 Time Zones
18:00 Time in Germany
more than 1 Mio.
less than 1 Mio.
Washington D.C. national capital
Austin capital of state
Miami
Nassau
BAHAMAS
CUBA
0 mile 125 25
0 km 250 500
HAITI

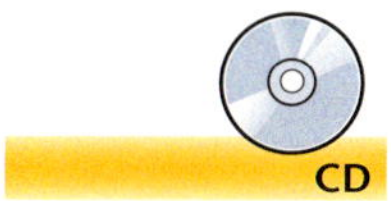

Dieser Text ist auf der Lehrer-CD.

Dieser Text ist auf der Schüler-CD.

Dieser Text ist auf beiden CDs.

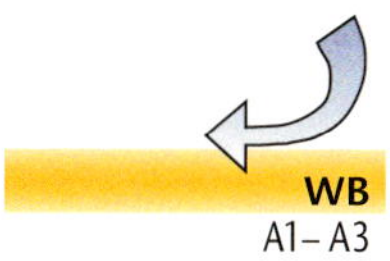

Hierzu gibt es Übungen im Workbook.

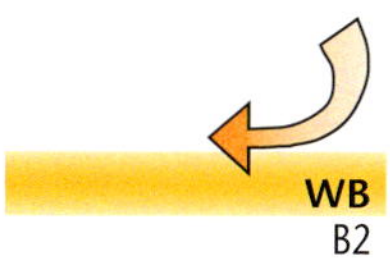

Zu dieser Übung gibt es eine Aufgabe im Workbook, die dir bei der Lösung hilft.

Auf den Skills-Seiten findest du Techniken, die dir beim Englischlernen helfen.

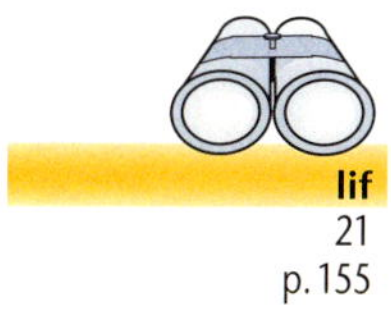

Hierzu gibt es eine Erklärung im LiF-Teil.

Diese Arbeit kannst du in deinem Portfolio-Ordner abheften.

Projekte sind Aufgaben, die ihr in Gruppen durchführen könnt.

Inhalt

Methodenkompetenzen (Skills)	Strukturen	People & places
How to read: Einen längeren Lesetext besser verstehen *How to look for information:* Im Internet nach Informationen suchen / recherchieren *How to work with words:* Das richtige englische Wort finden *How to write:* Eine kurze Meinungsäußerung / Einen Kurzkommentar schreiben *How to listen:* Einen Hörtext besser verstehen *How to mediate:* Informationen von einer Sprache in die andere übertragen	**R:** Signalwörter für die Zeiten **R:** *tenses (past perfect, present perfect, simple past, simple present, present progressive, future)* Gerundium als Subjekt des Satzes Gerundium als Objekt des Satzes **R:** Häufigkeitsadverbien Britisches und Amerikanisches Englisch	1 All about jeans
How to look for information: Im Internet nach Informationen suchen / recherchieren *How to listen:* Einen Hörtext besser verstehen *How to speak:* Etwas vortragen oder erzählen; Ein Interview vorbereiten und durchführen *How to mediate:* Informationen von einer Sprache in die andere übertragen *How to present something in class:* Eine Präsentation gestalten *How to read:* Einen längeren Lesetext besser verstehen; Einen Liedtext oder ein Gedicht interpretieren	*if*-Sätze Typ 2 Das *present perfect* mit *"since"* und *"for"* Das Gerundium nach präpositionalen Ausdrücken	
How to read: Einen Liedtext oder ein Gedicht interpretieren; Einen längeren Lesetext besser verstehen *How to listen:* Einen Hörtext besser verstehen *How to speak:* Etwas vortragen oder erzählen; Über ein Thema diskutieren *How to look for information:* Im Internet nach Informationen suchen / recherchieren *How to present something in class:* Eine Präsentation gestalten *How to work with words:* Die Bedeutung eines englischen Wortes finden *How to write:* Eine Zusammenfassung *(summary)* schreiben *How to mediate:* Informationen von einer Sprache in die andere übertragen	**R:** Die einfache Gegenwart / Die Verlaufsform der Gegenwart **R:** Die einfache Vergangenheit / Das Perfekt Das Passiv in der einfachen Gegenwart Das Passiv in der einfachen Vergangenheit Relativsätze ohne Pronomen	2 Where do these words come from?

Inhalt

Last year in Camden Town

I had forgotten to bring my compass.

JED MARSH
IN CONCERT
MARCH 14th EDINBURGH
16th NEWCASTLE
24th LONDON
27th MANCHESTER
29th LEEDS
Jed Marsh is coming to London soon.

When do we add the peas and carrots?

The Camden Gathering!
This year we thought of holding the games ourselves here at the school.

Camden Town Realschule

Classroom phrases

Wenn man mit dem Computer arbeitet

What's your e-mail address?	Wie ist deine E-Mail-Adresse?
You can click on this link.	Du kannst auf diesen Link klicken.
Can I print it out / download it?	Kann ich das ausdrucken / herunterladen?
I saved it.	Ich habe es gespeichert.
My computer has crashed.	Mein Computer ist abgestürzt.

Wenn man zusammen arbeitet oder spielt

Whose turn is it?	Wer ist dran?
I (don't) like this story.	Diese Geschichte gefällt mir (nicht).
I think it's good / interesting / funny.	Ich finde sie gut / interessant / komisch.
I think it's terrible / boring / sad.	Ich finde sie schrecklich / langweilig / traurig.
Can I be ...?	Kann ich ... sein / spielen?
Do you want to work with me?	Möchtest du mit mir arbeiten?
What do you think?	Was meinst du?
Can I borrow your pencil / dictionary / ..., please?	Kann ich mir bitte deinen Bleistift / dein Wörterbuch / ... ausleihen?
Can ... and I work together, please?	Können ... und ich bitte zusammenarbeiten?
I think we should ...	Ich finde, wir sollten / könnten ...
In my opinion ...	Meiner Meinung nach ...
What about ...?	Wie wäre es mit ...?

Wenn man Hilfe braucht

Can you spell "...", please?	Können Sie bitte „...“ buchstabieren?
Can you help me, please?	Können Sie / Kannst du mir bitte helfen?
I've got a question.	Ich habe eine Frage.
I don't understand this.	Ich verstehe das hier nicht.
How can I do this exercise?	Wie mache ich diese Aufgabe?
What's ... in English / German?	Was heißt ... auf Englisch / Deutsch?
What does ... mean?	Was bedeutet ...?
Can you write it on the blackboard, please?	Können Sie / Kannst du das bitte an die Tafel schreiben?
Can you say that again, please?	Können Sie / Kannst du das bitte noch einmal sagen?
Sorry, I don't know.	Tut mir leid, das weiß ich nicht.
What page is it on?	Auf welcher Seite ist es, bitte?

Diesterweg®

Wenn es ein Problem gibt

What's the matter with you?	Was ist mit dir los?
I'm fine.	Mir geht's gut.
I feel sick.	Mir ist schlecht.
I've got a headache.	Ich habe Kopfschmerzen.
Can I open the window, please?	Kann ich bitte das Fenster öffnen?
Can I go to the toilet, please?	Kann ich bitte zur Toilette gehen?
I'm sorry, I haven't done my homework.	Ich habe meine Hausaufgaben nicht gemacht.

Was die Lehrerin oder der Lehrer sagt

Open your books at page ...	Öffnet eure Bücher auf Seite ...
Turn to page ...	Blättert zu Seite ...
Look at line ...	Seht euch Zeile ... an.
Read the text on page ...	Lies / Lest den Text auf Seite ...
Work in pairs.	Arbeitet zu zweit.
Work in groups of four.	Arbeitet zu viert.
Sit in a circle.	Bildet einen Sitzkreis.
Listen to the CD.	Hör / Hört die CD an.
Write about ...	Schreibe / Schreibt über ...
Talk about ...	Sprich / Sprecht über ...
Ask questions about ...	Stelle / Stellt Fragen zu ...
Answer the question, please.	Beantworte / Beantwortet bitte die Frage.
Match the sentences.	Ordne / Ordnet die Sätze zu.
Who wants to read the text?	Wer möchte den Text vorlesen?
Write down the answers.	Schreibe / Schreibt die Antworten auf.
You don't have to understand everything.	Ihr braucht nicht alles zu verstehen.
Act it out.	Spiel / Spielt es vor.
Change roles.	Tauscht die Rollen.
Make your own dialogue.	Entwirf / Entwerft selbst ein Gespräch.
Take a card.	Nimm / Nehmt eine Karte.
Come to the blackboard, please.	Komm / Kommt bitte zur Tafel.
Collect the exercise books, please.	Sammelt bitte die Hefte ein.
Do this exercise at home, please.	Mache / Macht diese Aufgabe bitte zu Hause.
Please be quiet.	Sei bitte ruhig. / Seid bitte ruhig.
Please sit down.	Bitte setz dich. / Bitte setzt euch.
Please speak up.	Sprich bitte lauter.
You can do better.	Das kannst du besser.
Try again.	Versuch es noch einmal.
That's it.	Das ist alles.
Well done.	Gut gemacht.

Made in the USA 1

1

A1 American culture in your life

Have you ever been to the USA? Even if you haven't, you already know a lot about American leisure culture. This is because American inventions, free time activities and the media have always had a great influence on life in Europe.

Work in pairs. Collect information about the USA and make a word web on a poster. Use some pictures to illustrate your ideas. Then present your poster to the class.

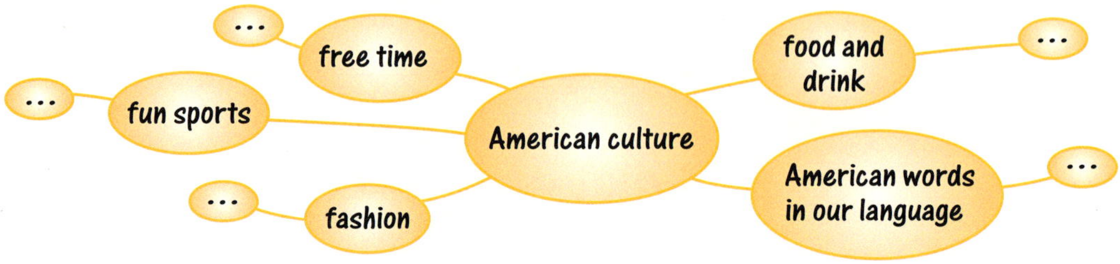

A2 How American are you?

a) Test how familiar you are with popular free time activities among teenagers in the USA. Read the following questions and answer them. Write down 0 to 5 items for each question in your exercise book.

SPORTS

Which of these sports have you played?

- O basketball
- O baseball
- O American football
- O field hockey
- O volleyball

MUSIC

Which of these singers and bands do you know?

- O REM
- O Red Hot Chilli Peppers
- O Destiny's Child
- O Madonna
- O Elvis Presley

CINEMA

Which of these movies have you seen?

- O Spider-Man
- O American Pie
- O The Matrix
- O Pirates of the Caribbean
- O Lord of the Rings

TV

Which of these shows have you watched on TV?
- O Emergency Room
- O The Simple Life
- O Charmed
- O Friends
- O The Simpsons

MEDIA

Which of these media do you often use?
- O Internet
- O TV
- O radio
- O cellphone
- O computer games

FOOD

Which of these kinds of food do you like?
- O Chinese food
- O Italian food
- O pancakes with maple syrup
- O hamburgers
- O donuts

SHOPPING

Have you ever heard of these places?
- O Gap
- O Woolworth
- O Subway
- O Foot Locker
- O Starbucks

**b) Work in groups of four.
Talk about your experiences.
Ask each other questions.
Take turns to read out your results to each other.**

Where did you see it?

I don't know The Matrix but I've seen Lord of the Rings.

lif
1, 2
p. 138

I have never / already done … • I know / don't know … • I sometimes / often / never use …

where? • what (for)? • when? • who with?

**c) Add up the number of items you have written down.
Then check how American you are:**

1. 35–24 items: Believe it or not, you are almost American.
2. 23–12 items: You have quite a lot of things in common with American teenagers.
3. 11 – 0 items: American leisure culture is not important for you.

WB
A1, A2

A3 Do all Americans eat burgers?

Rachel and Neil Mason from London are in the USA for the first time. They are spending the summer holidays with their cousins Lucy and Greg Baker in Chicago.
After a visit to the Field Museum in the morning, the children went to a busy fast food restaurant. Now they are standing in line.

CD

a) Listen to the teenagers' conversation at the restaurant. Find out
- **what Lucy and Greg think is typically British.**
- **what Rachel and Neil think is typically American.**

Take notes. Compare them to your partner's notes.

skills
How to listen
p. 122

Rachel: Not another queue! We seem to queue forever. We queued to get on top of the Sears Tower yesterday, we queued for the museum this morning and now we are queuing for something to eat.
Lucy: But queuing is typically British, isn't it? You guys must be used to it.
Neil: That's true, though it doesn't mean we always enjoy queuing.
Rachel: Right now I'm certainly not enjoying it because I'm starving.
Lucy: As you can see, we queue in the States too, but we call it "standing in line".
Greg: The food's worth it, you'll see. I know it really well because my buddy Mark has a part-time job here as a burger-flipper.
Neil: Funny, the way you say that. In England we would just say that someone works in a burger restaurant.
Rachel: I think I'll have a hot dog and an orange juice.
Neil: I'd like a double cheeseburger with fried onions, chips and a large coke. What about you?
Greg: I'll go for some nachos with salsa and cheese.
Lucy: I'll take a salad with olives and an orange juice.
Neil: What?! Don't you like burgers and coke, Lucy?
Lucy: Well, I don't go for burgers or fries and I don't like any sweet drinks. I like eating Italian food best, especially pasta.
Rachel: I thought eating burgers and drinking coke was typically American.
Greg: Maybe. But American food is more than that. At home we often eat traditional dishes like fried chicken, meat loaf or baked potatoes with vegetables. I like our mom's cooking very much.

Half an hour later they have finished lunch.
They are still sitting at their table and making plans for the afternoon.

Lucy: Mom said we could go check out the shops on North Michigan Avenue if we want to. It's very near and all the big stores are there.
Greg: Oh no, I knew you would say that!
Rachel: That's a great idea. I wanted to buy a new pair of jeans anyway, and I think they are cheaper here than at home.
Greg: Shopping is a girls' disease. What do you think, Neil?

Neil: Usually I don't mind shopping. But right now I'm a bit tired.
Lucy: You don't have to come with us, guys.
Rachel: It will be even more fun without you.
Greg: Well, how about if we went home, Neil? I could call some friends of mine and tell them to come over. You could meet Mark, the burger-flipper.
Neil: Meeting your friends would be cool. OK, let's put the trays back and make a move.
Greg: See you, girls. But don't forget to be home at five o'clock.
Lucy: What do you mean?
Greg: Mom said be home by five o'clock for tea.
Rachel: Very funny, Greg. You know I can't stand drinking tea.
Neil: Hey, the cheeseburger was really good, but I can still taste the onions.
Lucy: Want some chewing gum? I always have some with me.
Neil: Wow, I guess that's typically American.

b) Now read the story. Choose two of the four teenagers and say what you have learned about their likes and dislikes.

He / She likes ... / enjoys ...

He / She can't stand ... / hates ... / doesn't mind ...

I like our mom's cooking.
Shopping is a girls' disease.
Meeting your friends would be cool.
I can't stand drinking tea.

Language gym p. 16, ex. 1 – 3

lif 3, 4 p. 139

WB A3–A8

A4 How typical?

a) Look at the pictures and make a list of things that you think are
- **typically American and / or**
- **typically British.**

lif 3, 4, 6 p. 139, 140

1. eating fish and chips

2. drinking tea

3. cheerleading

4. gardening

5. playing baseball

6. driving big cars

7. playing soccer

8. eating sandwiches with peanut butter

9. queuing up

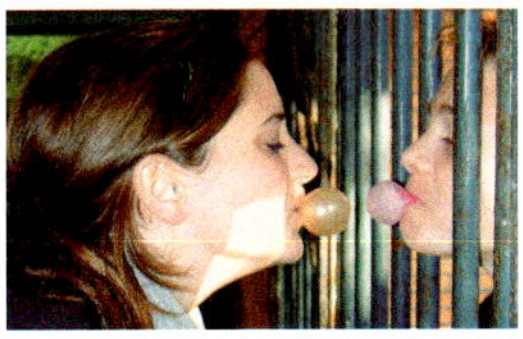
10. chewing bubble gum

... is typically American / British.
... is both typically American and typically British.
... is neither typically American nor typically British.

b) Give examples and reasons for your choices.

Example: *Eating fish and chips is typically British. You can get fish and chips everywhere in Britain.*

c) Make a list of things that you think are typical of your country and say whether or not you do them. Compare your list with your partner's.

Example: *Hiking is typically German but I never go hiking.*

WB A9

1 Language gym

1 **Look through A1–A3 and find words and phrases that mean the following:**

- comes from Britain
- something you can use to carry things
- 30 minutes after
- making food
- to queue in America
- a word for TV, radio, newspapers, magazines and the Internet
- a programme on TV in America
- you can buy things there

2 **Look at these pictures and make sentences. Use the switchboard for help.**

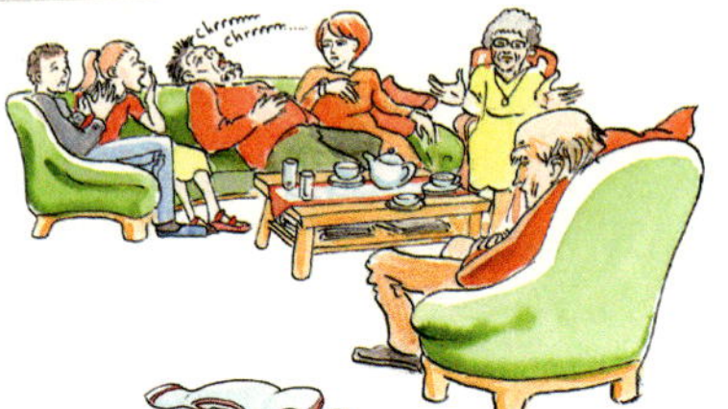

Example: *1. Chewing gum is not always fun.*

Chewing Eating Playing Being Working Having	in a shop a cheerleader American football visitors gum pasta	can be is not always	difficult. boring. easy. fun. dangerous.

portfolio

3 **Read the following poem. Then write a short poem on your own about things you love or hate doing.**

I enjoy sleeping long
But I hate waking up
to the sound of the alarm clock
I love having tea for breakfast
But I can't stand drinking it without milk
Sometimes I don't feel like going to school
But I don't mind reading all day

I enjoy ...
But I hate ...
I love ...
But I can't stand ...
Sometimes I don't feel like ...
But I don't mind ...

You have found out about how much influence American culture has on your life. You have listened to and talked about the likes and dislikes of different people. You have talked about what you think is typical of the USA, Britain and Germany.

Playing football is great.
Watching TV is boring.
I like sleeping long.
I hate cleaning my room.

Memory Box

B1 Thought bubbles

What can you do with chewing gum? Collect ideas in your class.

Start like this: *With chewing gum you can …*

B2 Chewing habits

a) Copy the table into your exercise book. Walk around in class and interview at least five classmates. Write their answers in your table. Find out who chews the most in your class.

How often do you chew gum?

name	never	rarely	sometimes	often	very often	all the time

lif 5 p. 140

b) Work in groups of four. Ask each other why you chew/don't chew chewing gum. Give reasons.

c) Report back to your class and compare the different reasons.

Simon Jenny and Derya …	never often sometimes …	chews chew	because	it's bad for the teeth. it looks silly. it helps me/him/her/them to concentrate. …

WB B1

skills
How to read
p. 124/1

B3 Something to chew on

a) Read the text and write down five things which are interesting for you. Tell your class about your ideas.

Believe it or not, chewing gum has a long history. People were chewing gum over 2,000 years ago. They all used resin from different types of trees.

In 1870 shops sold chewing gum as we know it today for the first time. Producers used *chicle,* a type of resin from the tropical South American rainforests, to make the gum. More and more companies began to enter the market with new kinds of chewing gum made from new ingredients, with new colorings and flavors.

20 years later a man named William Wrigley Jr. built a new factory in Chicago. He produced famous brands such as Wrigley's Spearmint and Juicy Fruit. The first attempts to produce bubble gum were not successful because the gum was too sticky.
Wrigley Jr. spent over $100 million on advertising. He was one of the pioneers to use ads to increase sales.
He was 29 years old and had only $32 in his pocket when he came to Chicago. William Wrigley Jr. was a millionaire when he died at the age of 71 in 1932.

Today people chew 100,000 tons of chewing gum altogether each year. And surprisingly you can find the most chewing gum factories in Turkey – not in the USA. Most people chew gum because they like the taste. Others want to lose a pound or two, so instead of eating cookies or potato chips, they chew gum. Lots of parents don't like it when their children chew gum because they don't say very much then.

By the way, this is how to keep your chewing gum fresh overnight: drop it into a glass of water!

b) Read the text again.
What do these numbers stand for?
Write complete sentences in your exercise book.

Example: William Wrigley Jr. was 29 years old when he came to Chicago.

29 | 1870 | 100,000,000 | 32

2,000 | 1932 | 20 | 100,000

WB
B2, B3

Language gym
p. 21, ex. 1+2

B4 Does your chewing gum lose its flavor on the bedpost overnight?

CD

a) Listen to the song and read along.

Oh me, oh my, oh you,
I don't know what to do.
Hallelujah! The question is peculiar.
It's got me on the go,
I'd give a lot of dough
if someone here would tell me
is it "yes" or is it "no"?

Does your chewing gum lose its flavor
on the bedpost overnight?
If you chew it in the morning,
will it be too hard to bite?
Can't you see I'm going crazy,
won't somebody put me right?
Does your chewing gum lose its flavor
on the bedpost overnight?

The nation rose as one
and sent its favorite son
to the White House,
this mighty country's lighthouse.
He saw the President,
he said that "I'd been sent
to solve the burning question
that involves the continent."

Does your chewing gum lose its flavor
on the bedpost overnight?
If you pull it out like rubber,
will it snap right back and bite?
If you paste it on the left side,
will you find it on the right?
Does your chewing gum lose its flavor
on the bedpost overnight?

Here comes the blushing bride,
the boob right at her side,
to the altar, as steady as Gibraltar.
The bridegroom has the ring,
it's such a pretty thing.
He puts it on her finger
and the choir begins to sing:

Does your chewing gum lose its flavor
on the bedpost overnight?
Would you use it on your collar
when your button's not in sight?
Put your hand beneath your seat.
And you will find it there alright.
Does your chewing gum lose its flavor
on the bedpost overnight?

b) Look at these pictures. Match them to the verses of the song. Put them in the correct order.

Ⓐ

Ⓑ

Ⓒ

c) Look at the text again. Choose the funniest lines and read them out.

WB
B4

B5 William Wrigley Jr.'s story

a) Read the story of William Wrigley Jr. Collect keywords that describe stages in his life that you think are important. Compare your results in class.

William Wrigley Jr. was born in 1861, the son of a soap maker in Philadelphia. As a boy, he walked the streets selling soap from a basket. In his early teens, he drove from town to town with a horse and wagon selling soap for his father.
At the age of 29, Wrigley arrived in Chicago with $32 and a great plan. He wanted to set up his own business. First he sold soap and later cans of baking powder. Then he started adding two packs of chewing gum to each can for free.
This was so successful that he decided to sell just chewing gum. There was strong competition but hard work and new ideas helped the company to grow. Between 1893 and 1914 Wrigley introduced Wrigley's Spearmint, Doublemint and Juicy Fruit chewing gums to the USA.
He opened factories in Canada (1910), Australia (1915) and Great Britain (1927). In 1921 he started to build the Wrigley Building, one of Chicago's first skyscrapers. It was finished in 1924 and is one of Chicago's most famous sights.
Wrigley died in 1932 as one of the most famous people in Chicago.

WB
B5, B6

skills
How to look for information
p. 133

b) Work in groups. Choose one of these people below and write a biography about their career. Check on the Internet for information. Present your results in class.

- Henry Ford
- Walt Disney
- Maurice and Richard McDonald
- John Harvey Kellogg
- Alexander Graham Bell
- John Stith Pemberton

Language gym
p. 21, ex. 3+4

B6 Ads, ads, ads

a) Look at the advertisement (ad) for chewing gum. What information does it give you? Think about the following aspects:
- modern / old-fashioned
- creative / boring / original / funny / eye-catching
- good / bad layout
- …

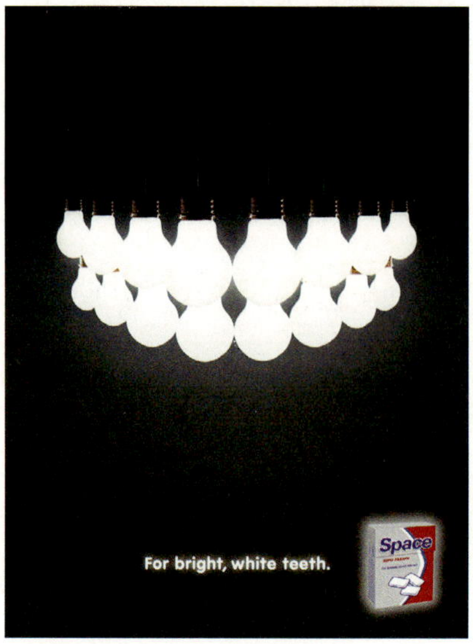

portfolio

b) Form groups of four and create an ad with a slogan for your famous person's product (B5b).

c) Show your ad to the other groups. Decide whether you would / wouldn't like to buy their product.

WB
B7–B9

1 Describe the meanings of the following words. Write them in complete sentences in your exercise book.

Example: *A pocket is like a small bag on your trousers.*

~~pocket~~ • attempt • to increase • company • pioneer • advertisement • successful

2 Some American words are different from British English. Some are just spelt differently. Make two lists under the following headings.

potato chips · cookies · colour · chips · flavor · color · film · mom · crisps · fries · flavour · mobile phone · cellphone · movie · mum · biscuits

American English (AE)	British English (BE)
flavor	flavour

3 Look at the verbs in the box. Write complete sentences. They can be silly.

Example: *Putting your chewing gum on the bedpost is great.*
I love watching …

listen to • watch • eat • drink • go • buy • play • write

4 You can find these words in B5.
Read them and write them in your exercise book.

[ˌkɒmpə'tɪʃn] · ['bɪldɪŋ] · ['bɪznəs] · ['fɑːðə] · ['bɑːskɪt] · ['fæktriz] · ['beɪkɪŋˌpaʊdə] · [ə'raɪvd] · ['skaɪˌskreɪpəz]

You have interviewed your classmates on their chewing habits. You have read about the history of chewing gum. You have written a biography and have created an ad for a product.

Memory Box

I sometimes chew chewing gum.
My parents often go to bed late.
Steven never works at home.

Going shopping is fun.
Sleeping long is my favourite hobby.
She loves reading books but she hates playing computer games.

CD

People and places 1 – All about jeans

a) How was the first pair of jeans invented? Read the text and find out.

Levi Strauss was 17 years old when he left Bavaria with his mother and two sisters and emigrated to the USA in 1847. He could only speak and understand a little English but his brothers had a job for him. He was to go from house to house selling things for kitchens in the towns near Louisville, Kentucky.

In 1849, Levi heard about the Californian Gold Rush. He decided to look for gold. He packed up everything he could sell: material used for making clothes and some canvas, a thick material used for making tents. With the money he intended to buy the equipment he would need to search for gold. However, the journey by ship from New York was so long that he had sold almost everything when he arrived in San Francisco. The canvas was all he had left. He decided to sell this cloth to people so that they could make tents – but nobody wanted to buy it. "What we need here are strong trousers," said the men who were looking for gold. Their overalls didn't last very long. So Strauss discovered his own goldmine – jeans!

He hired a tailor and started making overalls that were strong enough for the hard work. In 1853 Levi Strauss opened a warehouse and since thousands of people had already heard of his new overalls, orders started coming in from all over the country. Trying constantly to improve the quality of his jeans, Strauss started to work with a man named Jacob Davis in 1872. Together they patented a way to strengthen the jeans even more with round metal pieces (copper rivets). These jeans came out in 1873.

Strauss knew that there was an even stronger cloth made in a town in France, Nîmes, and decided to order some *serge de Nîmes* (cloth from Nîmes). But when it arrived in America, people couldn't pronounce the name and just called it denim instead. That's how his trousers became known as denims. Later, Strauss bought cloth from an Italian town, Genoa, and people called his trousers jeans.

In 1890 Strauss and his company decided to give the jeans numbers instead of names. With this, the famous jeans known as "501" were born.

Levi Strauss died on September 26, 1902, at the age of 73. But his company, Levi Strauss & Co., is still one of the largest clothing companies in the world today.

skills
How to work with words
p. 121/2

b) Explain in your own words what the statement "Strauss discovered his own gold mine" means.

c) What other products do companies make out of denim?

WB
C1

C1 Greg's summer vacation job

**a) Read Greg's letter to Neil.
Take notes of all the things Greg likes and doesn't like about his job.**

skills
How to read
p. 124/1

Dear Neil,
How are things going? Guess what? I found a summer vacation job in a department store! I can work there for all three vacation months. I know it's gonna be three really tough months but I can start saving money for next year's class trip to Florida. The department store is in a big shopping mall close to Chicago and I work on the first floor in the sports department. Everyone has to wear a black T-shirt, pants, sneakers and a baseball cap. It sure is a change from mowing lawns in the neighborhood.
I work several hours a day, five days a week and my pay is fair for my age. I work with other young people and it's a lot of fun. The work itself is usually pretty interesting. I don't like some jobs though, like taking care of the garbage, wiping shelves and cleaning the floor. That's boring. I prefer serving customers (although that can be tough sometimes too). The store motto is: 'Keep the customers satisfied!', so I always have to speak politely, help willingly and smile constantly. It can be hard sometimes, especially if I'm tired or in a bad mood.
What I don't like at all is when people come in, wander around and don't know what they want. Then I have to show them everything from ping-pong balls to golf tees. This being the States, everybody is interested in baseball. Last week an older man wanted to buy a baseball. After I had shown him several different brands, I waited patiently. He stood there in silence, looking at them. Then he quietly said: "I'd like to try them out in the dressing room." He meant it seriously! I wanted to laugh out loud, but I remembered the store's motto and stopped in time. Wanna guess what the man finally bought?
A baseball bat!
What I like most, Neil, is giving advice to customers who need me. It feels good to help out.
I'd like to work here next summer and I've already talked to the department manager about it. He said I could come back anytime I like. I'm going to, and I'll work hard. Who knows? Maybe someday I'll be the manager there.
Greetings from my family.
Greg

b) Could you imagine having a summer vacation job or part-time job? Think of possible advantages and disadvantages. Write your own list. You can work with your partner.

c) Would you like to have one of these jobs? Why? Why not? Use your notes to write a short text about the pros and cons of a summer vacation or part-time job.

babysitting
going shopping for elderly people
helping in a shop
walking dogs
mowing lawns
delivering newspapers

I prefer working …
I like … most.
I don't like … at all.
I would like to …
… but I wouldn't want to …
One of the advantages is …
A negative aspect is …
On the one hand …
On the other hand …
Finally …

lif
4
p. 139

WB
C2, C3

skills
How to write
p. 128/2

Language gym
p. 26, ex. 1+2

C2 In the sports department

CD

Greg is working in the department store.
He is helping a customer.

skills
How to listen
p. 122

a) Listen to the dialogue between Greg and the customer. What does the customer want to buy? What doesn't he buy?

b) Listen to the conversation again. Complete the following sentences.

1. The customer tells the shop assistant that he has already …
2. He wants to buy baseball equipment for his son Tom who …
3. Tom's school colors are …
4. The customer chooses red pants and a red shirt because Tom has always …
5. Finally the customer pays for …
6. He doesn't buy the … yet because next week there …

C3 Can I try it on?

skills
How to mediate
p. 126

You are in a department store in your area to buy some clothes. There is an American woman who talks in English to the shop assistant. You notice that the shop assistant doesn't understand English very well and you offer to help them.

Shop assistant: I'm sorry, aber ich verstehe Sie nicht.
You: Can I help you?
Customer: That would be very kind. I would like to try the blue skirt in size 8.
You: Die Dame möchte gerne …
Shop assistant: Das ist bei uns Größe 38. Aber wir haben diesen Rock leider nur noch in braun.
You: You need size …
Customer: Brown? Could you show me the skirt?
You: …
Shop assistant: Ja, natürlich. Einen Augenblick bitte.
You: …
Customer: I like the color. Where can I try it on?
You: …
Shop assistant: Die Umkleidekabinen sind hinten links.
You: …
Customer: Thanks for your help. Before you leave I have one more question. Can you tell me where I can find shoes?
You: …
Shop assistant: Die Schuhe befinden sich im ersten Stock.
You: …
Customer: Thanks a lot for your help. Bye.
You: …

WB
C4

C4 An unexpected present at the mall

a) Read the text. Who does Greg meet again?

It was a rather quiet day at the mall. As a matter of fact, Greg found it extremely boring. He had to sort baseball caps and he really preferred serving customers. Oh well, nothing anyone could do about it!
While he was humming to himself, Greg saw a teenage boy about his age enter the store and start to look around. "May I help you?" Greg asked him politely. The teenager shook his head and moved away. Greg kept looking at him. "I know I've seen him before. But where?" Suddenly he remembered. Of course! It was Ben. They were in the school band together last year. Greg saw Ben edge around one table. Suddenly Ben's hand slid out, grabbed a blue cap and hid it under his coat. Greg thought he wasn't seeing right. Ben was stealing the cap! He couldn't ignore it, but … What should he do?
Greg had an idea. He walked up to Ben and said: "Hey, Ben! How did you know I was going to get you that for your birthday? Now it's not a surprise anymore!" Ben's hand dropped. Greg took the cap and said: "At least let me wrap it up for you. Come on! The cash register is over there."
Greg went over to pay and Ben followed him with an astonished look on his face.
After Greg had paid for the present and wrapped it, he handed it to Ben. "Happy birthday, band-buddy!" Ben looked straight into Greg's eyes and thanked him. He told Greg that he had received much more than a cap from Greg that day.
Before they parted, they agreed to meet up the following Wednesday. Greg went back to work, whistling "Happy birthday to you!" He felt good.

WB
C5

**b) Imagine you are Greg.
How would you react?**

c) Write the story from Ben's point of view. Write five sentences and read them to your partner.

Yesterday I went …
I wanted to …
But then …

skills
How to write
p. 127/1

C5 A shopping day

a) Do you like shopping? Explain why or why not. Talk to your partner.

b) Describe your perfect shopping day. Think of things like
- money
- stores
- places to stop and rest
- food
- …

Language gym
p. 26, ex. 3

WB
C6, C7

1 Language gym

1 Copy the text into your exercise book. Put the verbs in the correct tense.

Last month I … (to begin) my part-time job in a burger bar. At the end of my first week I … (to feel) very tired. But now I … (to be) used to standing and serving customers. Ever since I started the job there I … (not to eat) any fries or burgers. The smell of fast food … (not to make) me hungry any more.
It … (to be) a very busy restaurant. There … (to be) customers who … (to come) three times a week. I have already … (to meet) lots of nice people there. Yesterday … (to be) a pretty bad day because I … (to have) no time to sit down for a minute. But I … (to know) I … (not to stay) forever. For the moment I … (to be) happy about the extra money.

CD

2 American English and British English sound different. Listen to a boy from London and a girl from New York saying the same words. Work with a partner and try to say the words the British way and the American way.

hot dog · dance · z · modern · after · bottle · address · problem · can · hospital · tomato

CD

3 a) Listen to an American girl and write down the American English words she says for the pictures. Write them in your exercise book.

b) Write down the British English words for these things.

You have read about working in a department store. You have written about the pros and cons of a part-time job. You have helped out an American woman in a department store in Germany.

stand in line	queue
burger-flipper	person working in a burger restaurant
stores	shops
cookies	biscuits
potato chips	crisps
garbage	rubbish

simple past	*last …, yesterday*
present perfect	*since …*
present progressive	*now, at the moment*
future	*forever*

Memory Box

New places, new faces

2

A1 Lots to see in the USA

a) Work in pairs. Look at the pictures. Find out what they show and where they were taken.

1. Did you know that the Statue of Liberty was a present the Franco-American Union gave to the USA in 1886? The statue is about 151 feet (46 m) tall. The foundation is another 154 feet (46,9 m) high. The statue commemorates the date of the United States Declaration of Independence on July 4, 1776.

2. Immigrants who came by ship to the USA between 1892 and 1954 had to go through Ellis Island Immigrant Station. Doctors examined these people to decide if they could enter the country. People called it "The Island of Hope" or "The Island of Tears". Guess why. Since 1990 the building has been a museum.

3. If you had the chance to go to Yosemite National Park, would you want to see a bear? The national park is located in the center of Sierra Nevada in California and has been a national park since October 1, 1890. It covers an area of 1,189 sq mi (3,081 km²). El Capitan is 7,569 feet (2,307 m) high, so would you try and climb up to its top?

4. The Mohawks are Native Americans. They settled on the banks of Lake Ontario. The Mohawks are one of the five nations of the Iroquois. Originally the tribe lived in large bark-covered houses, called "longhouses". A whole family – sons, daughters, cousins, aunts, grandparents etc – shared each "longhouse". How many people would live in your "longhouse" if you had one?

b) Read the texts and match them with the pictures. Explain your choice to your partner. Take turns.

I think picture … must be … because …

5. The White House in Washington DC is the residence and office of the President of the United States of America. It took eight years to build, from 1792 until 1800.
In 1901 Theodore Roosevelt gave it the name that we still use today.

6. On May 27, 1937 people walked across the Golden Gate Bridge for the first time. The next day vehicles crossed the bridge. Since then, more than a billion vehicles have crossed the bridge.

7. The Wrigley Building has been open since 1924 and is one of Chicago's most famous sights and one of the city's first skyscrapers. When W. Wrigley Jr. died in 1932, he had become a millionaire and one of the most famous people in Chicago. What do you know about his business?

8. Las Vegas is the largest city in the state of Nevada. The town began to grow in 1905 and became a city in 1911. Some people call it "The Entertainment Capital of the World". Las Vegas is famous for its great shows and many casinos. Gambling is legal – so be careful with your money …

9. In 1853 there was only one small house in Hollywood. At the beginning of the 20th century film companies began to settle there. It became the center of the American movie and TV industry. Today Hollywood is a district in the northwest of Los Angeles.

c) Imagine you had the chance to visit the USA. Where would you go? What would you do there? Tell your partner.

I would climb to the top of the Statue of Liberty if I had the chance to go to New York.

If I had the chance to visit the USA, I would go to Hollywood.

If I had the money, I would go and see the White House.

lif 7 p. 143

Language gym p. 33, ex. 1 + 2

WB A1–A3

skills
How to look for information
p. 133

A2 The USA quiz

Do the quiz and test your knowledge of the United States. Write the answers in your exercise book. Use an encyclopaedia or the Internet for help.

Look at page 40 to check your answers.

1. What is the capital of the United States?
   a) New York b) Washington DC c) Los Angeles
2. Which is the longest river in the USA?
   a) Mississippi b) Colorado c) Rio Grande
3. Imagine you were on the highest mountain of the USA. Where would you be?
   a) Blocksberg b) Harney Peak c) Mount McKinley
4. Who was the first president of the United States?
   a) George Bush b) George Washington c) George Clooney
5. What do the 50 stars on the US flag stand for?
   a) 50 presidents b) 50 time zones c) 50 states
6. What do the stripes represent?
   a) the original 13 states b) the 13 pilgrims c) the 13 rivers in the USA
7. Where would you go if you wanted to see the smallest state of the USA?
   a) Texas b) Rhode Island c) North Dakota
8. Where would you go if you wanted to see the largest state of the USA?
   a) Alaska b) Mississippi c) Maine
9. If you wanted to visit a city called Frankfort in the USA, where would you go?
   a) Kentucky b) Arizona c) Wyoming
10. What is the biggest city in the USA?
    a) Miami b) New York City c) Springfield
11. Which of these languages is not spoken by many Americans?
    a) English b) Spanish c) Danish
12. Which of these countries does not have a border with the USA?
    a) Peru b) Mexico c) Canada

A3 The USA – a vast country

New England

The USA is a vast country that is divided into six large regions: New England, the Mid-Atlantic, the Midwest, the West, the South and the Southwest. All six regions differ from each other.

a) Read the text about New England. What do you learn about this region?

New England was named after the English Protestants who settled in this area in the 17th century and devoted themselves to farming. Until the 19th century it was the center of culture and business. This region is also well-known for its universities and colleges, including Harvard and Yale. Harvard was America's first college and it was founded in Cambridge, Massachusetts in 1636.

b) Look at the photos. What is typical of the Mid-Atlantic, the Midwest and the West? Use the prompts to write complete sentences.
Example: *The Mid-Atlantic has become the center of ...*

The Mid-Atlantic

become • center of iron, glass and steel industries • in the past • thousands of immigrants • come to work hard • today • some of the most important industries • finances, communications and pharmaceuticals • capital • Washington DC

The Mid-West

famous for • agricultural areas • the nation's "breadbasket" • farmers harvest • cereal crops (wheat, oats and corn)

The West

scenic beauty • some areas • undeveloped land • not many people live here • areas for fishing, camping, hiking • California • most populous state • movie and high-technology industries • Spanish as language widespread • many inhabitants in California of Mexican origin

c) What do you know about the South and the Southwest? Find some information on one of these regions and present your ideas to the class.

skills
How to look for information
p. 133

WB
A4

The South

The Southwest

lif 7 p. 143

A4 Just a dream?

WB A5–A7

Match the following sentence halves and complete the two remaining sentences. Write them down in your exercise book.

If I spent my holidays in the USA, …
If I had a friend in the USA, …
If I were not afraid of flying, …
If I saved a lot of money, …
If I wanted to see wild bears, …
If I visited the White House, …

… I wouldn't …
… I would fly around the world.
… I would say hello to the US president.
… I wouldn't go to Disneyland.
… I would …
… I wouldn't spend it all in Las Vegas.

Language gym p. 33, ex. 3

A5 The USA in short

Read the facts on the United States of America. What is new and interesting for you?

Capital city: Washington, DC
States: 50 states
Political system: federal constitutional republic
National language: English
Currency: United States dollar ($; USD)
Religion: 76.5% Christian, 13.2% Nonreligious, 1.3% Jewish, 0.5% Muslim
National independence: July 4, 1776 (from Great Britain)
Motto: In God We Trust
Largest cities: New York, Los Angeles, Chicago
Largest state: Alaska
Smallest state: Rhode Island
Neighboring countries: Canada (north), Mexico (south)
States in other areas than the continental United States: Alaska, Hawaii

Population: about 301,487,000 (2007)
Land area: 3,718,695 sq mi (9,631,420 km^2); 3rd largest country in the world
Highest point: Mt McKinley, Alaska, 20,320 ft (6194 m) above sea level
Lowest point: Death Valley, California, 282 ft (86 m) below sea level
Mountains: the Appalachian Mountains, the Rocky Mountains
Rivers: Mississippi-Missouri, Rio Grande, Colorado
Time zones: 4 on continental United States
National bird: Bald Eagle
National flower: Rose
National anthem: The Star-Spangled Banner

Language gym p. 33, ex. 4

A6 What a beautiful state

CD

Each student in Madison's class has to present one of the 50 states of the USA. Today it is Madison's turn and she is going to give a presentation on her home state.

skills How to listen p. 122

a) Listen to Madison presenting her home state. Which state is she from?

b) Listen again and take notes on the following points in your exercise book. Compare them to your partner's.

nickname • capital • big cities • inhabitants • attractions • lakes

A7 A country of your choice

skills How to look for information p. 133

What do you know about your country? Use the Internet or an encyclopaedia and collect facts about your country or another country of your choice.

1 **a) Write the following phrases in your exercise book and find verbs with the same meaning.**

1. to play for money: …
2. to find a place to live: …
3. to divide among two or more people: …
4. to make you think of something in the past: …

b) Complete the following sentences.

Example: *1. A pedestrian is a person who goes on foot.*

2. A customer is a person who …
3. Hollywood is a district of Los Angeles which …
4. Immigrants are people …
5. A climber …

2 **Look at the map of the USA on the inside cover of your textbook. There are 50 states in the USA. Which state would you be in if you lived in the following cities?**

Example: *If I lived in Memphis, I would be in the state of Tennessee.*
If I lived in Denver, I would be in …

Harrisburg | Dallas | Chicago | Boston | St. Louis | Bismarck | Seattle | Frankfort | ~~Memphis~~ | Los Angeles | Denver | New York | Salt Lake City

3 **Imagine you know people in other countries. What would you do if you went there? Make complete sentences and write them in your exercise book.**

Example: *If I had a friend in California, I would visit him and go to see the Golden Gate Bridge.*

If I had	a friend an aunt an uncle a pen friend an e-mail friend	in the USA, in California, in France, in …,	I would visit him / her and go to … I would visit him / her and …

4 **Listen to the words and repeat them.**

CD

pharmaceuticals | national anthem | Appalachian Mountains | federal constitutional republic | National Independence | Massachusetts

If I had the chance to visit the USA, I would go to Hollywood.
If you lived in Memphis, you would be in the state of Tennessee.

Memory Box

You have found out about popular sights in the USA. You have read about some important facts and listened to a presentation on a popular US state.

B1 National parks in California

At Abraham Lincoln High School in San Francisco, all 9th grade students traditionally go on a field trip to a national park. Before the fall vacation Mr Seymour, a geography teacher, asked his students to collect some information about national parks in California.

Look at the map of California. What can you find out?
How many national parks are there and what are their names?
Where are they? Talk to your partner. Take turns.

in the north / south / east / west / northwest / southeast of …

B2 Planning a field trip

Today Mr Seymour would like to see what his students have found out.

a) Ashley has taken down notes on Death Valley National Park from the Internet. Read her notes and help her write complete sentences. Then compare with your partner.

Death Valley National Park

Founded:	*1933, national park since 1994*
Size:	*3,367,626 acres*
Climate:	*very hot and dry in summer, hottest temperature in July 1913 (134 °F)*
What to see:	*beautiful wild flowers in spring, more than 900 kinds of plants*
	ravens, ground squirrels, lizards, rattlesnakes, scorpions, black widow spiders,
	coyotes and mountain lions
Attractions:	*ghost towns, sand dunes, Dante's View or Zabriskie Point*
Mountains:	*Telescope Peak (11,049 feet), Dante's View (5,475 feet)*
Interesting:	*282 feet below sea level*
	in 1849, a group of pioneers got lost, one of them died,
	the rest of the team called the region Death Valley

b) Read the following entry from Zachary's travel guidebook on Yosemite National Park and find out what each paragraph is about. Write keywords and compare them with your partner.

Yosemite has existed as a national park for more than 100 years. It was established on October 1, 1890.
The area's first residents were Native Americans who inhabited the region 7,000 to 10,000 years ago. Various tribes lived in the area over the years, with the most recent being a Miwok tribe that called Yosemite Valley "Ahwahnee". People believe that it means "place of the gaping mouth". The Ahwahneechee, as they called themselves, gathered acorns and went hunting and fishing. The discovery of gold, however, meant that they had to give up their homes.
Yosemite National Park is in the center of Sierra Nevada. It covers an area of almost 1,200 sq mi of scenic wild lands. For years, people have been visiting Yosemite National Park for its wilderness, waterfalls and rocks. In order to see a lot of Yosemite some people go hiking, others attend a guided tour.
Climbing has been very popular among the visitors to Yosemite for many years. El Capitan is one of the rocks that are the most difficult to climb. Further beautiful attractions are Yosemite Valley with its high cliffs and waterfalls and Mariposa Grove with hundreds of giant sequoia trees.
The park is home to many different animals. There are squirrels, mule deer, bighorn sheep, mountain lions and coyotes, but also a variety of birds, such as falcons and eagles. Bears are also active everywhere in the park.

lif
8
p. 144

c) Now read Ashley's notes and the entry on Yosemite again. Match these sentence halves to get the main information. Compare your sentences with your partner.

*Death Valley has been a national park since 1994.
People have admired the waterfalls in Yosemite for more than 100 years.*

1. People have been visiting Yosemite Park for
2. Yosemite has been a national park
3. Climbing has been very popular
4. Death Valley has been a national park
5. 134 °F has been the hottest temperature
6. The park has been called Death Valley

a) since July 1913.
b) more than 100 years.
c) for over 150 years now.
d) for many years.
e) since 1994.
f) since 1890.

WB
B1, B2

d) With the help of your keywords, make a short presentation on Yosemite National Park. You may also look again at Ashley's notes.

Language gym
p. 37, ex. 1+2

skills
How to speak
p. 131/3

B3 Where to go

Mr Seymour and his students are going to decide where to spend their next field trip.

a) Have you got an idea where they might go? Discuss with your partner.

**b) Listen to the conversation in class.
Which of your ideas was right? Where do the students want to spend their field trip?**

CD

c) Listen again. Who wants to see what? Why? Complete the sentences in your exercise book.

lif
9
p. 144

Example: *1. Emily is not keen on meeting a bear.*
2. José is looking forward to seeing …
3. Zachary is interested in …
4. Zachary and Kaitlyn are interested in …
5. The class is looking forward to …

*The class is interested in visiting a national park.
They are looking forward to going on their field trip.*

Language gym
p. 37, ex. 3

WB
B3, B4

B4 Keen on more information

Mr Seymour's students need more information to plan their field trip. As they are going to stay there for two days, they are interested in getting some more information on camping facilities. They would also like to know what they can do there.
So they are going to write an e-mail to the park's information center.

Help them write the e-mail. Think about these aspects:

WB B5

date / season • accommodation • guide • places of interest • activities • costs • ...

B5 Rules in Yosemite

skills How to mediate p. 126

You are with your parents in Yosemite National Park. Your parents don't speak good English.

Look at the rules and tell your parents in German what you must or mustn't do in Yosemite.

WB B6, B7

YOSEMITE NATIONAL PARK – PARK RULES

- Plan your trip before you go and leave information about it at the visitors' center.
- Always carry plenty of water.
- Be prepared for sudden changes of weather.
- Do not hike on your own, always make sure another person is with you.
- Stay on trails to protect plant life.
- Be careful when driving along roads: wild animals crossing.
- Do not feed the animals.
- Throw garbage into cans that are available.

And last but not least: BE AWARE OF THE BEARS
- If you see a bear, report it to the ranger.
- Keep your food in the special bear-proof lockers.
- Do not approach a bear.
- Make as much noise as possible by yelling and clapping your hands to scare bears away.

Language gym p. 37, ex. 4

B6 Presenting a national park

skills How to present something in class p. 132

Make a leaflet about a national park in the USA.
How to do it:

- First choose one of the national parks in the USA.
- Use the link www.nps.gov to find information.
- Write about the location, the size and the attractions of the national park.
- Give some information on things you can do and animals you can see there.
- Write some rules on how to behave in the national park.
- Use photos to illustrate your leaflet.
- Present your leaflet to the class.

portfolio

1 **Copy the sentences into your exercise book and complete them with *for* or *since*.**

Most of the eight national parks in California have existed ... more than 100 years now. California's oldest national park is Sequoia which has been a national park ... 1890. It is famous for its giant sequoias which millions of tourists have visited ... many years. No one knows the ages of the large trees, but people think that the oldest have been there ... between 700 BC and 200 AD.

CD

2 **Choose the right form of the verb and copy the sentences into your exercise book.**

CD

1. I *have known / know* my best friend for three years.
2. Carla *got / has got* her bicycle last year.
3. We *have been / are* in 8th grade since the beginning of September.
4. I *have lived / live* in this town since I was born.
5. Jan *has played / played* football last weekend.
6. Patrick *doesn't eat / hasn't eaten* pizza since last Saturday.

3 **Imagine you are visiting a national park. There are many things you can do there. Look at the activities in the box and tell your partner what you are interested / not interested in doing in a national park.**

walking • climbing • riding • fishing • hiking • seeing • watching • going to • visiting

I'm interested in watching wild animals.

Do you like walking?

I'm looking forward to visiting the national park.

I like riding.

...

No, I'm not keen on walking. I prefer riding.

4 **Where is the stress in these words? Copy the table and write them in the correct column.**

CD

Sequoia · ~~Yosemite~~ · ~~national~~ · variety · California · approach · giant · information · attend · valley · established · pioneers · garbage

stress on ...		
1st syllable	2nd syllable	3rd syllable
national	Yosemite	...

You have read about different national parks. You have listened to a class planning their field trip and helped them write an e-mail for more information. You have also made a leaflet about a national park and presented it in class.

Emily is not keen on meeting a bear.
I'm interested in watching wild animals.

Death Valley has been a national park since 1994.
Yosemite has been a national park for over a hundred years.

Memory Box

C1 Famous people

a) There are a lot of famous people living in the USA. Look at these photos. Who are they? What do you know about them? What do you think they have in common? Talk about them in class.

b) Choose one person and find out more about him/her. You may use the library or the Internet. Present your information to the class.

skills
How to look for information
p. 133

C2 Ancestors

a) Look at the pie chart. What information does it give you? Which nation represents the largest group of immigrants in the USA? Talk about the figures with your partner.

Make comparisons:

- There are more Mexican immigrants than ...
- The biggest group are ...
- The fewest immigrants come from ...

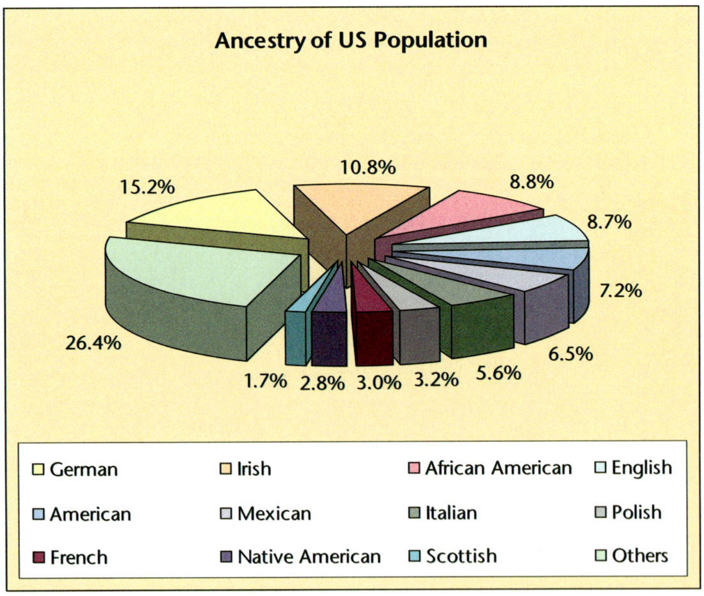

b) What do you find interesting or surprising? Why?

Language gym
p. 42, ex. 1

C3 Different reasons

What reasons do you think people have for leaving their home country and moving to another country? Collect your ideas in a word web and compare with your partner.

C4 Family histories

a) 9th graders Thomas, Kim and Antonio talk about their families and their experiences in the USA. Work in groups and choose one of the students. Copy the grid and complete it.

skills
How to read
p. 124/1

b) Use your notes to talk about the teenagers in class. Then listen to the other groups and complete your grid.

name	family from	reasons for immigrating	experiences
Antonio Vargas			

Hi, I'm Thomas Schneider. I'm 14 years old. My ancestors are from Germany. They came from Lower Saxony and settled in New York. They left their home country because they were afraid of political turmoil in Germany. Soon after the inflation crisis in 1923 they boarded the ship and entered the USA through Ellis Island. There they had to wait because they had to be examined. After three days they arrived in New York. New York City is very popular with German immigrants. Many small towns in the USA have German names, e.g. Mannheim and Oppenheim. Germans have emigrated to the USA since the 18th century. My ancestors were very happy when they arrived in New York. They were able to work as businessmen again. I love living in the USA. It's a great place.

Hi, I'm Kim Duong and I'm from Vietnam. My parents, my brother and I have been in the USA for three years. When we came I couldn't speak English at all, so I had a lot of problems at school. I couldn't understand the teachers and the students in my class but everybody was very nice to me. They helped me a lot. When my parents first told me that they wanted to go to the USA, I was very sad and I didn't like the idea at all. My parents both had a job in Vietnam and they earned well, but our relatives in the USA persuaded them to come here and join the family. We had a very long trip. First we flew to Hong Kong and then we had to change to another plane to New York. It took us about two days to reach our destination. At first I missed my friends from Vietnam a lot. But now I have made some good friends here too.

Hi, I'm Antonio Vargas. I'm 14 years old. My grandparents are from Mexico. They did not have a job in Mexico so they decided to come to the USA for a better life. They have lived here since 1975. In the beginning it was very hard for them. They couldn't speak English and they had to work in a meat factory for very little money. In spite of that they were happy that they were able to bring up their children, my father and his sister, in America. They wanted to offer them a better education. My father studied law at Nebraska University and he has been a lawyer since 1995. I like living in the USA. I love traveling to the national parks and I enjoy the big cities as well as the wilderness of this great country.

c) You have read about different reasons why people have immigrated to the USA. Add the information to the word web in C3.

Language gym
p. 42, ex. 2

WB
C1, C2

C5 The kids in school with me

CD

a) Listen to the poem by Langston Hughes. How many nationalities are mentioned? What are they? Write them down.

The Kids in School with Me

When I studied my A-B-C's
And learned arithmetic,
I also learned in public school
What makes America tick:
The kid in front
And the kid behind
And the kid across the aisle,
The Italian kid
And the Polish kid
And the girl with the Irish smile,
The colored kid
And the Spanish kid
And the Russian kid my size,
The Jewish kid
And the Grecian kid
And the girl with the Chinese eyes –
We were a regular Noah's ark,
Every race beneath the sun,
But our motto for graduation was:
One for All and All for One!
The kid in front
And the kid behind
And the kid across from me –
Just American kids together
The kids in school with me.

Langston Hughes (1902–1967)

skills
How to read
p. 125/2

b) Read the poem and find out what the poet says about his class.

c) What does the poet mean by "Noah's ark"? Discuss with your partner.

C6 The kids in my class

skills
How to speak
p. 130/1

a) Interview the pupils in your class. Do they or their parents come from different countries?

project

b) Create a "Noah's ark" of your class. Use photos of the pupils in your class to illustrate a poster or make a collage.

c) Write a poem of your own class.

In my grade, we're thirty-one,
Always having lots of fun.
Vanessa, sitting next to me,
She loves math and David Lee.

Answer key for A2, p. 30	1b; 2a; 3c; 4b, 5c; 6a; 7b; 8a; 9a; 10b; 11c; 12a

C7 A Mexican in California

WB
C3, C4

When Panchito left Mexico with his brother and his parents, he was about five years old and didn't speak English. The family hoped to make a good living in California. They moved around the country in their old van, the *Carcachita*, picking strawberries and harvesting grapes and cotton. They moved from one labor camp to the next, year after year ...

"*La frontera*" is a word I often heard when I was a child living in El Rancho Blanco, a small village in the middle of dry hills several miles north of Guadalajara, Mexico. I heard it for the first time back in the late 1940s when Papá and Mamá told me and Roberto, my older brother, that someday we would take a long trip north, cross *la frontera*, enter California, and leave our poverty behind. I did not know exactly what California was, but Papá's eyes sparkled whenever he talked about it with Mamá and his friends. "Once we cross *la frontera*, we'll make a good living in California," he would say, standing up straight and sticking out his chest. (...)

"We have work! Mr Sullivan said we can stay the whole season," Mamá said, pointing to an old garage near the stables. (...)
Early the next morning Mr Sullivan showed us where the crop was, and after breakfast Papá, Roberto and I headed for the vineyard to pick grapes.
Around nine o'clock the temperature was almost one hundred degrees Fahrenheit. I was covered with sweat and my mouth felt as if I had been chewing on a handkerchief. I walked over to the end of the row, picked up a bottle of water and drank. "Don't drink too much; you'll get sick," Roberto shouted. (...) I still didn't feel well when we took a break to eat lunch. It was past two o'clock and we sat under a large walnut tree that was on the side of the road. While we ate, Papá wrote down the number of boxes we had picked. Suddenly Papá looked down the road and his face turned pale. "Here comes the school bus," he whispered loudly in alarm. Roberto and I ran and hid in the vineyards. We did not want to get in trouble for not going to school. The neatly dressed boys about my age got off. They carried books under their arms. (...)
After lunch we went back to work. The sun was very hot. The insects, the wet sweat, the hot dry dust made the afternoon ever so long. Then the shadows grew and within an hour it was too dark to go on picking. "*Vámonos,*" said Papá, – it was time to leave. Papá then took out a pencil and began to figure numbers, crossed some out, wrote down some more. "*Quince,*" he murmured.
When we arrived home, we took a cold shower underneath a water hose. We then sat down to eat dinner. Mamá had cooked a special meal for us. We had rice and tortillas with "*carne con chile*", my favorite dish. (...)
It was Monday, the first week of November. The grape season was over and I could now go to school. I woke up early that morning and lay in bed, looking at the stars and was happy that I was not going to work and that I was starting sixth grade that year. I could not sleep so I decided to get up and join Papá and Roberto at breakfast. I sat at the table across from Roberto, but I kept my head down. I did not want to look up and face him. I knew he was sad. He was not going to school today. He was not going tomorrow, or next week, or next month. He would not go until the cotton season was over, and that was sometime in February.

From: Francisco Jimenéz, The Circuit: Stories from the life of a migrant child.

a) Read the text and answer these questions.
- Why do Panchito and his family move from Mexico to California?
- Where does Panchito work, and what is it like there?
- Why do you think Panchito's father is worried when they see the school bus?
- How does Panchito feel about going to school?
- Why is Roberto sad at the end of the story?

skills
How to read
p. 124/1

b) Can you imagine living like Panchito? Why? Why not?

Language gym
p. 42, ex. 3+4

Language gym

1 Look at the pie chart in C2 again.
Use the words in the boxes to make comparisons.

largest | biggest | fewer | Irish | Native Americans | Mexican | African Americans | more | as big as

1. The Germans are the … group.
2. The 2nd … group are the …
3. There are … Polish immigrants than …
4. There are … Italian immigrants than … immigrants.
5. The number of English immigrants is almost … that of …

2 Copy the words into your exercise book and find opposites or synonyms for them.
Use your dictionary for help.

Example: *1. Be afraid is a synonym for be frightened.*

2. ancestors / family
3. board a ship
4. enjoy
5. destination
6. enter

3 Read the text "A Mexican in California" (C7) again.
Copy the beginnings of the sentences into your exercise book and complete them.

Example: *1. When Panchito was a child, he lived in Mexico.*

2. One day Papá and Mamá told him …
3. It was very hot, so I …
4. Papá took out a pencil and …
5. Panchito could not sleep so …

CD

4 a) Same spelling – different sounds. Look at the words.
Copy the grid into your exercise book and write the words in the correct column.

underneath | early | meal | head | heard | season | speak | near | eat

/ɪə/ as in h<u>e</u>re	/iː/ as in d<u>ee</u>p	/ɜː/ as in b<u>i</u>rd	/e/ as in r<u>e</u>d	/eɪ/ as in th<u>ey</u>
…	…	…	…	…

neatly | sweat | year | break | leave | hear

b) Think of more words with *ea* and add them to your grid.

You have talked about famous people living in the United States and about a pie chart showing the ancestors of Americans. You have read about different reasons for immigrating to the USA. You have read and written a poem.
You have also read the story of a Mexican boy in California.

center
fall
public school
labor
9th grade

centre
autumn
state school
labour
year 9

The biggest group are the Germans.
There are more Mexican immigrants than Scottish immigrants.
There are fewer French immigrants than there are Italian immigrants.

Memory Box

The world in a city 3

A1 New York, New York

CD

a) Listen to Frank Sinatra. How does the song make you feel?

happy • sad • adventurous • curious • positive • negative • timid • excited

In my opinion it's a … song.

I think it's a … song.

The song makes me think of …

The song / It makes me feel …

I get … feelings.

Start spreading the news
I'm leaving today
I want to be a part of it, New York, New York
These vagabond shoes
Are longing to stray
Right through the very heart of it
New York, New York.

I want to wake up in a city that doesn't sleep
And find I'm king of the hill, top of the heap
These little town blues
Are melting away
I'll make a brand new start of it
In old New York
If I can make it there
I'll make it anywhere
It's up to you, New York, New York.

I want to wake up in a city that never sleeps
And find I'm a number one, top of the list
King of the hill, a number one
These little town blues
Are melting away
I'm gonna make a brand new start of it
In old New York
And if I can make it there
I'm gonna make it anywhere
It's up to you, New York, New York.

Lyrics: Fred Ebb
Music: John Kander

b) Listen to the song again and read along. Look at the expressions in the box. Try to find expressions with a similar meaning in the text.

skills
How to read
p. 125/2

tell everybody • traveling boots • go and see new places • a new beginning • I'm very successful • sad feelings • go away • I can succeed

c) Read the song text again. What does the singer want to do?

d) Would you like to go to New York? Why? Why not? Tell your partner. Then tell the class what your partners would like to do.

Yes. / No. Because I want to / I would like to …

… says that he / she would like to / wants to …

WB
A1

A2 Some famous sights

a) A tourist took these photos of famous places in New York. Do you know them? Talk in class.

Central Park

Statue of Liberty

Empire State Building

Macy's Department Store

WB A2–A4

lif 10 p. 146

Language gym p. 50, ex. 1

b) What do tourists or people normally do at such places?

CD

c) Look at the photos and listen. Where are these people and what are they doing? Take notes.

A3 The Big Apple

skills How to read p. 124/1

a) Read the text and find these dates and numbers. What do they stand for?

1790 | 1664 | 5 | April 30, 1789 | 7 | 1.5 | September 13, 1788 | 1,860 | 350

lif 11 p. 146

Did you know that New York used to have a different name? Before 1664 its name was New Amsterdam, but in that year the British conquered the area and named it New York. However, New Yorkers often call it "The Big Apple". In the 1930s, there was a famous jazz club in Harlem called the Big Apple. That is probably where the name came from. But no one is really sure.

New York became the first capital of the newly formed United States on September 13, 1788. George Washington became the first president of the United States on April 30, 1789 in Federal Hall on Wall Street in New York. New York remained the capital of the USA until 1790 with a population of 33,131.

350 years ago New York was only a large town. Today it is the largest city in the USA. Its population has grown to about seven million people. Many residents have lived in New York all their lives but their neighborhoods still have foreign sounding names like "Jamaica" or "Chinatown". However, no matter where their ancestors may have come from, New Yorkers have always had one thing in common – they love "The Big Apple".

There are five boroughs in New York City: Manhattan, Brooklyn, Queens, the Bronx and Staten Island. Manhattan is the most famous of the five. About one and a half million people live there but five million come to work there every day. For many years, Manhattan's most famous sight, the Empire State Building, was the tallest building in the world. You can take 1,860 steps up to the top. Broadway, with its many theaters, has become one of the best-known streets in the world.

Brooklyn has the largest population of all the boroughs. It has an interesting mixture of both modern skyscrapers and some older buildings.

New York has changed a lot in its short history. For example, the Bronx was once an area where rich people lived. Slowly, over the years it began to decay. Today, the Bronx is poor and still has some slums.

Richmond on Staten Island is a quiet area. It is home to many families whose ancestors came from Italy or Ireland. Although most residents have never lived outside the USA, they still call themselves Irish or Italian Americans. Richmond is not as famous as some of the other boroughs, but it is a nice place to live.

Have you ever been on a plane? If you come to see New York, you will probably land at JFK Airport or La Guardia Airport in the borough of Queens.

WB A5, A6

b) Read the text again. Write down eight quiz questions in your exercise book. Ask a partner. Answer your partner's questions.

When did ...?

What have most people already ...?

What has changed a lot?

Language gym p. 50, ex. 2 + 3

skills How to speak p. 131/3

c) Write down eight things about New York that you find most interesting. Prepare a short talk and present it.

A4 Something for everyone

Imagine you had the chance to visit New York yourself. What could you do?

a) Read the ads. Copy the table into your exercise book and complete it.

the tour	highlights	means of transport	costs
...	...	...	...

skills
How to read p. 124/1

Tours in New York

You'd like to see New York? Choose between different kinds of tours. There's something for everyone!

By boat – Sightseeing Cruises

Pier 83, West 42nd Street
The Full Island Cruise – 3 hours
Enjoy a relaxed 3-hour cruise as you discover the secrets of the city. You'll sail around Manhattan Island and see it all – 3 rivers, 7 major bridges, 5 boroughs and the magnificent Statue of Liberty. Drinks, food and souvenirs are available on board. The boat leaves from Pier 83 at 42nd Street on the Hudson River.

Adults $29 | Children $16 | Senior Citizens $24

By bus – Hop on Hop off Bus Tour

This tour includes 48 hours of touring within Manhattan. Hop on and hop off classic double-decker buses as you please at any of the 40 stops. Spend as much time as you wish to discover and enjoy some of New York's wonderful attractions. When you're ready to continue your tour, just hop back on the next bus! Tour includes a ticket for the ferry to the Statue of Liberty/Ellis Island and admission ticket to the Empire State Building Observatory.

Adults $71 | Children $51

By helicopter – New York helicopter sightseeing flights

The Big Apple
Experience Manhattan's famous skyline on board a helicopter flight. You will see the beautiful Statue of Liberty, Ellis Island and the Empire State Building just like birds see them.

Downtown Manhattan heliport, Pier 6 and the East River.
Monday through Friday from 9:00 am to 6:30 pm.
Saturdays from 9:00 am to 5:30 pm.
Phone 0150-7845287 for details of our special offers.

Walking the streets of Manhattan

Explore the streets of Manhattan on foot!

Walking tour of Lower Manhattan
This walking tour explores the historic sites and a wonderful river setting. Starting from Battery Park, you board a ferry for a harbor view of New York from the Staten Island Ferry, or one of the tour boats that sail to the Statue of Liberty and the Ellis Island Museum of Immigration. When you return to shore, you visit sites that show the city's history. Moving northwest along Wall Street, you will find the world's most important financial district. You will escape from the busy streets in the grounds of Trinity Church, City Hall Park, and the piers of South Street Seaport, where you can see tall ships.

Your kids will love it!

Guided Tours of New York TV and Movie Destinations
New York City is the most filmed city in the world. Come and see where the lights, camera and action happen. See where the world of movies meets real life while you shop, eat, drink, and dance at the sites you've seen on both the big and small screens.

Over 40 TV and movie sites, including *Friends*, *Will & Grace*, *Spider-Man*, and *Hitch*

- See the restaurant used in *Spider-Man*
- Visit the apartment building from *Friends* where Monica, Chandler and the others live
- Sit on the steps of the *Bill Cosby* house
- Go on location to the café used in *Men in Black*
- Visit one of the locations used in *Hitch*
- Take photos at the locations used in *Ghostbusters*

b) Read the ads again. Then read the sentences below. Which statements are true, false or not in the text?

1. If you get on the bus, you have to stay on it for 48 hours.
2. The boat leaves from Pier 83 at 42nd Street on the Rhine River.
3. You can sail to the Statue of Liberty on the walking tour.
4. If you go on the movie tour, you will see a ghost.
5. If you take the helicopter tour, you will fly over the big orange.
6. You will sail around Manhattan Island and see three rivers and seven major bridges if you take the boat tour.
7. The costs for the walking tour include a visit to the Museum of Immigration.
8. The buses on the bus tour are single deckers.

Language gym
p. 50, ex. 4

A5 Everybody wins

Fergus Flynn, a young American boy from Iowa, has found the ads in A4.
He is talking to his mum, dad and sister Betty.

a) What do you think their conversation is about? Listen and find out.

b) Listen to the conversation again. Choose one person (Fergus, his mum, dad or sister) and take notes. What do the Flynns want to do in New York?

CD

skills
How to listen
p. 122

A6 A day in New York

a) Plan a day in New York. Try to find some information about New York in your textbook or from websites like http://www.nyvisit.com/

- Think about these questions and make notes first: Where would you go? What sights would you like to see? What else would you do? Why?
- Think about transport, times, prices.
- Then work in groups of four and decide how your group would spend the day.

b) Present your plan. Don't forget to give reasons for your choice. Use posters, photos and brochures.

skills
How to look for information
p. 133

skills
How to present something in class
p. 132

project

portfolio

WB
A7–A9

Language gym

CD

1 Simple present or present progressive? Fill in the correct tense.

Mom: I … (to be) really glad. I … (to look forward to) going to New York again. I always … (to feel) so happy there. Dad often … (to go) there on business trips, but when he … (to be) there, he normally … (to have to) work hard. He … (not to have) time for sightseeing. But he sometimes … (to take) me with him. When Dad and I … (to walk) down Fifth Avenue I usually … (to look) out for famous movie stars. But I never … (to see) any.
Betty: Mom, we … (not to have) time to listen to you. We … (to pack) our suitcases right now.
Mom: Oh no, Betty, you … (not to take) *two* suitcases to New York!

2 a) Form correct questions and write them in your exercise book.

1. where / these pictures / you / have / taken /?
2. take / pictures / how many / did / you / you / there / when / were /?
3. most / like / what / you / did /?
4. your / why / it / favourite / is / sight /?
5. who / the statue / as a present / gave / to the USA /?

b) Match the questions to the answers.

b. Hundreds of pictures.

a. The Franco-American Union.

c. In New York.

d. Because it's a symbol of freedom.

e. The Statue of Liberty.

CD

3 Simple past or present perfect? Fill in the correct tense.

In 1979 it was very dangerous to travel on the subway in New York. People … (to be) also afraid of walking in the streets at night in some neighborhoods. Curtis Sliwa and 12 other teenagers … (to decide) to do something. They … (to start) an organization called "The Guardian Angels". Since then, the men and women have become a part of New York life. They … (to spread) to 28 cities around the world. They are a non-profit organization. They … (to raise) over $850,000 in 2002. The Guardian Angels … (to come) a long way from those 13 kids who … (to found) the organization nearly 30 years ago.

CD

4 Copy the table on the right into your exercise book. Then read out the words in the box. Where is the stress? Write the words in the correct column.

hundred • became • American • dangerous • neighbourhood • September • resident • capital • population • however • example • theatre

1st syllable	2nd syllable	3rd syllable

You have learned about New York and have made up a quiz. You have read about different tours, listened to a family planning their trip and have planned your own day in New York.

I have never been to New York.
I was in New York last year.

Memory Box

People and places 2 – Where do these words come from?

CD

All of these words came into English from other languages.
Most of them were first used in American English.

lasso
1808 Old French

moccasins
1612 Algonquian

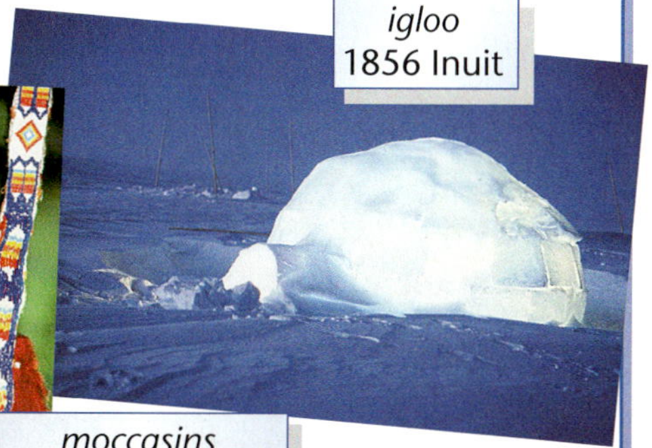

igloo
1856 Inuit

tepee
1872 Sioux or Dakota

dollar
1553 German

tobacco
1577 Spanish / possibly of Caribbean origin

raccoon
1608 Algonquian

In 1607 the British founded their first successful town in North America. They called it Jamestown. The people themselves were called settlers.
More and more people from other European countries moved to places like Jamestown. They all spoke different languages and couldn't talk to each other. Even the people who came from different parts of Britain could not always understand each other. But since the settlers lived in a very dangerous place, they had to be able to speak to each other to survive. After a few years most people were able to speak English.
There were many things in the "New World" that the settlers didn't know. They had to find new names for them. Sometimes they used words from the Native American languages like *moccasins* or *raccoon*. Sometimes they used words from other European languages like *Thaler* (dollar) or *lasso*.
They stopped using some words that people still used in Britain. Other words changed their meaning in British English but did not change in American English.
All of these changes meant that American English and British English slowly grew apart. Today however, with telephones, the Internet and the big American film industry some of these differences are disappearing. You can see a lot of American films in Britain and British people are using more and more American English words.

Which German words can you think of that come from other languages?

B1 Looking for liberty

**a) Look at the photos.
What do they show? You may guess.**

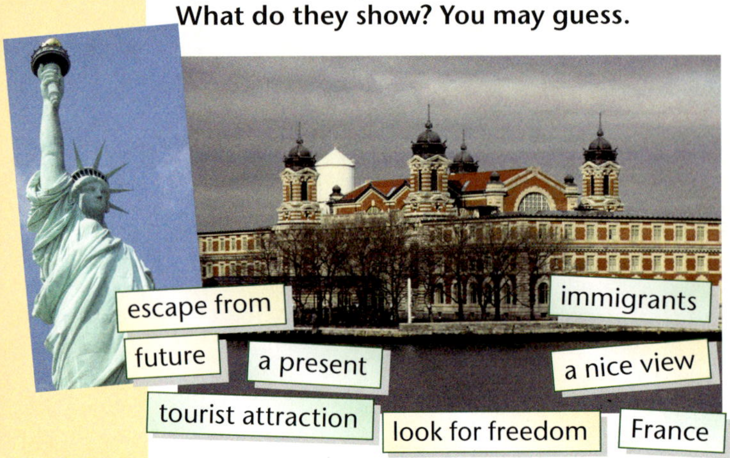

b) Read the text. Were your thoughts correct?

skills
How to read
p. 124/1

More than 12 million immigrants were brought to the United States by boat between 1892 and 1954. The first sight of America that the immigrants had was often the Statue of Liberty. On Ellis Island, an island in New York harbor, the new immigrants were checked and processed before they were allowed to enter the USA. The Ellis Island Immigrant Station was opened on January 1, 1892 and it was closed in November 1954. While most immigrants passed through Ellis Island in three to five hours, some were held back or refused entry. Those unfortunate people were sent back to the countries from which they had tried to escape.
Of course everyone wanted to stay in America. They dreamed of living in peace, of being free and of enough work to support themselves. It was an extremely difficult moment when the medical inspectors looked at the people and checked them. Signs of disease or insanity were looked for. English was tested. Language was important because a job could not be found without English. The poor immigrants had to show that they could survive. The rich immigrants were not inspected.

In Roddy Doyle's novel "Oh, play that thing" an eyewitness remembers:

WB
B1, B2

... Old men tried to straighten long-crooked backs and mothers rubbed rough color into the white cheeks of their children. Wild men ran fingers through long beards and regretted that they hadn't shaved. Jewish women caressed son's ringlets and tried to push them under hats. Fragments of new language were tried, and passed from mouth to mouth.
– Yes Sir
– No Sir
– My cousin, he have a house
– I am a farmer ...
... The medical inspector stared into my eyes. I knew what he was looking for. I'd been told all about it by a lame and wheezy anarchist who was making his seventh try at landing. "They see the bad leg, but never the brains behind it," he had said ...
... If you could afford first or second class, I told him, you wouldn't have to set foot on the island ...
He saw nothing that was going to send me back. To my left another inspector drew a large L on a person's shoulder with a brand new piece of chalk. L was for lung. I knew the sign ... The man with the brand new L had already given up. He collapsed and coughed out most of his remaining life. He had to be carried away. An E on a shoulder meant bad eyes, another L meant lameness. And behind those letters, other hidden letters, never chalked onto shoulders: J for too Jewish, C for Chinese, X was for mental ...

Ellis Island is still visited by millions of people today. Many of them are tourists who are usually taken by ferries from Battery Park in Manhattan. They are shown around the Ellis Island National Monument. The ancestors of over 40 percent of America's population were put through Ellis Island. The names of everyone who came through Ellis Island are kept in computer databases. Today those lists are looked at by many tourists.

c) Read and quote the line in the text where it says
- **how the people felt.**
- **what they had to fulfill.**
- **what they were dreaming of.**

is / are visited by tourists	*tourists visit*
was / were refused by inspectors	*inspectors refused*

B2 In other words

Find the phrases in B1 which mean the same as the following ones. Read them out and take turns.

1. Millions of people still visit Ellis Island today.
2. Ferries from Battery Park usually take tourists to Ellis Island.
3. They practised the new language.
4. Mothers rubbed the cheeks of children's faces.
5. The inspector denied entry to the person with the L on his shoulder.
6. They keep names of everybody who came through Ellis Island on computer databases.
7. Boats brought more than 12 million immigrants to the United States.
8. They sent those unfortunate people back.

Language gym
p. 56, ex. 1

lif
12, 13
p. 146 + 147

B3 Facts about some famous immigrants

Here are short profiles of some well-known people who emigrated to the USA.

a) Read the profiles and visit the websites about the people for further information.

**b) Look at the example of Annie Moore.
Choose one person and write a similar profile in your exercise book.**

Example: *Annie Moore was brought from Ireland on the SS Nevada. She was the first immigrant processed at Ellis Island on January 1, 1892, Annie's 15th birthday. Annie Moore was given a $10 gold coin by Colonel John Weber. The statue of Annie Moore was unveiled by President Mary Robinson of Ireland at a special ceremony in 1993.*

lif
12, 13
p. 146 + 147

skills
How to look for information
p. 133

- Annie Moore
- bring / Ireland
- process / Ellis Island / January 1, 1892 / 15th birthday
- give / $10 / Colonel John Weber
- unveil / statue / President Mary Robinson of Ireland / 1993
- http://www.coedu.usf.edu/culture/Story/Story_Ireland.html

- Lucky Luciano
- born / Sicily / 1897
- father of modern organized crime
- bring / USA / 1906
- first arrest / shoplifting / 1907
- sentence / 30 to 50 years / 1936
- release and deport / from USA / 1946
- http://crime.about.com/od/gangsters/a/luciano.html

- Maria Goeppert Mayer
- born / Katowice, Silesia / 1906
- marry / American / 1930
- take / USA / 1930
- award / doctorate in theoretical physics / 1930
- name / professor physics / University Chicago / 1946
- present / Nobel Prize Physics / 1963
- http://nobelprize.org/nobel_prizes/physics/laureates/1963/mayer-bio.html

- Arnold Schwarzenegger
- born / Austria / July 30, 1947
- award / Mr Universe title / 1968
- grant / American citizenship / 1983
- elect / Governor California / 2003
- http://en.wikipedia.org/wiki/Arnold_Schwarzenegger

Language gym
p. 56, ex. 2

WB
B3, B4

CD

skills
How to listen
p. 122

B4 Family history

a) Listen to Betty and her mother talking about the past. What are they talking about?

Planning a trip to Ellis Island

Finding information for a project

Searching on the Internet

Betty: Mom, we have been told to find information about our family history. I was instructed to ask you what you know about our family origins.
Mom: That's funny, darling. My teacher told me to do the same when I was in high school back in 1980. I have all the information in a box in the attic. I hope it didn't get lost. There are some great photos of the house where Grandma Pat was born.
Betty: Tell me, why did she decide to emigrate from Ireland?
Mom: Well, she did not have much choice. She was brought here by your great-grandparents in 1925 when she was very young.
Betty: Yes, but what made Great-Grandpa decide to leave?
Mom: As far as I remember, his house was destroyed during the rebellion in 1919. Guns had been hidden on the farm without his knowledge. He was forced to leave Galway and move to Dublin. He found an apartment in a slum in the middle of Dublin but he could not find regular work. Life was very hard back then.
Betty: So where did he get the money to come to America?
Mom: The money was sent to him. His older brother Matt had emigrated to Chicago a few years earlier. Matt sent him a ticket in 1921. That's the way a lot of families did it. They helped each other.
Betty: But you said Grandma Pat came here in 1925?
Mom: Yes! You see, she was still a baby in 1921 so she was taken back to her grandmother in Galway until she was old enough to travel.
Betty: Why?
Mom: Well, your great-grandma was turned back at Ellis Island. They said she was ill.
Betty: That must have been really hard.
Mom: Yes. She began to cry when she told me about that.
Betty: Did Grandma Pat miss Ireland when she got here?
Mom: No, she was too young. But her father did. Your great-grandpa didn't speak English very well so it was hard for him here. He was lonely.
Betty: I thought they spoke English in Ireland.
Mom: People do today. However, most Irish people used to speak another language called Gaelic. Most people today still speak a little but there are only a few native speakers left.
Betty: Wow! There is a lot I don't know about our family. I'm really looking forward to opening that box in the attic so I can find out more.

b) Listen to the conversation again. Answer the following questions.

1. What is Betty's homework?
2. What can Betty's mother give Betty for her homework?
3. Where is Betty's grandmother from?
4. When did Betty's grandmother arrive in America?
5. Who did Betty's grandmother come to America with?
6. Who had already emigrated to America a few years earlier?
7. Why didn't Betty's great-grandmother move to America?
8. What is Betty looking forward to?

B5 The Flynn family

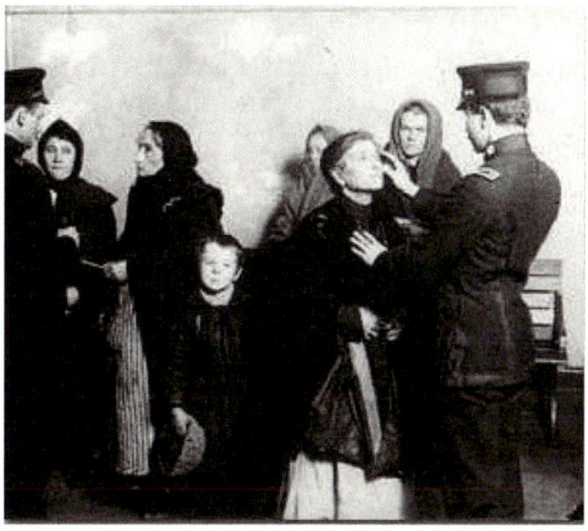

Here are some important events from the Flynn family history. Read the dialogue in B4. Then match the sentences to the right time expressions and put them in the correct order. Write them in your exercise book.

1. Matt Flynn emigrated to America
2. Grandma was brought back to her grandmother in Galway
3. Grandma was taken to America
4. Matt sent Betty's great-grandfather a ticket
5. Her great-grandfather's house was destroyed

a) in 1921.

b) during the rebellion in 1919.

c) a few years earlier.

d) in 1925.

e) in 1921.

Language gym
p. 56, ex. 3 + 4

B6 Your family history

a) Ask your grandparents or your parents about the history of your family. Make notes of events and dates. Then write a text about your family.

Example: *My mother's parents were born in a small village near ...*
They moved to ...
My father's parents lived in ...
Before my mother's parents went to ... they had lived in ...

**b) Sit in groups of four.
Put everybody's text face down on the table and mix them up.
One person reads a text aloud without saying the pupil's name.
The others have to guess whose family history is being read.**

- *grandparents: Selma and Mehmet*
- *year of birth: 1933 and 1929*
- *place of birth: Ankara and Konya*
- *immigrated to Germany in 1978*
- *...*

- *grandparents: Margarete and Jürgen*
- *year of birth: 1934 and 1930*
- *place of birth: Selbitz and Limburg*
- *moved to Oberjosbach in 1958*
- *...*

portfolio

WB
B5, B6

Language gym

1 **These are the meanings of some words from the text in B1. Which words are described? When you have found them, describe five more words and ask your partner to find them.**

1. People who come to a country to live there
2. All the people who live in a country or city
3. To not allow into a country
4. Not lucky
5. People who visit a city or country
6. A large collection of information

2 **What is meant here? Write complete sentences.**

Example: **Last of 12 million immigrants processed yesterday**

The last of 12 million immigrants was processed yesterday.

Bear shot – *Last week …*

Famous singer refused entry for USA – *At 12.30 today …*

Gangster caught – *Every day …*

Boat found in Atlantic Ocean – *Four days ago …*

3 **Active or passive? Fill in the right forms of the verbs.**

My grandparents … (to be born) in Poland. They … (not to have) much money. They … (to decide) to move to Germany in 1982. Money … (to send) by Grandpa's brother who was living in Essen. They … (to escape) across the border into the Czech Republic in 1981. From there they … (to smuggle) into Austria by friends. Grandpa's brother … (to meet) them and … (to drive) them to Essen. My grandma spoke good German but my grandpa … (not to speak) good German. Still, he … (to find) a job and … (to teach) by his colleagues. Three months later, their children … (to send) for. My mum … (to arrive) in Essen on 3rd March 1983. She … (to begin) school and … (to teach) German by a young German man. They … (to fall) in love and … (to marry) five years later. My older brother … (to be born) in 1994 and I … (to be born) in 1997.

CD

4 **American or British English? Listen to the words spoken with a typical American or British accent. Copy the table into your exercise book and note down which accent you hear each time.**

France | enter | unfortunate | tourist attraction | Statue of Liberty | processed | Mr Universe | inspector

American English	British English
…	…

You have read about the origins of different words. You have also read about the experiences of immigrants on Ellis Island. You have written a text about your own family history.

Ellis Island **is visited by** many tourists.
English **is spoken** in Ireland.
People **were sent back** to their countries.
Grandma **was turned back** at Ellis Island.

Memory Box

C1 Going to school in Harlem

Read the story. Who is telling it? Where is the person?

I spotted the guy from the opposite apartment. He was getting into the black limousine I had seen the day before. "Hey," the guy yelled, "wanna have a ride to school?" I didn't need a ride. It wasn't far from Strivers Row to West 138th Street so I should have known that something was up. There aren't many black limousines around here and even fewer would stop to give a kid a ride to school. I got into the car, which had waited for me. "Cool, man," I said as I sat in the back beside Leroy, the coolest dude on our block, who only wore the newest and the best.

"Hey, wait till the kids see me step out of this ride," I grinned cheerfully at Leroy. He didn't reply. But that was OK, I thought as the driver turned right on Seventh Avenue. "Those are some bad threads you got on bro," I said, trying to sound hip. "That shirt I saw you in yesterday must have cost $300." Leroy still didn't say anything. In fact, that guy, who was normally so cool, sure was looking pretty nervous. I started looking out the window. I felt uneasy.

"Hey dude, you just passed my street," I said as the driver flashed by 137th Street where he should have turned left.

"That's OK, kid," said a man I had not noticed from the passenger seat. "You can play hooky today."

"Hey, I can't man, we have final practice and a test today after school." I was starting to get pretty annoyed.

The man turned to look me in the eye. He didn't raise his voice. "You are not going to school today kid and I ain't gonna say it again. OK?"

Nobody ever said I was the sharpest knife in the drawer but even I knew you'd better not talk back to a guy like that. Sometimes, it's better to keep your mouth shut.

But you can't just shut your mind. All kind of thoughts were going through my head, like my mother saying, "Don't get into a car with a man you don't know." Others were questions like "What was I doing here?" I also thought of men shooting guns, men robbing a bank, men kidnapping children.

I saw cops arresting men, even shooting at them. I got more and more anxious.

After about 25 minutes, we passed Dr Martin Luther King Junior Blvd and ten minutes later, we turned left and pulled over. We were told to get out and stay quiet. I recognized Minton's Playhouse so I knew we were on 118th Street. My Uncle Tommy, who was an ex-marine, had a store nearby.

I paused for a second on the sidewalk to look around when I felt a hand push my left shoulder. "Move it, kid," someone shouted at me. The passenger was right behind me, on the left. The guy who had been driving was just in front of me on my right. I pretended to stumble. As I expected, the passenger tried to grab my arm to stop me falling. In one movement, I put a thumb lock on him and threw him over my shoulder against the driver. You see, I knew how to do that. I had practiced that for my black belt in judo. I felt good. But the driver, who was a strong man, was too fast. Somehow he was behind me. I saw something which was in his hand. The lights went out.

> *He was getting into the black limousine I had seen before.*
>
> *"That's OK, kid," said a man I had not noticed from the passenger seat.*

skills
How to read
p. 124/1

skills
How to work with words
p. 120/1

WB
C1

C2 What happened?

a) Read the story in C1 again. Put the pictures in the right order.

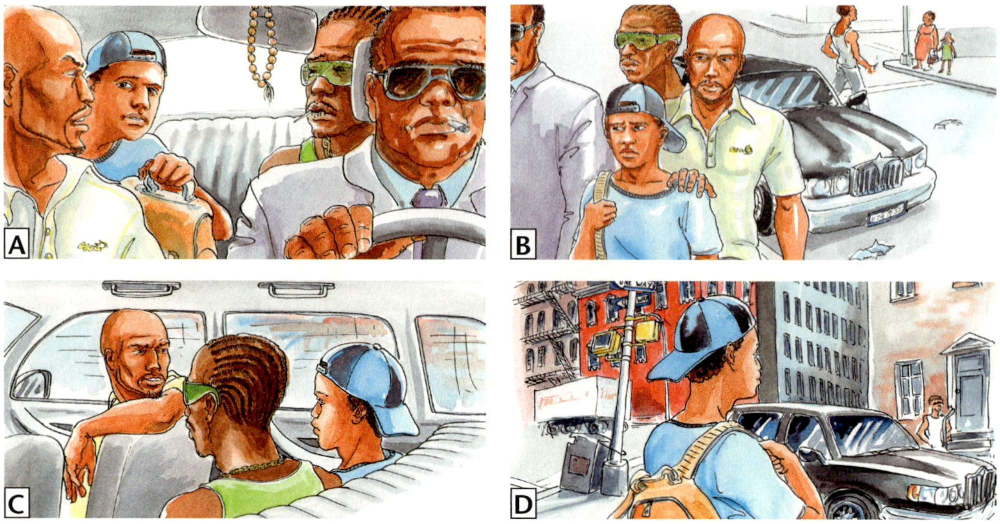

b) What do you think happened next? Discuss with your partner.

WB C2

c) Write an ending to the story. Read it out to the class.

C3 Just a dream

Here is the original ending to the story.

"Come on, wake up." My face was slapped. "Come on, open your eyes." I was awake but I kept my eyes closed. I was frightened. I remember thinking I should have walked to school.
I remember thinking how nice it was to save the bus fare and buy ice cream or a hot dog with the money. Would I ever get that chance again?
"Come on, wake up or you'll miss breakfast," said my mother as I finally realized I had been dreaming.

skills
How to write
p. 127/1

**a) Do you like the ending?
Why? Why not? Tell your partner.**

funny • unexpected • strange • stupid • boring • shocking • interesting • amusing

I think that … / In my opinion … / To my mind … / The way I see it … / I thought … / I believe that … / I expected …

Language gym
p. 60, ex. 1

WB C3

b) Write a summary of the whole story.

C4 Keeping safe

Read the statements. Decide whether you must add *who*, *which* or *that* or nothing at all.

lif
14
p. 147

1. Don't start a fight … you can't win.
2. Run away from people … are trying to attack you.
3. Never take sweets from people … you don't know.
4. Don't get into situations … nobody can control.
5. Be careful with dogs on the street … have no owner.

WB C4, C5

Language gym
p. 60, ex. 2

C5 Living in Harlem

a) Read the text, and give each paragraph a title.

b) Make a list of the girl's arguments for and against life in Harlem. Compare your list to your partner's list.

c) Make a list of the words and phrases the girl uses to introduce her ideas: *Firstly etc.*

d) Write a similar text with pros and cons about your neighbourhood.

You all know Harlem, and the stories about Harlem. It doesn't have a good reputation, but it is my home: I love it.

Sadly, Harlem is not perfect. Firstly, there is the poverty. A lot of people here are unemployed. My best friend's parents haven't had a job for years so my friend has to work as a waitress to help her family get by. Secondly, healthcare is very expensive and there aren't enough doctors here so we have to travel to get treatment. My neighbor can't afford to see a dentist and his teeth are in really bad shape. He must have terrible toothaches!

Finally, Harlem is still quite poor compared to the rest of New York so there is much crime.

A few days ago, two women were attacked and robbed just down the road from my house. Even at school we have problems with guns. There is a metal detector at school but that doesn't stop the worst guys. Teachers are sometimes attacked by students.

On the other hand, there is tons to do here and the culture is so rich. There is a lot of jazz, and New York's nickname "The Big Apple" comes from a famous jazz club in Harlem. We're really proud of this fact. In my opinion the music is the best thing about living here. I sing in a gospel choir twice a week. I sang my first solo the other week. I was so nervous, but I enjoyed it in the end. We do concerts every few weeks and we always have a big party afterwards.

Harlem is also really beautiful, but only people who live here seem to know that. Harlem was very poor for a long time so people couldn't keep up the buildings. My parents keep telling me how dirty and run-down everything was when they were young. Nowadays it is nice. I mean, it is still a little bit dirty but most of it is alright. Our apartment is old, but we try to make the best of it.

I think that the other great aspect of this neighborhood is the food. The restaurants here are second to none. I love it when my parents sometimes take me out to a restaurant – it is better than the food Mom cooks! My favorite is Bayou on Lenox Avenue, which serves Southern food. I really love it!

Last but not least is the sense of community in Harlem. Although there are different people from all over the world, we all stick together here. I have tons of friends at school and we are very close because we have to fight the same prejudices. My cousin lives in Brooklyn, but it isn't as friendly as here. The houses and stuff there are nicer, but she doesn't have as many friends.

To sum things up, there are advantages and disadvantages to living in Harlem. It suffers from unemployment and the problems this creates. However, this also creates the community spirit that I love. Since there is so much here that I love, I can put up with the rest.

skills
How to write
p. 128/2

C6 Fighting prejudices

Your grandma sees you reading this text but she doesn't understand English. She has heard of Harlem's bad reputation and wants to know if it's true.
Tell her in German what you found out about Harlem.

skills
How to mediate
p. 126

Language gym
p. 60, ex. 3 + 4

WB
C6

C7 For and against

a) Form two groups in class and look at C5b) and c) again. One group concentrates on keywords for arguments *for* Harlem, the other group concentrates on keywords *against* Harlem. Think of housing, relations, jobs, activities etc.

b) Discuss the pros and cons of living in Harlem with the help of your keywords. Which group has a better argumentation?

skills
How to speak
p. 130/2

3 Language gym

1 **a) Find words in the box that are used for people in the story in C1.**

passenger • fall • guy • ex-marine • turn • mother • stumble • cop • step • drive • driver

b) Write down the rest of the words. Which of the names below can you give this group of words?

adjectives of sport | verbs of giving opinion | verbs of movement

2 **a) The boy in the story (C1–C3) is telling his mother about his strange dream. Write correct sentences into your exercise book**

1. The man / into that huge car / before / was getting / which / I / had seen
2. got into / the car / I / that / for me / had waited
3. on our block / who / I / beside a guy / sat / is / dude / the coolest
4. the car / stopped / after half an hour / which / in a place / knew / I
5. the thing / afraid of / I / was / the driver / had / which / in his hand

CD

b) Look at your sentences again. Cross *who, which* or *that* out where possible.

3 **Read C5 again. Use the words in the switchboard and make sentences about Harlem.**

Poverty		a place	the girl loves to sing.
The Big Apple		the food	a lot of people have.
Southern Food	is	the music	people …
Harlem		a problem	she …
Gospel		the name	…

4 **Say the words. Listen for the odd one out.**

/əʊ/ shoulder, although, sound, though
/ʌ/ enough, through, country, double
/ɒ/ tons, along, job, cons
/iː/ mean, really, great, least
/ʊ/ cook, good, neigbourhood, school

You have read a story of a boy in Harlem and have written the ending of the story. You have also read an article about Harlem and talked about the pros and cons of living there. You have written an article about your own neighbourhood.

Monday through Friday	Monday to Friday
harbor	harbour
subway	underground
apartment	flat
cops	police
sidewalk	pavement
sick	ill
gotten	got

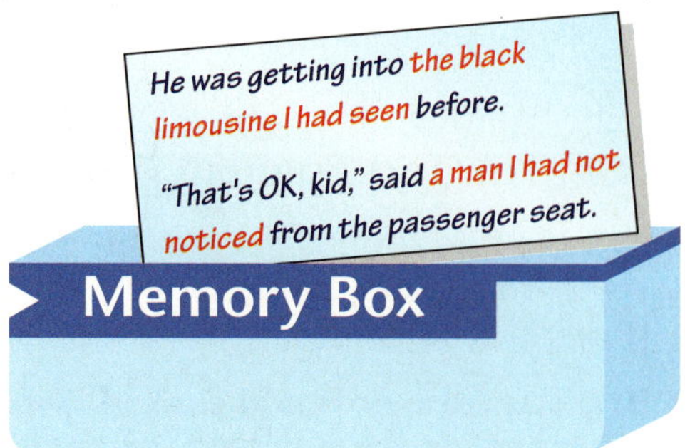

On the move

4

CD

A1 Return to innocence

a) Listen to the Native American song by Enigma. What does the singer tell you to do? Write down three things you can understand.

skills
How to listen
p. 122

b) Read Chief Tecumseh's statement. Think about it. Who are *they*? What do you think Chief Tecumseh means by *avarice* and *oppression*? Tell the class.

WB
A1

"They have vanished before the avarice and the oppression of the White Man, as snow before a summer sun."

Chief Tecumseh
(Shawnee tribe)
1768–1813

A2 Where are the Native Americans?

a) Read the text and find out if your ideas in A1b) are right.

Chief Tecumseh and his tribe, like other Native Americans, were robbed of their natural environment. Europeans pushed into the New World, hoping to find more space for themselves and their beliefs. By doing so, they forced many Native Americans to give up their culture and homes. They had to move into reservations. This was infertile land given to the tribe by the government, and was called 'Indian Territory'.
Not all Native Americans were warriors like the Chickasaws, who originally lived northeast of the Mississippi but were forced into reservations in Oklahoma. The Kickapoo tribe, located first on the shores of Lake Michigan was forced to settle in Kansas. Most of the tribes were simple farmers, hunters and fishermen, like the Seminoles, who settled in Florida. Other peaceful tribes include the Mohawks, located mostly in Ontario, Quebec and New York, and the Delaware tribe, originally from Delaware and New Jersey but forced to move to Oklahoma. Today there are about 300 reservations in the USA, and they are seen as totally separate from the rest of America.

b) Look at the map on the inside cover of your textbook. Write down the route and the distance each tribe had to travel in your exercise book. Name the states the Native Americans had to travel through. Work in groups.

skills
How to present
something in class
p. 132

c) One of your group presents the routes to the class. Check by following the route on the map.

A3 Then and now!

Look at the two maps and compare them. Tell the class what has changed.

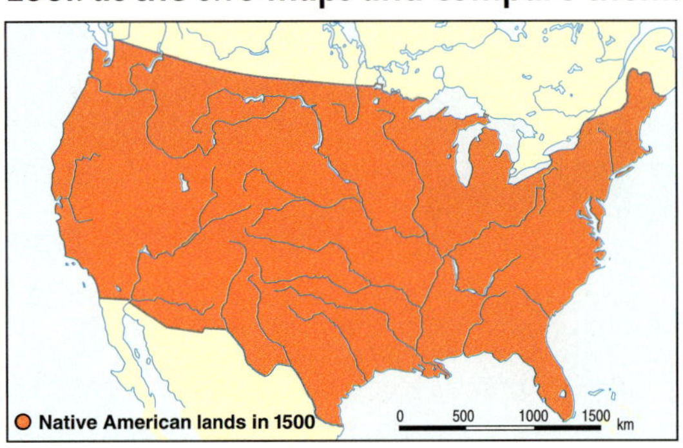

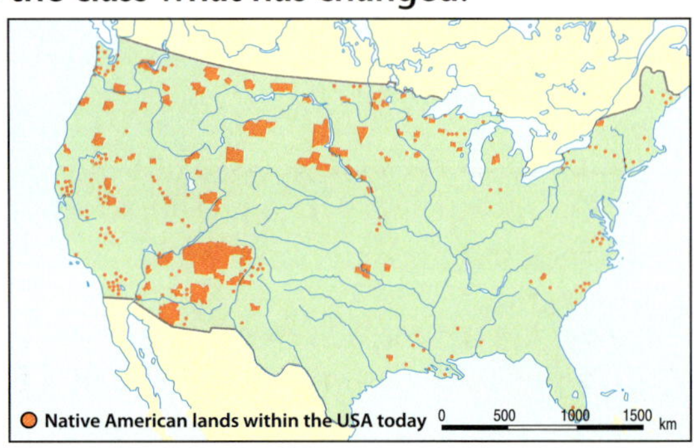

A4 Life on a reservation

Johnny Deermount is a member of a Native American tribe.

a) Read his story and find out
- **where his tribe has been living for many years.**
- **what he has been doing since he went to New York.**

Johnny used to live with his parents and his sister Shannaw on a reservation in Connecticut. The family has been living there for three generations. One year ago Johnny decided to move to New York City and study to become a lawyer. Since he went away Shannaw has been thinking of leaving too because there are hardly any jobs on the reservation. Mr and Mrs Deermount can understand their children well. Life has not improved over the years. Many members of their tribe suffer from poverty and, as a result, have become depressive or started to drink too much alcohol. There are hardly any doctors on the reservation. Despite all this, Mr and Mrs Deermount love their reservation land and would never want to move anywhere else.
For Johnny lots of things have changed since he started studying. He has been going to seminars on minority groups and Native Rights because he would like to help his tribe.
One day Johnny calls his father. He is very excited: "Dad, I've been thinking a lot about how we can tell people about our problems. Listen!"

Facts about Native Americans
Did you know that ...
- reservations are often compared to Third World Nations?
- about one third of all young adults living on reservations leave to find a job?
- infant mortality rates are much higher and life expectancy is much lower than the national averages?
- the suicide rate of Native Americans is three times the national average?
- the number of teenage pregnancies has increased by 15 % since the 1990s?
- to attract tourists and gain some money, many tribes have started up casinos?

skills
How to read
p. 124/1

WB
A2, A3

skills
How to work with words
p. 121/2

b) What could Johnny's idea be? Work in groups. Compare your ideas and write them on a poster. Present your poster to the class and hang it up on the wall.

c) Write your ending of the story in your exercise book.

Language gym
p. 66, ex. 1 + 2

I have been thinking
he has been going
they have been living

A5 At university

Johnny is talking to his friend David, another law student. David is very interested in the problems of Native Americans and asks Johnny some questions about his tribe.

Read A4 again. Complete the dialogue and write it in your exercise book.

David: How long has your family been living on the reservation?
Johnny: …
David: What do your parents and your sister think about your decision to leave the reservation?
Johnny: …
David: Have things on the reservation been improving or getting worse in the last few years?
Johnny: …
David: What are the main problems?
Johnny: …
David: Have you learned more about these things in your seminars here?
Johnny: …
David: Is that why you want to become a lawyer?
Johnny: …

lif
15
p. 149

A6 Johnny's idea

CD

skills
How to listen
p. 122

WB
A4, A5

a) You are going to listen to Johnny's conversation with his father about his idea. Here are three summaries of the phone call with his father. Find out which summary is the correct one.

1. Johnny tells his father about the organization 'Young Natives' which his ancestors founded in Oklahoma many years ago.

2. Johnny suggests that the Native Americans must try to make all Americans aware of their problems by writing about their situation in a magazine.

3. Johnny tells his father that they must get in touch with the other Native Americans. Johnny thinks it is important that they are finally seen the same way the white settlers are seen.

b) Listen again and take notes about the project Johnny is talking about.

c) If you had the opportunity to support Johnny Deermount, what would you do? Present your ideas to the class.

I would …

I suggest that …

Maybe …

It might be a good idea to …

A7 The Mohawk Trail

a) Which states does the Mohawk Trail go through?

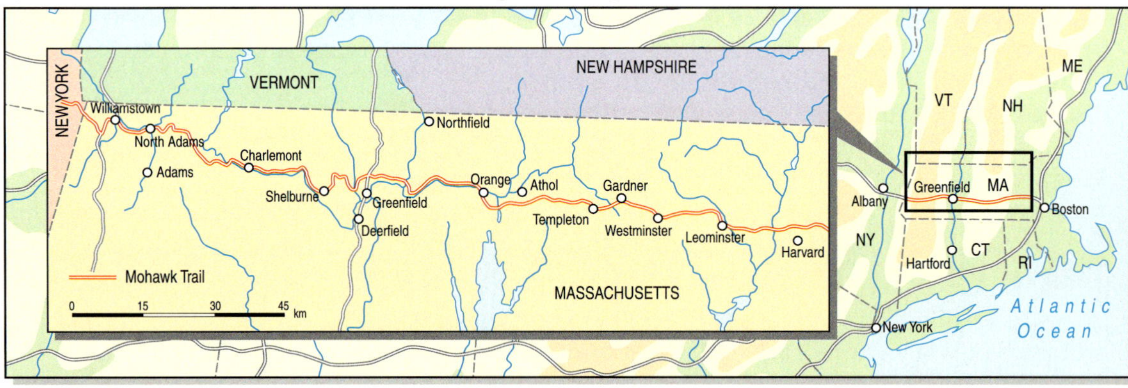

b) Read the text. Write down eight sentences you find the most important in your exercise book.

The Mohawk Trail:
Hundreds of years ago Native Americans used to travel vast distances so they made footpaths for themselves. One of these was the Mohawk Trail, which still exists and is visited by tourists who want to recapture the feeling of Native America. Only local tribes used the path until European settlers came to America. The settlers used it, too, to travel between the English settlements of Boston, Deerfield and the Dutch settlements in New York.

The original Mohawk Trail was only 18 inches wide, which is just enough space for one person to pass through. Native Americans walked behind each other. With the settlers and traders came the wheel so the path was widened. Before the settlers arrived, Native Americans from various tribes had shared land like hunting and fishing areas.
Through early contact with the Europeans, many Native Americans died from disease and wars. The Natives weren't strong enough to protect their land or their people. The settlers wanted land and thought of ways to get it.
For example, the British and the Dutch invited two Indian tribes, the Pocumtucks and the Mohawks, to a 'peace conference', where they killed an important Mohawk leader and told his tribe that the Pocumtucks were guilty. Then a war between the Mohawks and the Pocumtucks broke out in which both sides lost a lot of warriors. The British later marched up the Connecticut River and the Dutch took control of the Hudson River. Both groups killed Native Americans along the way and took over their land. Two tribes, once living in peace together, were almost totally wiped out.

c) Go through the text again. Find words with the same meaning as the following ones:

different | a narrow place to walk | to ask somebody to come | to have less strength | to be there | the ones to blame | a meeting aimed at stopping or avoiding a war

WB
A6, A7

Language gym
p. 66, ex. 3+4

A8 In a café in Boston

skills
How to mediate
p. 126

You and an American friend are sitting in a café in Boston, Massachusetts and are planning to go down the Mohawk Trail. A German tourist is sitting at the next table. He doesn't understand a lot of English but overhears your conversation and asks about the path.

Help your friend and the German tourist to understand each other.
Then act out the conversation.

German tourist: Guten Tag. Ich möchte nicht unhöflich sein, aber könnten Sie mir bitte etwas über diesen Mohawk Trail erzählen?
American friend: What did he say?
You: He said he would like to hear a little bit about the Mohawk Trail.
American friend: Well, it starts in New York and runs through to Massachusetts, almost to Boston.
You: …
American friend: Would he like to know some details about the towns? The history?
You: …
German tourist: Ich habe mich schon immer für Geschichte interessiert. Kann man den Pfad eigentlich an einem Tag laufen?
You: …
American friend: If he is driving, he can get to New York in a day. It would take him much longer to walk. How is he planning to travel?
You: …
German tourist: Ich hatte eigentlich vor zu laufen. Aber so eine lange Strecke werde ich mit dem Auto fahren.
You: …
American friend: Have a good time and enjoy the sights along the trail.
You: …
German tourist: Vielen Dank für Ihre Hilfe.
You: …

4 Language gym

1 Complete the following sentences using *since* or *for*. Write them in your exercise book.

1. Johnny Deermount has been living in New York … last April.
2. He has been interested in Native Rights … many years.
3. At university Johnny has met some students who have had the same thoughts and interests … a long time.
4. Johnny has been working on a presentation for a seminar about Native Rights … last week.
5. He has promised his family to improve their situation … he decided to move to New York.
6. Living a better life has been his dream … he was a little boy.

CD

2 Put the words in the right order and write the sentences in your exercise book.

1. since / has been studying / Johnny / law / he moved / to New York
2. the wars / in Connecticut / since / against the settlers / Johnny's tribe / on a reservation / has been living
3. for / have not been changing / Problems / many years / on the reservation
4. Johnny's tribe / farming / traditionally / has been living / from
5. Shannaw / a very long time / to find a job / has been trying / for / near her home
6. have been working / since / they started up casinos / for the gambling industry / Other Native Americans

3 Match the sentence parts and copy the sentences into your exercise book.

1. Before the settlers arrived,
2. Through contact with the Europeans
3. The Native Americans weren't strong enough
4. The British marched up the Connecticut River
5. The British and the Dutch

a. killing the Native Americans and taking over their land.
b. quietly killed an important Mohawk leader during the 'peace conference'.
c. a lot of Native Americans died.
d. the Native Americans had shared things.
e. to protect their land or their people.

CD

4 Say these words out loud. Write down the ones that have the /eɪ/ sound.

able, tribe, made, wipe, area, day, land, came, various, way, native, write, share, trader

I have been going
You have been thinking
He / She has been living
They have been changing

Memory Box

You have learned something about the history and the problems of Native Americans in the USA. You have also helped a German tourist find out about the Mohawk Trail.

B1 The gold rush

a) Look at the picture and describe it to your partner. Think of the situation, the people and the atmosphere.

b) Read the text and write down two arguments why you would / would not have liked to pan for gold. Compare the reasons in class.

In 1849 everybody was talking about the news: 'Gold in California!' A man named James Marshall had discovered a gold nugget in 1848 and people started spreading the news. Hundreds of thousands of people made their way across the country to find gold. Families went west, leaving their homes and relatives behind them. Wagon trains were formed. Between 1848 and 1854 the city of San Francisco grew from 14,000 to 230,000 inhabitants.

Companies had to close because the workers all ran off to search for gold.
Ships couldn't leave San Francisco's port because the sailors had left as well.
The main gold rush period was between 1848 and 1854. During this time, many people found their gold, while others just stayed there and kept on searching.
Gold made California rich. In 1850 it joined the Union (USA) as the 31st state.
James Marshall, who had originally discovered the gold, died a poor man.

WB B1, B2

B2 The El Dorado of the West

Henry has just arrived from England at the gold diggers' camp near San Francisco. He wants to start digging for gold immediately. Liam and Patrick, two Irishmen who came with the first wave of gold diggers, are telling him what to expect.

Read the dialogue. Find seven keywords that describe the diggers' experience at the camp. Quote three things that are interesting / surprising / boring for you.

CD

Henry: Well, it took me long enough to get here. I hope it's worth it. I left everything to come here. Wife, kids, job, everything. People said I could find enough gold to live easier for the rest of my life.

Liam: Ha! I think every digger around here would want that. That's if he gets out alive.

Henry: What do you mean?

Patrick: Well, have you seen the gold diggers? Have you seen the state of them? A lot of them have scurvy because of the stuff they eat.

Liam: Many of them will be lucky if they can pay their way home. One guy I knew went crazy and nearly died.

Henry: But isn't anyone finding gold?

Liam: Sure. You can find it along the riverbanks and streams. But most of them spend what they find on gambling.

Patrick: There aren't many that strike it rich.

Henry: They said the gold was just lying around in nuggets for anyone to pick up.

Patrick: Maybe, but no one I know has found nuggets. Most of them pan for it by the rivers.

Liam: Yeah. But it's pretty dangerous around here. Someone said that a guy had been murdered over a gold claim. It's crazy, there are people stealing, lying, gambling, murdering and no one to stop them.

Henry: So there's no sheriff here?

Liam: There are sheriffs, but the situation is really out of hand here. They can't cope with it. Especially the gambling. Some men make and lose thousands in a night.

Patrick: True. I've seen small boys bet $10, lose it and go back and dig some more. What they don't find in the goldfields, they will try and win at the gambling table.

Henry: Well, I guess the whole thing is a gamble. Nothing ventured, nothing gained.

WB B3

Language gym p. 70, ex. 1

*"There **are** sheriffs."*	→	*He said there **were** sheriffs.*
"... was ..."	→	*... had been ...*
"... spend ..."	→	*... spent ...*
"... have / has been ..."	→	*... had been ...*
"... had been ..."	→	*... had been ...*
"... can ..."	→	*... could ...*
"... will ..."	→	*... would ...*

B3 Who said what?

Look at B2 again. Find out who said these sentences. Write complete sentences in your exercise book.

lif 16 p. 149

Example: 1. Who said that it had taken him long enough to get there?
It was Henry. He said: "It took me long enough to get here."

2. Who told Henry that a lot of gold diggers had scurvy?
3. Who asked if there wasn't anyone finding gold?
4. Who mentioned that you could find the gold along the riverbanks and streams?
5. Who answered that the situation was really out of hand there?
6. Who explained that the gold diggers would try and win at the gambling table?

WB B4

B4 From St. Joseph to Sacramento

As the West of the USA became more and more populated, it was necessary to make communication possible between the East and the West.

a) In many towns across the West of the USA there are statues like these. Can you guess why? What do they commemorate?

I think ...

I know that ...

Perhaps they are ...

Maybe ...

b) Write down six questions with the help of these facts and figures. Work with a partner. Take turns to answer each other's questions.

c) Close your book. Write down what you remember about the Pony Express in your exercise book. Then check your results with your partner's.
Start like this: *The Pony Express was a mail service.*

PONY EXPRESS
MAIL SERVICE
between St. Joseph (Missouri) and Sacramento (California)
April 1860 - November 1861
about 80 riders, 400 - 500 horses
fresh horse every 10 - 15 miles,
fresh rider every 75 - 100 miles
about 10 days

B5 Riders wanted!

a) Read the advertisement and tell the class in German all the information it gives you.

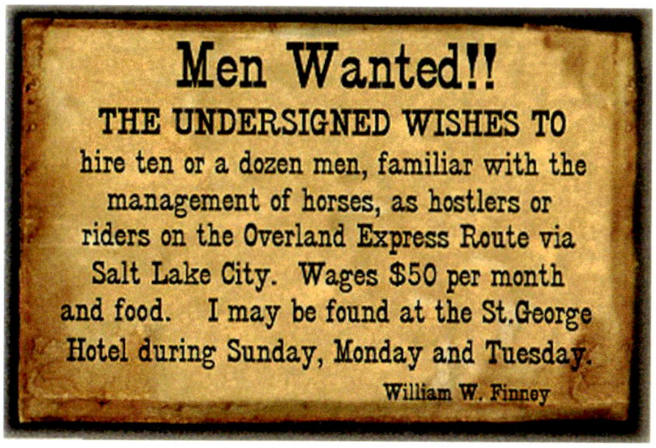

b) Billy, a young man, has just seen the advertisement pinned to a tree in town and talks to his friend Jack about it. Copy the beginning of the conversation into your exercise book and go on.

Billy: *Jack! Guess what I've just seen! They want men!*
Jack: *Who? Where? What are you talking about?*

skills
How to mediate
p. 126

WB
B5

B6 Life with the Pony Express

a) Read the text. Take notes about the things that Danny learned about the Pony Express. Then compare the results with your partner's and quote from the text.

Danny, a young boy of nine, lived with his father in a lonely area in the Rocky Mountains. After the boy's mother had died, his father took over the Pony Express station there. The Pony Express riders came to the station to quickly eat, drink, and change horses. Danny was fascinated and waited for each rider to arrive. He wanted to ask many questions. Maybe he could be a rider some day too. Danny liked being with these interesting men and was sad when they left their tired horses at the station and rode off again on fresh horses.
All in all, 75 ponies were needed. The Pony Express riders usually needed about ten days from east to west.
One day, Danny's favorite rider arrived at the station. Danny's father had a big bowl of hot soup ready for him.
Then he and Danny sat down at the table with him. Danny suddenly started talking to his favorite rider. "Sir, how long have you been a Pony Express man?" The rider smiled at him and answered: "I've been on the route for almost a year now but I haven't gotten used to it. It was hard from the start and many of my friends have been killed." He looked down at his soup bowl and added: "I have seen so many sad things." Suddenly Danny didn't want to be a rider anymore. He didn't want his friend to finish his route to Salt Lake City. Danny touched the man's arm and said: "Please don't finish this route. It's too dangerous!" His Pony Express friend smiled and replied: "I have only got one more ride to go. Then I'll stop. I've asked my girlfriend to marry me."

skills
How to read
p. 124/1

WB
B6, B7

b) Finish the story in a suitable way. Write four to five sentences.

skills
How to write
p. 127/1

c) Form groups of four. Read out your endings to your group members. Which story ending do you like best? Say why. Then listen to the original ending.

Language gym
p. 70, ex. 2+3

CD

4 Language gym

1 **Copy the lists into your exercise book. Then complete the lists with the help of a dictionary. Can you find more examples?**

verbs	nouns
win	***winner***
think	
murder	
lose	
dig	

adjectives	nouns
lucky	***luck***
rich	
crazy	
long	
successful	

2 A reporter interviewed some people about the gold rush and the Pony Express. After the interview he wrote an article for the local newspaper.
Complete his article. Start like this:
Last week I spoke to some people and asked them questions about the gold rush and the Pony Express. A student told me that ... A young woman said that ... A couple mentioned ...

3 Henry (B2) writes a letter to his family back home in England. He tells them about what he has heard. **Finish Henry's letter to his family.**

Dear Maude, Jane and Jack,
After a long journey to the El Dorado of the West, I finally arrived here. I spoke to two men called Liam and Patrick who told me that they had come from Ireland. I told them I had left everything behind to come to the United States. Patrick said that a lot of gold diggers here were sick because they didn't eat proper food. Liam said that many diggers would be lucky if they could pay for the trip home. He mentioned that you could find gold by the rivers.

Memory Box

"I'm very tired."	→	*She said she was very tired.*
"... was ..."	→	*... had been ...*
"... spend ..."	→	*... spent ...*
"... have been ..."	→	*... had been ...*
"... had been ..."	→	*... had been ...*
"... can ..."	→	*... could ...*
"... will ..."	→	*... would ...*

You have learned about the gold rush and the Pony Express in the USA. You have talked about a story and have made up your own ending to it.

C1 A long way to freedom

a) What does the word *freedom* mean to you?
Work in groups of four. Collect your ideas and write them on a piece of paper. Then decide on one statement and present it to the class.

b) Read the following text about the history of African Americans. Then find a headline for each paragraph. Work in pairs.

skills
How to read
p. 124/1

In the 16th century European slave traders started buying slaves in Africa. They took them to America in big ships. During the trip, which sometimes lasted six or seven weeks, many of the men, women and children died because they didn't have enough food to eat or fresh water to drink. There was so little room in the ships that they weren't able to stand up or move around.

In the New World, the slaves who had survived the trip were sold to white settlers. Most of them had to work on sugar, tobacco or cotton plantations. The slaves had no rights at all. If they didn't work hard enough, the settlers could beat them or even kill them. The slaves were neither taught English nor how to read and write. Their children, too, grew up and died as slaves.

Most Northern states took steps to end slavery in the first half of the 19th century. The growing industry in the North attracted many immigrants from Europe and slaves were not needed any more. In contrast to this, the Southern states still used slaves to work on their plantations. At that time a number of people successfully helped slaves to escape the South and enjoy freedom in the North. This movement was called the 'Underground Railroad' though it had nothing to do with trains. Hiding places were known as 'stations' and people who helped were called 'conductors'.

This difference between the Northern and Southern states led to the American Civil War in 1861. In 1863, President Abraham Lincoln declared the end of slavery. The South was defeated in this war and slavery was finally ended in 1865.
But black Americans continued to live in poverty. They also suffered from discrimination and laws which limited their freedom. Many Southern states passed laws which became known as the black codes. Some of these codes did not allow black people to own land and to choose the kind of work they wanted to do. Others did not allow them to enter a town without permission from their white employer or to go out at night. In some states they could even be arrested for not having a job.

37

c) Make up five questions about the text and write them in your exercise book. Work in pairs. Ask and answer each other's questions.

WB
C1

C2 Are all men equal?

lif 17, 18 p. 150

a) Look at the picture. What do you think the young men are talking about? Draw a speech bubble on a sheet of paper and write down your ideas. Then present them in class.

b) Read Phil's letter to the theater manager.

Dear theater manager,
I am really angry about the sign "Whites Only" in front of your theater. Why are there still separate theaters for black and white people?
Last weekend my friends and I decided to go to your theater. On our way there I felt really excited about seeing the play. But when we arrived the man at your box office told us to go to a theater for "Colored People". Why? We can pay the entrance fee to your theater just like anyone else. And it is so much closer to where we live. The only theater for colored people I know is miles away. You can guess how angry and disappointed we were. I just don't understand it.
I am the grandson of former slaves. My grandparents are very proud of me because I was the first person in my family who learned to read and write. My grandparents were never allowed to go to school and my parents still cannot read properly. Some rich white people down in Virginia forced my grandpa to spend many years of his life working on their tobacco plantations and they ordered Grandma to work as one of their housemaids. White children were told not to play with my mom and dad. My parents were not allowed to go to school. That's why they keep telling me how lucky I am to be a free man.
Free? I don't know if I am. Nowadays, laws officially apply to everyone, black or white. Why do the so-called "segregation laws" still exist? Wherever you go, there are signs saying "Whites Only" posted at the entrances. In public places, in front of restaurants, even at hospitals they ask black guys like me to leave and stay by ourselves. Why do you allow us to learn how to read? Just so we can read the signs? Can you guess how it feels to be sent away all the time, just because the color of your skin is different? These signs make me sad. They just show that we still live in a world full of prejudice. No, "freedom" doesn't seem the right word.
Thank you for taking the time to read my letter.
Very truly yours, Phil Johnson

c) Talk to your partner about Phil's experiences. How do you feel about them?

It's surprising / unfair / shocking …
I didn't know that … / I knew that …
I wouldn't have thought that …
I think it's good / important that …
Phil should / shouldn't …

They ordered Grandma to work.
They ask black guys like me to leave.

The man told us to go.
White children were told not to pl
with my mom and dad.

d) Compare Phil's life to his grandparents' life when they were young. Write eight sentences in your exercise book.

What Phil writes about his life:	What his grandparents' life was like when they were young:
White people often tell him to …	**White people forced them to …**
…	…

WB C2

C3 About a girl and a woman

a) Read the stories of Linda Brown and Rosa Parks. The stories are mixed. Choose one character and write the full story in your exercise book.

At the beginning of the 20th century a group of black and white citizens in New York City founded the National Association for the Advancement of Colored People (NAACP). They wanted to ensure the rights of minority groups and fight against racial discrimination. Black leaders began to use marches, demonstrations and the courts to stop racist laws. A very famous case was that of seven-year-old Linda Brown from Topeka, Kansas.

Another important case happened in Montgomery, Alabama. She was not allowed to go to a school which was just four blocks away from her home because she was black. Rosa Parks was asked to give up her bus seat to a white man. She refused and was arrested by the police. Linda's father went to the Supreme Court. In response to this, NAACP-leaders told black people not to use the buses in Montgomery any more. The boycott lasted 381 days and the bus companies lost a lot of money. In the end it was ruled that segregating races in public schools was against the Constitution. Finally the Supreme Court decided that Montgomery could no longer have a segregated public transportation system.

b) Choose one of the following tasks. Look at C2b) and c) for help.

1. Put yourself into the position of Linda Brown and write a diary entry about your troubles finding a school near your home and how you felt when your parents finally won at court.

2. Put yourself into the position of Rosa Parks and write a diary entry about your bad experience with the Montgomery buses and the success of the boycott.

Language gym
p. 76, ex. 1

WB
C3

C4 The March on Washington

a) Read the encyclopaedia entry about the March on Washington. Write down what made this march so important. Compare your statements with your partner's.

March on Washington: August 28, 1963, became a very important day for the civil rights movement. About 250,000 people of all ethnic origins, led by Martin Luther King Junior, marched to the Lincoln Memorial in Washington to protest against racial segregation and discrimination. At the march, King gave his famous 'I have a dream' speech. Two years later President Lyndon B. Johnson signed a law which promised equal rights for black Americans in jobs, voting, and the use of public facilities.
Since the 1970s job opportunities for minorities have further improved. Today a lot of black Americans hold important positions in society and government. But racism and poverty have not been defeated yet.

skills
How to speak
p. 131/3

WB
C4–C6

b) The March on Washington was not the only important march. Find out about other marches and leaders of the civil rights movement. Use the Internet.
(www.americaslibrary.gov)

project

People and places 3 – Martin Luther King

CD

Read the text about Martin Luther King and an extract from his famous 'I have a dream' speech. Then answer the questions in German. Talk to your partner and compare your results.

Fasse zusammen,
a) was du über die Bedeutung Martin Luther Kings für die amerikanische Bürgerrechtsbewegung erfährst.
b) womit Martin Luther King unzufrieden war.
c) was er sich für eine bessere Zukunft erhoffte.

skills How to mediate p. 126

skills How to work with words p. 120/1

Martin Luther King was a Baptist pastor and probably the most famous leader of the American civil rights movement. In 1964 he won the Nobel Peace Prize for his peaceful fight against racial discrimination. Four years later, at the age of 39, he was shot and killed in Memphis, Tennessee. A week of rioting in many cities across the nation followed this murder. The circumstances of King's death have never been solved completely. Every year, on the third Monday in January, there is a national holiday in the USA to honor the memory of Martin Luther King.

"(…) We cannot walk alone. And as we walk, we must make the pledge that we shall always march ahead. We cannot turn back. There are those who are asking the devotees of civil rights, 'When will you be satisfied?' (…) We can never be satisfied as long as our bodies, heavy with the fatigue of travel, cannot gain lodging in the motels of the highways and the hotels of the cities. We cannot be satisfied as long as the Negro's basic mobility is from a smaller ghetto to a larger one. (…) We cannot be satisfied as long as a Negro in Mississippi cannot vote and a Negro in New York believes he has nothing for which to vote. No, no, we are not satisfied, and we will not be satisfied until justice rolls down like waters and righteousness like a mighty stream. (…)

I have a dream that one day this nation will rise up and live out the true meaning of its creed: 'We hold these truths to be self-evident, that all men are created equal.' I have a dream that one day on the red hills of Georgia the sons of former slaves and the sons of former slave owners will be able to sit down together at a table of brotherhood. I have a dream that one day even the state of Mississippi, a state sweltering with the heat of injustice, sweltering with the heat of oppression, will be transformed into an oasis of freedom and justice. I have a dream that my four little children will one day live in a nation where they will not be judged by the color of their skin but by the content of their character. I have a dream today. (…)"

WB C7

Language gym p. 76, ex. 2+3

C5 Mr Cab Driver

a) Describe the singer's appearance and style of clothing. Would you notice a person with his looks in the street? Say why or why not.

b) Listen to the song and read along.

Mr Cab Driver won't stop to let me in
Mr Cab Driver don't like my kind of skin
Mr Cab Driver you're never gonna win
Mr Cab Driver won't stop to pick me up
Mr Cab Driver I might need some help
Mr Cab Driver only thinks about himself

(Chorus)
Mr Cab Driver, Mr Cab Driver
Mr Cab Driver, Mr Cab Driver

Mr Cab Driver don't like the way I look
He don't like dreads, he thinks we are all crooks
Mr Cab Driver reads too many story books
Mr Cab Driver pass me up with eyes of fire
Mr Cab Driver thinks we're all 165'ers*
Mr Cab Driver (...) I'm a survivor

Let me in

(Chorus)
Mr Cab Driver, Mr Cab Driver
Mr Cab Driver, Mr Cab Driver

© Music and lyrics by Lenny Kravitz

*165'ers refers to W165th street, a rough area in Harlem, NYC

CD

c) Find another title for the song. Say why you chose it.

d) Name some of the prejudices the cab driver has against the singer of the song.

He thinks ...

The cab driver doesn't ...

skills
How to read p. 125/2

e) Work in groups of four. Think about a conflict similar to the one described in the song. You may have seen it in your area or heard about it. Act out the scene.

WB C8

Possible conflicts:
- A foreign-looking guy – other teenagers call him names
- A new girl in class – her classmates don't like her because of her clothes
- A couple with small children looking for an apartment – the landlord doesn't want kids in the house
- ...

portfolio

You don't belong here ...

I don't agree with ...

We don't want ...

What's wrong with ...?

Why don't you ...?

project

4 Language gym

1 **These word pairs are mixed. Put them together correctly.**
Example: *slave traders*

slave Court · Supreme codes · Underground school · cotton Railroad
black traders · Northern boycott · public plantation · bus states

2 **Match the words with the definitions.**
Then write complete sentences.

Example: *A demonstration means a large group of people who protest against something.*
The Underground Railroad was an organization which …
Slaves are …

demonstration · political leader · racial segregation · civil rights movement · slaves · Underground Railroad

- a large group of people / protest against something
- laws / only allow white people to enter some restaurants, buses or schools
- person with a strong character / fight for their ideas
- movement / fight for equal rights for all
- people / are without any rights
- an organization / helped slaves to escape

CD

3 **Where is the stress in these words?**
Copy the table and write the words in the correct column.

~~facility~~ • ~~movement~~ • ~~transportation~~ • successful • poverty • permission • constitution • settler • ensure • plantation • industry • segregation • northern • conductor • survive • demonstration • arrest • decide

stress on the 1st syllable	stress on the 2nd syllable	stress on the 3rd syllable
movement	*facility*	*transportation*
…	…	…

favorite	favourite
color / colored	colour / coloured
honor	honour
traveled	travelled
mom	mum
theater	theatre

You have read about the history of African Americans in the USA. You have talked and written about their experiences and feelings.

They *wanted* me *to leave.*
They *ordered* her *to work.*
They *forced* them *to go.*

Memory Box

5

... and action!

lif 9 p. 144

A1 Sport in our class

a) Talk about these questions:

What is your favourite sport?
What sport are you fond of?
... are you interested in?
... are you good / bad / hopeless at?
... do you like watching live or on TV?
... do you play at school / outside school?
... would you like to learn?

b) Find out what sport two pupils in your class prefer. Write down four questions and interview them.

c) Tell your class what you have found out.

lif 19 p. 153

A2 A question of sport

a) Look at the photos and the switchboard. What sports do these people do? What sports did they use to do? Talk about the people and their sports to your partner.

I think Debi Thomas used to be a famous ice-skater.

Muhammad Ali

He She	is used to be was	a famous a successful the world-champion	golfer. ice-skater. tennis player. basketball player. boxer.

Tiger Woods

Serena Williams

Debi Thomas

Michael Jordan

skills How to look for information p. 133

b) Think of sport in your own country. What are the names of famous sportswomen and sportsmen? What can you say about them? Ask your friends or parents for help. Present your ideas to the class.

Debi Thomas used to be a famous ice-skater.
Muhammad Ali used to be a successful boxer.

c) Choose one of the personalities in a) or b) and write a profile about their career. Search on the Internet and find out:

- about important stages in their career
- what he / she is doing now
- where the person was born and brought up
- when he / she first became famous
- how he / she got interested in their sport

WB A1, A2

Language gym p. 82, ex. 1+2

A3 More American sport

a) What do you know about these sports? Have you ever watched or played one of them?

b) Look through the following four texts and answer the questions below.
- **What does a pitcher do?**
- **Which sport is mainly played indoors?**
- **Which sport is not a team sport? Why?**
- **What is a touchdown?**

In **American football** two teams with at least eleven players play against each other (only eleven players per team are allowed on the field at the same time, though). The idea is to get the ball across the opponent's goal line or kick it over the goal crossbar. Each team has an offensive and a defensive unit. The defensive players are allowed to tackle the ball carrier and to push other players out of the way. Offensive players are allowed to block the other team's players to keep them away from the ball carrier. A team gets six points for a touchdown, which is when they get the ball over their opponent's goal line. If they score a touchdown, they can also try to kick the ball over the crossbar for an extra point. And if they carry the ball across the goal line again, they get another two points. A team can get three points for a field goal, which is when a player has kicked the ball over the crossbar from open play without a touchdown first. The game is played in four quarters (4 × 15 minutes).

Baseball is a bat and ball game which is played between two teams. In each team there are usually nine players. A pitcher throws (or pitches) a hard, leather-covered ball toward a batter on the opposing team. The batter tries to hit the baseball with a bat, which is usually made of wood. A team scores runs when its players pass four markers, called bases, set up at the corners of a ninety-foot square.

Basketball is a sport in which two teams of five active players try to score points against each other by throwing a ball through a 10 foot high hoop (the basket).

Points are scored by passing the ball through the basket from above. The team with the most points at the end of the game wins.

The ball can be advanced on the court by bouncing it (dribbling) or passing it between teammates. Physical contact (foul) is not allowed and there are rules on how the ball can be handled.

Basketball is mainly an indoor sport played on a basketball court. But many variations of basketball have developed and have become popular as outdoor sports. In some countries, basketball is also a popular spectator sport. Basketball is especially popular in the United States.

Surfing is a water sport in which the participant (surfer) is carried by a breaking wave, usually on a surfboard, toward the shore. As well as surfboards, surfers use kneeboards, body boards, kayaks, surf skis and their own bodies. This means they can do tricks while they are being carried by the waves. In competitions surfers gain points for doing tricks – they score from 1 to 10 depending on how difficult the trick is and how good the wave was.

There are different surfboard designs, such as long-boards and short-boards. Surfboards were invented in Polynesia, and were traditionally made out of local wood. Today, however, more modern materials and shapes are used to make the surfboards easier to use.

Other water sports, which are similar to surfing, make use of other elements too, such as the wind. These include kitesurfing and windsurfing.

c) Use these ideas to write a text about volleyball. Use the text about basketball above and the Internet for help. You can start like this:

Volleyball is a team sport ...

hit the ball over the net | throw a ball | server | two teams of six players | serving team | opposing team | court | "ace" | pass – set – attack | volleyball | prevent from touching the ground | indoor and outdoor sport | 25 | points | set | error

WB A3–A8

Language gym
p. 82, ex. 3+4

People and places 4 – A sport for all seasons

Sport plays a very important part in American culture. This is especially true of American sports. Americans have always preferred their own sports: baseball, (American) football and basketball. But soccer – or football, as it is known in Europe – is becoming more and more popular in the United States.
The American sporting calendar has its own big events. For many Americans, spring begins with the opening day of the baseball season, when the American president traditionally pitches the first ball. The World Series – the professional baseball championship play-offs – marks the end of the summer sport season. During the fall, the football and basketball seasons start. As winter gets nearer, fans go to indoor stadiums for the tip-off (start) of the basketball season. Special sporting events are national festivals themselves: Opening Day and the Pennant Races (baseball); the World Series, college bowls and the Super Bowl (football). Other holidays are also famous for sporting events, like the New Year and Thanksgiving Day football games.

Baseball, American football and basketball developed from European ball games which settlers brought with them. Basketball was invented in 1891 in Springfield, Massachusetts, by the YMCA leader James Naismith. He wanted to give the boys something to do during the winter breaks. American football was first played at top colleges and universities.
Every team has its cheerleaders – young people (usually girls) who organize cheers for their team, shouting slogans, dancing, jumping and hand-clapping. Most schools also have a marching band. Football, baseball and basketball have become a very important part of school life for boys. For girls, the most popular sports are volleyball, field hockey and lacrosse – a game which was first played by Native Americans.
Success in sport is very important to most American students – as important as math, English or science. It is also just as important for the schools and colleges because it is often reported on TV or in newspapers and makes them famous.

Here are two typical cheerleading slogans. In groups make up your own slogan.

GEORGE, GEORGE, HE'S OUR MAN.
IF HE CAN'T DO IT, NO ONE CAN!

DRIBBLE DOWN THE COURT,
DON'T STOP SHORT,
SHOOT THE BALL,
LET'S WIN IT ALL!

Language gym

1 Write sentences about Liz.
What did she use to do eight years ago?
What does she do nowadays?

… didn't use to …   … used to …

Eight years ago:

I don't speak Spanish. I don't ride a bike.
I have a rabbit.

I play the guitar.
I eat a lot of ice cream.
I watch children's programs on TV.
I play with my brother.

Nowadays:

I speak Spanish. I ride a bike.
I have a dog.

I don't play the guitar.
I go to the movies.
I eat a lot of vegetables.
I play soccer.

Example: *Liz used to eat a lot of ice cream eight years ago. Nowadays she eats a lot of vegetables.*

CD

2 Copy the sentences into your exercise book and fill in the missing prepositions.

Example: *1. Tim was in Mexico last summer. Now he is interested in learning Spanish.*

2. Sarah is good … painting. She goes to an art class.
3. Ben doesn't go to football training anymore. He's hopeless … playing football.
4. I've bought a new CD. I'm keen … listening to music.
5. Ann doesn't go out in the evening. She's afraid … walking in the dark.
6. John is bad … dancing. He has decided to go to a dancing class.
7. Ben and Sarah are fond … watching films. They go to the movies once a month.

3 a) Look at these words and sort them into the grid.

touch · four · about · your · bouncing · court · country
through · out · you · would · outside · though

/ʌ/ as in b**u**t	/uː/ as in tw**o**	/aʊ/ as in m**ou**th	/ɔː/ as in d**oo**r	/əʊ/ as in c**o**ld	/ʊ/ as in c**ou**ld

b) Can you think of more words you could add?

You have talked about different sports and sportspeople. You have written a profile about a person's career. You have also read about famous American sports.

She *used to be* a famous ice-skater.
He *used to play* basketball.

Markus is *interested in playing* squash.
Jasmin *likes jogging.*

Memory Box

B1 I'm a loser

a) Read Logan's letter to a teenage magazine. What is his problem?

Deborah!

Can't I do anything right? All the kids in my class love sports, but I'm just no good at it. Ball games make me sick – really! I'm a flop at American football, for example. Whether I kick or catch, it's not worth two cents.
I flip out if a team player tries to pass the ball to me. Just plain panic! Before I know what's happened, the ball is somewhere else. If I manage to get the ball back, I fall on my face! The players on my team just yell at me, and that makes it all worse. They stand there laughing (ha, ha, very funny!).
Baseball is just as bad. Man, that ball always seems to slide through my fingers. The couple of times that I HAVE caught it, I haven't known where to throw it. Second base? Third base? I turn around in circles before I can decide on anything – or I drop the thing like it was on fire. No one in the team likes me. They laugh at me and call me 'ALIEN', because I can't play ANY game.
Whenever I play, our team always loses. I always feel sick before our sports class. So now, I just go and hide some place. Our sports teacher doesn't seem to mind. I think he's quite happy when I'm not around. All I'm good at is running to catch the bus in the morning. But you don't get any cheers for that.
What can I do?

Signed: I'd rather be in the classroom.

b) Match the sentence halves.

1. I'm a flop
2. I flip out
3. I fall on my face
4. That ball always seems to
5. I turn around in circles
6. Whenever I play,
7. I always feel sick
8. When I'm not around,
9. I don't get cheers

a) slide through my fingers.
b) our team always loses.
c) at American football.
d) for running to catch the bus in the morning.
e) before I decide on anything.
f) our sports teacher doesn't mind.
g) if a team player tries to pass the ball to me.
h) if I try to get the ball back.
i) before sports class.

WB
B1, B2

B2 An American schedule

Logan is in 9th grade at high school. This is his schedule.

a) Look at Logan's schedule. Talk about it with your partner. What do you find interesting / surprising / unusual?

Period		Monday	Tuesday	Wednesday	Thursday	Friday
	7.50–8.00	Home room	Home room	Home room	Home room	Home room
1st period	8.05–8.50	Science	Science	Science	Science	Science
2nd period	8.55–9.40	English	English	English	English	English
3rd period	9.45–10.30	Social Studies	Social Studies	Social Studies	Social Studies	Social Studies
4th period	10.35–11.20	Spanish I	Spanish I	Spanish I	Spanish I	Spanish I
	11.20–12.10	Lunch break	Lunch break	Lunch break	Lunch break	Lunch break
5th period	12.15–1.00	Math	Math	Math	Math	Math
6th period	1.05–1.50	P. E.	P. E.	P. E.	P. E.	P. E.
7th period	1.55–2.40	Elective	Elective	Elective	Elective	Elective

b) Compare Logan's schedule to yours. Think especially about the following questions:

1. How many subjects does he have?
2. Are they the same as yours?
3. How much time does he spend at school each day?
4. How many breaks does he have per day?
5. What do you think happens in the "home room"?
6. What is the main difference between Logan's schedule and yours?
7. Which schedule do you prefer?

c) Look at Logan's letter in B1 again. Think again about the problems he has at school. Why is sport such a big problem for him?

WB B3

d) A pen friend from the USA comes to visit you. He would like to know about school in Germany. What can you tell him?

lif 20 p. 153

B3 Pass me the ball

Logan writes in his letter on page 83:

I flip out if a team player tries to pass the ball to me.

He could also write.

I flip out if a team player tries to pass me the ball.

Text them a message.
Text a message to them.

Language gym p. 87, ex. 1

How can you say or write these sentences in a different way?

WB B4, B5

1. Throw the ball to her.
2. Did he give you the homework?
3. Deborah sent an answer to Logan.
4. He never shows his schedule to us.
5. Have you sent him an e-mail?
6. Deborah offered her help to me.
7. Logan lent me his dictionary.
8. I haven't texted the message to her yet.

B4 Electives

Logan's classmates Tami and Alexa have to choose their electives. Electives are part of everybody's schedule but students can decide what they would like to learn. Many students choose electives that will prepare them for a special job. Tami would like to work as an IT assistant and Alexa wants to become a social worker.

Look at the list. Choose suitable electives for Tami and Alexa. Then choose suitable electives for yourself. Give reasons for your choice.

Office Skills
Marketing
Health at Home
Home Economics
Work & Family
Electricity in the Home
IT (Information Technology)
French I
German I
Basic Design
Ceramics
Acting
Modern Dance

WB B6

B5 Personal decisions

Tami and Alexa are talking to Sarah, Alexa's sister, about their electives.

Read these questions. Then listen to the conversation and answer the questions.

- Which electives should Alexa take if she wants to be a social worker?
- Why does Alexa want to take the same elective as Tami?
- What can you do if you don't like your elective?
- Why does Alexa want to take Spanish?

CD

skills
How to listen
p. 122

B6 School clubs

American schools also have school clubs, which are always looking for new members. Here are some of the ads from Tami and Alexa's school.

WB B7, B8

DRAMA GROUP
Do you want to be a star? Do you plan to go into the film industry? We can help you get there. Join our drama group. We are looking for actors and actresses – but we also need technicians, costume designers and make-up artists. Join us Fridays at 4 pm in room 5.

Mural Designing
Come and help us make our school nicer. Our next project is the big wall in the cafeteria. Drop in next Thursday at 3 pm if you are creative, have good ideas and can paint in a team. Wear old clothes.

Chess
Are you a logical thinker, good at solving problems? If so, join us every Wednesday at 3 pm in room 1.

Astronomy Club
Interested in astronomy? Do you enjoy looking at the stars and comets? Do you know how to use a telescope? Join our club if you want to take part in field trips. Phone Bill at 389475 or drop in next Tuesday at 5 pm. We meet in room 101.

a) What kind of people are the clubs interested in?

The drama group is interested in people who
- want to be a star
- plan to go into the film industry

...

Continue the list.

b) Which of these clubs would you like to join and why? Try to persuade someone to join with you.

c) Design an ad for a club you would like to have at your school.

portfolio

CD

People and places 5 – Schools in the United States

Every child in the United States has to go to school from kindergarten to the 12th grade. Kindergarten starts at the age of five and is part of school life. The last four years of school are called "high school".
In the USA all students of the same age go to the same school. There are no *Hauptschulen, Realschulen, Gymnasien* and *Gesamtschulen* like in Germany. When they are at high school, students have to plan their schedules themselves. This includes choosing special classes called "electives". Although all high school students have to take English, they don't have to take math every year.
When students leave high school, they have a graduation ceremony, where they wear special clothes. Teenagers who leave school before 12th grade are called "dropouts" and do not receive any kind of school certificate at all.
In addition to classes, there are also a lot of school clubs to choose from like the drama group, chess, square dance, mural designing and many more.

Age	School	Class
3 4	Nursery School (optional)	
5	Kindergarten	
6 7 8 9 10 11	Elementary School	first grade second grade third grade fourth grade fifth grade sixth grade
12 13	Junior High School	seventh grade eighth grade
14 15 16 17	High School	ninth grade (freshman) tenth grade (sophomore) eleventh grade (junior) twelfth grade (senior)

skills
How to mediate
p. 126

Logan's teacher has invited his German friend Sabrina to come to school for a day. She doesn't know very much about school in the United States. Help her by telling her the most important facts in German.

Language gym
p. 87, ex. 2+3

CD

1 **Put the words into the right order. Write the sentences in your excercise book.**

Example: 1. text / them / will / a message / I
1. I will text them a message.

2. wrote / to Deborah / a letter / Logan
3. me / a lot of things / Amy / sent
4. the books / you / she / give / did / ?
5. to Logan / the ball / pass / you / ? / can
6. him / given / she / has / her present / ?
7. to our friends / I've / the invitations / given
8. shown / her homework / to me / has / Amy
9. offer / a drink / you / did / ? / him

2 **Read these answers and look through 5B again. Then make up questions in your exercise book which match the answers.**

1. That's another word for timetable.
   What does schedule mean?
2. They are subjects that students must take but they have a variety to choose from.
3. They usually take place in the afternoon.
4. It is a board game for two players.
5. Because he can't play any game.
6. When students leave school.
7. At the age of five.

3 **How do you pronounce the following words? Copy the grid into your exercise book and fill in the words.**

stress on 1st syllable	stress on 2nd syllable
subject	designer

~~subject~~ technician telescope drama schedule assistant logical creative costume ceramics ~~designer~~ Wednesday marketing industry elective

You have heard from someone who doesn't like sport. You have read and talked about the differences between school in the United States and Germany. You have also listened to US pupils talking about their electives.

A team player passes the ball to me.
A team player passes me the ball.

Memory Box

C1 Favorite movies

skills
How to speak
p. 131/3

a) Look at the movie posters. Choose one of the posters and talk to your partner. Think about the following points and present your ideas in class.

actor / actress

action seen in the poster

title

director of the movie

WB
C1, C2

b) Read the following summaries of the movies.
Do you know which summary belongs to which movie poster? Why?

Summary 1:
Captain Barbossa kidnaps the beautiful Princess Elizabeth Swann and takes her onto his ship. The blacksmith Will Turner follows Captain Barbossa to rescue Elizabeth. The adventurous pirate Captain Jack Sparrow helps him.

Summary 2:
An ogre is asked by Lord Farquaad to rescue Princess Fiona from a dragon, because he wants to marry her. The ogre, however, falls in love with the princess and flees into a fairytale world with her. A talking donkey travels with them on their adventures.

Summary 3:
Peter Parker, a shy young man, has a secret nobody knows about. He is bitten by a spider and develops supernatural powers. He becomes a superhero and fights evil.

skills
How to look for information
p. 133

c) Work in pairs. What is the best movie you have ever seen? Design a leaflet for the movie. Think about:
- why you like the movie
- the title of the movie
- the setting of the movie
- the plot of the movie
- the actors / actresses in the movie

Add pictures from magazines or from the Internet. Then present your leaflet to the class.

portfolio

The title of ... is ...

We think the best scene is ... where ...

We've decided on ...

You might know the actor / actress ... who plays the role of ...

...

C2 An interview with a movie star

a) What do you know about Tobey Maguire? Use the fact file and write complete sentences in your exercise book. Then compare your ideas with your partner's.

Example: *Tobey Maguire was born on June 27, 1975.*

Full name: Tobias Vincent Maguire
Date of birth: June 27, 1975
Place of birth: Santa Monica, California, USA
Height: 5'8" (1.73 m)
Good friend: Leonardo DiCaprio
Start of television career: at the age of 13, appearing in advertisements for McDonald's etc
Start of movie career: at the age of 15
Blockbusters: Spider-Man 1–3
Food: vegetarian

**b) Read the interview with Tobey Maguire.
Add all the information you find to your own sentences in a).**

When did you start acting?
At the age of 13 I was cast in several TV ads for McDonald's and Doritos. Two years later I started playing small parts in American series, e.g. "Roseanne". But it was only in 1998 that I was given a major part in "Pleasantville" and "The Cider House Rules".

You have become well-known around the world for playing "Spider-Man". Why did you decide to play this role? Were you interested in reading the comics when you were a boy?
Not at all. I had never read the comics when I was a child. But I was thrilled when I was asked by Sam Raimi, the director of the film, whether I was interested in playing "Spider-Man". I liked working on all the little details and trying to bring the character to life.

Do you like working with Sam Raimi?
Oh, yes. When I started working with Sam I realized how wonderful he was as a director. He had been a fan of Spider-Man since his childhood and it was his enthusiasm that made me want to continue playing this role.

Did you do any special training before you started to play Spider-Man?
I spent five months doing an intensive training in sports and also in martial arts. And I was on a special diet.

Your father is a chef. Did you miss any special dishes during your diet?
(He laughs) I missed peanut M&Ms.

Thank you for the interview, Mr Maguire. Wishing you the greatest success ever.

WB
C3–C6

**c) Report what you know about Tobey Maguire.
What were his answers to the reporter's questions?**

Example: *Tobey Maguire said that he had been cast in several TV ads at the age of 13.*

lif
16
p. 149

**d) If you had the chance to meet and interview your favourite movie star, what would you like to ask him / her? Prepare five questions. Write them in your exercise book and compare your ideas with your partner.
Your partner takes the role of your favourite movie star and gives the answers. Swap your roles. Then present your interview to the class.**

Language gym
p. 92, ex. 1+2

skills
How to speak
p. 130/1

C3 A tour of Universal Studios in Hollywood

The students of 9th grade are visiting Universal Studios with their drama class. Their drama teacher, Mrs Chapman, has arranged a tour with a guide.

CD

a) Listen to the guide's talk and write down what jobs she mentions.

Hi boys and girls. I'm your guide today. Welcome to Universal Studios in Hollywood. As you can see, Elvis Castano and his team are shooting a film right now. So boys and girls you are lucky to witness how a film is shot. Please try to keep quiet and be careful not to stumble over anything and hurt yourself. Well, I'm going to tell you something about the different people who work on a set. Do you see the person over there with the blue cap sitting on the director's chair? That's Elvis Castano. He's the director of the film and is responsible for making a movie out of a script. He tells the actors and the production crew what to do. Josh, the person behind the camera, is the director of photography. He plans the shots. A number of cameras are used on a set. And Joe, who is operating the clapperboard, is the assistant camera person. He is also responsible for keeping the camera clean, loading film and keeping a camera report.

Do you see Liz and Tom over there setting the lights? Well, they are the gaffers. They put the lights where the director of photography wants them to be. Tony, the boy with the blue jumper, is still a student but he sometimes works as the best boy here on the set. He helps the gaffers and carries the wires for them. There are a number of other helpers though. They are called grips. They move the gear and the camera.
Not only cameras and lights but also sound is very important on the set. Cathleen, the girl you see over there, is the boom operator. She's holding the microphone in the right place and is directed by the sound recordist. He's responsible for recording sounds. Well, I hope you could get an overview of the people who work on a movie set.
Let's go to the cafeteria and get something to drink. We can talk about your impressions there.

WB C7

b) How many jobs did you write down? What have you learned about them? Listen again and take notes.

Language gym
p. 92, ex. 3+4

c) Look at these jobs. What are the people responsible for?
Match the jobs to their job descriptions.

Example: *The producer is responsible for raising money for the production.*

writer • composer • special effects designer • make-up artist • costume designer • ~~producer~~

creates stunts • changes how an actor looks • ~~raises money for production~~ • writes script • composes music • creates the actor's clothes

C4 Reviewing a movie

a) Read the movie review on Spider-Man and find out what each paragraph is about. Then present your ideas to the class.

Spider-Man On a school trip to a laboratory, Peter Parker, a high school student, is bitten by a genetically engineered spider. As a result he is able to transform himself into Spider-Man. Wearing his special suit he uses great strength to fight evil and help people. He can leap great distances and climb buildings. No one knows about his secret, not even those people who are close to him such as his aunt Mary and his secret love Mary Jane Watson.

Tobey Maguire plays the role of Peter Parker brilliantly. His performance carries most of the movie. The bad guy is played by Willem Dafoe, who plays his part wonderfully. Another great actor is Rosemary Harris, who plays Aunt Mary. On the other hand the performance of Kirsten Dunst is not on the same level. This, however, has nothing to do with her acting skills but with her minor role.

Sam Raimi, the director of the film, has successfully made a movie out of the Spider-Man comics. He uses lots of action scenes and special effects to create and keep the suspense until the end of the movie.

The movie is worth seeing and deserves three stars. ★★★

b) Copy the grid into your exercise book and fill in what you have read about the movie.

c) Write a review of a movie you like / don't like.

MOVIE REVIEW	
Title of the movie:	
Plot of the movie:	
The main actors / actresses in the movie:	
Performance of the actors / actresses:	
Director of the movie:	
Why is the movie interesting?	
Do you recommend the movie? Give a star rating.	

(★= bad, ★★= average, ★★★= above average)

WB
C8, C9

skills
How to write
p. 128/2

portfolio

C5 You, the movie director

You are the director of a movie. Think about:
- **a good story: western, love, action, horror, science fiction, thriller, …**
- **a place where you would shoot the movie and**
- **the actors you would like to have for your movie.**

Write down your ideas and present them to the class.

skills
How to present
something in class
p. 132

lif
7
p. 143

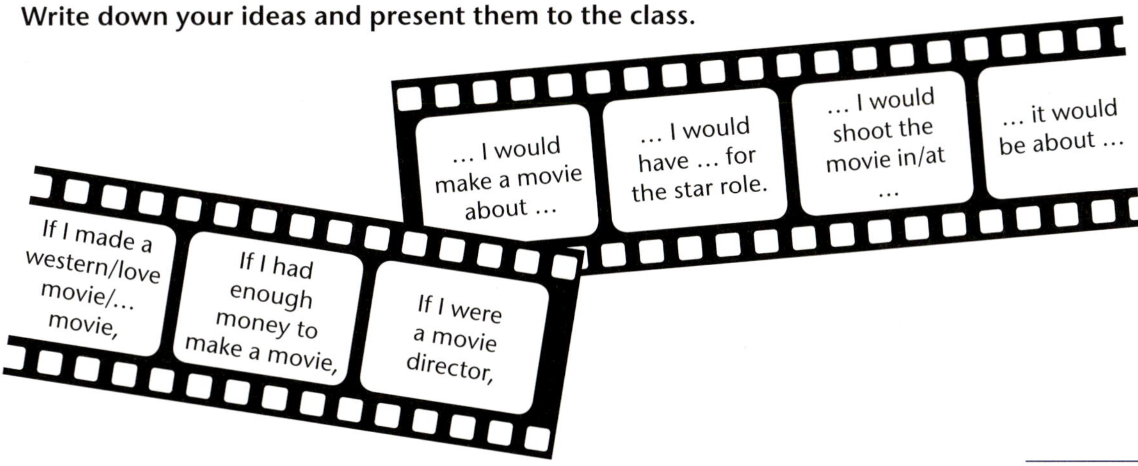

5 Language gym

1 **Ben Gibbons, a movie journalist working with the New York Times newspaper, is interviewing actress Jennifer Perkins. Find suitable questions for the answers and copy the interview into your exercise book.**

Example: *BG: When did you start acting?*

JP: I started acting at the age of 12.
BG: …
JP: I loved books at school. So I joined our drama group.
BG: …
JP: We did some pantomimes at Christmas and some plays by Shakespeare and Tennessee Williams.
BG: …
JP: The most interesting play I have ever acted in is "A Streetcar Named Desire" by Tennessee Williams.
BG: …
JP: I started making movies six years ago.
BG: …
JP: I love acting because I can play a lot of different roles and I travel a lot. Whenever I read a script, I try to imagine my part and identify with that special part. Acting is a challenge and I love it.
BG: …
JP: Yes, I have. I played a murderer once. That was in the movie "Dusk in the City."
BG: …
JP: I'd like to work as a director one day.
BG: Well, Miss Perkins, thank you very much for the interview. All the best with your new movie.

CD

2 **Fill in the missing prepositions.**

at | next to | in front of | on | behind

1. A number of people are busy … the set.
2. Ben, who is … the camera, is the director of photography.
3. Sarah, who is standing … Ben, helps him.
4. Tom and Linda, who are sitting … the desk, are the script writers.
5. John and Ann are standing … the curtain and arranging the lights.

3 **Say the words. Listen for the odd one out.**

/ɑː/ glass, part, drama, leap, aunt	/uː/ suit, movie, lots, new, blue
/aɪ/ shy, gear, spider, try, guide	/ɜː/ worth, load, were, hurt, deserves
/ɔː/ talk, board, though, all, story	/iː/ seen, clean, this, keep, team

You have talked about movies and designed a leaflet for the best movie you have ever seen. You have also interviewed a movie star and been on a tour of a movie set.

soccer
pitch
schedule
math
movie
show

football
throw
timetable
maths
film
programme

A bite to eat

6

A1 Fast food

a) What comes to your mind when you think of fast food? Work with your partner and collect words. Compare your words with the words of another pair.

b) Organize your findings in a word web.

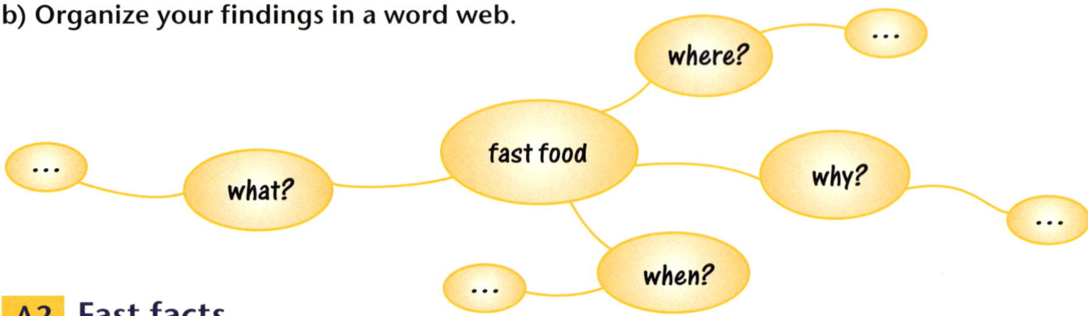

A2 Fast facts

Did you know that ...

... today there are at least 500,000 restaurants in the world that offer fast food?
... Americans eat at fast food places about four times a week?
... Americans eat approximately 5 billion pounds of fast food each year?
... about 157 million times a month fast food is eaten by kids who are 6–14 years old?
... the amount of money which is spent by Americans on fast food is higher than on movies, books, magazines, newspapers, videos and CDs altogether?
... fast food can be healthy?

Which fact do you find most interesting or surprising? And what do your classmates think? Ask each other questions and give answers.

Did you know that ...?
What do you think about the fact that ...?
Are you surprised that ...?

I think it is absolutely ...
In my opinion it is ...
I am surprised / not surprised that ...

A3 Fast answers

Radio One reporter Hugh Miller from Newburyport, Massachusetts, has interviewed people on the street. He wanted to find out if people like eating in fast food places.

a) Here are some of the comments which the interviewed people made. Which comments are positive? Which are negative? Put the comments into two groups. Write the answers in your exercise book.

WB
A1–A3

- I never eat anywhere else.
- Sure, it's good value for money.
- Well, I work there, but I would never eat there!
- Well, it's not bad, but I wouldn't eat there every day. It's too spicy for me.
- Yeah sure, if I want a quick snack.
- I wouldn't be caught dead in the place.
- I could eat it till it comes out of my ears.

b) Would you like to eat in one of these places? Give a fast answer. Use the phrases from a).

1

2

3

A4 What about you?

a) Do you often eat fast food? When do you go to a fast food restaurant? Who do you go with? What fast food do you like? Have you got a favourite fast food restaurant? Answer the questions. Make notes.

b) Work with a partner. Think of pros and cons of fast food. You can use the information given in A1, A2 and A3. Collect all the arguments in class.

c) Now make up your own mind. Write down what you think about fast food. Start your comment with an introduction using your answers given in a). Mention the pros and cons. Finish your comment by expressing your own opinion.

skills
How to write
p. 128/2

A5 Burgerland

Amy is recording an interview about fast food places for her school magazine.

CD

a) Help her prepare the interview. Make a list of topics she might talk about.

b) Read Amy's interview. Find out if you have the same topics. Do you agree with Cathy's answers? Why do you think she answers like this?

lif 16, 21 p. 149+155

Amy: Well, I'm here at Burgerland in Brooklyn, New York. And with me is Cathy, who is the manager here. How long have you been a manager, Cathy?

Cathy: Just over two years, I think. Before that I was the assistant manager.

Amy: OK. So Burgerland is open 24 hours a day. Is that right?

Cathy: Yeah, correct.

Amy: And are there many customers at night?

Cathy: Oh sure! They come all the time. This is a major highway, you know.

Amy: So how many hamburgers do you sell a day?

Cathy: Oh, well. Some days are busier than others. Saturday is our busiest day. We sell over seven thousand hamburgers most Saturdays.

Amy: Wow! Which is the most popular one?

Cathy: Well, I'd say it's the Giant New Yorker Special. It's pretty hot. Here, have a bite!

Amy: Wow! But Cathy, I know all this fast food is very popular, but is it very healthy?

Cathy: Sure! We use only the very best meat in our burgers. And our salads are really nice and fresh.

Amy: Is it OK for your kids to eat here every day?

Cathy: Well, maybe not every day. But when I don't have much time to cook, why not?

Amy: Another thing I wanted to ask you was about the garbage. You must produce tons of plastic and aluminium foil here. Is it all really necessary? I mean, can't you use real plates and cups and knives and forks?

Cathy: Well, you have to remember that lots of our customers use our drive-thru service. So we need to wrap their food up.

Amy: But what about the people who eat in here?

Cathy: It's not so easy. With the thousands of customers we get, we'd need lots of dishwashers. And they're expensive to use. So our prices would have to go up.

Amy: Well, aren't there any other ways you could reduce the garbage? I mean, surely ... Oh, sorry, can you wait a minute please? Something is wrong with the equipment.

Later that day Amy told her parents about the interview:

c) Read the interview again. Then read what Amy is telling her parents about the interview. Match the direct questions from the interview to the reported questions in the speech bubble.

I asked Cathy how long she had been a manager. And I asked her if Burgerland was open 24 hours. I asked whether there were many customers at night. I wanted to know how many hamburgers they sold a day. I also wanted to know which the most popular one was. I asked Cathy if it was OK for her kids to eat there every day. I asked if they couldn't use real plates and cups.

"... here ..." → *there*
"... yesterday ..." → *the day before*

"How many burgers do you sell?"	→	*I asked how many burgers they sold.*
"Is Burgerland open 24 hours?"	→	*I asked if it was open 24 hours.*
"How long have you been ...?"	→	*... had been ...*
"... did ... sell ...?"	→	*... had sold ...*
"... will ...?"	→	*... would ...*
"... can ...?"	→	*... could ...*

d) What else did Amy ask Cathy? Look at the interview again. Then tell your partner. Use the switchboard for help.

Amy asked her	if	this garbage	was	use real plates and cups and knives and forks.
Amy wanted to know	whether	all this fast food	weren't	very healthy.
		they	couldn't	any other ways they could reduce the garbage.
		there		necessary.

lif 21 p. 155
WB A4, A5
Language gym p. 98, ex. 1

A6 Nothing but questions

When Amy had finished her interview in Burgerland, she was really happy. She phoned her friend Chris. This is what Chris asked her straight after the interview.

lif 21 p. 155

Amy really likes Chris and she thinks about the questions Chris has asked her.

Complete the sentences.

Language gym p. 98, ex. 2–4
WB A6, A7

A7 A food diary

a) What do you eat? When and where do you eat? Do you eat healthily? Talk about a way of keeping a food diary for one week. You will compare the diaries later on (in B6).

b) Keep a record of everything you eat and drink for a week in a table like this.

breakfast	lunch	evening meal	snacks	drinks

Language gym

CD

1 Last week a reporter interviewed some people about fast food.

What did he want to know? Put the words into the right order.

He wanted to know …

1. fast food / if / ate / they
2. they / a fast food restaurant / went / to / how often
3. they / how much / a month / fast food / spent on
4. liked / what / they / best / fast food
5. to / had / they / a fast food restaurant / ever / been / if
6. fast food / why / like / some people / didn't
7. young people / so / fast food / was / among / popular / why
8. in town / where / fast food restaurant / the best / was

2 Grandma is talking about how she and Grandpa first met. Grandpa asked many questions when he met Grandma for the first time 30 years ago.

Complete what Grandma said.

He wanted to know what my name was.

Grandpa: What is your name?
Where do you live?
Have you ever been to Italy?
Do you like Italian food?
Will you come to an Italian restaurant with me?
Can you dance?
Will you marry me?

3 **How do you spell these words in British English? Write them in your exercise book.**

gotten

organization | math | traveling | theater | drive-thru service

4 **What are these words? Read and write them down.**

/ˈbɜːgə/ | /ˈgɑːbɪdʒ/ | /ˈfeɪv(ə)rət fuːd/ | /snæk/

/ˈkʌstəmə/ | /ˈplæstɪk pleɪt/ | /gʊd ˈvæljuː/

"Would you allow your kids …?"
→ I asked Cathy if she would allow …

"Is Burgerland open 24 hours?"
→ I asked if it was open 24 hours.

"How many burgers do you sell?"
→ I asked how many burgers they sold.

Memory Box

You have read about fast food facts and talked about fast food places. You have also discussed the pros and cons of fast food. You have talked about Amy's questions in her interview with the manager of a fast food restaurant. You have started keeping a food diary.

People and places 6 – It's not all fast food in America

CD

Cooking in the USA – it's more than just fast food like hamburgers, pizza or tacos. Generally, American cooking includes traditional dishes like spare ribs, turkey, clam chowder, baked potatoes, corn, baked beans and apple pie. Regional cooking varies from state to state depending on the ingredients which are locally available and the cultural background of the people who have settled in the area.
Southern cooking has an African influence. Around the New Orleans area you can find Cajun cooking, a spicy combination of Spanish, French and African styles. Californian cooking uses a lot of fresh fruits and vegetables with Asian, Spanish and Mexican flavorings.
As you can see, American food is as varied as the American people and their culture.

a) Look on the Internet and find out how two different dishes are prepared. What ingredients do you need for each dish? Can you cook the dishes?

b) Plan an American party at school. Think of food and drinks and design a menu for the day.

clam chowder

grilled steak and baked potato

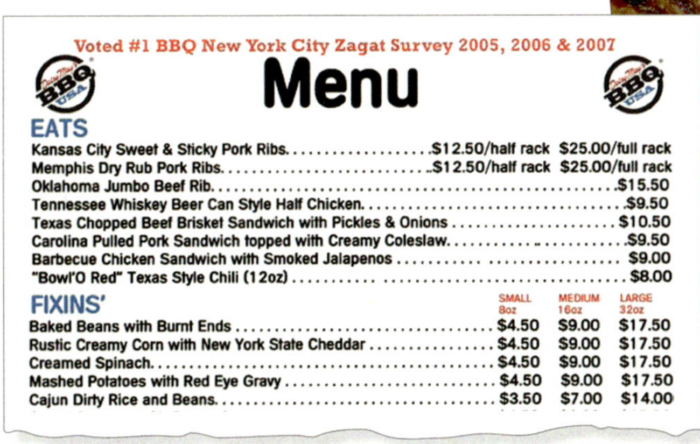

Voted #1 BBQ New York City Zagat Survey 2005, 2006 & 2007

Menu

EATS

Kansas City Sweet & Sticky Pork Ribs	$12.50/half rack	$25.00/full rack
Memphis Dry Rub Pork Ribs	$12.50/half rack	$25.00/full rack
Oklahoma Jumbo Beef Rib		$15.50
Tennessee Whiskey Beer Can Style Half Chicken		$9.50
Texas Chopped Beef Brisket Sandwich with Pickles & Onions		$10.50
Carolina Pulled Pork Sandwich topped with Creamy Coleslaw		$9.50
Barbecue Chicken Sandwich with Smoked Jalapenos		$9.00
"Bowl'O Red" Texas Style Chili (12oz)		$8.00

FIXINS'	SMALL 8oz	MEDIUM 16oz	LARGE 32oz
Baked Beans with Burnt Ends	$4.50	$9.00	$17.50
Rustic Creamy Corn with New York State Cheddar	$4.50	$9.00	$17.50
Creamed Spinach	$4.50	$9.00	$17.50
Mashed Potatoes with Red Eye Gravy	$4.50	$9.00	$17.50
Cajun Dirty Rice and Beans	$3.50	$7.00	$14.00

pork ribs on barbecue

B1 CFC – The facts

Amy picked up a flyer from Burgerland after she had done her interview with the manager.

a) Read the text. Choose the best heading.

Caring for the environment | Protection from the sun | Explanation of the term "ozone layer"

Chlorofluorocarbons (CFCs) – the facts

Because at Burgerland we have always cared about the environment, we have stopped using CFCs in our packaging.

CFCs can be found in sprays, fridges, air conditioners and foam packaging. Other companies have also banned CFCs from their products, and it is expected that in the next few years the use of CFCs will be greatly reduced.

The news about the ozone hole above the Antarctic has rightly caused international alarm. Ozone is constantly produced and destroyed in the upper atmosphere by the sun's radiation. In fact, it is this layer of ozone which protects us from the ultraviolet radiation from the sun. Now this balance has been disturbed by the CFCs which modern man puts into the atmosphere.

We, too, share this concern about CFC danger to the ozone layer. So we asked our packaging specialists to find the best alternative to CFCs for our packaging. For three years now, all Burgerland foam packaging has been CFC-free and now carries the CFC-free sign.

Ask for further information at your local Burgerland restaurant.

b) Read the text again. Then read the statements. Are they true, false or not in the text?

1. Burgerland restaurants have banned CFCs from their products.
2. People all around the world are concerned about the ozone holes.
3. Ozone destroys the sun's radiation.
4. We are protected from the ultraviolet radiation from the sun by the ozone layer.
5. Burgerland isn't concerned about CFC danger to the ozone layer.
6. At your local Burgerland restaurant you can go to an information evening.

WB B1

B2 What is it all about?

Find the definitions.

The upper atmosphere …
Ozone holes …
CFC …
Packaging specialists …
Foam packaging …
The CFC-free sign …

- are people who produce containers for all kinds of things.
- can only be printed on articles which do not contain chlorofluorocarbons.
- are caused by chemicals that are produced by industry.
- is a layer which is 35,000 metres above the earth.
- is a gas often used in packaging which causes damage to the ozone layer.
- is a method of packaging that keeps food warm or cold.

WB B2

Language gym
p. 104, ex. 1

B3 What a waste

a) Look at the items in the dustbin and answer the questions.

1. Who lives in each house? Say as much as you can.
2. What kind of food do they eat?
3. What kind of pets do they own?
4. What magazines / newspapers do they read?
5. What are their hobbies or interests?
6. What kind of holidays do they have?

b) Listen to the dialogues.
Try to work out which household each of the dialogues is from.

CD

c) Look at the contents of the three bags again. How should the rubbish be separated? Copy and complete the table. Compare your list to that of three other pupils. Is it the same? Discuss the differences.

packaging	paper	glass	biodegradable	other

skills
How to listen
p. 122

WB
B3, B4

Language gym
p. 104, ex. 2

skills
How to read
p. 124

B4 A healthy diet

a) Look at the picture. What do you expect to read? Talk to your partner.

b) Read the text and find out if you were right.

Do you usually eat white bread, rice or pasta instead of whole grain?
Do you sometimes skip meals, especially breakfast?
Do you eat meat or dairy products most days?

And on and on! These were some of the questions I had to answer the day my life suddenly changed. My mother had gone shopping and returned with her usual complaint: "Why can't somebody open the door?" I remember that I was concentrating hard on my X-Box game when she came into my room. She asked sweetly what I had had for breakfast. "I'll grab something later," I had innocently replied.
"Oh no you won't," she said quietly. "Things are going to change around here and they are going to begin to change right now." Then she told me to turn off my game and have breakfast with her. When my mom's voice was quiet, I knew she was serious.
"Oh Mom, if I turn off the game, I'll lose all the points I have collected."
"Well, young man," said my mom, "if you didn't spend so much time playing PC games, you would not have to be so careful about what you eat."
"OK, let me finish this part and I'll join you."
"OK, but finish it quickly," she said in a way that I knew she was serious.
When I got to the kitchen, the table was laid with things that looked suspiciously healthy. Instead of toast, there was whole grain bread. My mom asked me if I would prefer cereal with yoghurt or milk. "Actually, I'm starting a diet," I answered cleverly.
That was when she first opened 'The Book'. "It says here that breakfast does not make you fat. When you feed your body at regular times, it learns to burn fuel at a steady pace. When you don't eat regularly, your body holds onto food and converts it to fat. So eat regularly if you want to lose weight, young man."
I think I would have slowly starved to death over the following weeks if I hadn't spent all my pocket money in the school cafeteria. Instead of slices of pizza and jelly sandwiches, my mom started packing my lunchbox with green and red peppers, apples, pears, bananas and nuts. It was good for the brain, so 'The Book' said.
"Don't you feel less tired?" she asked me when I protested. Well I certainly didn't sleep in class anymore. The hunger kept me awake!
One day last week, I was sitting comfortably in my room dreaming of ice cream, hamburgers and fries with lots of ketchup and mayonnaise when my mom told me she was going away for two days to visit her sister in Kansas. She said: "I've made a carrot cake and some barley pancakes for you and your dad so you won't be hungry."
That night as Dad and I unhappily sat down to supper, he reluctantly asked me whether I wanted fresh beetroot juice or carrot juice to start with. "Neither," I answered. "I want a coke." "Me too," he said, "and would you prefer pizza or a hamburger to go with it?" I looked up hopefully. Dad was smiling.
"How about both?" I replied happily.
Dad and I ordered the biggest takeout ever and ate it happily while watching TV. Later we carefully tore up all the pizza boxes and made sure there was no evidence of our crime. As we were clearing up, I knocked 'The Book' off the table and it opened on the page with questions like those above.
My answer to them all was "Yes I do, but only when my mom is away."

c) Find phrases in the text that mean the same as the following sentences. Write them in your exercise book.

1. I said I would find something to eat later.
2. Everything is going to be different from now on.
3. If you did more exercise, you wouldn't have to worry about what you eat.
4. Eating breakfast doesn't make you gain weight.
5. I bought snacks at school to stop myself feeling so hungry.
6. We threw away all the clues of our unhealthy meal.

d) Read the text again. What advice does the boy's mother give him for living healthily?

You should eat breakfast.

Don't spend so much time playing on your X-Box.

…

WB
B5

e) Make five more sentences.
Pretend you are giving advice to a friend who wants to live a healthy life. Think of what you would say.

Language gym
p. 104, ex. 3+4

B5 Mom's point of view

Look at B4 again. Write the story from the mother's point of view.
Begin the story as follows:

A few weeks ago I found a wonderful book called "Healthy Food".

B6 Your food diary

a) In A7 you talked about what you usually eat and kept a food diary. Look at your food diaries in groups of four. Then collect the information for the whole class on a large sheet of paper and hang it up on the wall.

name	breakfast	lunch	evening meal	snacks	drinks

b) Talk about the results.

More than / Less than → one half / one third / a quarter / … → of the → class / boys / girls → have / don't have / eat / don't eat → …

15 out of *25* people don't have any …

c) Can you remember who said what?

Elif said she ate ice cream every day.

That's not true. I said I ate / didn't eat …

That's right. And Guiseppe said he …

lif
16
p. 149

6 Language gym

CD

1 a) Look at B1 again and find the active form of the following sentences. Write them in your exercise book.

Example: 1. CFCs can be found in sprays. *You can find CFCs in sprays.*
2. International alarm has been caused by the news about the ozone hole above the Antarctic.
3. This concern about CFC danger to the ozone layer is shared by Burgerland.
4. CFCs have been banned by other companies.
5. We are protected by the ozone layer.

b) Find three more sentences in B and change them from active to passive or passive to active.

2 Copy the text into your exercise book and complete the sentences with the simple past or past progressive.

Yesterday … (to be) my lucky day. I … (to walk) across the road when I … (to find) a bag of candy. I … (to pick) it up. As I … (to look) inside it, a car … (to come) around the corner. It … (to stop) before hitting me and the driver … (to get) out. He … (to shout) at me as he … (to walk) towards me. "Why … you … (to stand) in the middle of the road?" Then he … (to see) the bag of candy in my hand. "That is mine," he said. "I … (to think) I had lost it." The man … (to take) the candy, … (to give) me one and … (to drive) away.

3 Adjective or adverb? Choose the correct form.

1. Dad and I *happy / happily* ate the pizza.
2. My mother is very *sweet / sweetly*.
3. My friend Tom learns very *quick / quickly*.
4. Dad drives *careful / carefully*.
5. I was very *happy / happily* when I found the bag of candy.
6. My mother told me to be *careful / carefully* on my way to school.
7. *Lucky / Luckily*, the teacher didn't ask to see my homework.
8. You were *lucky / luckily* not to be hit by the car.
9. I'm a *quick / quickly* learner.
10. I asked *sweet / sweetly* if I could have the money for the movies.

4 a) Find words in the B4 text that rhyme with the following words:

pass | head | end | me | socks | younger | September

b) How many silly rhymes like the following can you make?

Example: *There were some socks in my lunchbox.*

"My mom gave strange food to me. It looked suspiciously healthy."

You have read an article about chorofluorocarbons and the ozone layer. You have talked about different people's rubbish and tried to help them separate their rubbish. You have read a story on healthy food and written the story from another point of view. You have talked about your food diaries and made a list for the whole class.

CFCs can be found in sprays.
The use of CFCs will be greatly reduced.

Memory Box

C1 What's on the menu?

CD

a) Listen to the sounds. Which of the three photos match the sounds?

skills
How to listen
p. 122

b) Do you know this food? Match the names to the food items.

smoothie | squash | quiche | hash browns

c) Now listen to the dialogues and see what you can learn about the food items.

CD

1. Squash is a type of …
2. Quiche is originally from …
3. Hash browns are made from …
4. Smoothies are …

d) Read the statements below. Are they right, wrong or not in the dialogues? Correct the wrong sentences in your exercise book.

skills
How to listen
p. 122

1. Greg doesn't like squash.
2. Fabian knows a sport called squash.
3. Halloween is a type of dessert.
4. There is a game called squash.
5. Quiche isn't a typical American dish.
6. Quiche isn't served in a nutshell.
7. Fabian recognizes hash browns when he sees them.
8. The hash browns are under the tomatoes.
9. A big cheese is somebody important.
10. A smoothie is something to eat.

e) Greg wants to write an e-mail to a friend telling him about his conversation with Fabian. Help him write his e-mail.

I had lunch with my German friend Fabian yesterday. At first he did not recognize …
But then …
The same thing happened with …
He thought … came from …
He had never tasted a …

WB
C1, C2

skills
How to work with words
p. 120/1

C2 What would you like?

a) Look at Greg's school menu and find the translation of any food items you don't recognize. Check your dictionary and / or the Internet.

PENN MANOR SCHOOL DISTRICT FOOD SERVICES

A LA CARTE PRICES-ELEMENTARY & SECONDARY

ENTREES

Bagel Sandwiches	$1.50
BBQ/Roll	$1.25
Breaded Chicken	$1.25
Cheese Steak	$1.65
Chicken BBQ/Roll	$1.25
Chicken Croquettes (2)	$1.25
Chicken Fajitas	$1.25
Chicken Nuggets (6)	$1.50
Chicken Stir Fry/Rice	$1.25
Chilli	$1.00
Croissant Sandwiches	$1.50
Double Decker Burger	$1.50
Egg McComet	$1.50
Fish Sandwich	$1.50
French Toast Sticks	$1.25
Grilled Cheese	$1.25
Ham & Cheese Supreme	$1.25
Ham Boat	$1.50
Hamburger	$1.50
Hot Dog	$1.25
Hot Turkey Sandwich	$1.25
Macaroni & Cheese	$1.25
Pancakes (3)	$1.25
Pizza	$1.75
Pizza Hot Pocket	$1.65
Pizza Sticks	$1.50
Pork Rib/Roll	$1.50
Ravioli	$1.25
Roast Chicken	$1.25
Roast Turkey	$1.25
Spaghetti	$1.25
Stuffed Shells (2)	$1.50
Tacos (2) or Taco Bowl	$1.25

VEGETABLES

All vegetables – corn, peas, green beans, mashed potatoes, baked beans	$0.40
Baked potato w/ toppings	$1.00
Potato items – french fries, potato rounds, waffle fries, dino tots	$1.25

BEVERAGES

Canned Drinks	$0.75
Capri Sun	$0.50
Fruit Juice	$0.40
Iced Tea – 1/2 Pint	$0.40
Milk – 1/2 pint	$0.40
Turkey Hill pint drinks	$0.60
Water	$0.60

BREAD

Bread-Slice	$0.10
Crackers (4pk or 2/2pk)	$0.10
Peanut Butter Crackers (3)	$0.25
Roll	$0.10
Soft Pretzel	$0.40
Steamed Pasta	$0.40

McCOMET LINE

Bacon Cheeseburger	$2.00
BBQ Chicken Filet	$1.65
BLT	$1.65
Chicken Filet	$2.00
Chicken Wings	$1.75
Domino's Pizza	$1.75
French Fries	$1.25
Hamburger	$1.65
Pizza – 5 inch round	$1.75
Shrimp Basket	$2.00
Subway 6 inch sub	$2.00
Wafer Steak	$1.65
Nachos	$1.25
Onion Rings	$1.25

DESSERTS

Baked items	$0.50
Cake or Pie	$0.50
Canned Fruit	$0.50
Cookies – doz.	$2.50
Cookies – ea.	$0.25
Donuts – doz.	$3.50
Donuts – ea.	$0.50
Fresh Fruit	$0.50
Gelatin	$0.50
Juicy Gels	$0.50
Pudding	$0.50
Dessert Sundae	$0.50

MISCELLANEOUS

BBQ Sauce	$0.25
Cheese Sauce	$0.25
Cheese Sticks (2)	$0.75
Honey Mustard	$0.25
Honey	$0.25
Jelly	$0.10
Popcorn, bag	$0.50
Poptart (2)	$0.75
Salad Dressing	$0.25
Sausage Patty (1)	$0.75
Soup	$1.25
Steak Sauce	$0.25
String Cheese	$0.50
Yoghurt	$0.75

BREAKFAST

Bagel	$0.75
Hash Brown (each)	$0.40
Muffin	$0.50
Sausage Patty	$0.75
Sticky Bun	$0.75
Breakfast Sandwich	$1.00

SANDWICHES

Bread Sandwiches	$1.50
Croissant Sandwiches	$1.50
Bagel Sandwiches	$1.50

**b) Imagine you have a budget of $12 for the week.
Plan your food for the week. Think of a different meal for each day.**

WB
C3, C4

**c) If you have a school cafeteria, compare the menus.
What is the same? What is different? Discuss with your partner.**

C3 Attention, please!

Fabian's mother is visiting him in the USA. He takes her to the school cafeteria where they hear some announcements. Fabian's mother doesn't understand English very well.
Help her by telling her in German what you have understood.

CD

Language gym
p. 108, ex. 1–3

C4 A piece of cake

a) Look at these food idioms from the conversation in C1. Match them to the pictures.

skills
How to mediate
p. 126

- butter somebody up
- the big cheese
- hot potato
- spill the beans
- use your noodle
- have a sweet tooth
- as cool as a cucumber

1
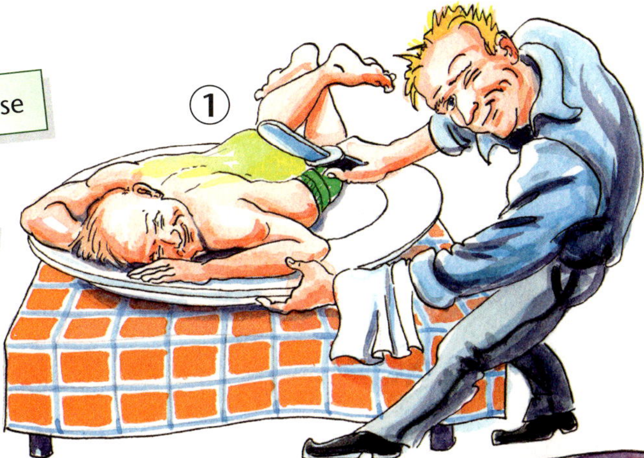

2

3

4
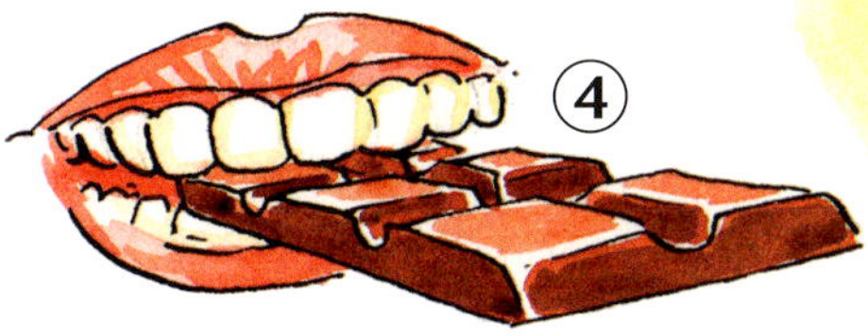

5

6

7

b) What do the idioms mean?

c) Do you know any other food idioms? Try to explain them in English.

WB
C5

Language gym

1 Which is correct? Write the correct sentence in your exercise book.

CD

1. I've never *eat / ate / eaten* hash browns.
2. I *drink / drank / drunk* a smoothie last week.
3. My sister *works / working / worked* in the cafeteria.
4. I've never *be / was / been* to America.
5. I've *becoming / became / become* interested in soccer.
6. I'm going to *visit / visiting / visited* my aunt.

2 American or British English? Listen to the words spoken with a typical American or British accent. Copy the table into your exercise book and note down which accent you hear each time.

CD

~~popcorn~~

British English	American English
popcorn	

yoghurt

pasta

butter

sausage

sandwich

waffle

tomato

3 Write the following text in American English. You will find the words you need in the boxes below.

A funny thing happened yesterday on my way home from secondary school. I was on the pavement outside a shop in the city centre when a taxi stopped. A guy who was talking on his mobile phone as he was getting out of the taxi asked if I had a biro. I gave him one and he said: "Thanks mate." Then he handed me a bag of chips while he wrote an address. He told me he was going to see a new flat but he was new to the neighbourhood. He had got lost on the underground and so he decided to take a taxi. Before he went to see the flat, he needed to post a letter, so I pointed out the post office across the street. As he was crossing, I told him he had forgotten his chips. He told me I could eat them.

mail

high school

gotten

ball point pen

cellphone

subway

store

cab

buddy

neighborhood

sidewalk

french fries

downtown

apartment

You have listened to dialogues at a school cafeteria and learned about different food items. You have looked at a menu and planned your food for the week. You have also compared the food plan with that of your own school.

jelly	jam
railroad	railway
pants	trousers
truck	lorry
meter	metre
neighborhood	neighbourhood
mail service	postal service

1 Signs in the States

a) What do these signs tell you about similarities / differences between Germany and the USA?

b) Choose the most surprising and / or the most interesting sign. Say why you chose this sign and compare your ideas with your partner's.

2 Groovy Gum

There are some things which are so much a part of our lives that we don't think twice about them. Take chewing gum, for example. Chewing gum has always been, hasn't it? I mean, what would we chew if we didn't have chewing gum? But if you think about it, someone must have invented it.
It doesn't grow on trees, like nuts or apples, does it?
I often wonder how it was invented – and

who invented it? Did some American cowboy sit down one day and suddenly say to himself, "Wow, I sure need something to chew!" – and then start looking for the ideal gum? Somehow, I don't think it was quite like that. But someone must have discovered it. Too bad it wasn't me – I would have been a millionaire now!
Lying in bed one night, I chewed these thoughts over. Waiting for sleep to come, I silently counted the lumps of used chewing gum on my bedpost. One, two, three, four, chew, chew, five, six, seven, chew, chew …
When I opened my eyes, I found myself lying sleepily in a dark forest, surrounded by strange, giant trees. I felt anxious. The air was filled with the frightening sounds of unknown animals. Birds were singing more sweetly than I had ever heard. It was hot and sticky. The sweat was dripping from my face. The mist which hung heavily over everything smelled pleasant and sweet – a little bit like mint sauce.

Suddenly there were different sounds. Human voices – shouting, singing, laughing. But I couldn't understand what they were saying. Then I saw them, two men at first. They looked handsome. And then two pretty women. I hid behind a large tree as they came nearer. Now I could see their dark skins and bright white eyes. One of the men was climbing a tree. He had a knife in his hand. Then he carefully began to cut away the bark of the tree. He threw a piece down to his companions below. One of them cut it into smaller pieces and passed it out to the others. Then they each put a piece into their mouths and began to chew happily.
It seemed to be very tough, because they chewed and chewed on it for at least ten minutes. It seemed to make them very happy. The longer they chewed, the bigger the smiles on their faces became. But it also appeared to make them very tired. When they had chewed their third piece, one after the other they all fell asleep.
I waited a moment or two, then quietly crept over to the place where they were lying. They all looked peaceful, and their faces were still smiling, as if they were dreaming the most beautiful dreams.
On the ground lay a few more pieces of the sticky stuff which they had been chewing.

Curious, I picked up a piece and put it into my mouth. At first it tasted bitter, but as I slowly chewed, my mouth was filled with a strange but wonderful taste. Very soon my head began to feel as light as a feather. With every chew, my body floated softly away in a cool, refreshing breeze …
Suddenly I was sitting in an ultramodern air-conditioned office on the 35th floor of a skyscraper in Chicago. Across from me a large man in a smart suit was sitting behind his desk, puffing a fat cigar.

"Let's get down to business, Mr Raleigh. If you can get me another fifty tons of your gum, you got a deal. Just take a look at these sales figures for last month! I'm telling you – we just can't get enough of the stuff."
"But wait a minute, Mr Grigley, you've read those medical reports. The dentists are all complaining that their patients' teeth are falling out. And it's making people so sleepy that they just don't want to do any work anymore."
"That's not our problem, is it? It's a free world. Nobody's making them chew the stuff."
"But once they start, they can't stop chewing," I said. "They can't get enough of the stuff. They're hooked."
"Yeah, brilliant, isn't it? A businessman's dream! I promise you, if you can supply fifty tons a month, you'll be a millionaire by the end of the year."
I secretly felt in my pocket for the little blue packet, took out a piece and began to chew …

The bright spotlights in the TV studio are switched on, and the smart interviewer holds out her microphone towards the president.
"Mr President, how much longer can you ignore the doctors' warnings? Groovy Gum is clearly a dangerous and addictive product. Thousands of people say it should be banned."
The president takes a deep breath. "Well, it's not so simple, Ms Whitney. Not all doctors agree that Groovy Gum is harmful. Indeed, many doctors chew it themselves. And anyway, we have agreed to put a Surgeon General's warning on every pack of Groovy Gum. We don't like to tell people what to do and what not to do. We believe the people should decide for themselves."
"So you will not agree to ban Groovy Gum. Mr President, could this have anything to do with the taxes that Groovy Gum brings in every year?"
"You might think that, Ms Whitney, but I couldn't possibly comment," answers the president with a smile, at the same time slipping something into his mouth and beginning to chew …

BEEPEEEPEEPEEP … !!!
I woke to the sound of my radio alarm. 6.30. Why was I so tired? What were all those chewing gum wrappers doing on the floor? Why were the bed sheets sticking to my pyjamas? What was that music the DJ was playing? "Does your chewing gum lose its flavor on the bedpost overnight?"

Choose one of the following tasks:

1. **Make notes about Raleigh, Grigley and the president and talk about them.**
2. **Imagine you are Mr Raleigh and talk about your dream.**
3. **Imagine you are Mr Grigley and tell your business partners about your difficulties with Mr Raleigh and the doctors.**
4. **Imagine you are a newspaper reporter and write an article about the dangers of Groovy Gum.**

1 What a trip(p)!

a) Read Ryan's amazing adventure!

He was tired and sunburned, but Ryan Tripp had had ... the trip of his life! It took the 12-year-old boy 42 days to cross the USA from Salt Lake City to Washington, DC. He traveled 3,116 miles, setting a record for the longest trip on a lawnmower.

"I knew about the old world record," said Ryan. "So we planned a new route for about 3,200 miles." But the trip wasn't just about setting records or missing five weeks of school. Ryan raised over $15,000 for Whitnie Pender, a baby who needed an organ transplant.

When planning the route, Ryan and his father had to avoid busy roads and large cities. This wasn't always easy, especially in Massachusetts, New Jersey and Maryland. In Boston many people were surprised to see a boy riding a lawn mower along the city's harbor! Ryan also had to go around the Uintah and Ouray Native American Reservation because he didn't have permission to drive through the area.

Ryan usually woke up at 6 am and drove at 10 mph until 9 pm. But it was even slower in the skiing areas of Colorado, Vermont, Maine and New Hampshire. "At the top of Green Mountain I had Vermont's speciality – maple syrup on pancakes," said Ryan. "It was a real treat."

Most difficult of all was the hot weather of Utah, Colorado and Nebraska. Although he lives in a state where temperatures can change from summer to winter by 150°F, this boy from Utah found the desert very hard. But after crossing the Mississippi in Missouri, Ryan was able to breathe a little easier. He enjoyed the forests, the view of Lake Erie and the cool weather of Vermont. When Ryan reached Maine and New Hampshire, he had his first lobster! "I'm not a fish guy, but the lobster was really great," said Ryan.

There wasn't much time for sightseeing, but Ryan didn't want to miss out on a few more stops. There was New York State's world famous

Niagara Falls; the Massachusetts' Basketball Hall of Fame; and the nation's historical sights in DC: the White House, the Lincoln Memorial and Capitol Hill.

But at 8–10 mph, most of Ryan's sightseeing was done on the lawnmower. He had lots of time to see the great plains and deserts of Nebraska and Missouri; the open fields and lakes of Illinois, Indiana and Ohio; the cool mountain areas of New York State and Colorado; the famous seaside resorts of Maine and Massachusetts. Sadly, Ryan also saw a lot of dead animals on the road. "At 8 mph they smelled awful!" he said.

"But the most exciting part was meeting lots of different people who gave money and good wishes," said Ryan. "When I arrived in Fairbury, Nebraska, everyone came to the town center to welcome me. It was so nice."

And the people that welcomed Ryan to Washington, DC on September 26, 1997 were fantastic. While he was mowing the lawn of Capitol Hill, Ryan's sunburned face was watched by millions of people on TV. He even appeared on The Late Show with David Letterman.

Ryan's biggest lesson was learning "how to set goals and reach them and to realize how good it makes you feel to do things for other people." But the next time his parents ask him to mow the lawn, Ryan said he's going to tell them no!

b) Draw an outline of the USA. Note down information about the areas that Ryan drove through (e.g. landscape, sights, specialities).

c) Compare your outline with your partner's and add more information.

1 Oh, play that thing

Roddy Doyle, born in May 1958 in Dublin, is an Irish writer. His novel "Oh, play that thing" describes the life and adventures of the Irishman Henry Smart in the United States. He had to leave Ireland in 1925 for political reasons.

Read the extract from "Oh, play that thing". Why do you think Henry did not say where he was really from and what his real name was?

The guards stood back and I walked the few steps to the next desk. I let my heels clip the Spanish tiles. Two beautiful sisters held each other as they were pushed back. Without parents or children they were too likely to fall into bad hands waiting for them on the Manhattan or New Jersey wharfs. If they were lucky they'd be kept on the island until relatives were found to take them; less lucky, they'd be pawed, then let through: less lucky still, they'd be deported, sent back before they'd arrived.
I handed my passport and papers to the Immigration Bureau officer. He opened the passport and found the ten-dollar note I'd left in its centre. The note was gone before I saw it missing. I'd taken it from the wheezy anarchist; its loss didn't sting. Then came the catechism, the questions I couldn't get wrong.
– What is your name?
– Henry Drake.
– Where are you from?
– London.
– Why have you come to the United States?
– Opportunity.
So far, so easy.
But he stopped. He looked at me.
– Where are you travelling from, sir? he asked me.
It wasn't one of the questions.
– London, I said.
He seemed to be staring at the word as I spoke it.
– You are a born Englishman, sir?
He read my latest name.
– Mister Drake?
– Yes.
– Henry Drake.
– Yes.
– And where is Missis Drake, sir?
– She's in my dreams.
– So you're travelling alone, sir, is that right? You are an unmarried man.
– That's right.
– And how do you intend supporting yourself, sir?
We were back on track.
– By working very hard.
– Yes, and how, sir?
– I'm a salesman.
– And your speciality?
I shrugged.
– Everything, and anything.
– Alright. And do you have sufficient funds to sustain you until you commence selling everything?
– I do.
He handed me a sheet of paper.
– Could you read this for me, sir?
– We, the people of the United States, in order to form a more perfect union –
And as I strolled through the literacy test, I could feel Victor, my brother, beside me, his leg pressed against mine at the school desk, and Miss O'Shea at my shoulder, my teacher and wife, the mother of the daughter I suddenly missed, her wet fingers on my cheek.
– and secure the blessings of liberty to ourselves and our posterity, do ordain and establish this Constitution of –
He took the paper from my fingers. He picked up a rubber stamp and brought it down on top of a card. I read the stamp: ADMITTED.
– Welcome to America, he said.
It was America, not just the U.S.A. America was bigger than the states, bigger than the world. America was everything possible.
He handed me the passport and registration card, then held them back.
– But you'd want to work on your accent, sir: Slán leat.*
That shook me, but only until I climbed the last few steps and walked out into my first American sunshine.

** Irish Gaelic for 'Goodbye'*

1 Legends

CD

Animals and plants have always played a very important role in Native American legends.

The earth on turtle's back

Long ago, before the Earth was here, all was water. Many creatures lived in the water, swimming about. Far above the clouds, there was, however, a land where lived a powerful chief. His wife was going to have a baby. In that Skyland was a great tree with four large roots, stretching out to each of the four sacred directions, and bearing many kinds of fruits and flowers.

One night the chief's wife dreamed that the great tree had been uprooted. The chief perceived that this was a dream of great power, and thus must be fulfilled. With great effort, the tree was uprooted, leaving a large hole in the sky. The chief's wife leaned to look through the hole, but lost her balance and fell. Grasping at the tree as she fell, she only managed to hold on to a handful of seeds. The water creatures below saw her falling. They realized that she was not a water creature and tried desperately to think of a way to help her.

"I have heard," said one, "that there is earth far below the waters. Perhaps we should try to get some for her to stand upon." One by one the animals tried to dive down far enough to retrieve land, but one by one they failed. Finally brave little Muskrat tried one last time. Deeper and deeper she dived until her little lungs almost burst. Suddenly she found a bit of land. Scooping it up, she frantically swam to the surface. But alas, where to put the land? Turtle said, "Put it on my back. I will hold up the Land and the Sky Woman." And so they did. Sky Woman landed safely on Turtle's back and was very thankful. She cast the seeds about. The Land became ever so beautiful. Some people call that land "America". Others call it, in honor of the brave and faithful Turtle, "Turtle Island".

Tell a legend you know to your class.

CD

How the raven got its black feathers

At the beginning of time the raven flew high up into the sky to the home of the birds. The birds all looked the same. The raven wanted to make all the birds look different so he went to the four Great Spirits in the sky with his idea. He said, "The birds are all the same colour and shape. They look so uninteresting. I will paint all of the birds different colours if you will give me the paints and the brushes."

The Spirits agreed and then the clever raven said, "If I do all of this work for you, I would like you to paint me so that I am the most beautiful bird in the world." The Spirits agreed again and the raven started painting the birds. When he had finished, each bird was different from all the other birds and their feathers were all the colours of the rainbow: red, orange, yellow, blue, green, indigo and violet.

The raven went to the four Great Spirits and said, "I have kept my promise, now you must keep yours." So the first Great Spirit painted the raven with wonderful colours and made him the most beautiful bird in the world. The clever raven said, "I don't think you have painted me very well. I'm no different from the other birds."
The raven hoped the Spirits would make him even more beautiful. So each of the other three Great Spirits added even more beautiful colours to the first Great Spirit's work but the raven still said, "I'm no different from the other birds."

After the fourth Great Spirit had finished painting, the raven said, "You have cheated me. I kept my promise and painted all the birds. You haven't kept your promise to make me the most beautiful bird in the world." When the Great Spirits heard this they were angry with the clever raven. They poured all of their paint over him so that all the colours mixed together. The result was a deep, deep black. Then they sent the raven back down to the earth.

That is how the raven got its black feathers.

Why does the raven say he wants to paint the other birds?
What do you think of the raven?

1 Marathon Macho

a) Read the text. Discuss the following questions in groups of four:
- **What kind of person is Ned? What is Ned and Erin's relationship?**
- **Why does Ned take part in the race? Is it good for him that he takes part?**
- **What do you think is funny / surprising / silly / ...?**

Present your ideas to the class.

So here I was at the big annual race organized by this huge bank. But how had I got here? Well, it started in the morning. I was working in my parents' office in the summer. They have this factory, you know. Along came Erin – red hair, glasses. Fantastically pretty. Too old for me, I know, but wow!

"Hi, Ned," she said. "Do you want to run today?"
"Sure!" I thought she meant a little office softball game. "Er ... where do I run?"
"In Central Park."
"And how far?"
"Three miles. The race starts after work. And bring a raincoat." She looked at me. She was going to make eye contact. "Ned," she said, "thank you for doing this." Wow!

I left the office at five, taking two T-shirts and my jacket. I also had an umbrella, a walkman and a book to read. OK, so the book wasn't really necessary for the race. Guys from my office were standing around and one said, "So, Ned, why are you wearing sandals and socks?" Everyone thought that was funny. I didn't see the joke. I was wearing them because I couldn't find my shoes. That happens quite often. Someone puts them behind a heater or in a corner and I can't find them for a day or two. "Er ... I just had them on today. I didn't know about the race until this afternoon."

"Where's your number?" There was no way to fix my running number to my shirt. I took my T-shirts and jacket and tied them round my waist. I pushed my running number under this ring of clothes, put the walkman and book in my pocket and the umbrella down the front of my jeans.
"And now – on your marks ... get set ... go!"
I started jogging. My sandals flip-flopped all over the place and the umbrella started to rub my leg.
"How far have we come?" I asked a kind-looking gentleman.
"Oh, a quarter of a mile."
A quarter of a mile! This was harder than I thought. The walkman was getting heavy. My jeans were soaked. I had to hold them with one hand to stop them falling down.

I stopped running and started walking. I wanted to give up but three things kept me going. One, all these bald guys of about fifty who were overtaking me. Second, those adverts for running shoes where the runner says "Believe in yourself!" And then, of course, Erin. She must be somewhere, perhaps at the finishing line. I didn't want her to see me looking like a tired, wet, sweaty idiot. I wanted to hold my head high and be a real man.

So I kept running. Every time I was given a drink of water, I poured it over my head. I ran through every puddle. I sang *L. A. Woman* as I ran. It was just the right song because it had the right rhythm for my flapping sandals. Sometimes I sang quietly, never sure if I'd see Erin. And then I was at the finishing line. I was just one wet blob. Some sporty types patted me on the back and said "Well done!" and gave me another T-shirt and some soda and Power Bars®. I looked around. Erin was nowhere in sight. I tried to think that the race had been a good thing. After all, I had got free T-shirts, a running number, water, soda, Power Bars® and exercise. On my way home I dropped by a local hamburger place and looked in the mirror there. I was a teenage Frankenstein – dirty face, sweat and rain mixed all over my shirt, socks and sandals covered in mud.

The next day, Erin was at work, all smiles. "So, Ned, how did you do in the race?"
"OK, I guess."
"Great, great. Did you hear how well Jack did?"
Jack was her boyfriend, who also worked here. I tried not to think about him.
"Come and look!" The other runners had made a note of how long they'd taken and reported back to Erin. I guessed this chart was something she did every year.
"There's Jack. 27 minutes! How long did you take, Ned? So I can put you on the chart."
I had probably run for an hour. "40 minutes," I said.
"Oh, great. Great job. And I hope you do it again if you work here next summer."
She put my name on the chart, poured herself a cup of coffee, and sipped, leaving lipstick all over the rim.

b) Have you ever been in a similar situation to Ned? What happened? Tell your partner.

Adapted from: Teen Angst? Naaah ... A Quasi-Autobiography by Ned Vizzini, © 2000. Used with permission from Free Spirit Publishing Inc., Minneapolis, MN; All rights reserved. 001-800-735-7323; www.freespirit.com

1 The story of the first Thanksgiving

a) Do you know any American festivals and holidays?

b) What do you think is correct in these four sentences about Thanksgiving? Write down all your guesses.

1. At Thanksgiving
   a) the children thank their parents.
   b) everyone gives thanks for the food they have.
   c) the white Americans thank the Native Americans.

2. Thanksgiving is celebrated in
   a) spring.
   b) summer.
   c) fall.

3. At Thanksgiving people often eat
   a) turkey.
   b) steaks.
   c) hamburgers.

4. The first American Thanksgiving was celebrated
   a) about 40 years ago.
   b) about 400 years ago.
   c) about 4000 years ago.

**c) This is how the story is told to American children.
Read the story and see if your guesses were right.**

On September 16, 1620, the Pilgrim Fathers set sail from Plymouth in England towards Virginia, USA. They were leaving to find a new home, far across the ocean in America. There they hoped to be free to worship God in their own way.

The journey was long and stormy. Huge waves washed across the deck of the Mayflower. The Pilgrims were sick and frightened. But they did not lose hope. On November 21 they reached land at Cape Cod which they later named Plymouth Rock. At last the tired Pilgrims had arrived in America.

Winter had begun, and the Pilgrims needed homes. They wanted to begin building. On land they found fields and a dark green forest. They cut down huge trees to make roofs. Then, on Christmas Day, they began to build.

Outside all was white with frost and snow. But inside each house a fire burnt. The women cooked soup over the fire. At the end of the day, the fire welcomed the cold and tired men.

That winter many of the Pilgrims became very sick. Some of them died. Those who could, cared for the others. Then, in March, they had a surprise.

Native Americans came to offer friendship. The Pilgrim leader and the native leader Chief Massasoit met. They feasted and talked. Then they made a promise to help each other. One Native American, who spoke English, decided to stay with the Pilgrims. His name was Squanto.

Spring had come. It was time to plant. The Pilgrims planted peas and barley brought from England. But they knew nothing about growing corn. Squanto showed them. He also told them where to hunt and how to fish in this new land.

The forest had many things the Pilgrims needed. It gave them wood for their homes and fires. There were deer and nuts and berries. But the forest was also dark and frightening. At night the Pilgrims could hear the howling of the wolves.

One summer day, young John Billington went berry picking. But he left the forest path and got lost. John walked through the forest for many days. He had only berries and wild plants to eat. At night he slept under the trees. Finally some Native Americans found him and sent word to Plymouth. Governor Bradford sent a boat to bring John home. The Native Americans sang and danced, and everyone exchanged presents. The Pilgrims were happy that young John had been found.

The green trees of summer turned red and gold. The corn grew tall and became dry and yellow. Huge orange pumpkins covered the fields. Wild geese filled the sky and turkeys gobbled everywhere. The Pilgrims began to gather the corn and pumpkins. It was time to give thanks to God for a good harvest.

On a sunny October day in 1621, Governor Bradford declared a time for thanksgiving. The women and children roasted fat geese and wild turkeys slowly over the fires. Pies and corn bread baked in the outdoor ovens.

Chief Massasoit and his people came with presents. Then, with songs and prayers, the Thanksgiving celebration began. For three days everyone ate, sang, and played games. Together the Pilgrims and Native Americans lived in peace and grew in friendship.

With the Pilgrims' journey began the largest migration of peoples in history. By the end of the 19th century about 11 million people had followed the Pilgrims across the Atlantic.

How to work with words

1 Die Bedeutung eines englischen Wortes herausfinden

Du verstehst ein Wort oder einen Ausdruck in einem Satz im Text nicht. Bevor du zum Wörterbuch greifst, versuche es so:

- Lies zwei Sätze vor dem unverständlichen Wort/Ausdruck und zwei danach. Versuche, die Lücke auf Englisch oder auf Deutsch inhaltlich zu füllen, z. B. *There are hardly any jobs on the reservation. Mr and Mrs Deermount can understand their children well. Life has not ... over the years. Many members of their tribe suffer from poverty.* ***(improved)*** Es könnte „geändert" *(changed)* oder „besser geworden" *(got better)* heißen. Beide Begriffe ändern nicht den Inhalt der Aussagen. Man nennt das „intelligentes Raten".
- Schau dir die Illustrationen an, die den Text begleiten. Sie helfen oft, den Sinnzusammenhang des Textes zu erkennen und helfen bei Verstehenslücken.
- Vielleicht erinnert dich die Schreibweise des unbekannten Wortes auch an ein deutsches Wort und du kannst so den Sinn erkennen.
- Manchmal gibt es auch Ähnlichkeiten zwischen dem deutschen und dem englischen Wort, in der Rechtschreibung und in der Bedeutung. Das erkennst du auf den ersten Blick, z. B. bei Wörtern wie *tourist – Tourist, catastrophe – Katastrophe, period – Periode, station – Station.*
- Manche Wörter im Englischen und im Deutschen haben ihren Ursprung in der lateinischen Sprache. Deren Bedeutung ist in Englisch und Deutsch auch gleich, z. B. *distance – Distanz, energy – Energie, irrational – irrational.*

Natürlich ist das Englisch-Deutsche Wörterbuch die zuverlässigste Hilfe, die Bedeutung eines Wortes herauszufinden.
Schlage es z. B. bei ***improve*** auf. Da findest du viele Bedeutungen. Welche ist die richtige?

im·prove [ɪm'pruːv] **I.** *vt* ▪ **to ~ sth** etw verbessern; ▪ **to ~ oneself** an sich *dat* arbeiten, sich *akk* verbessern
II. *vi* besser werden, sich *akk* verbessern; ***I hope the weather ~s*** ich hoffe, es gibt besseres Wetter; ▪ **to ~ on** [*or* **upon**] **sth** etw [noch] verbessern; ***you can't ~ on that!*** da ist keine Steigerung mehr möglich!; **to ~ with age** mit dem Alter immer besser werden; **to ~ in French/mathematics** sich *akk* in Französisch/in Mathematik verbessern; **to ~ with practice** mit der Übung immer besser werden; **to ~ dramatically** sich *akk* entscheidend [*o* erheblich] verbessern
◆**improve on** *vi (fig)* ▪ **to ~ on sth** *a price* etw übertreffen [*o* überbieten]

Nimm nicht die erstbeste Bedeutung. Lies sie alle und füge diejenige in den Satz ein, die inhaltlich passt. Das wäre *verbessern*, im Satz also: „hat *sich* nicht *verbessert*".
Mit ein wenig Übung wirst du sicher im Finden der richtigen Wortbedeutung.

2 Das richtige englische Wort finden

a) Du willst etwas sagen, aber dir fehlt das Wort. Bevor du zum Wörterbuch greifst, versuche es so:

- Du willst z. B. auf Englisch sagen: „Es wäre gut, die Menschen in den Reservaten mit Lebensmitteln zu unterstützen": *It would be good to* – Was heißt unterstützen? Finde ein anderes Wort mit sehr ähnlicher Bedeutung in Deutsch, z. B. „helfen" oder „geben", *help* oder *give*.

- Du kannst das Wort auch umschreiben. Du willst z. B. sagen: „Die Regierung muss den Menschen im Reservat helfen." Was heißt hier „Regierung"? *The people in Washington / The President … / The leaders of …*

Natürlich hilft dir in dieser Situation das Deutsch-Englische Wörterbuch zuverlässig, aber Vorsicht Falle! Du musst den Sinnzusammenhang deines Satzes vor Augen haben, wenn du ein Wort nachschlägst. Wenn du z. B. sagen willst: „Ich finde es **gemein**, wie die Indianer behandelt werden" und du schaust **gemein** nach, findest du mehrere Wörter mit unterschiedlichen Bedeutungen. Welches ist das richtige Wort? Du kannst es schnell finden, wenn du alle Einträge liest und sie mit deinem Satzinhalt vergleichst. So kommst du auf *mean* oder *nasty*.

b) Du möchtest einen Text schreiben, einen Brief, einen Bericht oder eine Zusammenfassung und du suchst für einen Satz das passende Wort.

Hier sind ein paar Tipps für dich, wie du in einem Wörterbuch nachschaust:
- Fange beim sogenannten Haupteintrag (dem *headword*) an.
- Die unterschiedlichen Bedeutungen sind durch Nummern angezeigt.
- Du findest in manchen Wörterbüchern auch Beispielsätze, an denen du erkennen kannst, ob die Bedeutung auch für deinen Satz zutrifft.
- Wenn du eine bestimmte Wortart, ein Nomen (*noun*) oder Adjektiv (*adjective*) suchst, findest du es unter den Folgeeinträgen, wenn du beim Ersteintrag anfängst.

1 Einen Hörtext besser verstehen

Du hast bisher schon viele Texte hörend erarbeitet und immer besser verstanden.
Du weißt, dass du nicht jedes einzelne Wort zu verstehen brauchst, um den Inhalt des Textes aufzunehmen.
Aber – die Texte werden mit deiner zunehmenden Erfahrung länger und schwieriger.
Hier bekommst du weitere Tipps, die dir das Verstehen erleichtern können.

Vor dem Hören:

- Stelle dir vor, in welcher Situation, in welchem thematischen Zusammenhang der Hörtext (z. B. eine Rede, ein Bericht, eine Geschichte) angesiedelt ist oder, wenn der Hörtext ein Dialog ist, wer mit wem worüber sprechen könnte.
- Denke an die Vokabeln und Redewendungen, die zu dem Thema des Hörtextes passen könnten. Sprich mit deinem Partner darüber oder schreibe sie auf.
- Denke daran, welche Art von Sätzen zu dem Hörtext passen könnten, z. B. Fragen, Ausrufe, Gefühlsäußerungen (Gespräch, Interview), sachliche Aussagesätze (Bericht), schmückende und ausführlichere Sätze in einem Erzähltext (Geschichte).
- Versuche vorauszusagen, wie das Thema des Hörtextes lauten könnte.

Während des Hörens:

- Wenn du einen Film oder eine DVD siehst, können dir die Bilder helfen. Der Hintergrund, die Umgebung, die Sprecher und deren Mimik und Gestik unterstützen dich beim Verstehen.
- Wenn du mit jemandem über etwas sprichst und du verstehst etwas nicht, kannst du nachfragen (z. B. *Could you please explain what … means?*).
- Wenn du eine Rede, einen Bericht oder eine Geschichte von der CD hörst, kannst du dir Notizen machen von dem, was du verstehst. Beim zweiten Hören ergänzt du die Notizen, und so verstehst du immer mehr. Dabei helfen dir die sogenannten *graphic organizers*, d. h. Übersichten und Tabellen, in die du deine Notizen einträgst. Du kannst z. B. die Vor- und Nachteile einer Situation, wie Leben in der Stadt oder auf dem Land (*the pros and cons*), schon geordnet in Notizen aufschreiben.

+	–
- fast food very popular - very quick service - drive-thru service	- not very healthy - lots of plastic garbage

Du kannst deine Notizen auch unter bestimmten Aspekten / Überschriften, die du beim ersten Hören mitbekommst, ordnen, wie z. B. *friends / sports / free time activities / school etc.*

friends	sports	free time activities	school

Wenn du einen Dialog hörst, kannst du z. B. die Namen der Gesprächsteilnehmer in eine Übersicht schreiben und deine Notizen in die entsprechenden Abteilungen eintragen.

Nach dem Hören:

- Jetzt kannst du deine Notizen durchgehen und versuchen, das eine oder andere Detail zu ergänzen. Auf jeden Fall solltest du versuchen, aus den Notizen sinnvolle Aussagen zu machen, mündlich oder schriftlich. Dabei fällt dir auch noch manches Gehörte wieder ein.
- Im Unterricht hast du auch die Möglichkeit, deine Notizen mit denen deines Nachbarn zu vergleichen. Dabei fällt dir auch meistens wieder etwas ein, was du verstanden, aber nicht notiert hattest.
- Versuche auch, dir nach dem gehörten Text Vokabeln / Ausdrücke in einer Liste zu notieren, die du benutzen würdest, um jemandem vom Inhalt des Gehörten zu berichten.

1 Einen längeren Lesetext besser verstehen

Du hast dir schon viele kürzere Lesetexte mit unterschiedlicher Zielsetzung erarbeitet:
Du hast
- dir einen allgemeinen Überblick über den Inhalt verschafft (*reading for gist*),
- nach bestimmten Informationen zu einem Thema gesucht (*selective reading*),
- alle Einzelheiten erfasst (*reading for detail*).

Hier bekommst du weitere Tipps, wie du auch längere Texte lesend erarbeiten und verstehen kannst:

Vor dem Lesen:

Mache dir klar, warum du den Text lesen wirst: Was ist dein Leseziel? Zum Beispiel, weil dich das Thema interessiert, weil du bestimmte Informationen zu einem Thema darin finden kannst oder weil du dein Wissen über das Thema mit den Informationen und Ideen des Textes vergleichen möchtest.
Schaue dir die Überschrift an und schreibe die Ideen auf, die dir dazu in den Sinn kommen. Eventuell ist der Text illustriert oder eine Tabelle oder Grafik sind in den Text eingebaut. Auch sie geben Einblick in den Inhalt. Du versuchst, Anteile des Inhalts „vorauszusehen".

Während des Lesens:

- Lies den Text einmal ganz durch und versuche, deine vorausgesagten Gedanken mit denen des Textes zu vergleichen. Was ist gleich? Was ist ganz anders in Bezug auf das Thema?
- **Fange nicht an, an dieser Stelle Vokabeln nachzuschlagen. Entdecke erst alles, was du verstehst!**
- Nahezu jeder Text ist in Abschnitte unterteilt. Versuche, entsprechend der Überschrift des Textes, eine Überschrift zu jedem Abschnitt zu formulieren.
- Versuche nun, der Überschrift entsprechend, dir das Gelesene auf Deutsch ins Gedächtnis zu rufen. Lies danach jeden Abschnitt noch einmal.
- Wenn du eine Kopie von dem Text hast (das wäre in jedem Fall sinnvoll), unterstreiche jetzt alles, was du verstehst. Wenn du keine Kopie hast, mache dir die Mühe, die Stellen herauszuschreiben.

Nach dem Lesen:

- Mithilfe von Tabellen, Übersichten oder Listen kannst du dir den Inhalt sortieren, z. B. Wesentliches / nicht so Wichtiges, dir Bekanntes, für dich Neues zum Thema, usw. in Notizform aufschreiben.
- Dazu brauchst du auch die Vokabeln, deren Bedeutung du noch nicht verstehst. Schlage sie jetzt in deinem Wörterbuch nach.
- Lege dir eine Liste mit den Ausdrücken an, die du brauchst, um den Inhalt des Textes mündlich oder schriftlich auf Englisch wiederzugeben. Du möchtest ja auch vom Gelesenen berichten können.
- Wenn du jetzt den Inhalt des Textes in Kurzform auf Englisch wiedergeben kannst, hast du neben dem Leseverstehen auch dein Sprechen oder Schreiben trainiert!

2 Einen Liedtext oder ein Gedicht interpretieren

Lieder und Gedichte haben einiges gemeinsam. Sie drücken Gefühle oder Erfahrungen anders aus als eine *short story* oder ein Roman. Die Sprache wird anders – auch freier – eingesetzt. Ein Gedicht / Lied nutzt Laute, Rhythmus oder Reime, um Stimmungen zu vermitteln. Die üblichen Sprachregeln, sogar die der Grammatik, werden in Gedichten / Liedern häufig verändert.

Die folgenden Leitfragen können dir helfen, ein Gedicht / Lied besser zu verstehen:

- **Thema (Topic):** Was ist das Thema? Wird es in der Überschrift genannt?
- **Geschichte (Story):** Erzählt das Gedicht / Lied eine Geschichte? Kannst du sie in ein paar Worten zusammenfassen?
- **Erfahrung (Experience):** Berichtet es von einer Erfahrung? Welche Schlüsselwörter beschreiben es? Hast du ähnliche Erfahrungen gemacht?
- **Gefühle (Feelings):** Welche Gefühle drückt es aus? Mit welchen Worten / Phrasen werden die Gefühle ausgedrückt? Werden konkrete Bilder benutzt, um die Gefühle darzustellen?
- **Erzähler (Narrator):** Gibt es in dem Gedicht / Lied direkte oder indirekte Hinweise auf die Person, die die Erfahrungen gemacht hat?
- **Klang (Sound):** Lies das Gedicht laut oder spiele das Lied und konzentriere dich auf die Klänge. Markiere die betonten Silben und schreibe die Wörter auf, die sich reimen. Gibt es Alliterationen (d.h. Wörter, die mit dem gleichen Laut beginnen)? Gibt es einen bestimmten Klang, der auffallend oft vorkommt?
- **Ungewöhnlicher Sprachgebrauch (Unusual language):** Kommen ungewöhnliche Wortkombinationen vor? Oder eine ungewöhnliche Wortstellung? Oder grammatikalische Konstruktionen, die wiederholt werden? Gibt es personifizierte Dinge oder Ideen?
- **Wirkung (Critique):** Wie fühlst du dich, wenn du das Gedicht / Lied liest bzw. hörst? Was drückt es für dich aus? Welche Wörter drücken für dich das meiste aus?

1 Informationen von einer Sprache in die andere übertragen

Du weißt schon, dass es beim Sprachmitteln darum geht, für jemanden aus englisch- oder deutschsprachigen Texten die wichtigen Informationen in die gewünschte Sprache, Englisch oder Deutsch, zu übertragen.
Du weißt auch schon, dass du diese Informationen manchmal für jemanden aufschreiben musst. Ein anderes Mal musst du etwas mündlich übermitteln oder spontan im Gespräch übertragen (dolmetschen).
Rufe dir die folgenden Dinge noch einmal in Erinnerung:

- Du musst auf keinen Fall jedes Wort übersetzen. Es reicht, wenn du den Sinn einer Aussage oder Information wiedergibst. Das kannst du auch in deinen eigenen Worten machen.

- Da du in solchen Situationen oft kein Wörterbuch zur Hand hast, kannst du wichtige Wörter auch umschreiben.

- Wenn du vom Deutschen ins Englische dolmetschst, solltest du am besten kurze Sätze benutzen. Das ist einfacher für dich und für denjenigen, den du informieren willst.

1 Eine Zusammenfassung (summary) schreiben

Eine Zusammenfassung verkürzt längere Texte, die neben dem Handlungsstrang noch Anteile beinhalten, die Situationen, Menschen und Stimmungen näher beschreiben, z. B. durch ausschmückende Einzelheiten oder wörtliche Rede.
Texte werden zusammengefasst, um einem Leser möglichst knapp und klar den wesentlichen Inhalt zu vermitteln.

Hier findest du Tipps, wie eine Zusammenfassung gelingen kann. Du folgst dem dir bekannten Konzept:
Planen, Gestalten, Überarbeiten.

Planen und Gestalten

Inhaltliche Aspekte:

- Lies den ganzen Text einmal oder mehrmals durch, um dir einen Überblick zu verschaffen: Worum geht es? Erkennst du einen „roten Faden", kannst du wichtige von unwichtigen Informationen unterscheiden?
- Wenn du eine Kopie des Textes hast, nimm einen Marker und kennzeichne die Stellen, die du für unverzichtbar hältst, damit der Leser deiner Zusammenfassung später nicht nachzufragen braucht, um Klarheit über den Inhalt zu gewinnen.
- Mithilfe eines Rasters, z. B. mit den Überschriften / Unterteilungen *place, time, people, action,* machst du dir jetzt Notizen. Vokabeln, deren Bedeutung dir noch unklar erscheint, schlägst du noch einmal nach.

place	time	people	action

Sprachliche Aspekte:

- Du kannst eine Zusammenfassung im Präsens oder in der Erzählzeit des Textes, meistens *past tense,* schreiben. Letzteres ist einfacher.
- Versuche, lange Nebensätze oder sogenannte „Bandwurmsätze" zu vermeiden. Setze lieber einen Punkt, wenn ein Gedanke ausgeführt ist.
- Wörtliche Rede gehört nicht in eine Zusammenfassung. Wenn der Inhalt der wörtlichen Rede wesentlich ist, schreibe den Text um, z. B. mit diesen Redewendungen:

He / She / They said, stated, announced, asked, made clear that …
He / She / They tried to …
He / She expressed his / her opinion on … and …

- Satzanfänge helfen, den Handlungsablauf zu strukturieren, z. B.:

The article / letter / story is about …
The writer / narrator / people is / are …
When …, the / a …
After that … / Then …
Some time later … / Afterwards …
In the end … / Finally …

- Du formulierst deine Zusammenfassung mithilfe deiner Notizen, Redewendungen und Satzanfänge.

Überarbeiten

Lies deine Zusammenfassung – ruhig laut – und versuche, dabei die Position deines Lesers einzunehmen. Dieser hat den Text, dessen Inhalt du zusammengefasst hast, nicht gelesen. Er weiß also bis jetzt nichts von dessen Inhalt.

- ☐ Sind alle wesentlichen Informationen wiedergegeben?
- ☐ Sind sie in der richtigen Reihenfolge angeordnet? Ergeben sie einen Sinn?
- ☐ Sind die Sätze verständlich gebildet? Stimmt der Satzbau?
- ☐ Sind Verbformen und Pluralformen richtig gebildet?
- ☐ Ist Abwechslung in den Satzanfängen gelungen?
- ☐ Kann, ohne etwas vom Inhalt aufzugeben, gekürzt werden?
- ☐ Ist die Rechtschreibung korrekt?

2 Eine kurze Meinungsäußerung / Einen Kurzkommentar schreiben

In einer Meinungsäußerung nimmst du Stellung zu einem bestimmten Thema oder Problem, das in einem Text dargestellt ist. Du vergleichst unterschiedliche Lebensweisen, die Vor- und Nachteile, z. B. *School life in the USA and in Germany, life in town and in the country.* Oder du drückst aus, was du von den amerikanischen Einflüssen auf unser tägliches Leben hältst, z. B. *How American are you?* Oder du sagst deine Meinung zu bestimmten grundsätzlichen Thesen wie z. B. *All men are equal* oder *Fast food makes you ill.*

Hier sind ein paar Tipps, wie du eine Meinungsäußerung schreibst. Du folgst wieder dem Konzept: Planen, Gestalten, Überarbeiten.

Planen und Gestalten

Inhaltliche Aspekte:
Schreibe dir die Ideen, die dir zum Thema einfallen, in Notizen auf. Und zwar so, wie sie dir in den Sinn kommen. Eine Tabelle mit *pros and cons (for and against)* oder *examples and reasons* hilft, deine Ideen zu ordnen.
Ehe du schreibst, mache dir klar, welche Position / Meinung du vertrittst. Entscheide dich: Bist du dafür? Bist du dagegen? Wenn du dir nicht sicher bist, zähle Beispiele dafür und dagegen auf und wäge sie mit Begründungen gegeneinander ab.

Sprachliche Aspekte:
Bestimmte Redewendungen leiten deine Meinungsäußerung / deinen Kommentar ein, z. B.:

- *In the text about … I have read that …*
- *The text … says that …*
- *I want to say something about …*

Folgende Redewendungen drücken deine Meinung grundsätzlich aus:

- *I think …*
- *I believe …*
- *In my opinion …*
- *I'm sure that …*
- *From my point of view I'd say …*

Die folgenden Redewendungen drücken deine Zustimmung bzw. Ablehnung aus:

- *It's (not) true that …*
- *I (don't) like the idea that …*
- *I think so too. / I don't think so.*
- *I (don't) agree with …*

Abwägende Redewendungen sind z. B.:

- *On the one hand … but on the other hand …*
- *Although I can understand …, I believe …*

Zum Abschluss kannst du diese Redewendungen benutzen:

- *To sum up, …*
- *I hope I've been able to make clear that …*

Formuliere jetzt deine Meinung mithilfe deiner Notizen und der Redewendungen. Folgende Ausdrücke sind hilfreich, um deine Ideen in eine gute Reihenfolge zu bringen:

- *Firstly, I …*
- *Secondly, …*
- *Finally, …*

Überarbeiten
Stelle dir die folgenden Fragen:

- ☐ Habe ich in der Einleitung verständlich ausgedrückt, worum es geht?
- ☐ Zeigt mein Text klar meine Entscheidung pro oder kontra bzw. mein Bemühen, Argumente gegeneinander abzuwägen?
- ☐ Habe ich Beispiele mit Begründungen genannt?
- ☐ Habe ich einen Schluss formuliert, der zeigt, dass ich offen bin für andere Argumente?
- ☐ Stimmen Satzbau, Grammatik und Rechtschreibung?

How to speak

1 Ein Interview vorbereiten und durchführen

Du hast schon häufig Interviews gehört und weißt, dass sie dem Zweck dienen, etwas vom Interviewpartner zu erfahren, das man selbst noch nicht weiß.

- Zuerst solltest du überlegen, warum du das Interview führen möchtest, z. B. um etwas über die Person zu erfahren, über einen bestimmten Anlass zu sprechen oder zu einem bestimmten Thema Informationen zu erhalten.
- Du solltest dich auf die Person, die du befragen möchtest, vorbereiten (Alter, Familienstand, Beruf etc.), damit du gute Fragen stellen kannst.
- Stelle dich immer höflich vor und sage, warum du das Interview durchführen möchtest.
- Gute und sinnvolle Fragen zu stellen ist wesentlich für das Gelingen eines Interviews. Du möchtest ja, dass dein Interviewpartner dir etwas erzählt und nicht nur „Ja" oder „Nein" sagt. Wenn du z. B. fragst *Do you like this town?*, musst du auch mit *yes* oder *no* zufrieden sein. Wenn du aber fragst *What would you like to tell me about your visit in our town?*, wird der Interviewpartner dir etwas erzählen.
- Versuche, deine Fragen so aufzubauen, dass du sie in einer sinnvollen Reihenfolge stellen kannst. Aber reagiere auch auf die Antworten, z. B. *Well, does that mean that you …?* oder *That sounds interesting. Could you tell me more about that, please?*
- Vermeide zu persönliche Fragen. Du wirst keine oder nur eine abwehrende Antwort erhalten.

In dem Kasten findest du Redewendungen, die dir helfen, dich freundlich, höflich und interessiert auszudrücken:

- *Thank you for coming here / being my guest today.*
- *May I ask you a few questions?*
- *Could you please tell me …?*
- *I'm sorry, I didn't quite understand. Could you say / explain that again, please?*
- *That sounds interesting. Could you tell me a bit more about …?*
- *Thank you very much for talking to me. / Thank you for your time.*
- *I enjoyed the interview. I hope to see you again sometime.*

2 Über ein Thema diskutieren

Diskussionen finden täglich über alle möglichen Themen statt. Oft sind solche Diskussionen spontan und ungeplant. Wenn es um ernsthaftere Themen geht, ist es jedoch sinnvoll, sich zunächst Gedanken über mögliche Argumente zu machen.

- Stichpunkte und *word webs* sind eine gute Hilfe, um nichts Wichtiges zu vergessen.
- Ein Diskussionsleiter ist wichtig, damit alle zu Wort kommen können. Er / Sie sollte auch darauf achten, dass alle beim Thema bleiben.
- Zuhören ist genauso wichtig wie selbst reden. Jeder hat das Recht, etwas zu sagen.

Wie du mündlich deine Meinung äußern, jemandem zustimmen und widersprechen kannst, kannst du unter *How to write* (Eine kurze Meinungsäußerung / Einen Kurzkommentar schreiben) auf Seite 128–129 nachlesen. Wichtig für eine mündliche Diskussion ist aber auch das gezielte Nachfragen: *Pardon? Could you say that again, please? What do you mean by that? Could you explain that, please? Is it true that …?*

3 Etwas vortragen oder erzählen

Du wirst häufiger (nicht nur in der Schule) aufgefordert, von einem Erlebnis, einem Ereignis, einer Fernsehsendung oder von etwas, das du gelesen oder gehört hast, zu erzählen.
Du hast schon ein wenig Erfahrung darin gesammelt, wenn du mit deiner Nachbarin / deinem Nachbarn Ergebnisse eurer Arbeit ausgetauscht oder der Klasse von etwas berichtet hast.
Hier sind noch ein paar Tipps, die dir bei deinem Vortrag helfen können:

- Sammle die Ideen, Gedanken und Informationen, die in deinem Vortrag vorkommen sollen, auf Englisch. Was du nicht ausdrücken kannst, schaust du im Wörterbuch nach. (Beachte dabei die unterschiedlichen Bedeutungen eines Wortes.)
- Plane jetzt, in welcher Reihenfolge du die Ideen, Gedanken oder Informationen vortragen möchtest. Was ist wichtig, was ist nicht so wichtig?
- Ordne die Notizen in dieser Reihenfolge:

Thema *(topic)*
Einleitung *(introduction)*
Ort *(place)*
Zeit *(time)*
Personen *(people)*
Handlung / Aktionen *(action)*
Schluss *(ending)*

- Mache dir eine Liste von den Satzanfängen (Redewendungen), die deutlich machen, wie dein Vortrag aufgebaut ist, z. B.:

- *Today I'd like to give you a report on … / … to tell you about …*
- *I have chosen the topic … (because) / I'd like to talk about … / My report / story is about …*
- *It happened in / at … / That was in / at …*
- *That was … (yesterday / last year / week / …)*
- *There was … / There were …*
- *He / She / They …*
- *When …*
- *After that …*
- *Later …*
- *At last / In the end …*
- *I hope you have enjoyed my report / story …*

- Formuliere jetzt mündlich, d. h. verbinde die Satzanfänge mit den Notizen, die du vorher gemacht hast. Sprich laut vor dich hin, z. B. vor dem Spiegel, oder suche dir jemanden zum Zuhören.
- Übe deinen Vortrag mehrmals. Es macht nichts, wenn du bestimmte Dinge jedes Mal anders sagst. (Du sollst ja nichts auswendig lernen.) Es ist auch kein Problem, wenn du Fehler machst oder etwas wiederholst. Sprechen ist auch mit Vorbereitung immer etwas Spontanes. Aber Üben macht dich sicherer.

How to present something in class

1 Eine Präsentation gestalten

Du hast schon so manches Arbeitsergebnis, ob in Partner- oder Gruppenarbeit gestaltet, der Klasse vorgestellt. Zu zweit, zu dritt oder zu viert habt ihr kleine Texte vorgetragen und Bilder oder Poster dazu gezeigt.

Du weißt, dass es wichtig ist,
- eure Präsentation so zu organisieren und zu gestalten, dass die Zuhörer euch folgen und das präsentierte Thema verstehen können,
- eure Präsentation einzuüben (Reihenfolge – wer präsentiert welchen Teil? –, welche Bilder, Karten, Poster werden während des Vortrags gezeigt?),
- nicht zu schnell, sondern langsam und deutlich zu sprechen,
- immer der Klasse zugewandt zu stehen, aufrecht und selbstbewusst, sie beim Sprechen anzuschauen, damit ihr merkt, ob die Mitschüler alles verstehen.

Grundsätzlich gilt bei jeder Präsentation folgender Ablauf:

- Sage, worüber du sprechen willst *(introduction)*.
- Sprich über dein Thema *(main part)*.
- Fasse zusammen, was du gesagt hast *(summary)*.

So gelingt dir mit deiner Gruppe eine Präsentation:

Das Material:

- Die Bilder und die Schrift auf dem Poster oder auf der Folie sind so groß, dass jeder im Raum sie sehen und lesen kann. Es ist besser, mehrere Poster und Bilder in größerem Format zu zeigen als alles auf ein Poster zu „quetschen".
- Zum Zeigen bestimmter Einzelheiten auf Postern oder einer Folie nimm einen Stift, nicht deine Hand. So kannst du Abstand halten und den Blick auf Poster oder Folie für alle frei halten.
- Wenn du Einzelheiten nacheinander zeigen möchtest, kannst du die übrigen Dinge mit einem Stück Papier zudecken (Papier und Klebematerial bereit halten).
- Überprüfe vor der Präsentation deine Materialien und lege sie dir in der benötigten Reihenfolge bereit. Überprüfe auch die Technik.

Redewendungen, die dir beim Präsentieren helfen:

- *Good morning. I'd / We'd like to talk about …*
- *We are going to talk about …*
- *First we want to tell you about …*
- *As you can see …*
- *The picture shows …*
- *Let me show you on the poster / in the picture how …*
- *Look at that detail at the top / in the top left-hand corner / right-hand corner / at the front / at the back / on the left / on the right / in the middle …*
- *Thank you for listening.*
- *Are there any questions? / Do you have any questions?*
- *It has been a pleasure to tell and show you something about …*

1 Im Internet nach Informationen suchen / recherchieren

Du weißt, dass das Internet nahezu alles anbietet. Aber wie findest du das, was du für dein Vorhaben brauchst?
Wenn du also das Internet sinnvoll und effektiv nutzen willst,

- solltest du in der Lage sein, für deine Zwecke brauchbare Informationen zu finden.
- müsstest du dich in einem gefundenen Text möglichst schnell orientieren können: Welches ist das Thema? Oder du müsstest den gefundenen Text sorgfältig auf bestimmte Informationen „durchforsten" können.

Use English pages. They may be more difficult to read but it is easier to use them for your English text.

Suchmaschinen nutzen

Wenn du nach etwas im Internet suchst, kannst du Suchmaschinen nutzen, wie z. B.:

www.google.com

www.yahooligans.yahoo.com

www.kidsclick.org

www.askforkids.com

Da du meistens sehr viel Text angeboten bekommst, ist es wichtig, dass du weißt, wie du die Textfülle begrenzen kannst. Dafür musst du die von dir gewählte Suchmaschine und ihre Funktionen kennen und deine Suchergebnisse eingrenzen.

Tipps:
Wähle sehr sorgfältig dein sogenanntes Suchwort aus. Wähle inhaltlich spezielle Ausdrücke, nicht nur allgemeine Einzelwörter, um die Anzahl der Beiträge zu verringern: z. B. *The Mohawk Trail today* statt *Native Americans*. Probiere andere Suchausdrücke, wenn dir das Ergebnis nicht zusagt oder dich vom Thema wegführt.

Klicke auf:

- **Help**, um zu sehen, wie die von dir gewählte Suchmaschine arbeitet.
- **Englisch**, um nicht andere fremdsprachliche Ergebnisse präsentiert zu bekommen.
- **News**, um Zeitungsartikel zu deinem gewünschten Thema zu finden.
- **Images**, wenn du z. B. Bilder für eine Präsentation brauchst.
- **Advanced Search**, wenn du mehr Informationen finden möchtest.

Das Auswerten der Suchergebnisse ist schwierig, aber Üben macht fit!

Tipps:

- Du verfährst grundsätzlich wie auf den **How to read**-Seiten in deinem Buch.
- Gehe den Text durch mit dem Leseziel, die Informationen, die du für dein bestimmtes Thema brauchst, herauszufiltern. Markiere die Stellen.
- Mache dir Notizen und sortiere sie (siehe dazu ‚**Nach dem Lesen**' auf den **How to read**-Seiten).
- Schlage nur wirklich für das Detailverstehen notwendige Wörter nach.
- Notiere dir die Internet-Adresse, unter der du die Informationen gefunden hast, damit du die Quelle nennen kannst.

C Classroom phrases

Wenn man mit dem Computer arbeitet

What's your e-mail address?	Wie ist deine E-Mail-Adresse?
You can click on this link.	Du kannst auf diesen Link klicken.
Can I print it out / download it?	Kann ich das ausdrucken / herunterladen?
I saved it.	Ich habe es gespeichert.
My computer has crashed.	Mein Computer ist abgestürzt.

Wenn es ein Problem gibt

What's the matter?	Was ist mit dir los?
I'm fine.	Mir geht's gut.
I feel sick.	Mir ist schlecht.
I've got a headache.	Ich habe Kopfschmerzen.
Can I open the window, please?	Kann ich bitte das Fenster öffnen?
Can I go to the toilet, please?	Kann ich bitte zur Toilette gehen?
I'm sorry, I haven't done my homework.	Ich habe meine Hausaufgaben nicht gemacht.

Wenn man Hilfe braucht

Can you help me, please?	Können Sie / Kannst du mir bitte helfen?
I've got a question.	Ich habe eine Frage.
I don't understand this.	Ich verstehe das hier nicht.
How can I do this exercise?	Wie mache ich diese Aufgabe?
What's … in English / German?	Was heißt … auf Englisch / Deutsch?
What does … mean?	Was bedeutet …?
Can you write it on the blackboard, please?	Können Sie / Kannst du das bitte an die Tafel schreiben?
Can you say that again, please?	Können Sie / Kannst du das bitte noch einmal sagen?
Can you spell "…", please?	Können Sie bitte „…" buchstabieren?
Sorry, I don't know.	Tut mir leid, das weiß ich nicht.
What page is it on, please?	Auf welcher Seite ist es bitte?

Wenn man zusammen arbeitet oder spielt

Whose turn is it?	Wer ist dran?
I (don't) like this story.	Diese Geschichte gefällt mir (nicht).
I think it's good / interesting / funny.	Ich finde sie gut / interessant / komisch.
I think it's terrible / boring / sad.	Ich finde sie schrecklich / langweilig / traurig.
What do you think?	Was meinst du?
Can I be …?	Kann ich … sein / spielen?
Do you want to work with me?	Möchtest du mit mir arbeiten?
Can I borrow your pencil / dictionary / …, please?	Kann ich mir bitte deinen Bleistift / dein Wörterbuch / … ausleihen?
Can … and I work together?	Können … und ich bitte zusammenarbeiten?
I think we should / could …	Ich finde, wir sollten / könnten …
In my opinion …	Meiner Meinung nach …
What about …?	Wie wär's mit …?

Was die Lehrerin oder der Lehrer sagt

Open your books at page …	Öffnet eure Bücher auf Seite …
Turn to page …	Blättert zu Seite …
Look at line …	Seht euch Zeile … an.
Read the text on page …	Lies / Lest den Text auf Seite …
Work in pairs.	Arbeitet zu zweit.
Work in groups of four.	Arbeitet zu viert.
Sit in a circle.	Bildet einen Sitzkreis.
Listen to the CD.	Hör / Hört die CD an.
Write about …	Schreibe / Schreibt über …
Talk about …	Sprich / Sprecht über …
Ask questions about …	Stelle / Stellt Fragen zu …
Answer the question, please.	Beantworte / Beantwortet bitte die Frage.
Match the sentences.	Ordne / Ordnet die Sätze zu.
Who wants to read the text?	Wer möchte den Text vorlesen?
Write down the answers.	Schreibe / Schreibt die Antworten auf.
You don't have to understand everything.	Du brauchst / Ihr braucht nicht alles zu verstehen.
Act it out.	Spiel / Spielt es vor.
Change roles.	Tauscht die Rollen.
Make your own dialogue.	Entwirf / Entwerft selbst ein Gespräch.
Take a card.	Nimm / Nehmt eine Karte.
Come to the blackboard, please.	Komm / Kommt bitte zur Tafel.
Collect the exercise books, please.	Sammelt bitte die Hefte ein.
Do this exercise at home, please.	Mache / Macht diese Aufgabe bitte zu Hause.
Please be quiet.	Sei bitte ruhig. / Seid bitte ruhig.
Please sit down.	Bitte setz dich. / Bitte setzt euch.
Please speak up.	Sprich bitte lauter.
You can do better.	Das kannst du besser.
Try again.	Versuch es noch einmal.
That's it.	Das ist alles.
Well done.	Gut gemacht.

Language in focus

Im Lif-Anhang wird die englische Sprache ganz genau unter die Lupe genommen.

Say it in English

Hier findest du zu jedem Kapitel Sätze und Ausdrücke, die du benutzen kannst, um dich mit jemandem auf Englisch zu unterhalten.

Word fields

Die neuen Wörter, die du in einem Kapitel gelernt hast, lassen sich nach Themen ordnen und so zu Wortfeldern zusammenstellen. Wenn du Wörter, die zusammengehören, auch zusammen lernst, kannst du sie dir ganz leicht einprägen.

Grammar

Immer, wenn du dieses Symbol lif vorne in deinem Buch siehst, kannst du im Anhang nachsehen, welche Regeln es in der englischen Sprache gibt.
Um dir die Regeln besser einzuprägen, kannst du sie noch einmal in dein eigenes Grammatikheft schreiben. Dort kannst du sie in deinen eigenen Worten notieren und weitere Beispielsätze finden.

1R

Wenn ein R hinter der Zahl steht, kennst du die Regel schon aus Band 3. R steht für das englische Wort *revision* und bedeutet „Wiederholung". Das heißt, wenn du dir nicht mehr ganz sicher bist, kannst du hier noch einmal nachlesen.

Theme 1 • Made in the USA

Say it in English

So kann man …

sagen, was man lieber mag	I prefer salad or pizza.
sagen, was man gerne macht	I enjoy meeting friends. I like buying new clothes. I love playing baseball.
sagen, was man nicht gerne macht	I can't stand cleaning my room. I hate queuing.
sagen, dass einen etwas nicht stört	I don't mind getting up early.
sagen, dass etwas typisch für ein Land ist	Eating fish and chips is typically British.

Word fields

American …

sports	fashion	food and drink	words in our language	free time
basketball	T-shirts	hamburgers	cool	skateboard
baseball	sneakers	coke	easy	in-line skate
American football	baseball caps	fries	cheerleader	…
…	…	chewing gum	shopping	
		candy	…	
		…		

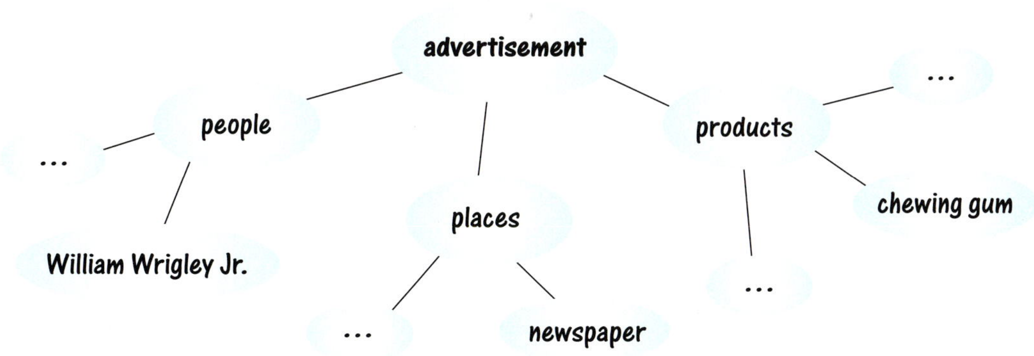

Grammar

1R Signalwörter (Signal words)

Es gibt ein paar Signalwörter für die Zeiten, die du kennst:

- **The future:** tomorrow, next week/month/year/time, in a minute/an hour, …
- **The present progressive:** now, at this moment, …
- **The present**: sometimes, often, normally, usually, …
- **The simple past:** yesterday, last week/month/year, …
- **The present perfect:** ever, never, yet, already, just, …
- **The past perfect:** after

2R Die Zeitformen des Verbs (Verb tenses)

future	Greg **will work** there the whole summer.
↓	
present progressive	Right now I'**m** certainly **not enjoying** it.
↓	
simple present	Mark **has** a part-time job as a burger-flipper.
↓	
simple past	Two weeks ago he **started** his new job.
↓	
present perfect	Greg **has** never **worked** as a burger-flipper.
↓	
past perfect	Greg **had sold** newspapers before he found a job in a department store.

- Das **will-future** benutzt man, wenn man darüber sprechen möchte, was in der Zukunft passieren wird. So kann man Vermutungen, Vorhersagen oder Versprechen ausdrücken. Es wird gebildet mit **will** und dem Infinitiv des Verbs.

- Das **present progressive** benutzt man, wenn man sagen möchte, was gerade passiert oder was man gerade tut. Es wird gebildet mit einer Form von **to be** (*am, are, is*) und der **-ing**-Form des Verbs.

- Das **simple present** benutzt man, wenn man über Gewohnheiten oder über regelmäßige Ereignisse spricht. Man benutzt es auch, wenn man beschreibt, dass jemand mehrere Dinge nacheinander tut (z.B. in einer Geschichte). Bei *I, you, we, they* hat das **simple present** dieselbe Form wie der Infinitiv. Wenn man im **simple present** von einer dritten Person (*he, she, it*) sprechen möchte, hängt man ein **-s** an das Verb. Endet das Verb mit einem Zischlaut /-s/, /-z/, /-ʃ/, /-tʃ/, /-dʒ/, muss bei *he, she, it* ein **-es** angehängt werden.

- Das **simple past** braucht man, wenn man sagen will, *wann* etwas passiert ist. Es drückt Ereignisse und Handlungen aus, die vergangen und abgeschlossen sind. Bei regelmäßigen Verben bildet man es, indem man **-ed** an den Infinitiv anhängt. Bei den unregelmäßigen Verben ist das **simple past** die zweite Form in der Tabelle auf Seite 238/239.

- Das **present perfect** drückt aus, *dass* etwas passiert bzw. nicht passiert ist. Es drückt aus, dass eine Handlung, die in der Vergangenheit begann, noch andauert oder nachwirkt. Es wird gebildet mit **have / has** und dem **past participle** des Verbs.

- Man verwendet das **past perfect**, wenn eine Handlung vor einer anderen in der Vergangenheit stattgefunden hat. Die zweite Handlung steht dann im **simple past**. Man bildet es mit **had** und dem **past participle** des Verbs.

Tipp
Die drei Formen (infinitive, simple past, past participle) der unregelmäßigen Verben kannst du dir besser merken, wenn du ähnliche Formen zusammen lernst, z. B. in Reimform: *bring, brought, brought* goes with *buy, bought, bought*.

3 Das Gerundium als Subjekt des Satzes (The gerund as subject of the sentence)

Man verwendet das Gerundium (auch **-ing**-Form genannt), wenn man über Tätigkeiten, Gewohnheiten und Hobbys spricht. Man macht dazu aus dem Verb ein Nomen (Substantiv), indem man **-ing** an das Verb hängt.

- **Queuing** is a typically British activity.
  Schlangestehen ist eine typisch britische Beschäftigung.

- **Eating burgers and drinking coke** is typically American.
  Hamburger Essen und Cola Trinken ist typisch amerikanisch.

4 Das Gerundium als Objekt des Satzes (The gerund as object of the sentence)

Oft folgt die **-ing**-Form nach bestimmten Verben. Dazu gehören **like**, **love**, **enjoy**, **hate** und **start**.

Lucy likes **eating** Italian food.
Lucy isst gerne italienisches Essen.

Rachel hates **drinking** tea.
Rachel hasst es, Tee zu trinken.

I love I like I enjoy	I don't mind	I can't stand I hate

5R Häufigkeitsadverbien (Adverbs of frequency)

Wenn man sagen will, wie *oft* man etwas macht, benutzt man Häufigkeitsadverbien. Diese Wörter stehen meistens zwischen Subjekt und Objekt.

Subjekt	Adverb	Verb	Objekt	
wer	*wie oft*	*tut*	*was*	*wo, wann usw.*
I	always	meet	my friends	at school.
We	sometimes	play	football	on Saturdays.

6 Britisches und Amerikanisches Englisch (British and American English)

Unterschiede zwischen Britischem (BE) und Amerikanischem Englisch (AE) findet man vor allem in drei Bereichen.

- **Aussprache**
  Deutlich zu hören ist das **r**, das im AE auch am Wortende und vor Konsonanten ausgesprochen wird. In der amerikanischen Popmusik hört man oft den [æ]-Laut, wo im BE normalerweise [ɑː] gesprochen wird. Weitere Unterschiede in der Aussprache gibt es bei diesen Wörtern:

Aussprache Britisches Englisch		Aussprache Amerikanisches Englisch
[hɑːt]	**heart**	[hɑːrt]
[hɪə]	**here**	[hɪr]
['betə]	**better**	['betər]
[dɑːns]	**dance**	[dæns]
[lɑːf]	**laugh**	[læf]
[hɒt]	**hot**	[hɑːt]

- **Schreibung**
  Im Amerikanischen Englisch haben sich für viele Wörter vereinfachte Schreibweisen entwickelt.

Britisches Englisch	Amerikanisches Englisch
favour, colour	favor, color
centre, theatre	center, theater
travelling	traveling

- **Wortschatz**
  Nur wenige Wörter kommen *ausschließlich* im BE oder AE vor. Teilweise werden Wörter in beiden "Englishes" unterschiedlich gebraucht, was manchmal zu Missverständnissen führen kann.

Britisches Englisch	Amerikanisches Englisch
film	movie
sweets	candy
chips	(French) fries
crisps	chips
pupil	student

BE: chips

AE: fries

BE: fall

AE: autumn

Theme 2 • New places, new faces

Say it in English

So kann man …

über eine Reise sprechen	It took him five days to get there. He / She traveled … miles a day. When I arrived in …
ausdrücken, dass etwas besonders schön war	This day was one of the most exciting in my life. What a lovely sight!
jemanden um Rat fragen	What would you do if you were me?
über Pläne und Wünsche sprechen	I would go to / visit …
eine imaginäre Reise beschreiben	If you traveled down the river, …
sagen, wie lange jemand etwas schon tut	He / She has eaten packed food for months.
sagen, seit wann jemand etwas schon tut	He / She has been alone since 1999.
sagen, dass einen etwas interessiert	I'm interested in visiting old buildings.
über Hoffnungen sprechen	He / She hoped to find … He / She dreams of having … He / She has great plans to …
erklären, warum jemand etwas tut	He / She went to the museum to find out about … They had come to start a better life.

Word fields

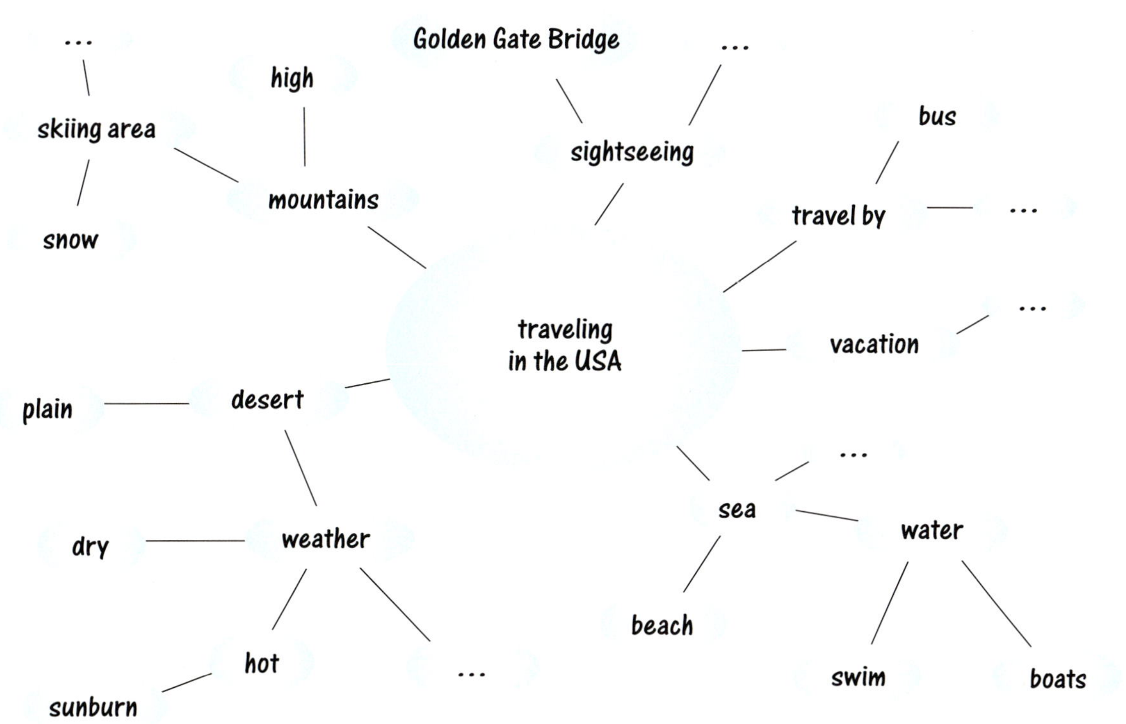

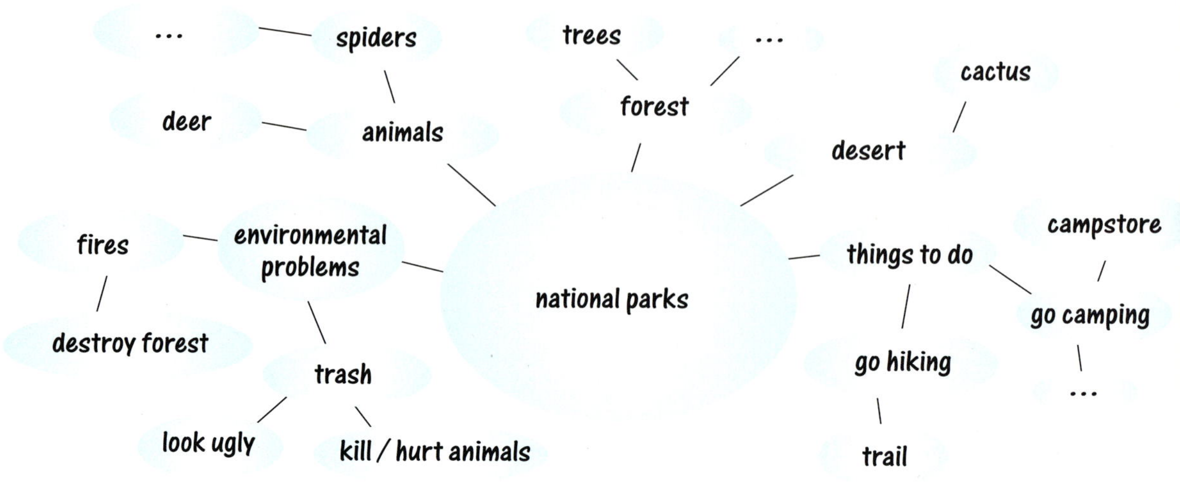
national parks
animals
spiders
...
deer
forest
trees
...
desert
cactus
environmental problems
fires
destroy forest
trash
look ugly
kill / hurt animals
things to do
campstore
go camping
...
go hiking
trail

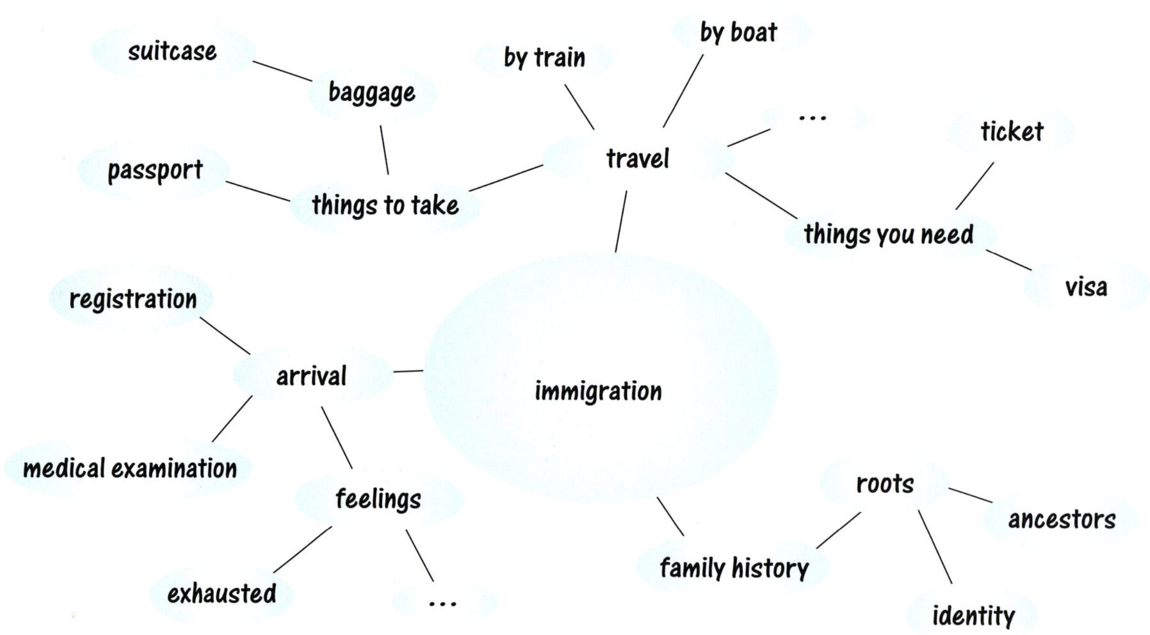
immigration
travel
by train
by boat
...
things to take
baggage
suitcase
passport
things you need
ticket
visa
arrival
registration
medical examination
feelings
exhausted
...
family history
roots
ancestors
identity

Grammar

7 If-Satz Typ 2 (Conditional clause type 2)

- Bedingungssätze können realistische oder unrealistische Bedingungen nennen:

  You'll make Grandmom very happy **if you buy her that picture**.
  Du wirst Oma sehr glücklich machen, wenn du ihr das Bild kaufst.

  Hier ist die Bedingung erfüllbar, denn die angesprochene Person braucht das Bild nur für die Großmutter zu kaufen.

  If I had an aunt in California, I would visit her and go to Yosemite National Park.
  Wenn ich eine Tante in Kalifornien hätte, würde ich sie besuchen und in den Yosemite Nationalpark gehen.

  Wer das sagt, hat keine Tante in Kalifornien, sonst würde er oder sie anders sprechen. Die Bedingung für einen (kostengünstigen!) Besuch in Kalifornien ist also nicht erfüllbar. Die Idee bleibt also Wunschtraum.

- Wenn du ausdrücken willst, dass eine Bedingung unerfüllbar ist, benutzt du im **if**-Satz ein Verb im **simple past**. Im Hauptsatz muss dann entweder **would** (Kurzform **'d**) oder **could** oder **might** stehen – mit einem Hauptverb im Infinitiv:

  If I **lived** in Memphis, I **would** be in the state of Tennessee.
  Wenn ich in Memphis lebte, würde ich im Staat Tennessee sein.

IF-SATZ *if-clause*	HAUPTSATZ *main clause*		
If I **had** an e-mail friend in the USA,	I	**would** **could** **might**	**visit** her and **climb** El Capitan.

8 Das Perfekt mit "since" und "for" (The present perfect with "since" and "for")

- Wenn man über das Ereignis eines Vorgangs oder eines Zustands reden möchte, der in der Vergangenheit begonnen hat und immer noch andauert oder gerade erst beendet wurde, verwendet man das **present perfect**.
- Spricht man von einem genauen Zeitpunkt, an dem dieser Vorgang oder Zustand begonnen hat, so verwendet man **since**.

  Death Valley has been a national park **since** 1994.
  Death Valley ist seit 1994 ein Nationalpark.
- Gibt man hingegen einen Zeitraum an (Tage, Wochen, Monate usw.), so benutzt man **for**:

  Yosemite has been a national park **for** more than 100 years.
  Yosemite ist seit mehr als 100 Jahren ein Nationalpark.

9 Das Gerundium nach präpositionalen Ausdrücken (The gerund after prepositions and phrasal verbs)

- Das Gerundium wird auch nach bestimmten Ausdrücken mit Präpositionen wie **keen on**, **afraid of**, **good at**, **bad at**, **interested in**, **look forward to** und **hopeless at** gebraucht.

  They are **interested in** watch**ing** wild animals. *Sie haben Interesse am Beobachten von wilden Tieren.*

  Emily is not **keen on** see**ing** a bear.
  Emily hat wenig Lust darauf, einen Bären zu sehen.

Theme 3 • The world in a city

Say it in English

So kann man …

sagen, was man fühlt	I get … feelings / It makes me feel …
wiedergeben, welche Wünsche eine Person äußert	… says that he/she would like to / wants to …
sagen, was man gerne tun würde	… would like to do / want to do …
seine Meinung ausdrücken	In my opinion… / I think … / To my mind … / The way I see it … / I believe that …
sagen, was mit einer Person / einer Sache / einem Tier passiert / passierte	Gaelic is spoken in Ireland. / Grandma was brought to America.

Word fields

Feelings

positive
happy
excited
adventurous
curious
relaxed

negative
sad
depressed
desperate
frightened
worried

New York

Where to go	**What to see**	**What to do**
Statue of Liberty	a monument	take photos
Ellis Island	a museum	look at the database
The Empire State Building	a skyscraper	climb up the steps
Central Park	trees and paths	have a picnic, sunbathe, go for a walk
Macy's Department Store	lots of different products	buy something, look for souvenirs
…	…	…

Grammar

10R Die einfache Gegenwart / Die Verlaufsform der Gegenwart (Simple present / Present progressive)

- Wenn man über Gewohnheiten oder regelmäßige Ereignisse spricht, verwendet man das **simple present**. Oft benutzt man dabei Häufigkeitsadverbien wie *always, usually, often, sometimes, never, every morning / day / month / year.*

  Tourists **usually take** photos of the Statue of Liberty.
  Touristen fotografieren gewöhnlich die Freiheitsstatue.

- Im Gegensatz dazu benutzt man das **present progressive**, wenn man sagen möchte, was in diesem Moment passiert oder was man gerade macht. Wenn man Fotos oder Bilder beschreibt, benutzt man das **present progressive**, da ein Bild eine Momentaufnahme ist. Signalwörter sind z. B. *at the moment* oder *now.*

  Tourists **are taking** photos of the Statue of Liberty in that picture / now.
  Touristen fotografieren auf diesem Bild / gerade die Freiheitsstatue.

11R Die einfache Vergangenheit / Das Perfekt (Simple past / Present perfect)

- Das **simple past** braucht man, wenn man sagen will, *wann* etwas passiert ist.

  New York **remained** the capital of the USA until 1790.

- Beim **present perfect** ist es dagegen wichtig, *dass* etwas ohne genaue Zeitangabe passiert ist.

  Washington DC **has been** the capital of the USA since then.

12 Das Passiv in der einfachen Gegenwart (The passive voice in the simple present)

- Wenn mit einer Person oder einer Sache etwas geschieht, kann man das durch das Passiv ausdrücken.

  Ellis Island **is** still **visited** today.
  Ellis Island wird heute immer noch besichtigt.

- Im Deutschen übersetzt man das englische Passiv oft mit „man" + Verb.

  The names of the people **are kept** in computer databases.
  Die Namen der Menschen bewahrt man in Computerdatenbanken.

- Man bildet das Passiv in der Gegenwart mit **am / is / are** und dem Partizip des Verbs.

- Im Passiv kann man auch den Urheber der Handlung angeben. Man benutzt dazu eine Angabe mit **by**:

  Ellis Island is still visited **by** millions of people today.
  Ellis Island wird heute immer noch von Millionen Menschen besichtigt.

am / is / are	taken called visited kept told

13 Das Passiv in der einfachen Vergangenheit (The passive voice in the simple past)

- Möchte man darüber sprechen, was mit einer Person oder einer Sache in der Vergangenheit passiert ist, dann verwendet man das Passiv im **simple past**.

  The new immigrants **were checked**.
  Die neuen Immigranten wurden untersucht.

- In der Vergangenheit bildet man das Passiv mit **was / were** und dem **past participle** des Verbs.

was / were	checked closed put refused tested

14 Relativsätze ohne Pronomen (Relative clauses without pronouns)

- Das Relativpronomen (*who, which, that*) kann im Englischen weggelassen werden, wenn es das Objekt des Relativsatzes ist. Im Deutschen ist dies nicht möglich.

  He was getting into a **car (that) I had seen the day before**.
  Er stieg gerade in ein Auto ein, das ich am Tag davor gesehen hatte.

  "That's OK, kid," said a man **(who) I had not noticed**.
  „Das ist OK, Junge", sagte ein Mann, den ich nicht bemerkt hatte.

Relativsätze mit Pronomen

- Wenn man Personen beschreiben möchte, kann man dies in einem Nebensatz ausdrücken. Ein solcher Nebensatz heißt Relativsatz und beginnt mit dem Pronomen **who**.

  A pedestrian is a person **who** goes on foot.
  Ein Fußgänger ist eine Person, die zu Fuß geht.

- Wenn man Sachen oder Tiere näher beschreiben möchte, kann man dies in einem Relativsatz mit dem Pronomen **which** oder **that** ausdrücken.

  The Statue of Liberty, **which** was a present from the Franco-American Union to the USA, is in New York.
  Die Freiheitsstatue, die ein Geschenk der Franco-Amerikanischen Union an die USA war, ist in New York.

  That shirt, **which** I saw you in yesterday, must have cost $300.
  Das Shirt, in dem ich dich gestern gesehen habe, muss $300 gekostet haben.

  The first sight of America **that** the immigrants had was often the Statue of Liberty.
  Der erste Anblick von Amerika, den die Immigranten hatten, war oft die Freiheitsstatue.

Theme 4 • On the move

Say it in English

So kann man …

Wege und Routen beschreiben	The original Mohawk Trail was only 18 inches wide. The Pony Express riders needed about ten days from east to west.
Trauer oder Begeisterung über Ereignisse ausdrücken	I've seen so many sad things. We would love to have you as our guests!
erzählen, seit wann jemand etwas tut	They've been living on that reservation for many years. Since Johnny moved to New York, he has been studying to become a lawyer.
Aussagen anderer indirekt wiedergeben	Jack said that they had been there for about a year. We heard that a man called Marshall had discovered gold in this area.
über Verbote und Zwänge sprechen	My parents weren't allowed to go to school. Rosa Parks was asked to give up her bus seat to a white man. He told us to go to a theater for colored people.
über die Rechte von Menschen sprechen	They wanted to ensure the rights of minority groups and fight against racial discrimination. Today a lot of black Americans hold important positions in society and government.
über Vorurteile sprechen	He doesn't like my kind of skin. Her classmates don't like her because of her clothes.

Word fields

Movement

what	by	on the
travel	foot	(foot)path
move	wagon trains	Mohawk Trail
pass	horses	trail
march (up / to / ahead)	ship	way
escape	buses / public transportation	"Underground Railroad"
turn back	cabs	street
…	…	…

Grammar

15 Die Verlaufsform des Perfekts (Present perfect progressive)

- Wenn man ausdrücken möchte, dass ein (längerer) Vorgang oder Zustand in der Vergangenheit begonnen hat und in die Gegenwart hineinreicht oder gerade eben beendet ist, dann benutzt man das **present perfect progressive**.
- Das **present perfect progressive** wird mit **have / has been** und der **-ing**-Form des jeweiligen Verbs gebildet.

Johnny **has been living** in New York since last April.
Johnny wohnt seit letztem April in New York.

Lots of things **have been changing** since he started his studies.
Viele Dinge haben sich seit Beginn seines Studiums geändert.

Ich warte jetzt schon seit zwei Stunden hier. Vielleicht kommt sie doch nicht.

16 Die Zeitverschiebung in der indirekten Rede (Backshift of tenses in reported speech)

- Wenn du berichten willst, was jemand sagt, benutzt du die Form der indirekten Rede. Hier ändert sich die Zeitform nicht.

	BEGLEITSATZ	WIEDERGEGEBENE AUSSAGE
"It took me long enough to get here."	Henry says (that)	it took him long enough to get there.

- **Berichtete Rede** besteht aus einem Begleitsatz und der wiedergegebenen Aussage. Beide Satzteile können, müssen aber nicht durch *that* verbunden werden.

- Wenn die Originalaussage Wörter enthält, die nur aus dem Zusammenhang richtig zu verstehen sind, musst du sie bei der Wiedergabe anpassen:

"One guy **I knew** went crazy." *"Einer, den ich kannte, drehte durch."*	Liam says one guy **he knew** went crazy. *Liam sagt, einer, den er kannte, drehte durch.*

- Wenn man berichtet, was jemand gesagt hat, steht das Verb im Begleitsatz der indirekten Rede in der Vergangenheit (*said, told, asked*). Die Zeitform der indirekten Rede rückt dann sozusagen eine Stufe weiter zurück in die Vergangenheit. Diesen Vorgang nennt man Zeitverschiebung (**backshift of time**).

Liam: "The situation is really out of hand."
Liam said **the situation was** really out of hand.

Henry: "It took me long enough to get here."
Henry mentioned that it **had taken him** long enough to get **there**.

Patrick: "No one has found nuggets."
Patrick told him that no one **had found** nuggets.

- Wenn das einleitende Verb in einer Vergangenheitsform steht, müssen auch die Modalverben eine Stufe zurück in die Vergangenheit gesetzt werden:

  Liam: "They can't cope with it."
  Liam said that they **couldn't** cope with it.

  Patrick: "Gold diggers will try and win at the gambling table."
  Patrick explained that gold diggers **would** try and win at the gambling table.

- Hier eine Übersicht über **backshift of tenses**:

simple present	→	simple past
present progressive	→	past progressive
present perfect	→	past perfect
simple past	→	past perfect
going-to-future	→	was / were going to
will-future	→	would + Infinitiv
can	→	could + Infinitiv

- Zeitangaben wie **tomorrow**, **yesterday** … müssen in der indirekten Rede je nach Logik verändert werden.

tomorrow	→	today
yesterday	→	the day before

17 Aufforderungen und Verbote in der indirekten Rede (Commands and prohibitions in reported speech)

- Aufforderungen und Verbote in der indirekten Rede werden meist mit dem einleitenden Verb **tell** und einem **to**-Infinitiv wiedergegeben. Der oder die Angesprochene bildet das Objekt des einleitenden Verbs:
  The man: "Go!"
  The man **told us to go**.

- Wenn die Aufforderung oder das Verbot negativ ist, steht vor dem **to**-Infinitiv **not**:
  Mother: "Don't ride that old bike."

18 Der Infinitiv mit "to" (Infinitive with "to")

- Nach bestimmten Verben, die eine Erlaubnis, einen Ratschlag, eine Warnung oder ein Verbot ausdrücken (*ask, advise, allow, order, permit, tell, warn*), oder die einen Wunsch oder einen Willen ausdrücken (*force, want / would like*) wird der Infinitiv mit **to** verwendet. **To** steht in diesen Fällen nach dem Objekt.

  The man at the box office **told us to go**.
  Der Mann an der Theaterkasse befahl uns zu gehen.

  White people **forced them to work**.
  Weiße zwangen sie zu arbeiten.

Theme 5 • … and action!

Say it in English

So kann man …

über Lebensläufe sprechen	… was born in … As a boy / girl, he / she … First, he / she … and then he / she … In his / her early teens, he / she … … was a pioneer in … When … died in …, there was … At the age of …, he / she … As a very talented athlete, he / she has to …
eine Schule (oder eine Organisation) beschreiben	The school offers …
besondere Ereignisse beschreiben	When we have …, we usually …
über Filme sprechen	The ending was one of the worst I have seen in a long time. I wouldn't waste my money on it if I were you. It's a perfect flop. … really captured me with non-stop action. The stunts are really well done.
fragen, welche Aufgabe(n) jemand hat	Do you compose the music for a film? Do you have to carry the cables?
eine Vermutung äußern	You must be the sound recordist.
sagen, was passieren würde, wenn …	If I made a film, it would be about love. If I had enough money to make a film, I would shoot it in Miami.

Word fields

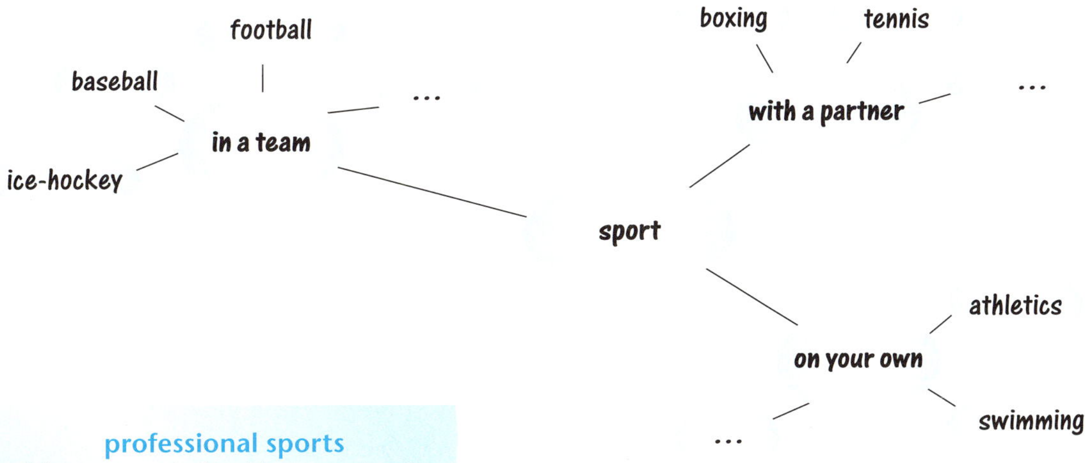

professional sports

athlete	scholarship	contract
career	pressure	scout
potential	stadium	teammate

What you do at school

attend classes
try to improve your marks
concentrate on an exercise
do sports
study for exams
talk to classmates
have lunch at the cafeteria
learn about history
read books in the library

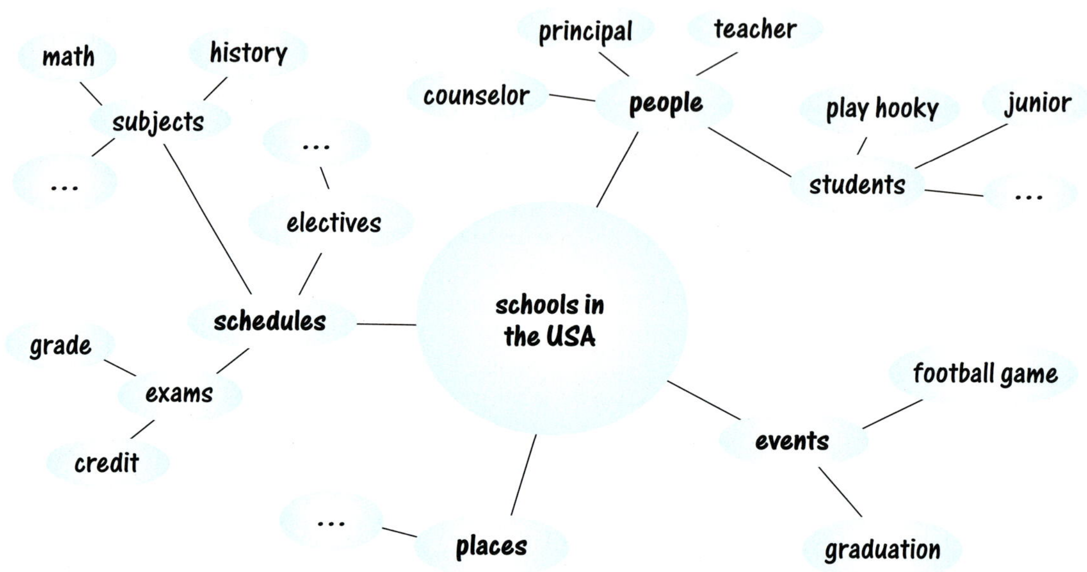

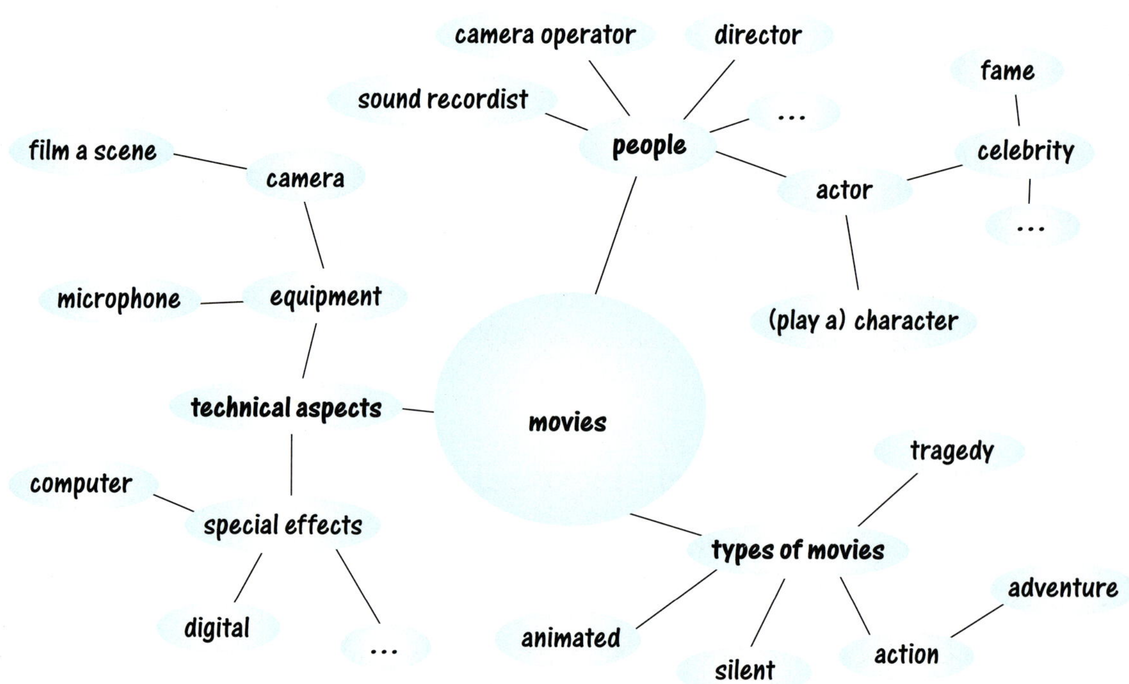

Grammar

19 Used to

Einen Zustand, der über längere Zeit in der Vergangenheit bestanden hat und abgeschlossen ist, kann man auch mit **used to** beschreiben.

Debi Thomas **used to be** a famous ice-skater.
Debi Thomas war früher mal eine berühmte Eiskunstläuferin.

I started playing hockey two years ago. I **used to play** in a volleyball team before that.
Ich habe vor zwei Jahren angefangen, Hockey zu spielen. Davor spielte ich in einer Volleyballmannschaft.

20 Verben mit zwei Objekten (Verbs with two objects)

- Wie im Deutschen, so gibt es auch im Englischen viele Verben, die zwei Objekte haben können:

  Whenever a teammate passes **the ball** to me, I panic.
  Jedesmal wenn ein Mitspieler mir ***den Ball*** *zuspielt, gerate ich in Panik.*

- Man unterscheidet dann **direkte** und indirekte Objekte. Das indirekte Objekt bezeichnet meistens eine Person, das **direkte** hingegen eine Sache.

	indirektes Objekt	**direktes Objekt**
Please get	Grandma	a cup of coffee.
Let me show	you	my new bike.

- Das indirekte Objekt steht entweder vor dem **direkten Objekt** oder es folgt ihm unmittelbar. Wenn das indirekte Objekt hinter dem **direkten** steht, muss es durch **to** oder **for** eingeleitet werden:

	direktes Objekt	indirektes Objekt
She left	a note	**for** me
Hand	your matches	**to** me.

- Man benutzt die Form mit **to** oder **for** vor allem, wenn das indirekte Objekt hervorgehoben werden soll oder es von einem Pronomen gebildet wird:

	indirektes Objekt	**direktes Objekt**	indirektes Objekt	
Whenever a teammate passes	him			he panics.
		the ball		
			to him,	

- Wenn beide Objekte von Pronomen gebildet werden, steht das indirekte Objekt fast immer hinter dem **direkten**:

  Whenever a teammate passes **it** to him, he panics.
  Jedesmal wenn ein Mitspieler ihm ihn zuspielt, gerät er in Panik.

Theme 6 • A bite to eat

Say it in English

So kann man …

sagen, was man gemacht hat, als etwas anderes passiert ist	I was concentrating on my X-Box when she came into my room.
über ein Gespräch mit jemandem berichten	I asked Cathy how long she had been a manager. I wanted to know which burger was most popular.
über ein neutrales Thema sprechen	CFCs can be found in sprays.
sagen, auf welche Art und Weise etwas passiert ist	Dad and I ate the pizza happily. I was sitting comfortably.

Word fields

Grammar

21 Indirekte Rede: indirekte Fragesätze mit Zeitverschiebung (Reported speech: reported questions with backshift of tenses)

- Wenn du eine Frage wiedergeben willst, die jemand anderes gestellt hat, benutzt du **if** oder **whether**:

  "Is Burgerland open 24 hours?"
  She asked **if** Burgerland was open 24 hours.

  "Are there many customers at night?"
  She wanted to know **whether** there were many customers at night.

- Wenn die Frage mit einem Fragewort eingeleitet wird, übernimmst du einfach das Fragewort:

  "**How long** have you been a manager?"
  She asked **how long** she had been a manager.

- Die Zeitform der indirekten Rede rückt eine Stufe weiter zurück in die Vergangenheit, wenn eine Frage indirekt wiedergegeben wird.

  "**Is Burgerland** open 24 hours?"
  She asked if **Burgerland was** open 24 hours.

  "**Are** there **many customers** at night?"
  She wanted to know whether there **were many customers** at night.

  "How long **have you been** a manager?"
  She wondered how long **she had been** a manager.

- Hier zur Erinnerung noch einmal die **backshift of tenses** (siehe lif 16):

simple present	→	simple past
present progressive	→	past progressive
present perfect	→	past perfect
simple past	→	past perfect
going-to-future	→	was / were going to
will-future	→	would + Infinitiv
can	→	could + Infinitiv

G Grammar glossary

			Lif
Adjektiv	adjective ['ædʒɪktɪv]	young, short, cheap …	
Adverbien der Art und Weise	adverbs of manner [ˌædvɜːbz‿əv 'mænə]	angrily, loudly, quickly …	
Adverbien der Häufigkeit	adverbs of frequency [ˌædvɜːbz‿əv 'friːkwənsi]	always, sometimes, never …	5R
Adverbien der Zeit	adverbs of time [ˌædvɜːbz‿əv 'taɪm]	this morning, on Saturday …	
Bedingungssatz	conditional clause [kən'dɪʃnəl ˌklɔːz]		
(Typ 1)	(type 1) [taɪp 'wʌn]	If it rains, I will stay at home.	
(Typ 2)	(type 2) [taɪp 'tuː]	If I had the money, I would buy a car.	7
Bestätigungsfragen	tag questions ['tæg ˌkwestʃ(ə)nz]	It's a good idea, isn't it?	
Indirekte Frage	indirect questions [ˌɪndərekt 'kwestʃ(ə)nz]	Can you tell me …?	
Ja-/Nein-Frage	yes/no-questions [jes'nəʊˌkwestʃ(ə)nz]	Did you like the film?	
Wh-Fragen	wh-questions [dʌbljuː'eɪtʃˌkwestʃ(ə)nz]	What is your favourite food?	
Futur	future ['fjuːtʃə]		
(mit *going to*)	(going to-future) ['gəʊɪŋ tʊˌfjuːtʃə]	He is going to buy a burger.	
(mit *will*)	(will-future) ['wɪlˌfjuːtʃə]	We will always be best friends.	2R
Gegenwart	present tense [ˌpreʒnt‿'tens]		2R
(einfache Form)	(simple present) [ˌsɪmpl 'preznt]	Tourists usually take photos.	10R
(Verlaufsform)	present progressive [ˌpreznt prəʊ'gresɪv]	Tourists are taking photos now.	10R
Gerundium	gerund ['dʒerənd]		
(als Subjekt des Satzes)	(as subject of the sentence) [æz 'sʌbdʒɪkt‿əv ðə ˌsentəns]	Eating burgers is typically American.	3
(als Objekt des Satzes)	(as object of the sentence) [æz 'ɒbdʒɪkt‿əv ðə ˌsentəns]	Rachel hates drinking tea.	4
(nach präpositionalen Ausdrücken)	(after prepositions and phrasal verbs) [ɑːftə prepə'zɪʃnz‿ən freɪzl ˌvɜːbz]	He is good at playing football.	9
Infinitiv	infinitive [ɪn'fɪnətɪv]	(to) be, (to) sit, (to) listen …	
Infinitiv mit *"to"*	infinitive with "to" [ɪn'fɪnətɪv wɪθ ˌtʊ]	White people forced them to work.	18
Indirekte Rede:	reported speech [rɪˌpɔːtɪd 'spiːtʃ]		
(Aufforderungen und Verbote)	(commands and prohibitions) [kə'mɑːndz‿ən prəʊɪˌbɪʃn]	I told you not to ride that old bike!	17
(Zeitverschiebung)	(backshift of tenses) ['bækʃɪft‿əv ˌtensɪz]	Liam said that they couldn't cope with it.	16
Indirekte Fragesätze mit Zeitverschiebung	reported questions with backshift of tenses [rɪˌpɔːtɪd 'kwestʃ(ə)nz wɪθ ˌbækʃɪft‿əv tensɪz]	He asked me if I would marry him.	21
Konjunktion	conjunction [kən'dʒʌŋkʃn]	and, because, where, if, although …	
Modalverb	modal verb ['məʊdl ˌvɜːb]	can, must, need, may, should …	
Nomen	noun [naʊn]	Rachel, table, movie, sister …	
Objekt	object ['ɒbdʒɪkt]	I miss my mother.	
Partizip	past participle [ˌpɑːst 'pɑːtɪsɪpl]	visited, brought, fallen …	
Passiv	passive voice ['pæsɪv ˌvɔɪs]		
(in der einfachen Gegenwart)	(in the simple present) [ɪn ðə ˌsɪmpl 'preznt]	Ellis Island is still visited today.	12
(in der einfachen Vergangenheit)	(in the simple past) [ɪn ðə ˌsɪmpl 'pɑːst]	New immigrants were checked.	13
Perfekt	present perfect [ˌpreznt 'pɜːfɪkt]		2R
(Verlausform)	(present perfect progressive) [preznt ˌpɜːfɪkt prəʊ'gresɪv]	Johnny has been living here since May.	15
(mit *"since"* und *"for"*)	(with "since" and "for") [wɪð 'sɪns‿ən ˌfɔː]	I've known him for 10 years.	8, 11R
Personalpronomen	personal pronoun [ˌpɜːsnəl 'prəʊnaʊn]	I, you, he, she …	

			Lif
Plural/Mehrzahl	plural ['pluərəl]	houses, brothers, children …	
Possessivbegleiter	possessive determiner [pəˌzesɪv dɪ'tɜːmɪnə]	my, your, his, her …	
Reflexivpronomen	reflexive pronoun [rɪˌfleksɪv 'prəʊnaʊn]	We bought ourselves some cokes.	
Relativpronomen	relative pronoun [ˌrelətɪv 'prəʊnaʊn]	who, that, which …	
Relativsatz	relative clause [ˌrelətɪv 'klɔːz]	It was a car which/that I had not seen before.	
Relativsatz ohne Pronomen	relative clause without pronoun [relətɪv 'klɔːz wɪðaʊt ˌprəʊnaʊn]	It was a car (which/that) I had not seen before.	14
s-Genitiv	s-genitive ['esˌdʒenətɪv]	Greg's idea, the Flynns' holiday …	
Singular/Einzahl	singular ['sɪŋgjʊlə]	house, brother, child …	
Signalwörter	signal words ['sɪgn(ə)l wɜːdz]	tomorrow, sometimes, after, yesterday, never, just …	1R
Steigerung/Vergleich	comparison [kəm'pærɪsn]	Logan is faster than Amy.	
Subjekt	subject ['sʌbdʒɪkt]	Susan is my sister. We've got a cat.	
Used to	"used to" ['juːst‿tuː]	She used to be a famous ice-skater.	19
Verb	verbs [vɜːbz]		
(regelmäßig)	(regular) ['regjʊlə]	(to) play, (to) clean, (to) like …	
(unregelmäßig)	(irregular) [ɪ'regjʊlə]	(to) come), (to) do, (to) eat …	
Verb-Adverb-Verbindung	phrasal verb [ˌfreɪzl 'vɜːb]	(to) look after, (to) work out	
Verben mit zwei Objekten	verbs with two objects ['vɜːbz wɪθ tuː‿ˌɒbdʒɪkts]	She left a note for me.	20
Vergangenheit	past tense [ˌpɑːst‿'tens]		
(einfache Form)	(simple past) [ˌsɪmpl 'pɑːst]	New York remained the capital of the USA until 1790.	2R, 11R
(Verlaufsform)	(past progressive) [ˌpɑːst prəʊ'gresɪv]	He was taking a photo.	11R
Verneinung	negation [nɪ'geɪʃn]	No, I don't like it.	
Vorvergangenheit	past perfect [ˌpɑːst 'pɜːfɪkt]	They had walked for hours.	2R
Wortbildung	word formation ['wɜːd fɔːˌmeɪʃn]	healthy – unhealthy	

Numbers

0	oh, zero, nil [əʊ, 'zɪərəʊ, nɪl]
1	one [wʌn]
2	two [tuː]
3	three [θriː]
4	four [fɔː]
5	five [faɪv]
6	six [sɪks]
7	seven ['sevn]
8	eight [eɪt]
9	nine [naɪn]
10	ten [ten]
11	eleven [ɪ'levn]
12	twelve [twelv]
13	thirteen [ˌθɜː'tiːn]
14	fourteen [ˌfɔː'tiːn]
15	fifteen [ˌfɪf'tiːn]
16	sixteen [ˌsɪks'tiːn]
17	seventeen [ˌsevn'tiːn]
18	eighteen [ˌeɪ'tiːn]
19	nineteen [ˌnaɪn'tiːn]
20	twenty ['twenti]
21	twenty-one [ˌtwenti'wʌn]
22	twenty-two [ˌtwenti'tuː]
⇓	⇓
30	thirty ['θɜːti]
40	forty ['fɔːti]
50	fifty ['fɪfti]

60	sixty ['sɪksti]
70	seventy ['sevnti]
80	eighty ['eɪti]
90	ninety ['naɪnti]
100	a/one hundred [ə/wʌn 'hʌndrəd]
101	one hundred and one [ˌwʌn hʌndrəd‿ənd 'wʌn]
⇓	⇓
110	one hundred and ten [ˌwʌn hʌndrəd‿ənd 'ten]
⇓	⇓
200	two hundred [ˌtuː 'hʌndrəd]
⇓	⇓
1000	a/one thousand [ə/wʌn 'θaʊznd]
1001	one thousand and one [ˌwʌn θaʊznd‿ənd 'wʌn]
⇓	⇓
1111	one thousand one hundred and eleven [ˌwʌn θaʊznd wʌn hʌndrəd‿ənd‿ɪ'levn]
⇓	⇓
2000	two thousand [tuː θaʊznd]
⇓	⇓
1000000	a/one million [ə/wʌn 'mɪljən]

1st	first [fɜːst]
2nd	second ['sekənd]
3rd	third [θɜːd]
4th	fourth [fɔːθ]
5th	fifth [fɪfθ]
6th	sixth [sɪksθ]
7th	seventh ['sevnθ]
8th	eighth [eɪtθ]
9th	ninth [naɪnθ]
10th	tenth [tenθ]
11th	eleventh [ɪ'levnθ]
12th	twelfth [twelfθ]
13th	thirteenth [ˌθɜː'tiːnθ]
⇓	⇓
20th	twentieth ['twentiəθ]
21st	twenty-first [ˌtwenti'fɜːst]
22nd	twenty-second [ˌtwenti'sekənd]
23rd	twenty-third [ˌtwenti'θɜːd]
⇓	⇓
30th	thirtieth ['θɜːtiəθ]
⇓	⇓
100th	hundredth ['hʌndrədθ]
1/2	a/one half [ə/wʌn hɑːf]
1/3	a/one third [ə/wʌn θɜːd]
1/4	a/one quarter [ə/wʌn 'kwɔːtə]
1/8	an/one eighth [ən/wʌn‿eɪtθ]
3/4	three quarters [θri 'kwɔːtəz]

W Words

So funktionieren die Wortlisten

Es gibt alphabetische Wortlisten und Wortlisten nach Kapiteln.

Alphabetische Wortlisten

Wenn du nicht mehr weißt, wo ein Wort zum ersten Mal aufgetaucht ist (und es nicht findest), kannst du es in der alphabetischen Wortliste ab **Seite 200** nachschlagen.
Dort findest du auch die Wörter aus allen Arbeitsanweisungen und aus den Optionals.
Wörter mit einem * gehören zu Texten aus den Optionals.
Wenn du mal eine Aufgabe machst, bei der du ein „neues" englisches Wort brauchst, kannst du in der deutsch-englischen Wortliste ab **Seite 228** nachgucken.

Wortlisten nach Kapiteln

Hier siehst du, wie du diese Wortlisten (ab **Seite 160**) benutzen kannst:

Die Lautschrift zeigt an, wie man ein Wort ausspricht.

Hier findest du die Übersetzungen.

Hier stehen die englischen Wörter mit ihrer Lautschrift.

Fett gedruckte Wörter solltest du dir merken.

(AE): Dies ist die amerikanische Schreibweise für ein englisches Wort bzw. ein Wort, das vor allem im amerikanischen Englisch benutzt wird.

(npl) bedeutet: Dieses Wort wird nur in der Mehrzahl benutzt.

(no pl): Dieses Wort wird nur in der Einzahl benutzt.

Zu dieser Aufgabe gehören die folgenden Wörter.

(pl) weist auf eine unregelmäßige Mehrzahlform hin.

Kleine Bilder und Beispielsätze helfen dabei, dir Wörter besser einzuprägen.

Hier sind die verschiedenen Schreibweisen im amerikanischen und britischen Englisch gegenübergestellt.

Hier findest du wichtige Vokabel-Lerntipps.

(informal) bedeutet: Dieses Wort ist umgangssprachlich.

Theme 3 — Words — W

as you please [ˌæz_jə ˈpliːz]	wie es Dir/Ihnen gefällt	
continue [kənˈtɪnjuː]	fortführen; fortsetzen	
admission [ədˈmɪʃn]	Eintritt	
helicopter [ˈhelɪˌkɒptə]	Hubschrauber	
experience [ɪkˈspɪəriəns]	erleben; kennen lernen	
downtown [ˌdaʊnˈtaʊn]	Innenstadt-	
through *(AE)* [θruː]	*hier:* bis	
am (= ante meridiem) [eɪ em]	morgens, vormittags *(nur hinter Uhrzeit zwischen Mitternacht und 12 Uhr mittags)*	
pm (= post meridiem) [ˌpiːˈem, ˈpəʊst məˌrɪdiəm]	nachmittags, abends *(nur hinter Uhrzeit zwischen 12 Uhr mittags und Mitternacht)*	*pm* = in the afternoon or in the evening
Saturdays [ˈsætədeɪz]	samstags	
special offer [ˌspeʃl ˈɒfə]	Sonderangebot	
offer [ˈɒfə]	Angebot	
explore [ɪkˈsplɔː]	erforschen, erkunden	*to explore* = to travel around an area to learn about it
historic [hɪˈstɒrɪk]	historisch	
site [saɪt]	Stelle, Platz	
setting [ˈsetɪŋ]	Lage; Schauplatz	harbor *(AE)* = harbour *(BE)*
harbor *(AE)* [ˈhɑːbə]	Hafen	
immigration [ˌɪmɪˈgreɪʃn]	Einwanderung	
shore [ʃɔː]	Küste; Ufer; Strand	He's standing on the *shore.* 
financial district [faɪˈnænʃl ˌdɪstrɪkt]	Finanzbezirk	
grounds *(npl)* [graʊndz]	Anlagen	
seaport [ˈsiːˌpɔːt]	Seehafen	
movie *(AE)* [ˈmuːvi]	Kino-, Film-	
destination [ˌdestɪˈneɪʃn]	(Reise)ziel; *hier:* Schauplatz	*destination* = the place where someone is going
film [fɪlm]	filmen, drehen	
camera [ˈkæm(ə)rə]	Kamera, Fotoapparat; *hier:* Aufnahme	
screen [skriːn]	Leinwand; Bildschirm	What you see on a *screen* is not always reality.
see [siː]	*hier:* ansehen, besichtigen	
apartment [əˈpɑːtmənt]	Wohnung	
false [fɔːls]	falsch	*false* ≠ true
the Rhine *(no pl)* [ðə ˌraɪn]	der Rhein	
single decker [ˌsɪŋgl ˈdekə]	Bus *(mit einem Deck)*	
A6 transport [ˈtrænspɔːt]	Transport; Verkehrsmittel	**Reimwörter** Damit du dir besser merken kannst, wie bestimmte Wörter ausgesprochen werden, suche Reimwörter für sie. Dir wird auffallen, dass die Reimwörter nicht immer dieselbe Schreibweise haben.
L1 present progressive [ˌpreznt prəʊˈgresɪv]	Verlaufsform (des) Präsens	
L3 present perfect [ˌpreznt ˈpɜːfɪkt]	Perfekt	
subway *(AE)* [ˈsʌbˌweɪ]	Unterführung, U-Bahn	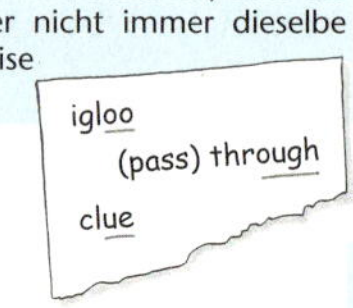
organization [ˌɔːgənaɪˈzeɪʃn]	Organisation	
non-profit [ˌnɒnˈprɒfɪt]	gemeinnützig	
PP2 lasso *(pl -s or -es)* [læˈsuː]	Lasso	
French [frentʃ]	Französisch	
igloo [ˈɪgluː]	Iglu	

English Sounds

Im Englischen spricht man Wörter oft anders aus, als man sie schreibt. Das ist aber kein Problem. Denn die Aussprache der Wörter ist in jedem Wörterbuch angegeben. So kann man auch neue Wörter richtig aussprechen, ohne sie vorher gehört zu haben.
Dazu nimmt man die so genannte Lautschrift zu Hilfe. Das ist eine Schrift, deren Symbole jeden Laut genau bezeichnen. Die Lautschrift wird in jedem Wörterbuch benutzt.

Hier ist eine Liste mit den Symbolen dieser Lautschrift zusammen mit Beispielwörtern, in denen der entsprechende Laut vorkommt.

Vokale

[ɑː]	arm
[ʌ]	but
[e]	desk
[ə]	a, an
[ɜː]	girl, bird
[æ]	apple
[ɪ]	in, it
[i]	happy
[iː]	easy, eat
[ɒ]	orange, sorry
[ɔː]	all, call
[ʊ]	look
[u]	January
[uː]	boot

Doppellaute

[aɪ]	eye, by, buy
[aʊ]	our
[eə]	air, there
[eɪ]	take, they
[ɪə]	here
[ɔɪ]	boy
[əʊ]	go, old
[ʊə]	you're

Konsonanten

[b]	bag, club
[d]	duck, card
[f]	fish, laugh
[g]	get, dog
[h]	hot
[j]	you
[k]	can, duck
[l]	lot, small
[m]	more, mum
[n]	now, sun
[ŋ]	song, long
[p]	present, top
[r]	red, right
[s]	sister, class (scharfes s)
[z]	nose, dogs (weiches s)
[t]	time, cat
[ʒ]	television
[dʒ]	sausage
[ʃ]	fresh
[tʃ]	child, cheese
[ð]	these, mother (weicher Laut)
[θ]	bathroom, think (harter Laut)
[v]	very, have
[w]	what, word

[ˈ]	Betonungszeichen für die folgende Silbe (Hauptbetonung)
[ˌ]	Betonungszeichen für die folgende Silbe (Nebenbetonung)

The English Alphabet

[eɪ]	[biː]	[siː]	[diː]	[iː]	[ef]	[dʒiː]	[eɪtʃ]	[aɪ]
a	b	c	d	e	f	g	h	i
[dʒeɪ]	[keɪ]	[el]	[em]	[en]	[əʊ]	[piː]	[kjuː]	[ɑː]
j	k	l	m	n	o	p	q	r
[es]	[tiː]	[juː]	[viː]	[ˈdʌbljuː]	[eks]	[waɪ]	[zed]	
s	t	u	v	w	x	y	z	

Theme 1 – Made in the USA

	made in ['meɪd‿ɪn]	hergestellt in	
A1	**culture** ['kʌltʃə]	Kultur	The manners, customs, arts and sciences of a country are its *culture*.
	the USA (= United States of America) [ðiˌjuːes'eɪ, juːˌnaɪtɪd ˌsteɪts‿əv‿ə'merɪkə]	die USA (= Vereinigte Staaten von Amerika)	
	leisure culture ['leʒə ˌkʌltʃə]	Freizeitkultur	 This is Mr Smith's wonderful *invention*!
	invention [ɪn'venʃn]	Erfindung; Fantasie	
	the media *(pl)* [ðə 'miːdɪə]	die Medien	*the media* = radio, TV, the Internet, newspapers and magazines
	have influence on [ˌhæv‿'ɪnfluəns‿ɒn]	Einfluss haben auf	
	word web ['wɜːd ˌweb]	Wortnetz	**Zehn Minuten** Übe die Vokabeln immer nur fünf bis zehn Minuten, aber dafür regelmäßig! Das ist viel wirkungsvoller als eine ganze Stunde, die aber nur zweimal im Monat. Probiere dabei die Vokabeltipps auf den nächsten Seiten aus.
	sports *(AE)* [spɔːts]	Sport; Sportart	
A2	basketball ['bɑːskɪtˌbɔːl]	Basketball	
	field hockey ['fiːld ˌhɒki]	(Feld)hockey	
	volleyball ['vɒliˌbɔːl]	Volleyball	
	movie ['muːvi]	(Kino)film	
	cellphone ['selˌfəʊn]	Mobiltelefon, Handy	
	Chinese [ˌtʃaɪ'niːz]	Chinese/Chinesin; chinesisch	
	Italian [ɪ'tæliən]	Italiener/in; italienisch	
	pancake ['pænˌkeɪk]	Pfannkuchen, Omelette	*pancake* 
	maple syrup *(no pl)* [ˌmeɪpl 'sɪrəp]	Ahornsirup	
	what for? ['wɒt fɔː]	wofür?, warum?	
	who with? ['huː wɪð]	mit wem?	
	add up [æd‿'ʌp]	addieren	
	have sth in common with [hæv ˌsʌmθɪŋ‿ɪn 'kɒmən wɪð]	etw gemein(sam) haben mit	
A3	for the first time [fə ðə 'fɜːst‿ˌtaɪm]	zum ersten Mal	
	busy ['bɪzi]	*hier:* gut besucht	The shop was very *busy*.
	stand in line *(AE)* [stænd‿ɪn 'laɪn]	anstehen, Schlange stehen	
	British ['brɪtɪʃ]	britisch	Someone who is *British* comes from England, Scotland, Wales or Northern Ireland.
	forever [fər'evə]	ewig	
	queue [kjuː]	anstehen, Schlange stehen	
	you guys *(AE, informal)* [jə 'gaɪz]	ihr	
	be used to sth [biː 'juːzd tə ˌsʌmθɪŋ]	etw gewohnt sein	*be used to sth* = be familiar with sth
	be starving *(informal)* [bi‿'stɑːvɪŋ]	ausgehungert sein, vor Hunger sterben	
	the States *(informal)* [ðə 'steɪts]	die Staaten *(Amerika)*	
	be worth it [biː 'wɜːθ‿ɪt]	die Mühe wert sein	
	buddy *(AE, informal)* ['bʌdi]	Kumpel	
	burger-flipper *(AE, informal)* ['bɜːgəˌflɪpə]	*jd, der in einem Fastfood-Restaurant arbeitet*	
	that [ðæt]	dass	

	fried [fraɪd]	gebraten	*fried* = cooked in hot oil
	go for sth ['gəʊ fə ˌsʌmθɪŋ]	etw holen	
	salsa ['sælsə]	Salsasoße	
	olive ['ɒlɪv]	Olive	
	go for sth *(informal)* ['gəʊ fə ˌsʌmθɪŋ]	*hier:* mögen	
	fries *(AE, pl)* [fraɪz]	Pommes frites	mom *(AE)* = mum *(BE)*
	meat loaf ['miːt ˌləʊf]	Hackbraten	
	baked potatoes *(pl)* [ˌbeɪkt 'pə'teɪtəʊz]	Ofenkartoffeln	
	cooking ['kʊkɪŋ]	Kochen	
	half an hour [ˌhɑːf‿ən‿'aʊə]	eine halbe Stunde	*half an hour* = 30 minutes
	later ['leɪtə]	später	
	check out sth *(AE)* ['tʃek‿aʊt ˌsʌmθɪŋ]	sich etw ansehen	
	store *(AE)* [stɔː]	Laden; Geschäft	 There are many different *stores* in this street.
	not mind sth [ˌnɒt 'maɪnd sʌmθɪŋ]	nichts gegen etw einzuwenden haben	
	How about …? [ˌhaʊ‿ə'baʊt]	Was ist mit …?, Wie wäre es mit …?	
	come over [ˌkʌm‿'əʊvə]	herüberkommen; vorbeischauen	
	tray [treɪ]	Tablett	
	make a move *(informal)* [ˌmeɪk‿ə 'muːv]	sich auf den Weg machen	
	See you (soon)! *(informal)* [ˌsiː jə 'suːn]	Bis bald!	
	not (be able to) stand sth [nɒt 'stænd ˌsʌmθɪŋ]	etw nicht ertragen/leiden (können)	He *can't stand* eating burgers. = He hates eating burgers.
	chewing gum *(no pl)* ['tʃuːɪŋ ˌgʌm]	Kaugummi	
	with [wɪð]	*hier:* bei, dabei	
	guess [ges]	denken; annehmen	*guess* = think
	likes and dislikes *(pl)* [ˌlaɪkz‿ən dɪs'laɪkz]	Vorlieben und Abneigungen	
A4	fish and chips [ˌfɪʃ‿ən 'tʃɪps]	Fisch und Chips	
	cheerleading ['tʃɪəˌliːdɪŋ]	*Cheerleaden*	 Our neighbour loves to do the *gardening*.
	gardening *(no pl)* ['gɑːdnɪŋ]	Gartenarbeit, Gärtnern	
	soccer *(AE)* ['sɒkə]	Fußball	
	peanut ['piːnʌt]	Erdnuss	
	gum [gʌm]	(Kau)gummi	
	neither … nor [ˌnaɪðə 'nɔː]	weder … noch …	*Neither* my dad *nor* my mum like chewing gum. = My dad doesn't like chewing gum and my mum doesn't like chewing gum.
	Britain ['brɪtn]	Großbritannien	
	hiking ['haɪkɪŋ]	Wandern	
	go hiking [gəʊ 'haɪkɪŋ]	wandern gehen	
L2	switchboard ['swɪtʃˌbɔːd]	Satzschalttafel	
L3	wake up [weɪk‿'ʌp]	aufwachen	
B1	**thought** [θɔːt]	Gedanke	You think *thoughts*.
	bubble ['bʌbl]	Blase	
B2	chewing ['tʃuːɪŋ]	Kau-	
	all the time [ˌɔːl ðə 'taɪm]	die ganze Zeit	

report back to [rɪˌpɔːt 'bæk tə]	jdm Bericht erstatten	
B3 chew on sth ['tʃuː‿ɒn ˌsʌmθɪŋ]	auf etw herumkauen; sich etw gründlich durch den Kopf gehen lassen	
resin *(no pl)* ['rezɪn]	Harz	produce producer product
producer [prə'djuːsə]	Hersteller/in; Produzent/in	
tropical rainforest [ˌtrɒpɪkl 'reɪnˌfɒrɪst]	tropischer Regenwald	
more and more [mɔːr‿ən 'mɔː]	mehr und mehr, immer mehr	
ingredient [ɪn'griːdiənt]	Zutat	
coloring *(no pl, AE)* ['kʌlərɪŋ]	Farbstoff	coloring *(AE)* = colouring *(BE)* flavor *(AE)* = flavour *(BE)*
flavor *(AE)* ['fleɪvə]	Geschmack, Aroma	
produce [prə'djuːs]	herstellen, produzieren	
brand [brænd]	Marke	This is John's *attempt* to cut his sister's hair. 
attempt [ə'tempt]	Versuch	
sticky ['stɪki]	klebrig	
advertising ['ædvəˌtaɪzɪŋ]	Werbung, Reklame	
pioneer [ˌpaɪə'nɪə]	Pionier/in, Wegbereiter/in	
ad (= advertisement) [æd, əd'vɜːtɪsmənt]	Werbung, Reklame; Anzeige	
increase [ɪn'kriːs]	erhöhen, verstärken	*to increase* = to get *more and more*
sales *(pl)* [seɪlz]	Absatz; Umsatz	
millionaire [ˌmɪljə'neə]	Millionär	
at the age of [ˌət ðɪ'eɪdʒ‿əv]	im Alter von	
ton [tʌn]	Tonne	**Wortnetze ergänzen** Inzwischen weißt du ja schon, wie man Wortnetze (word webs) zusammenstellt. Du lernst immer mehr neue Wörter und es sind bestimmt einige dabei, die in Wortnetze passen, die du früher schon angelegt hast. Ergänze deine alten Wortnetze und sieh dir die Wörter noch einmal an. Sicherlich kannst du dich noch gut an sie erinnern, oder?
surprisingly [sə'praɪzɪŋli]	überraschenderweise	
taste [teɪst]	Geschmack	
lose *(weight)* [luːz]	abnehmen	
instead of [ɪn'sted‿əv]	(an)statt	
cookie ['kʊki]	Keks, Plätzchen	
potato chip [pə'teɪtəʊ ˌtʃɪp]	Kartoffelchip	
by the way [ˌbaɪ ðə 'weɪ]	übrigens	
how to ['haʊ‿tə]	wie man	
overnight [ˌəʊvə'naɪt]	in der Nacht, über Nacht	
B4 bedpost ['bedˌpəʊst]	Bettpfosten	
read along [ˌriːd‿ə'lɒŋ]	mitlesen	
Hallelujah! [ˌhælɪ'luːjə]	Halleluja!, Gott sei Dank!	
peculiar [pɪ'kjuːliə]	seltsam, merkwürdig	*peculiar* = strange
It's got me on the go. *(informal)* [ɪts ˌgɒt me ən ðə 'gəʊ]	Es macht mich noch wahnsinnig.	
dough *(AE, informal)* [dəʊ]	Kohle, Knete	*"Dough"* is an informal American English word for "money".
would [wʊd]	würde(st/n/t)	
bite [baɪt]	beißen	
go crazy [gəʊ 'kreɪzi]	verrückt werden	favorite *(AE)* = favourite *(BE)*
put sb right *(informal)* [pʊt ˌsʌmbədi 'raɪt]	jdn eines Besseren belehren	
the White House [ðə 'waɪt ˌhaʊs]	das Weiße Haus	
mighty ['maɪti]	gewaltig; mächtig	

Theme 1

	lighthouse ['laɪtˌhaʊs]	Leuchtturm	
	involve [ɪn'vɒlv]	beinhalten; betreffen	Her job *involves* working with the computer.
	continent ['kɒntɪnənt]	Kontinent, Erdteil	
	pull out [pʊl‿'aʊt]	(heraus)ziehen; *hier:* auseinanderziehen	
	rubber ['rʌbə]	Gummi; Radiergummi	
	snap back [snæp 'bæk]	zurückschnellen	
	paste [peɪst]	kleben; einfügen	
	blush [blʌʃ]	erröten, rot werden	
	bride [braɪd]	Braut	
	boob *(AE, informal)* [buːb]	Trottel	
	right at his/her side ['raɪt‿ət‿ɪz/hə ˌsaɪd]	direkt neben ihm/ihr	They are sitting *right at each other's sides.* 
	altar ['ɔːltə]	Altar	
	steady ['stedi]	fest, stabil	
	bridegroom ['braɪdˌgruːm]	Bräutigam	
	put on [pʊt‿'ɒn]	*hier:* stecken an	
	choir [kwaɪə]	Chor	
	collar ['kɒlə]	Kragen	
	button ['bʌtn]	Knopf	
	be in sight [biː‿ɪn saɪt]	in Sichtweite sein	
	beneath [bɪ'niːθ]	unter	 Micky is *beneath* the cheese.
	verse [vɜːs]	Dichtung; Strophe	
B5	**keyword** ['kiːˌwɜːd]	Schlüssel(wort), Stichwort	
	stage [steɪdʒ]	Etappe, Station	
	soap [səʊp]	Seife	
	maker ['meɪkə]	Hersteller/in, Produzent/in	
	basket ['bɑːskɪt]	Korb	
	teens *(pl)* [tiːnz]	Jugendjahre	
	wag(g)on ['wægən]	Wagen; Karren	
	can [kæn]	Dose; Büchse	This is a *can.* 
	baking powder ['beɪkɪŋ ˌpaʊdə]	Backpulver	
	pack [pæk]	Packung	
	for free *(informal)* [fə 'friː]	gratis, umsonst	*for free* = £ 0.00
	competition [ˌkɒmpə'tɪʃn]	*hier:* Konkurrenz	
	introduce (to) [ˌɪntrə'djuːs]	einführen (in)	
	skyscraper ['skaɪˌskreɪpə]	Wolkenkratzer	
	biography [baɪ'ɒgrəfi]	Biografie	
B6	creative [kri'eɪtɪv]	kreativ, schöpferisch	
	eye-catching ['aɪˌkætʃɪŋ]	auffällig	
	bright [braɪt]	*hier:* strahlend	
	create [kri'eɪt]	erschaffen; *hier:* gestalten	to *create* sth = to make sth new or original
L2	be spelt [biː 'spelt]	geschrieben/buchstabiert werden	
	heading ['hedɪŋ]	Überschrift; Titel	Another word for *"heading"* is "title".
L3	verb [vɜːb]	Verb	
PP1	was invented [wəz‿ɪn'ventɪd]	wurde erfunden	
	Bavaria [bə'veəriə]	Bayern	
	emigrate (to) ['emɪgreɪt]	auswandern (nach)	*emigrate to* another country = leave your country to live in another country
	Californian [ˌkælɪ'fɔːniən]	Kalifornier/in; kalifornisch	
	gold rush ['gəʊld ˌrʌʃ]	Goldrausch	
	pack up (sth) [pæk‿'ʌp]	(etw) zusammenpacken	
	make clothes [meɪk 'kləʊðz]	Kleider nähen	She's *making clothes.* 

	canvas *(no pl)* ['kænvəs]	Segeltuch; Leinwand	
	tent [tent]	Zelt	
	intend [ɪn'tend]	beabsichtigen	*intend* = have a plan in one's mind to do sth
	search for ['sɜːtʃ fə]	suchen nach	
	cloth [klɒθ]	Tuch, Stoff	
	strong [strɒŋ]	*hier:* robust, stabil	
	overalls *(pl, AE)* ['əʊvərˌɔːlz]	Latzhose	
	last [lɑːst]	(an)dauern; halten	Something that is *strong lasts* long.
	goldmine ['gəʊldˌmaɪn]	Goldmine	
	hire sb ['haɪə ˌsʌmbədi]	jdn einstellen	
	tailor ['teɪlə]	Schneider/in	
	warehouse ['weəˌhaʊs]	Lagerhaus, Lagerhalle	
	order ['ɔːdə]	*hier:* Bestellung	
	come in [kʌm‿'ɪn]	*hier:* eintreffen	
	constant ['kɒnstənt]	dauernd, ständig	
	quality ['kwɒləti]	Qualität	
	patent ['peɪtnt]	sich patentieren lassen	
	strengthen ['streŋθ(ə)n]	kräftigen, (ver)stärken	To *"strengthen"* means to "make stronger".
	copper ['kɒpə]	Kupfer	
	rivet ['rɪvɪt]	Niete	
	France [frɑːnts]	Frankreich	
	America [ə'merɪkə]	Amerika	How do you *pronounce* the word "English"? — English? That's ['ɪŋglɪʃ].
	pronounce [prə'naʊns]	aussprechen	
	denim ['denɪm]	Denim®; blauer Jeansstoff	
	instead [ɪn'sted]	stattdessen	
	denims *(pl)* ['denɪmz]	Jeans	
	clothing company ['kləʊðɪŋ ˌkʌmp(ə)ni]	Bekleidungsfirma	Co. = company
C1	vacation *(AE)* [və'keɪʃn]	Ferien, Urlaub	
	How are things going? *(informal)* [ˌhaʊ‿ɑː θɪŋz 'gəʊɪŋ]	Wie geht's?	
	Guess what! [ges 'wɒt]	Stell dir vor!	
	(department) store ['stɔː]	Kaufhaus	
	for all [fər‿'ɔːl]	*hier:* die ganzen	
	gonna *(AE, informal* = going to) ['gɒnə]	werden	
	tough [tʌf]	*hier:* schwierig, hart	He's having a *tough* time with his dog.
	(shopping) mall [mɔːl]	*überdachtes Einkaufszentrum*	
	floor [flɔː]	*hier:* Stock(werk)	
	sports department ['spɔːts dɪˌpɑːtmənt]	Sportabteilung	
	pants *(AE)* [pænts]	(lange) Hose	
	sneaker ['sniːkə]	Turnschuh	
	cap [kæp]	Mütze, Kappe	
	It sure is a change from … *(AE, informal)* [ɪt ʃɔːr‿ɪz‿ə 'tʃeɪndʒ frəm]	Das ist echt eine Abwechslung vom …	neighborhood *(AE)* = neighbourhood *(BE)*
	mow [məʊ]	mähen	
	lawn [lɔːn]	Rasen	
	several ['sev(ə)rəl]	einige; verschiedene; *hier:* mehrere	There were *several* books lying on the desk. 
	pay *(no pl)* [peɪ]	Lohn, Gehalt	
	fair [feə]	*hier:* angemessen	

	pretty *(informal)* ['prɪti]	ziemlich	
	garbage *(no pl)* ['gɑːbɪdʒ]	Müll, Abfall	
	wipe [waɪp]	abwischen, abputzen	
	serve sb ['sɜːv ˌsʌmbədi]	jdn bedienen	
	motto *(pl* -s *or* -es) ['mɒtəʊ]	Motto, Wahlspruch	
	satisfied ['sætɪsˌfaɪd]	zufrieden	
	polite [pə'laɪt]	höflich	
	willingly ['wɪlɪŋli]	gern(e); freiwillig	This lady is not in a good *mood.*
	mood [muːd]	Laune, Stimmung	
	wander around ['wɒndər‿əˌraʊnd]	umherstreifen	to *wander* = to walk slowly
	tee [tiː]	Tee, Abschlagstelle *(Golf)*	
	This being the States, … [ðɪs 'biːɪŋ ðə ˌsteɪts]	Da wir in den Staaten sind, …	
	patient ['peɪʃnt]	geduldig	
	in silence [ɪn 'saɪləns]	still	
	try out [traɪ‿'aʊt]	ausprobieren	We're *trying out* a new secretary.
	dressing room ['dresɪŋ ˌruːm]	Ankleideraum, Umkleidekabine	
	serious ['sɪəriəs]	ernst	 He's a *serious* person.
	laugh out (loud) [lɑːf‿'aʊt laʊd]	(laut) auflachen	
	in time [ɪn 'taɪm]	rechtzeitig	
	wanna *(informal)* (= want to) ['wɒnə]	wollen	
	bat [bæt]	Schläger, Schlagholz	
	department manager [dɪ'pɑːtmənt ˌmænɪdʒə]	Abteilungsleiter/in	
	anytime ['eniˌtaɪm]	jederzeit	
	someday (= some day) ['sʌmˌdeɪ]	eines Tages, irgendwann (einmal)	
	greetings *(pl)* ['griːtɪŋz]	Grüße	
	the pros and cons [ðə ˌprəʊz‿ənd 'kɒnz]	das Für und Wider, das Pro und Kontra	*the pros and cons* = arguments for and against something
	on the one hand [ɒn ðə 'wʌn ˌhænd]	einerseits	
	on the other hand [ɒn ði‿'ʌðər ˌhænd]	andererseits	You use *"on the one hand … on the other hand …"* when you give two different opinions on something.
C2	**summary** ['sʌməri]	Zusammenfassung	
	shop assistant ['ʃɒp‿əˌsɪst(ə)nt]	Verkäufer/in	
C3	leave [liːv]	*hier:* weggehen	color *(AE)* = colour *(BE)*
C4	unexpected [ˌʌnɪk'spektɪd]	unerwartet	
	rather ['rɑːðə]	ziemlich	
	as a matter of fact [əz‿ə ˌmætər‿əv 'fækt]	übrigens; *hier:* ehrlich gesagt	
	extremely [ɪk'striːmli]	äußerst	This girl is concentrating *extremely* hard.
	Nothing one could do about it! ['nʌθɪŋ wʌn kəd‿duː‿əˌbaʊt‿ɪt]	Nichts zu machen!	
	hum [hʌm]	brummen; *hier:* summen	
	teenage ['tiːnˌeɪdʒ]	jugendlich, im Teenageralter	
	look around [ˌlʊk‿ə'raʊnd]	sich umsehen	

shake one's head ['ʃeɪk wʌnz ˌhed]	den Kopf schütteln	
keep (on) doing sth [kiːp 'duːɪŋ ˌsʌmθɪŋ]	etw weiter(hin) tun	She has breakfast every morning. She always goes for a run *before* (that). 
before [bɪ'fɔː]	vorher	
edge [edʒ]	*hier:* sich langsam bewegen	
slide [slaɪd]	rutschen; gleiten	
grab sth ['græb ˌsʌmθɪŋ]	sich etw schnappen	
ignore [ɪg'nɔː]	ignorieren	
walk up to sb ['wɔːk‿ʌp tə ˌsʌmbədi]	auf jdn zugehen	
drop [drɒp]	(herunter)fallen	
wrap (up) [ræp]	einwickeln, einpacken	 This present is *wrapped.*
Come on! [kʌm‿'ɒn]	Komm(t) jetzt!, Mach(t) schon!	
cash register ['kæʃ ˌredʒɪstə]	Registrierkasse	
astonished [ə'stɒnɪʃt]	erstaunt	
hand sth to sb ['hænd sʌmθɪŋ tə‿ˌsʌmbədi]	jdm etw übergeben	
Happy birthday (to you)! [ˌhæpi 'bɜːθdeɪ]	Alles Gute zum Geburtstag!	
receive [rɪ'siːv]	erhalten	Charlie *received* an e-mail. Now he's answering it.
agree [ə'griː]	*hier:* vereinbaren	
meet up ['miːt‿ʌp]	sich treffen	
whistle [wɪsl]	pfeifen	
react [rɪ'ækt]	reagieren	
point of view [ˌpɔɪnt‿əv 'vjuː]	Gesichtspunkt, Standpunkt	*point of view* = opinion
C5 rest [rest]	(sich) ausruhen	
L1 tense [tens]	Zeitform, Tempus	
L3 simple past [ˌsɪmpl 'pɑːst]	einfache Form der Vergangenheit	
simple present [ˌsɪmpl 'preznt]	Präsens, einfache Gegenwart	
rubbish *(no pl)* ['rʌbɪʃ]	Müll	*rubbish*

Die Vokabeln aus den OPTIONAL-Teilen findest du im englisch-deutschen Dictionary auf den Seiten 200–227!

Theme 2 – New places, new faces

A1	**lots (= a lot)** [lɒts]	viel; sehr; oft	He knows *lots* about it. I like her *lots*.
	Statue of Liberty [ˌstætʃuː‿əv ˈlɪbəti]	Freiheitsstatue	
	Franco- [fræŋkəʊ]	französisch- *(in Komposita)*	
	union [ˈjuːnjən]	Union, Staatenbund	*union* = a group of states or countries
	statue [ˈstætʃuː]	Statue, Standbild	
	foot (ft) (*pl* **feet**) [fʊt, fiːt]	Fuß; *Längenmaß = 30,48 Zentimeter*	
	foundation [faʊnˈdeɪʃn]	Fundament	
	another [əˈnʌðə]	*hier:* weitere(r, s)	
	commemorate [kəˈmeməˌreɪt]	gedenken	
	the United States [ðiˌjuːˈnaɪtɪd ˌsteɪts]	die Vereinigten Staaten	
	the Declaration of Independence [ðə ˌdekləˌreɪʃn‿əv‿ɪndɪˈpendəns]	*die Unabhängigkeitserklärung der USA*	center *(AE)* = centre *(BE)*
	immigrant [ˈɪmɪɡrənt]	Einwanderer/in	
	go through [ɡəʊ ˈθruː]	durchgehen	
	decide [dɪˈsaɪd]	entscheiden; bestimmen	*decide* = choose what you're going to do
	hope [həʊp]	Hoffnung	
	tear [tɪə]	Träne	
	bear [beə]	Bär	Her eyes were full of *tears*. 
	be located [bi ləʊˈkeɪtəd]	sich befinden	
	cover [ˈkʌvə]	*hier:* sich erstrecken über	
	sq mi (= square mile) [skweə ˈmaɪl]	Quadratmeile	
	Native American [ˌneɪtɪv‿əˈmerɪkən]	amerikanische/r Ureinwohner/in	*Native American* 
	settle [ˈsetl]	(be)siedeln	
	bank [bæŋk]	Ufer	
	nation [ˈneɪʃn]	*hier:* Stamm	*"Nation"* can mean "a group of people who share the same culture".
	the Iroquois [ðɪ‿ˈɪrəkwɔɪz]	die Irokesen *(Indianer)*	
	tribe [traɪb]	Stamm; Sippe	
	bark-covered [ˈbɑːkˌkʌvəd]	mit Rinde gedeckt	
	residence [ˈrezɪd(ə)ns]	Wohnsitz	
	vehicle [ˈviːɪkl]	Fahrzeug	
	billion [ˈbɪljən]	Milliarde	The president was in no *state* to think of the *state*. 
	state [steɪt]	Zustand; Verfassung; *hier:* (Bundes)staat	
	entertainment [ˌentəˈteɪnmənt]	Unterhaltung, Unterhaltungs-	
	casino [kəˈsiːnəʊ]	(Spiel)kasino	
	gambling [ˈɡæmblɪŋ]	Glücksspiel	
	legal [ˈliːɡl]	legal, gesetzlich zulässig	
	at the beginning [ət ðə bɪˈɡɪnɪŋ]	am Anfang, zu Beginn	*at the beginning* ≠ in the end
	district [ˈdɪstrɪkt]	Gebiet; Bezirk	
	northwest [ˌnɔːθˈwest]	(nach) Nordwesten	
A2	quiz [kwɪz]	Quiz, Ratespiel	
	knowledge *(no pl)* [ˈnɒlɪdʒ]	Kenntnisse; Wissen	What someone knows about a subject is his/her *knowledge*.

	encyclopaedia [ɪnˌsaɪklə'piːdiə]	Lexikon, Enzyklopädie
	star [stɑː]	Stern
	(the) US (= United States) [ˌjuː'es, juːn'aɪtɪd steɪts]	die USA
	zone [zəʊn]	Zone, Region
	stripe [straɪp]	Streifen
	represent [ˌreprɪ'zent]	vertreten; symbolisieren
	pilgrim ['pɪlgrɪm]	Pilger/in
	Spanish ['spænɪʃ]	spanisch
	Danish ['deɪnɪʃ]	Dänisch
A3	vast [vɑːst]	gewaltig, riesig
	is divided into [ɪz dɪ'vaɪdɪd ˌɪntə]	ist aufgeteilt in
	region ['riːdʒ(ə)n]	Region, Bezirk
	mid- [mɪd]	Mitte *(in Komposita)*
	the Atlantic (Ocean) *(no pl)* [ðiˌət'læntɪk]	der Atlantik
	the Midwest [ðə ˌmɪd'west]	der Mittelwesten
	(the) south [saʊθ]	(der) Süden
	the Southwest [ðə ˌsaʊθ'west]	der Südwesten
	differ (from sth) ['dɪfə]	sich (von etw) unterscheiden
	learn about [ˌlɜːnˌə'baʊt]	erfahren von/über
	was named after [wɒz 'neɪmdˌˌɑːftə]	wurde nach … benannt
	Protestant ['prɒtɪstənt]	Protestant/in, protestantisch
	devote oneself to sth [dɪ'vəʊt wʌnˌself tə ˌsʌmθɪŋ]	sich etw widmen
	farming ['fɑːmɪŋ]	Ackerbau und Viehzucht
	university [ˌjuːnɪ'vɜːsəti]	Universität
	college ['kɒlɪdʒ]	*Bildungseinrichtung; hier:* Hochschule
	was founded [wɒz 'faʊndɪd]	wurde gegründet
	prompt [prɒmpt]	Stichwort
	iron ['aɪən]	Eisen
	steel [stiːl]	Stahl
	finances *(pl)* ['faɪnænsɪz]	Finanzen
	communications *(pl)* [kəˌmjuːnɪ'keɪʃnz]	Fernmeldewesen
	pharmaceuticals *(pl)* [ˌfɑːmə'sjuːtɪklz]	Pharmaka
	agricultural [ˌægrɪ'kʌltʃ(ə)rəl]	landwirtschaftlich
	breadbasket ['bredˌbɑːskɪt]	Brotkorb; Kornkammer
	harvest ['hɑːvɪst]	ernten
	cereal *(no pl)* ['sɪəriəl]	Getreide
	crop [krɒp]	Feldfrucht; Ernte
	wheat *(no pl)* [wiːt]	Weizen
	oats *(pl)* [əʊts]	Haferkörner
	corn [kɔːn]	Getreide, Korn

star

These are *stripes.*

region = an area of land

Probier's mal mit Gemütlichkeit
Nicht nur für das Vokabellernen gilt: Du solltest dich an dem Ort, an dem du arbeitest, wohl fühlen und durch nichts abgelenkt sein! Eine gewisse Ordnung erleichtert das Arbeiten. Mache regelmäßig Pausen, in denen du z. B. das Fenster öffnest, etwas trinkst und dich bewegst. So kannst du dich besser konzentrieren.

He *devotes himself to farming.*

Im amerikanischen Englisch bezeichnet *college* eine Universität oder den Fachbereich einer Universität, im britischen Englisch dagegen ist ein *college* eine Art Berufsschule oder Fach(hoch)schule, kann aber auch eine Universität sein.

an *agricultural* job = a job that has something to do with farming

to *harvest* = to collect a *crop* from the field

	scenic ['siːnɪk]	landschaftlich (schön)	
	beauty ['bjuːti]	Schönheit	
	undeveloped [ˌʌndɪ'veləpt]	unerschlossen, unbebaut	
	fishing ['fɪʃɪŋ]	Fischerei, Fischen	My hobby is *fishing*.
	populous ['pɒpjʊləs]	bevölkerungsreich, dicht besiedelt	
	widespread ['waɪdˌspred]	weit verbreitet	
	inhabitant [ɪn'hæbɪtənt]	Einwohner/in; Bewohner/in	
	Mexican ['meksikæn]	Mexikaner/in, mexikanisch	
	origin ['ɒrɪdʒɪn]	Ursprung; Herkunft	*origin* = the country that someone comes from or the place or moment where something begins
A4	remaining [rɪ'meɪnɪŋ]	übrig, restlich	
	visit ['vɪzɪt]	*hier:* besichtigen	
A5	in short [ɪn 'ʃɔːt]	kurz gesagt	*in short* = not with many details
	facts (on/about) *(pl)* [fækts]	Fakten (über)	
	federal ['fed(ə)rəl]	föderativ	
	constitutional [ˌkɒnstɪ'tjuːʃn(ə)l]	konstitutionell	
	republic [rɪ'pʌblɪk]	Republik	
	nonreligious [nɒnrə'lɪdʒəs]	*ohne Glaubenszugehörigkeit*	*nonreligious* = without a religion
	independence *(no pl)* [ˌɪndɪ'pendəns]	Unabhängigkeit, Selbstständigkeit	
	God [gɒd]	Gott	
	trust in (sb/sth) ['trʌst‿ɪn]	vertrauen auf (jdn/etw)	
	neighboring *(AE)* ['neɪbərɪŋ]	benachbart, Nachbar-	neighboring *(AE)* = neighbouring *(BE)*
	north [nɔːθ]	Norden	
	continental [ˌkɒntɪ'nentl]	Kontinental-	
	area ['eəriə]	*hier:* Fläche	
	Mt (= Mount) *(no pl)* [maʊnt]	*erster Teil eines Bergnamens*	
	sea level ['siː ˌlevl]	Meeresspiegel	
	low [ləʊ]	niedrig	
	below [bɪ'ləʊ]	unter; unterhalb	
	bald eagle [bɔːld‿'iːgl]	weißköpfiger Seeadler	
	national anthem [ˌnæʃn(ə)l‿'ænθəm]	Nationalhymne	
	the Star-Spangled Banner [ðə ˌstɑː ˌspæŋgld 'bænə]	das Sternenbanner	*Star-Spangled Banner* bezeichnet sowohl die Nationalhymne als auch die Nationalflagge der USA.
A6	what … [wɒt]	was für …	
	home state [həʊm 'steɪt]	Heimat(bundes)staat	
	attraction [ə'trækʃn]	Anziehung(skraft); Attraktion	What attracts many people is an *attraction*.
	nickname ['nɪkˌneɪm]	Spitzname; Kosename	
L1	divide [dɪ'vaɪd]	(auf)teilen	
	pedestrian [pə'destriən]	Fußgänger/in	A *pedestrian* is someone who goes on foot.
	climber ['klaɪmə]	Bergsteiger/in	
L2	cover ['kʌvə]	Buchdeckel	
L3	pen friend ['pen ˌfrend]	Brieffreund/in	A *pen friend* is a friend you don't often see but write to.
L4	repeat [rɪ'piːt]	wiederholen	
B1	grade [greɪd]	Klasse	
	traditionally [trə'dɪʃn(ə)li]	traditionell; üblicherweise	
	field trip ['fiːld trɪp]	Exkursion	

fall *(AE)* [fɔːl]	Herbst	*"Fall"* is the American English word for "autumn".
in the north (of) [ɪn ðə 'nɔːθ]	im Norden (von)	
in the south (of) [ɪn ðə 'saʊθ]	im Süden (von)	
in the east (of) [ɪn ði‿'iːst]	im Osten (von)	
in the west (of) [ɪn ðə‿'west]	im Westen (von)	
southeast *(no pl)* [ˌsaʊθ'iːst]	Südosten	
B2 acre ['eɪkə]	Morgen *(altes Feldmaß)*	
climate ['klaɪmət]	Klima	
F (= Fahrenheit) ['færənhaɪt]	Fahrenheit *(Maßeinheit für Temperatur)*	
wild flower ['waɪld ˌflaʊə]	wild wachsende Blume	
raven ['reɪvn]	Rabe	
ground squirrel ['graʊnd ˌskwɪrəl]	Erdhörnchen	
lizard ['lɪzəd]	Eidechse, Echse	
rattlesnake ['rætlˌsneɪk]	Klapperschlange	
scorpion ['skɔːpiən]	Skorpion	
black widow [blæk 'wɪdəʊ]	schwarze Witwe	
coyote [kɔɪ'əʊti]	Kojote	
mountain lion ['maʊntɪn ˌlaɪən]	Puma	
sand dune ['sænd ˌdjuːn]	Sanddüne	
paragraph ['pærəˌgrɑːf]	Absatz, Abschnitt	A *paragraph* is a part of a text that begins on a new line.
Find out what each paragraph is about. [faɪnd‿'aʊt wɒt‿iːtʃ ˌpærəgrɑːf ɪz‿əˌbaʊt]	Finde heraus, worum es in jedem Abschnitt geht.	
exist [ɪg'zɪst]	existieren, bestehen	*to exist* = to be real
was established [wɒz‿ɪ'stæblɪʃt]	wurde gegründet	
resident ['rezɪd(ə)nt]	Bewohner/in	A *resident* is someone who lives in a place.
inhabit [ɪn'hæbɪt]	bewohnen	
various ['veəriəs]	verschiedene(r, s)	*various* = different and more than a few
over the years [ˌəʊvə‿ðə‿'jɪəz]	mit den Jahren, im Laufe der Jahre	
recent ['riːsnt]	kürzlich; neueste(r, s); jüngste(r, s); letzte(r, s)	
gape [geɪp]	starren; *hier:* offen stehen	*"gape"* can mean "stare at" but also "be open".
gather ['gæðə]	sammeln	
acorn ['eɪkɔːn]	Eichel	
hunting ['hʌntɪŋ]	Jagen, Jagd	
discovery [dɪ'skʌv(ə)ri]	Entdeckung	
give up [gɪv‿'ʌp]	aufgeben; überlassen	
for years [fə‿'jɪəz]	seit Jahren; jahrelang	
wilderness ['wɪldənəs]	Wildnis	
waterfall ['wɔːtəˌfɔːl]	Wasserfall	
rock [rɒk]	*hier:* Fels(en)	
in order to [ɪn‿'ɔːdə tə]	um zu	
attend [ə'tend]	teilnehmen (an)	
guided tour ['gaɪdəd tʊə]	Führung	
climbing *(no pl)* ['klaɪmɪŋ]	Bergsteigen; Klettern	
among [ə'mʌŋ]	unter	

southeast

$32°F = 0°C$
$0°F = –17{,}8°C$
$50°F = 10°C$

Wenn du Fahrenheit in Celsius umrechnen willst, musst du 32 abziehen und mit 5/9 multiplizieren. Umgekehrt geht es auch: Du multiplizierst die Gradzahl in Celsius mit 9/5 und addierst 32. Probier's mal aus!

$0°C = 32°F$
$100°C = 212°F$

rock

	cliff [klɪf]	Klippe, Kliff	
	giant ['dʒaɪənt]	riesig	*giant* = huge
	sequoia (tree) [sɪ'kwɔɪə]	Sequoia, Mammutbaum	
	squirrel ['skwɪrəl]	Eichhörnchen	
	mule deer ['mjuːl ˌdɪə]	Maultierhirsch	
	bighorn sheep ['bɪghɔːn ˌʃiːp]	Dickhornschaf	
	a variety of [ə və'raɪəti‿əv]	verschiedene	*a variety of* = various
	falcon ['fɔːlkən]	Falke	
	eagle ['iːgl]	Adler	
	admire [əd'maɪə]	bewundern	
B3	**be keen on doing sth** [bi 'kiːn‿ɒn ˌduːɪŋ sʌmθɪŋ]	etw mit Begeisterung tun	
	look forward to doing sth [lʊk 'fɔːwəd tə ˌduːɪŋ sʌmθɪŋ]	sich auf etw freuen	When you're planning to have a party, you're certainly *looking forward to* it.
B4	facilities *(pl)* [fə'sɪlətiz]	Einrichtungen, Anlagen	
	information center *(AE)* [ɪnfə'meɪʃn ˌsentə]	Informationsstelle	information center *(AE)* = information centre *(BE)*
	accommodation *(no pl)* [əˌkɒmə'deɪʃn]	Unterkunft	
B5	carry ['kæri]	*hier:* mitnehmen	
	hike [haɪk]	wandern	
	trail [treɪl]	Weg, Pfad	A *trail* is a narrow road.
	protect [prə'tekt]	schützen	
	can [kæn]	*hier:* Mülleimer	
	last but not least [ˌlɑːst bət nɒt 'liːst]	nicht zu vergessen	 *Protect* the animals!
	ranger ['reɪndʒə]	Aufseher/in, Ranger/in	
	-proof [pruːf]	-sicher	
	locker ['lɒkə]	Schließfach	
	yell [jel]	(laut/gellend) schreien	
	clap one's hands [ˌklæp wʌnz 'hændz]	in die Hände klatschen	
	scare away [ˌskeər‿ə'weɪ]	verscheuchen, abschrecken	
B6	leaflet ['liːflət]	Prospekt	
	location [ləʊ'keɪʃn]	Lage; Standort	This is not the best *location* to have a party. 
	behave [bɪ'heɪv]	sich verhalten	
L1	copy into ['kɒpi‿ˌɪntə]	abschreiben in	
	BC (= before Christ) [ˌbiː'siː]	v. Chr. (vor Christus)	
	AD (= Anno Domini) [ˌeɪ'diː]	n. Chr. (nach Christus)	
L2	form [fɔːm]	Form	
L4	stress [stres]	Stress; *hier:* Betonung	
	syllable ['sɪləbl]	Silbe	The word *syllable* has got three *syl-la-bles.*
C2	ancestor ['ænsestə]	Vorfahr(e)/Vorfahrin	
	pie chart ['paɪ ˌtʃɑːt]	Tortendiagramm	
	figures ['fɪgəz]	*hier:* Zahlen	
	make a comparison [ˌmeɪk‿ə kəm'pærɪsn]	einen Vergleich anstellen	*to make a comparison* = compare
	ancestry ['ænsestri]	Abstammung	
	African American [ˌæfrɪkən‿ə'merɪkən]	Afroamerikaner/in; afroamerikanisch	

	French [frentʃ]	französisch	
	Scottish ['skɒtɪʃ]	schottisch	
C3	home country [həʊm 'kʌntri]	Heimatland	to come into a country because you want to live there = *to immigrate*
	immigrate ['ɪmɪˌgreɪt]	einwandern	
C4	grader ['greɪdə]	*hier:* -klässler	
	Lower Saxony [ˌləʊə 'sæksəni]	Niedersachsen	The capital of *Lower Saxony* is Hanover.
	turmoil ['tɜːmɔɪl]	Tumult, Aufruhr	
	inflation [ɪn'fleɪʃn]	Inflation, Preisauftrieb	
	crisis ['kraɪsɪs]	Krise	
	board a ship [ˌbɔːd‿ə 'ʃɪp]	ein Schiff besteigen	
	e. g. [ˌiː'dʒiː]	z. B. (zum Beispiel)	When you try to *persuade* someone, you often say "please", *e. g.*: Oh, please, come to the party! I don't want to go without you!
	businessman (*pl* -men) ['bɪznəsmæn, 'bɪznəsmen]	Geschäftsmann	
	persuade [pə'sweɪd]	überreden; überzeugen	
	change [tʃeɪndʒ]	*hier:* umsteigen	
	destination [ˌdestɪ'neɪʃn]	(Reise)ziel, Bestimmungs-ort	
	education [ˌedjʊ'keɪʃn]	(Aus)bildung	
	lawyer ['lɔːjə]	Rechtsanwalt/-anwältin	
	traveling (*AE*) ['trævliŋ]	Reisen	traveling (*AE*) = travelling (*BE*)
C5	**nationality** [ˌnæʃə'nælɪti]	Nationalität; Staats-angehörigkeit	
	arithmetic (*no pl*) [ə'rɪθmətɪk]	Arithmetik	
	public school (*AE*) [ˌpʌblik 'skuːl]	staatliche Schule	nation national nationality
	what makes sb tick [wɒt meɪks ˌsʌmbədi 'tɪk]	was jdn bewegt	
	aisle [aɪl]	Gang, Korridor	
	Polish ['pɒlɪʃ]	polnisch	
	Irish ['aɪrɪʃ]	irisch	
	colored (*AE*) ['kʌləd]	farbig	colored (*AE*) = coloured (*BE*)
	Russian ['rʌʃn]	Russe/Russin; russisch	
	Grecian ['griːʃn]	griechisch	
	Noah's ark [ˌnəʊəz‿'ɑːk]	die Arche Noah	
	graduation [ˌgrædʒu'eɪʃn]	Abschluss	
	race [reɪs]	Rasse	
	across from [ə'krɒs frəm]	gegenüber	
	poet ['pəʊɪt]	Dichter	
C6	collage ['kɒlɑːʒ]	Collage	
	math (*AE* = maths *BE*, *informal* = mathematics) [mæθ(s), ˌmæθə'mætɪks]	Mathe	
C7	**make a living** (*no pl*) [meɪk‿ə 'lɪvɪŋ]	seinen Lebensunterhalt verdienen	
	move around [muːv‿ə'raʊnd]	herumgehen; umherreisen	
	van (*AE*) [væn]	Kleinbus, Minibus	
	cotton ['kɒtn]	Baumwolle	
	labor camp (*AE*) ['leɪbə kæmp]	Arbeitslager	labor camp (*AE*) = labour camp (*BE*)
	year after year [jɪə‿ˌɑːftə‿'jɪə]	Jahr für Jahr	
	back in (+ *Jahreszahl*) ['bæk‿ɪn]	schon …	

I live in a house *across from* the park.

She *makes a living* as a teacher.

leave behind [liːv bɪ'haɪnd]	zurücklassen	 This woman is living in *poverty*.
poverty ['pɒvəti]	Armut	
sparkle ['spɑːkl]	funkeln, glitzern	
whenever [wen'evə]	jedes Mal, wenn …	
stick out [stɪk‿'aʊt]	(her)ausstrecken	
garage ['gærɑːʒ]	Garage	
stable ['steɪbl]	Stall, Box	
head for ['hed fə]	zusteuern auf	
vineyard ['vɪnjəd]	Weinberg	He *is covered in sweat.* 
pick grapes [pɪk 'greɪpz]	Trauben lesen	
degree [dɪ'griː]	Grad; Maß	
be covered in/with sweat [bi 'kʌvəd ɪn/wɪð ˌswet]	in Schweiß gebadet sein	
handkerchief ['hæŋkəˌtʃɪf]	Taschentuch	
row [rəʊ]	Reihe	
have/take a break [hæv/teɪk‿ə 'breɪk]	eine Pause machen	 He's *having a break.*
walnut tree ['wɔːlnʌt triː]	Walnussbaum	
number ['nʌmbə]	*hier:* Anzahl	
turn pale [tɜːn 'peɪl]	blass werden	
whisper ['wɪspə]	flüstern	
alarm [ə'lɑːm]	Angst, Beunruhigung	
get in(to) trouble [ˌget‿ɪn 'trʌbl]	in Schwierigkeiten geraten	When you steal, you will *get into trouble.*
neat [niːt]	ordentlich, sauber	
dressed [drest]	angezogen; gekleidet	
insect ['ɪnsekt]	Insekt	
dust *(no pl)* [dʌst]	Staub	
ever so *(informal)* ['evə səʊ]	wahnsinnig *(als Verstärkung)*	
shadow ['ʃædəʊ]	Schatten	A *shadow* is a dark area.
within [wɪð'ɪn]	innerhalb	
figure ['fɪgə]	*hier:* ausrechnen	
cross out [krɒs‿'aʊt]	aus-, durchstreichen	
take a shower [teɪk‿ə 'ʃaʊə]	duschen	
underneath [ˌʌndə'niːθ]	unter	
water hose ['wɔːtə həʊz]	Wasserschlauch	
wake up [weɪk‿'ʌp]	aufwachen	
keep one's head down ['kiːp wʌnz ˌhed‿daʊn]	den Kopf einziehen	
look up [lʊk‿'ʌp]	nach oben sehen	
face sb ['feɪs ˌsʌmbədi]	sich jdm zuwenden, zu jdm blicken	
be over [bi‿'əʊvə]	vorbei sein	
sometime ['sʌmtaɪm]	irgendwann	*sometime* = at a time that you do not know exactly
migrant ['maɪgrənt]	Wanderarbeiter-	
L2 synonym ['sɪnənɪm]	Synonym	
L4 spelling ['spelɪŋ]	Rechtschreibung	
grid [grɪd]	Gitter; *hier:* Tabelle	
state school ['steɪt ˌskuːl]	staatliche Schule	
labor *(AE)* ['leɪbə]	Arbeit	labor *(AE)* = labour *(BE)*
year [jɪə]	*hier:* Klasse	

Die Vokabeln aus den OPTIONAL-Teilen findest du im englisch-deutschen Dictionary auf den Seiten 200–227!

Theme 3 – The world in a city

A1	adventurous [əd'ventʃ(ə)rəs]	abenteuerlich; abenteuerlustig	If you are *adventurous*, you love to have adventures.
	curious ['kjʊəriəs]	neugierig	
	timid ['tɪmɪd]	ängstlich, schüchtern	
	vagabond ['vægəˌbɒnd]	Vagabunden-	
	long (to/for) [lɒŋ]	sich sehnen (nach)	
	stray [streɪ]	streunen; umherstreifen	 The tiger *has strayed.*
	right through the very heart ['rɑɪt θruː ðə ˌveri hɑːt]	genau mitten durch	
	be (at the) top of the heap [biː 'tɒp‿əv ðə ˌhiːp]	zu den Gewinnern zählen	
	little town blues ['lɪtl taʊn ˌbluːz]	*hier etwa: kleinstädtischer Frust*	
	melt (away) [melt]	(dahin)schmelzen	My ice cream *is melting* in the sun.
	brand-new [brændnjuː]	brandneu	
	make it *(informal)* ['meɪk‿ˌɪt]	es schaffen	
	be up to sb/sth [biː‿'ʌp tə ˌsʌmbədi, sʌmθɪŋ]	von jdm/etw abhängen	
	lyrics *(pl)* ['lɪrɪks]	(Lied)text	
	expression [ɪk'spreʃn]	Ausdruck, Äußerung	
	boot [buːt]	Stiefel	A *boot* is a type of shoe that covers your foot and part of your leg.
	succeed [sək'siːd]	Erfolg haben, erfolgreich sein	
A2	**take a photo** [ˌteɪk‿ə 'fəʊtəʊ]	fotografieren, ein Foto machen	
A3	The Big Apple *(informal)* [ðə‿bɪg‿'æpl]	New York	
	the British *(pl)* [ðə 'brɪtɪʃ]	die Briten	
	conquer ['kɒŋkə]	erobern; besiegen	
	no matter where … from [nəʊ 'mætə weə frəm]	ganz gleich woher …	*"No matter where* you come *from …"* = It makes no difference where you come from.
	borough ['bʌrə]	Verwaltungsbezirk	
	step [step]	*hier:* Stufe	
	both … and ['bəʊθ ˌənd]	sowohl … als auch …	*Both* he *and* his brother work at the theatre.
	decay [dɪ'keɪ]	verfallen	
	Italy ['ɪtəli]	Italien	theater *(AE)* = theatre *(BE)*
	Ireland ['aɪələnd]	Irland	
A4	means of transport [ˌmiːnz‿əv 'trænspɔːt]	Transportmittel	
	cruise [kruːz]	Kreuzfahrt	
	pier [pɪə]	Pier, Hafendamm; Landungsbrücke	
	sail [seɪl]	*(mit dem Schiff)* fahren; segeln	 This man often *sails* to America.
	magnificent [mæg'nɪfɪsnt]	wunderbar, großartig	
	on board [ɒn bɔːd]	an Bord	
	senior citizens *(pl)* [ˌsiːniə 'sɪtɪznz]	ältere Menschen	
	hop on [hɒp‿'ɒn]	schnell einsteigen	
	hop off [hɒp‿'ɒf]	schnell aussteigen	
	touring ['tuːrɪŋ]	Reisen	
	classic ['klæsɪk]	klassisch	
	double-decker bus [ˌdʌbldekə 'bʌs]	Doppeldecker(bus)	A *double-decker bus* has got two decks.

as you please [ˌæz‿jə 'pliːz]	wie es dir/Ihnen gefällt	
continue [kən'tɪnjuː]	fortführen; fortsetzen	
admission [əd'mɪʃn]	Eintritt	
helicopter ['helɪˌkɒptə]	Hubschrauber	
experience [ɪk'spɪəriəns]	erleben; kennen lernen	
downtown [ˌdaʊn'taʊn]	Innenstadt-	
through *(AE)* [θruː]	*hier:* bis	
am (= ante meridiem) [eɪ em]	morgens, vormittags *(nur hinter Uhrzeit zwischen Mitternacht und 12 Uhr mittags)*	
pm (= post meridiem) [ˌpiː'em, 'pəʊst məˌrɪdɪəm]	nachmittags, abends *(nur hinter Uhrzeit zwischen 12 Uhr mittags und Mitternacht)*	*pm* = in the afternoon or in the evening
Saturdays ['sætədeɪz]	samstags	
special offer [ˌspeʃl 'ɒfə]	Sonderangebot	
offer ['ɒfə]	Angebot	
explore [ɪk'splɔː]	erforschen, erkunden	*to explore* = to travel around an area to learn about it
historic [hɪ'stɒrɪk]	historisch	
site [saɪt]	Stelle, Platz	
setting ['setɪŋ]	Lage; Schauplatz	harbor *(AE)* = harbour *(BE)*
harbor *(AE)* ['hɑːbə]	Hafen	
immigration [ˌɪmɪ'greɪʃn]	Einwanderung	He's standing on the *shore.* 
shore [ʃɔː]	Küste; Ufer; Strand	
financial district [faɪ'nænʃl ˌdɪstrɪkt]	Finanzbezirk	
grounds *(npl)* [graʊndz]	Anlagen	
seaport ['siːˌpɔːt]	Seehafen	
movie *(AE)* ['muːvi]	Kino-, Film-	
destination [ˌdestɪ'neɪʃn]	(Reise)ziel; *hier:* Schauplatz	*destination* = the place where someone is going
film [fɪlm]	filmen, drehen	
camera ['kæm(ə)rə]	Kamera, Fotoapparat; *hier:* Aufnahme	
screen [skriːn]	Leinwand; Bildschirm	What you see on a *screen* is not always reality.
see [siː]	*hier:* ansehen, besichtigen	
apartment [ə'pɑːtmənt]	Wohnung	
false [fɔːls]	falsch	*false* ≠ true
the Rhine *(no pl)* [ðə ˌraɪn]	der Rhein	
single decker [ˌsɪŋgl 'dekə]	Bus *(mit einem Deck)*	
A6 transport ['trænspɔːt]	Transport; Verkehrsmittel	**Reimwörter** Damit du dir besser merken kannst, wie bestimmte Wörter ausgesprochen werden, suche Reimwörter für sie. Dir wird auffallen, dass die Reimwörter nicht immer dieselbe Schreibweise haben.
L1 present progressive [ˌpreznt prəʊ'gresɪv]	Verlaufsform (des) Präsens	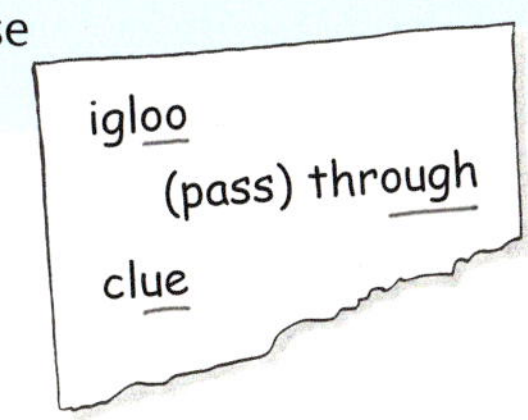
L3 present perfect [ˌpreznt 'pɜːfɪkt]	Perfekt	
subway *(AE)* ['sʌbˌweɪ]	Unterführung, U-Bahn	
organization [ˌɔːgənaɪ'zeɪʃn]	Organisation	
non-profit [ˌnɒn'prɒfɪt]	gemeinnützig	
PP2 lasso *(pl -s or -es)* [lə'suː]	Lasso	
French [frentʃ]	Französisch	
igloo ['ɪgluː]	Iglu	

tepee ['tiːpiː]	Indianerzelt	
Sioux [suː]	*(indian. Sprache)*	
Dakota [de'kəʊtə]	*(indian. Sprache)*	
moccasin ['mɒkəsɪn]	Mokassin	
Algonquian [æl'gɒŋkwiən]	Algonkin *(indian. Sprache)*	
tobacco *(no pl)* [tə'bækəʊ]	Tabak	
possibly ['pɒsəbli]	möglicherweise, vielleicht	*possibly* = perhaps = maybe
Caribbean [ˌkærɪ'biːən]	karibisch	
raccoon [rə'kuːn]	Waschbär/in	
settler ['setlə]	Siedler/in	A *settler* is someone who goes to live in a place where not many people live.
European [ˌjʊərə'piːən]	Europäer/in, europäisch	
survive [sə'vaɪv]	überleben	
in English [ɪn‿'ɪŋglɪʃ]	auf Englisch	
grow apart [grəʊ ə'pɑːt]	sich auseinander leben; *hier:* sich voneinander entfernen	

B1

liberty ['lɪbəti]	Freiheit	
sight [saɪt]	*hier:* Anblick	
process sb ['prəʊses ˌsʌmbədi]	jdn abfertigen	
pass through [pɑːs 'θruː]	durchlaufen; *hier:* passieren	
refuse [rɪ'fjuːz]	ablehnen; verweigern	
entry ['entri]	*hier:* Einreise	
unfortunate [ʌn'fɔːtʃ(ə)nət]	unglücklich; bedauerlich	
support oneself [sə'pɔːt wʌnˌself]	seinen Lebensunterhalt bestreiten	
medical ['medɪkl]	medizinisch; ärztlich	
inspector [ɪn'spektə]	Inspektor/in	
insanity *(no pl)* [ɪn'sænəti]	Wahnsinn, Geisteskrankheit	
inspect [ɪn'spekt]	untersuchen; kontrollieren	
novel ['nɒvl]	Roman	
eyewitness ['aɪˌwɪtnəs]	Augenzeuge/-zeugin	
straighten ['streɪtn]	gerade machen	
-crooked ['krʊkɪd]	krumm	
rub [rʌb]	reiben	
cheek [tʃiːk]	Wange, Backe	
run through sth [rʌn 'θruː ˌsʌmθɪŋ]	durchgehen; *hier:* durch etw durchfahren	
beard [bɪəd]	Bart	
regret [rɪ'gret]	bedauern	
shave [ʃeɪv]	sich rasieren	
caress [kə'res]	streicheln	
ringlet ['rɪŋlət]	Locke	
push [pʊʃ]	schieben	
fragment ['frægmənt]	Splitter; Brocken	
Sir [sə]	(mein) Herr *(Anrede)*	
by [baɪ]	*hier:* von	
lame [leɪm]	lahm	
wheezy ['wiːzi]	keuchend	
anarchist ['ænəkɪst]	Anarchist/in	
make/have a try at [meɪk/hæv‿ə 'traɪ‿ət]	versuchen	
brains *(pl)* [breɪnz]	Intelligenz, Grips	
afford [ə'fɔːd]	sich leisten	

The *unfortunate* people who were living here had to leave their homes.

They had to *push* the car.

	chalk [tʃɔːk]	Kalkstein; Kreide
	lung [lʌŋ]	Lungenflügel
	collapse [kə'læps]	zusammenbrechen
	cough [kɒf]	husten
	lameness *(no pl)* ['leɪmnes]	Lähmung
	chalk [tʃɔːk]	mit Kreide schreiben
	mental ['mentl]	geistig; *hier:* verrückt
	percent *(AE)* [pə 'sent]	Prozent
	database ['deɪtəˌbeɪs]	Datenbank
	quote [kwəʊt]	zitieren; nennen
	fulfill *(AE)* [fʊl'fɪl]	erfüllen
B2	in other words [ɪn‿'ʌðər ˌwɜːdz]	mit anderen Worten
	deny [dɪ'naɪ]	abstreiten; *hier:* verweigern
B3	profile ['prəʊfaɪl]	Profil; Porträt
	who [huː]	*hier:* der/die/das
	SS (= steamship) [ˌes'es]	Dampfschiff
	coin [kɔɪn]	Münze, Geldstück
	Colonel ['kɜːnl]	(Herr) Oberst
	unveil [ʌn'veɪl]	enthüllen
	ceremony ['serəməni]	Zeremonie, Feier
	Austria ['ɒstriə]	Österreich
	award [ə'wɔːd]	verleihen
	universe ['juːnɪˌvɜːs]	Universum
	grant [grɑːnt]	gewähren
	citizenship ['sɪtɪznʃɪp]	Staatsbürgerschaft
	elect [ɪ'lekt]	wählen
	Governor ['gʌv(ə)nə]	Gouverneur
	Sicily ['sɪsɪli]	Sizilien
	organized crime *(no pl)* [ˌɔːgənaɪzd 'kraɪm]	organisiertes Verbrechen
	shoplifting *(no pl)* ['ʃɒpˌlɪftɪŋ]	Ladendiebstahl
	sentence sb to sth ['sentəns ˌsʌmbədi tə ˌsʌmθɪŋ]	jdn zu etw verurteilen
	release [rɪ'liːs]	freilassen; entlassen
	deport [dɪ'pɔːt]	ausweisen
	Silesia [saɪ'liːziə]	Schlesien
	doctorate ['dɒkt(ə)rət]	Doktor, Doktortitel
	theoretical [ˌθɪə'retɪkl]	theoretisch
	physics ['fɪzɪks]	Physik
	name [neɪm]	*hier:* ernennen
	professor [prə'fesə]	Professor/in
	Nobel Prize [nəʊˌbel 'praɪz]	Nobelpreis
B4	**search (on) the Internet** [ˌsɜːtʃ ði‿'ɪntənet]	im Internet suchen
	instruct [ɪn'strʌkt]	anweisen
	darling ['dɑːlɪŋ]	Liebling, Schatz
	attic ['ætɪk]	Dachboden, Speicher
	make sb do sth [ˌmeɪk sʌmbədi 'duː sʌmθɪŋ]	jdn dazu bringen, etw zu tun
	great-grandpa *(informal)* [ˌgreɪt'grænpɑː]	Uropa
	as far as [əz 'fɑːr‿əz]	soweit
	rebellion [rɪ'beljən]	Rebellion; Aufstand
	gun [gʌn]	(Schuss)waffe, Pistole

percent *(AE)* = per cent *(BE)*
fulfill *(AE)* = fulfil *(BE)*

Spiel: Relativsatz-Rallye
Mit Relativsätzen kannst du Dinge oder Gegenstände näher beschreiben – dass diese Beschreibung nicht nach einem Satz enden muss, beweist dieses Spiel!
Ihr könnt entweder in einer kleinen Gruppe (z. B. zu viert) oder in zwei größeren Gruppen gegeneinander spielen. Ein Mitspieler bzw. eine Gruppe beginnt einen Satz, danach hängt der nächste Spieler einen Relativsatz an, usw. Welche Gruppe fährt das längste Rennen?
Beispiel: This is Mr Miller – who teaches English – which is my favourite subject – …

These people would like to *be released.*

Many people who work at universities are *professors.*

Your grandfather's father is your *great-grandpa.*

	force sb (to do sth) ['fɔːs ˌsʌmbədi]	jdn zwingen (etw zu tun)	 Look, this is my *great-grandma*!
	great-grandma *(informal)* [ˌgreɪt'grænma]	Uroma	
	turn back sb [ˌtɜːn 'bæk sʌmbədi]	jdn zurückschicken, zurückweisen	
	used to … (+ *infinitive*) ['juːsd tə]	früher …	When I was young, I played tennis. I *used to* play tennis.
	Gaelic ['geɪlɪk]	gälisch	
	native speaker [ˌneɪtɪv 'spiːkə]	Muttersprachler/in	
B5	great-grandfather [ˌgreɪt'grænˌfɑːðə]	Urgroßvater	*great-grandfather* = great-grandpa
B6	face down [ˌfeɪs 'daʊn]	mit dem Gesicht nach unten; *hier:* mit dem Text nach unten	
	year of birth [ˌjɪər‿əv 'bɜːθ]	Geburtsjahr	
	place of birth [ˌpleɪs‿əv 'bɜːθ]	Geburtsort	What's your *place of birth*?
L3	passive ['pæsɪv]	Passiv	
	Poland ['pəʊlənd]	Polen	
	the Czech Republic [tʃek rɪ'pʌblɪk]	die Tschechische Republik	
	smuggle ['smʌgl]	schmuggeln	
	colleague ['kɒliːg]	(Arbeits-)kollege/kollegin, Mitarbeiter/in	
	fall in love (with) [ˌfɔːl‿ɪn 'lʌv]	sich verlieben (in)	They *have fallen in love.* 
L4	accent ['æksnt]	Akzent; Betonung	
	note down [nəʊt 'daʊn]	(sich) notieren	
C1	spot [spɒt]	entdecken	
	opposite ['ɒpəzɪt]	gegenüber(liegend)	*opposite* = across from
	get into sth [get‿'ɪntə ˌsʌmθɪŋ]	in etw (ein)steigen	
	limousine [ˌlɪmə'ziːn]	(Luxus)limousine; Kleinbus	
	have a ride *(AE, informal)* [ˌhæv‿ə 'raɪd]	mitgenommen werden	
	ride [raɪd]	*hier:* Mitfahrgelegenheit	
	sth is up *(informal)* [ˌsʌmθɪŋ‿ɪz‿'ʌp]	hier stimmt etw nicht	
	man [mæn]	Mensch!, Mann!	
	beside [bɪ'saɪd]	neben	*beside* = at the side of someone or something and close to them
	dude *(informal)* [duːd]	*feiner Pinkel; Typ*	
	block [blɒk]	Block; *hier:* Häuserblock	
	step out [step‿'aʊt]	weggehen; *hier:* aussteigen	
	ride *(AE, informal)* [raɪd]	fahrbarer Untersatz	
	grin [grɪn]	grinsen	
	cheerfully ['tʃɪəf(ə)li]	fröhlich, vergnügt	
	reply [rɪ'plaɪ]	antworten, erwidern	*reply* = answer
	threads *(informal)* [θreds]	Zeug	
	bro (= brother, *AE informal*) [brəʊ, 'brʌðə]	Bruder	
	in fact [ɪn 'fækt]	tatsächlich	*In fact*, she's right! = What she says is really true.
	sure *(AE, informal)* [ʃʊə]	echt	
	feel uneasy [fiːl 'ʌn'iːzi]	sich unbehaglich fühlen	

	flash by [flæʃ 'baɪ]	vorbeirasen	 He's sitting on the *passenger seat.*
	passenger seat ['pæsɪndʒə siːt]	Beifahrersitz	
	play hooky *(informal)* [pleɪ 'hʊki]	die Schule schwänzen	
	final ['faɪnl]	letzte(r, s)	
	practice ['præktɪs]	Übung(sstunde)	
	annoyed [ə'nɔɪd]	verärgert	
	voice [vɔɪs]	Stimme	
	be the sharpest knife in the drawer *(informal)* [bi ðə ˌʃɑːpəst naɪf ɪn ðə 'drɔːə]	*etwa: der/die Hellste sein*	She's *annoyed* because her neighbour is talking all the time.
	talk back [tɔːk 'bæk]	eine freche Antwort geben	
	keep one's mouth shut ['kiːp wʌnz ˌmaʊθ ʃʌt]	den Mund halten	
	shut [ʃʌt]	schließen, *hier:* abstellen	
	rob [rɒb]	bestehlen; (aus)rauben	He *is robbing a bank.* 
	bank [bæŋk]	Bank *(Geld)*	
	kidnap ['kɪdnæp]	entführen	
	anxious ['æŋkʃəs]	besorgt	
	Blvd (= boulevard) ['buːləˌvɑːd]	Boulevard, Prachtstraße	
	pull over [pʊl‿'əʊvə]	zur Seite fahren	
	marine [mə'riːn]	Marinesoldat/in	
	nearby [ˌnɪə'baɪ]	in der Nähe gelegen	
	pause [pɔːz]	eine (kurze) Pause machen, innehalten	*to pause* = to stop for a moment
	second ['sekənd]	Sekunde	A *second* is one of the 60 parts in a minute.
	sidewalk *(AE)* ['saɪdˌwɔːk]	Bürgersteig	*"Sidewalk"* is the American English word for "pavement".
	left [left]	linke(r, s)	
	Move it! *(informal)* ['muːv‿ɪt]	Beweg dich!	
	shout at sb ['ʃaʊt‿æt ˌsʌmbədi]	jdn anschreien	In a minute, she'll probably *shout at* her neighbours. 
	passenger ['pæsɪndʒə]	Fahrgast; *hier:* Beifahrer	
	right [raɪt]	völlig; *hier:* genau, direkt	
	pretend [prɪ'tend]	vorgeben, vortäuschen	
	stumble ['stʌmbl]	stolpern, straucheln	
	thumb lock ['θʌm ˌlɒk]	*Technik beim Judo*	
	practice *(AE)* ['præktɪs]	üben	
	belt [belt]	Gürtel	
	judo ['dʒuːdəʊ]	Judo	practice *(AE)* = practise *(BE)*
	somehow ['sʌmhaʊ]	irgendwie	
	The lights went out. *(informal)* [ðə ˌlaɪts went‿'aʊt]	*hier:* Ich kippte um.	
C2	ending ['endɪŋ]	Ende, Schluss	*ending* ≠ beginning
C3	slap [slæp]	schlagen; ohrfeigen	
	awake [ə'weɪk]	wach	
	closed [kləʊzd]	geschlossen, zu	*closed* ≠ open
	fare [feə]	Fahrpreis	When something is *closed*, you can't get in.
	shocking ['ʃɒkɪŋ]	schockierend; völlig überraschend	
	amusing [ə'mjuːzɪŋ]	amüsant, unterhaltsam	
	to my mind [tə maɪ 'maɪnd]	meiner Meinung nach	*to my mind* = in my opinion
C4	**attack** [ə'tæk]	angreifen	
	control [kən'trəʊl]	kontrollieren	

C5	**reputation** [ˌrepjʊ'teɪʃn]	Ruf	He doesn't have a good *reputation.* = People don't think that he is a good person.
	sadly ['sædli]	bedauerlicherweise, leider	
	firstly ['fɜːstli]	erstens	
	get by (with) [get 'baɪ]	auskommen (mit)	
	secondly ['sekəndli]	zweitens	
	healthcare *(no pl)* ['helθˌkeə]	Gesundheitsfürsorge	
	treatment ['triːtmənt]	Behandlung	neighbor *(AE)* = neighbour *(BE)*
	dentist ['dentɪst]	Zahnarzt/ärztin	*Dentists* look after your teeth.
	be in bad shape [bi‿ɪn 'bæd ˌʃeɪp]	in schlechtem Zustand sein	
	toothache ['tuːθeɪk]	Zahnschmerzen	I've got really bad *toothache. (BE)* I've got really bad *toothaches. (AE)*
	crime [kraɪm]	Verbrechen; Kriminalität	
	metal detector ['metl dɪˌtektə]	Metalldetektor	
	tons *(informal)* [tʌnz]	jede Menge	
	rich [rɪtʃ]	*hier:* vielfältig	
	in the end [ɪn ði‿'end]	letzten Endes; schließlich	*in the end* = finally
	every few ... *(informal)* ['evri‿fjuː ...]	alle paar ...	
	afterwards ['ɑːftəwədz]	später, danach	When you eat in a restaurant, you often have an ice cream or another dessert *afterwards.*
	keep up [kiːp‿'ʌp]	hoch halten; *hier:* erhalten	
	run-down [ˌrʌn'daʊn]	heruntergekommen	
	nowadays ['naʊəˌdeɪz]	heutzutage	
	be second to none [bi ˌsekənd tə 'nʌn]	unvergleichlich sein	
	southern ['sʌðən]	südlich, Süd-	*southern* = in or from the south of a country or region
	sense of community [sens‿əv kə'mjuːnəti]	Gemeinschaftsgefühl	
	stick together ['stɪk təˌgeðə]	zusammenhalten	
	be close to sb [bi‿'kləʊs tə‿ˌsʌmbədi]	jdm (sehr) nahestehen	
	prejudice ['predʒʊdɪs]	Vorurteil	
	sum up [ˌsʌm‿'ʌp]	zusammenfassen	
	suffer from ['sʌfə frəm]	leiden an/unter	
	unemployment *(no pl)* [ˌʌnɪm'plɔɪmənt]	Arbeitslosigkeit	
	community spirit [kə'mjuːnəti ˌspɪrɪt]	Gemeinschaftsgeist	
	put up with [pʊt‿'ʌp wɪð]	sich abfinden mit	*put up with* = accept someone or something that is not nice
C7	**housing** *(no pl)* ['haʊzɪŋ]	Wohnungen	
	argumentation *(no pl)* [ˌɑːgjʊmen'teɪʃ(ə)n]	Argumentation	
L1	give an opinion (on sth) [gɪv‿ən‿ə'pɪnjən]	seine Meinung (zu etw) äußern	
L4	the odd one out [ði‿ˌɒd wʌn‿'aʊt]	das fünfte Rad am Wagen; *hier: das Wort, das nicht zu den anderen passt*	
	pavement ['peɪvmənt]	Gehsteig, Bürgersteig	

Randolph is *suffering from* a bad cold.

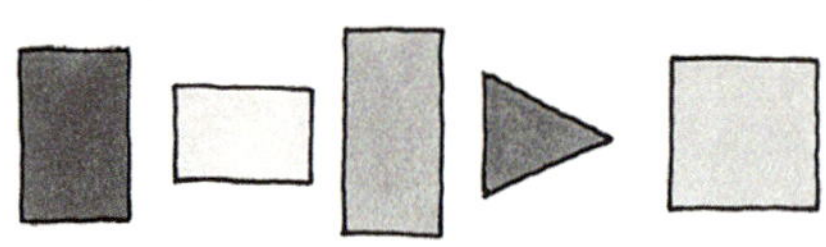

Which is the *odd one out?*

Die Vokabeln aus den OPTIONAL-Teilen findest du im englisch-deutschen Dictionary auf den Seiten 200–227!

Theme 4 – On the move

	be on the move [bi‿ɒn ðə 'muːv]	unterwegs sein; sich im Umbruch befinden	
A1	**return** [rɪ'tɜːn]	Rückkehr	*return* = a situation in which you go back to a place or come back from a place
	innocence *(no pl)* ['ɪnəs(ə)ns]	Unschuld, Arglosigkeit	
	vanish ['vænɪʃ]	verschwinden; verloren gehen	
	avarice *(no pl)* ['ævərɪs]	(Hab)gier, Habsucht	
	oppression *(no pl)* [ə'preʃn]	Unterdrückung	
A2	**natural** ['nætʃ(ə)rəl]	natürlich	
	environment [ɪn'vaɪrənmənt]	Umgebung; Umwelt	The *natural environment* of a penguin is water and ice.
	push into sth ['pʊʃ ˌɪntə sʌmθɪŋ]	sich Zugang zu etw verschaffen	
	belief [bɪ'liːf]	Glaube; Überzeugung	
	by [baɪ]	*hier:* indem	
	reservation [ˌrezə'veɪʃn]	Reservat	
	infertile [ɪn'fɜːtaɪl]	unfruchtbar	
	Indian ['ɪndiən]	Indianer/in, indianisch	
	territory ['terətri]	Gebiet, Territorium	
	warrior ['wɒriə]	Krieger	
	simple ['sɪmpl]	einfach	I am a man of *simple* taste. I only accept the best. *(Oscar Wilde)*
	hunter ['hʌntə]	Jäger/in	
	fisherman (*pl* -men) ['fɪʃəmən]	Fischer; Angler	
	mostly ['məʊstli]	meistens; größtenteils	
	be seen as [biː 'siːn‿əs]	angesehen werden als	
	separate ['sep(ə)rət]	getrennt, separat	
A3	**now** [naʊ]	*hier:* heute	
A4	**member** ['membə]	Angehörige/r; Mitglied	
	for (+ *Zeitspanne*) [fə]	seit …; … lang	 There are three *generations* of our family in this picture.
	generation [ˌdʒenə'reɪʃn]	Generation	
	improve [ɪm'pruːv]	besser werden; sich verbessern	
	depressive [dɪ'presɪv]	depressiv	
	alcohol ['ælkəˌhɒl]	Alkohol	
	despite [dɪ'spaɪt]	trotz	
	not anywhere else [nɒt ˌeniweər‿'els]	nirgendwo anders (hin)	
	seminar ['semɪˌnɑː]	Seminar	
	minority [maɪ'nɒrəti]	Minderheit, Minderheiten-	A *minority* is a small number of people or things that are part of a larger group but different in some way from most of the group.
	Native Rights [neɪtɪv 'raɪts]	*hier:* Rechte der amerik. Ureinwohner/innen	
	one day [wʌn 'deɪ]	eines Tages	
	Third World [ˌθɜːd 'wɜːld]	Dritte Welt	
	one third [wʌn 'θɜːd]	ein Drittel	
	infant [ˌɪnfənt]	Säugling	
	mortality rate [mɔː'tæləti reɪt]	Sterblichkeitsrate	
	life expectancy [ˌlaɪf ɪk'spektənsi]	Lebenserwartung	
	average ['æv(ə)rɪdʒ]	Durchschnitt	
	suicide rate ['suːɪsaɪd ˌreɪt]	Selbstmordrate	
	pregnancy ['pregnənsi]	Schwangerschaft	

	attract [ə'trækt]	anziehen	Nessie *attracts* many tourists. 
	gain [geɪn]	bekommen	
	start up [stɑːt‿'ʌp]	gründen; *hier:* aufmachen	
A5	**law** [lɔː]	Jura, Jura-	
A6	make sb aware of sth ['meɪk sʌmbədi‿əˌweər‿əv ˌsʌmθɪŋ]	jdm etw bewusst machen	
	get in touch with [get‿ɪn 'tʌtʃ wɪð]	in Kontakt treten mit	
	opportunity [ˌɒpə'tjuːnəti]	Gelegenheit	
A7	footpath ['fʊtˌpɑːθ]	Fußweg	
	exist [ɪg'zɪst]	existieren, bestehen	
	recapture sth [riː'kæptʃə ˌsʌmθɪŋ]	*hier:* etw wieder lebendig werden lassen	
	path [pɑːθ]	Weg, Pfad	
	settlement ['setlmənt]	Siedlung	
	Dutch [dʌtʃ]	holländisch, niederländisch	
	inch [ɪntʃ]	Zoll (2,54 cm)	
	which [wɪtʃ]	*hier:* was	 one *inch*
	pass through [pɑːs 'θruː]	*hier:* durchkommen	
	trader ['treɪdə]	Händler/in	
	widen ['waɪdn]	verbreitern; erweitern	
	contact ['kɒntækt]	Kontakt	Das Längenmaß "inch" (Zoll) entspricht 2,54 cm. Man sieht es oft abgekürzt dargestellt: 1″ = 1 inch
	from [frəm]	wegen, aufgrund von	
	the Dutch *(pl)* [ðə 'dʌtʃ]	die Holländer/Niederländer	
	peace conference ['piːs ˌkɒnf(ə)rəns]	Friedenskonferenz	
	leader ['liːdə]	Leiter/in, Führer/in	A *leader* is someone who is responsible for a group or in control of a group. He or she leads it.
	guilty ['gɪlti]	schuldig	
	break out [breɪk‿'aʊt]	ausbrechen	
	march [mɑːtʃ]	marschieren	
	take control of sth [teɪk kən'trəʊl‿əv ˌsʌmθɪŋ]	die Gewalt über etw übernehmen	
	take over [teɪk‿'əʊvə]	übernehmen	
	once [wʌns]	*hier:* früher, einst	
	totally ['təʊtli]	völlig, total	*totally* = completely
	wipe out [waɪp‿'aʊt]	auswischen; auslöschen	
	strength *(no pl)* [streŋθ]	Kraft, Stärke	
	blame (sb for sth) ['bleɪm ˌsʌmbədi fə ˌsʌmθɪŋ]	(jdm) die Schuld (an etw) geben	
	aim (at) [eɪm]	zielen (auf)	
	avoid [ə'vɔɪd]	(ver)meiden	*avoid* = keep away from
A8	overhear [ˌəʊvə'hɪə]	zufällig mithören	
B1	atmosphere ['ætməsˌfɪə]	Atmosphäre; Stimmung	
	argument ['ɑːgjʊmənt]	Argument	This man is *panning for gold*. He hopes to find a big *gold nugget*. 
	pan for gold [pæn fə 'gəʊld]	nach Gold schürfen	
	gold nugget ['gəʊld nʌgɪt]	Goldnugget	
	hundreds of thousands of [ˌhʌndrədz‿əv 'θaʊzndz‿əv]	Hunderttausende von	
	make one's way [meɪk wʌnz 'weɪ]	sich auf den Weg machen	
	across [ə'krɒs]	*hier:* quer durch	*across* = from one side to the other
	west [west]	westwärts, nach Westen	A *port* is an area of water where ships stop. A harbour is the same thing, but a *port* is bigger than a harbour.
	wagon train ['wægən ˌtreɪn]	Wagenkolonne	
	worker ['wɜːkə]	Arbeiter/in	
	port [pɔːt]	Hafen	

	English	German	Example
	sailor ['seɪlə]	Matrose, Seemann	
	period ['pɪəriəd]	Zeitspanne, Zeitraum	The dog *is digging for* a bone.
	the Union [ði‿'juːnjən]	die Nation	
B2	(gold) digger ['dɪɡə]	Goldgräber	
	dig (for) [dɪɡ]	graben (nach); *hier:* schürfen	
	Irishman (*pl* -men) ['aɪriʃmæn, 'aɪriʃmen]	Ire	
	wave [weɪv]	Welle	
	alive [ə'laɪv]	lebendig, lebend	*to be alive* = to live
	state [steɪt]	Zustand; körperliche Verfassung	
	scurvy *(no pl)* ['skɜːvi]	Skorbut *(Krankheit)*	
	riverbank ['rɪvəˌbæŋk]	Flussufer	
	stream [striːm]	Bach	A *stream* is a small narrow river.
	strike it rich *(informal)* ['straɪk‿ɪt rɪtʃ]	einen Glückstreffer landen und reich werden	
	yeah *(informal)* [jeə]	ja(wohl)	
	murder ['mɜːdə]	ermorden, umbringen	
	claim [kleɪm]	*Anteil an einem Goldgräberunternehmen*	
	lie [laɪ]	lügen	tell the truth ⟷ *lie*
	gamble ['ɡæmbl]	(um Geld) spielen	
	stop [stɒp]	*hier:* abhalten	
	be out of hand [biˌaʊt‿ɒf 'hænd]	außer Kontrolle sein	
	cope (with) [kəʊp]	zurechtkommen, fertig werden mit	
	make [meɪk]	*hier:* gewinnen	
	bet [bet]	setzen, wetten	
	goldfield ['ɡəʊldˌfiːld]	Goldfeld	
	gamble ['ɡæmbl]	Risiko, Wagnis	
	Nothing ventured, nothing gained. [nʌθɪŋ ˌventʃəd nʌθɪŋ 'ɡeɪnd]	Wer wagt, gewinnt., Frisch gewagt ist halb gewonnen.	
B4	populated ['pɒpjʊˌleɪtɪd]	bevölkert	
	communication [kəˌmjuːnɪ'keɪʃn]	Kommunikation, Verständigung	
	across [ə'krɒs]	*hier:* überall in	
	mail *(AE, no pl)* [meɪl]	Post	
	rider ['raɪdə]	Reiter/in	 She's a *rider*.
B5	wanted ['wɒntɪd]	erwünscht; gesucht	
	the undersigned [ðə 'ʌndəˌsaɪnd]	der/die Unterzeichnete *(förmlich)*	
	dozen ['dʌzn]	Dutzend	 a *dozen* eggs
	management of *(no pl)* ['mænɪdʒmənt‿əv]	Umgang mit	
	hostler (= ostler) ['ɒslə]	Stallknecht, Stallbursche *(historisch)*	
	overland ['əʊvəˌlænd]	Überland-, Land-	
	via ['vaɪə]	über	
	wage(s) [weɪdʒ(ɪz)]	Lohn	
	pin (on/to) [pɪn]	befestigen (an)	
B6	**change** [tʃeɪndʒ]	*hier:* (aus)wechseln	
	fascinated ['fæsɪneɪtɪd]	fasziniert	
	wait for ['weɪt fə]	warten auf	
	ride off [raɪd‿'ɒf]	*hier:* weiterreiten	

	bowl [bəʊl]	Schüssel; Schale	
	get used to sth [get 'juːsd tə ˌsʌmθɪŋ]	sich an etw gewöhnen	
	ride [raɪd]	Fahrt; *hier:* Ritt	
	girlfriend ['gɜːlˌfrend]	Freundin	
L1	noun [naʊn]	Hauptwort, Substantiv	
	adjective ['ædʒɪktɪv]	Adjektiv	"good" is an *adjective*: This is a good book.
C1	**headline** ['hedˌlaɪn]	Schlagzeile	
	slave [sleɪv]	Sklave/Sklavin	
	Africa ['æfrɪkə]	Afrika	
	trip [trɪp]	*hier:* Reise, Fahrt	
	room [ruːm]	Platz; Raum	
	the New World [ðə 'njuː ˌwɜːld]	die Neue Welt (*veraltet für* Amerika)	*"The New World"* is an old expression for "America".
	plantation [plɑːn'teɪʃn]	Plantage, Pflanzung	
	northern ['nɔːð(ə)n]	nördlich	*northern* ≠ southern
	take steps [teɪk 'steps]	Schritte unternehmen	
	slavery ['sleɪvəri]	Sklaverei	
	in contrast (to) [ɪn 'kɒntrɑːst]	im Gegensatz (zu)	
	at that time [ˌæt ðæt 'taɪm]	zu diesem Zeitpunkt	
	underground ['ʌndəˌgraʊnd]	unterirdisch; Untergrund-	
	railroad *(AE)* ['reɪlˌrəʊd]	Schienen; (Eisen)bahn	*"Railroad"* is the American English word for "train".
	hiding place ['haɪdɪŋ ˌpleɪs]	Versteck	
	known [nəʊn]	bekannt	
	conductor *(AE)* [kən'dʌktə]	Zugführer/in	
	civil war [ˌsɪvl 'wɔː]	Bürgerkrieg	
	declare [dɪ'kleə]	verkünden, bekannt machen	*to declare* = to announce
	defeat sb [dɪ'fiːt ˌsʌmbədi]	jdn besiegen	
	discrimination [dɪˌskrɪmɪ'neɪʃn]	Diskriminierung, Benachteiligung	
	limit ['lɪmɪt]	einschränken	
	code [kəʊd]	Kode; Gesetzbuch; *hier:* Gesetz	
	own [əʊn]	besitzen	
	permission [pə'mɪʃn]	Erlaubnis, Genehmigung	
	employer [ɪm'plɔɪə]	Arbeitgeber/in	
C2	**equal** ['iːkwəl]	gleich; *hier:* gleichberechtigt	
	speech bubble ['spiːtʃ ˌbʌbl]	Sprechblase	
	box office ['bɒks‿ˌɒfɪs]	Kasse *(im Kino, Theater)*	
	entrance fee ['entrəns ˌfiː]	Eintritt(sgeld)	
	grandson ['grænˌsʌn]	Enkel	
	former ['fɔːmə]	ehemalige(r, s), frühere(r, s)	
	order ['ɔːdə]	anordnen, befehlen	
	housemaid ['haʊsˌmeɪd]	Hausmädchen	The job as a *housemaid* is very hard.
	apply to [ə'plaɪ tə]	gelten für, betreffen	
	so-called ['səʊ kɔːld]	so genannt	
	segregation *(no pl)* [ˌsegrɪ'geɪʃn]	Trennung	
	wherever [wer'evə]	wo(hin) auch immer	
	post [pəʊst]	per Post schicken; durch Aushang bekannt geben	
	yours truly ['jɔːz 'truːli]	mit freundlichen Grüßen *(in Briefen)*	Americans often end a letter with *"yours truly"*.

C3	**citizen** ['sɪtɪzn]	(Staats)bürger/in	
	advancement [əd'vɑːnsmənt]	Vorrücken, Vorankommen	
	ensure [ɪn'ʃɔː]	sicherstellen, garantieren	
	racial ['reɪʃl]	rassisch, Rassen-	
	march [mɑːtʃ]	Marsch	
	demonstration [ˌdemən'streɪʃn]	Demonstration	
	court [kɔːt]	Gericht	
	racist ['reɪsɪst]	rassistisch	
	case [keɪs]	Fall	
	refuse [rɪ'fjuːz]	*hier:* sich weigern	
	Supreme Court [sʊˌpriːm 'kɔːt]	oberstes Bundesgericht (in den USA)	The judge is in *court*.
	in response to [ɪn rɪ'spɒns tə]	in Erwiderung auf	
	boycott ['bɔɪˌkɒt]	Boykott	
	rule [ruːl]	regieren; *hier:* entscheiden	
	segregate ['segrɪˌgeɪt]	absondern; trennen	
	constitution [ˌkɒnstɪ'tjuːʃn]	Verfassung	A *constitution* is a set of laws.
	segregated ['segrɪˌgeɪtɪd]	nur für Weiße oder Schwarze	
	public transport(ation) *(no pl)* [ˌpʌblɪk ˌtrænspɔː'teɪʃn]	öffentliche Verkehrsmittel	
	position [pə'zɪʃn]	Platz, Stelle, Lage	*position* = the place where somebody or something is
C4	civil rights movement [ˌsɪvl ˌraɪts 'muːvmənt]	Bürgerrechtsbewegung	
	ethnic ['eθnɪk]	ethnisch	
	protest (against) [prə'test]	protestieren (gegen)	
	speech [spiːtʃ]	Sprache; Rede	
	give a speech [ˌgɪv‿ə 'spiːtʃ]	eine Rede halten	He's *giving a speech.*
	sign [saɪn]	unterschreiben	
	voting *(no pl)* ['vəʊtɪŋ]	Wählen, Wahl	
	use [juːz]	Benutzung; Verwendung	
	hold a position ['həʊld‿ə pəˌzɪʃn]	einen Posten innehaben	
	racism *(no pl)* ['reɪˌsɪz(ə)m]	Rassismus	
PP3	extract ['ekstrækt]	Auszug, Exzerpt	An *extract* is a small part of a text.
	Baptist ['bæptɪst]	Baptisten-	
	pastor ['pɑːstə]	Pfarrer, Pastor	
	Nobel Peace Prize [nəʊˌbel piːs 'praɪz]	Friedensnobelpreis	
	rioting ['raɪətɪŋ]	Randalieren, Krawalle	
	murder ['mɜːdə]	Mord	
	circumstance ['sɜːkəmstəns]	Umstand	*circumstance* = the facts or conditions that have influence on a situation
	completely [kəm'pliːtli]	völlig	
	national holiday *(AE)* [ˌnæʃn(ə)l 'hɒlɪdeɪ]	gesetzlicher Feiertag; Nationalfeiertag	A *national holiday* is a day when most businesses in a country close.
	honor *(AE)* ['ɒnə]	in Ehren halten	honor *(AE)* = honour *(BE)*
	make a pledge ['meɪk‿ə ˌpledʒ]	geloben	
	ahead [ə'hed]	vorn; *hier:* vorwärts	

	turn back [ˌtɜːn 'bæk]	umkehren, zurückgehen	
	devotee [ˌdevəʊ'tiː]	Verehrer/in; Anhänger/in	
	civil rights *(pl)* [ˌsɪvl 'raɪts]	Bürgerrechte	
	fatigue *(no pl)* [fə'tiːg]	Ermüdung; Anstrengung, Strapaze	*fatigue* = a feeling of being extremely tired
	lodging ['lɒdʒɪŋ]	Unterkunft	
	Negro ['niːgrəʊ]	Neger	*Negro* bzw. Neger ist ursprünglich ein neutrales Wort. Es wird heute aber nur noch selten benutzt, weil es zu oft als abfällige und diskriminierende Bezeichnung missbraucht worden ist. Martin Luther King benutzte es in seiner Rede jedoch als völlig neutrales Wort.
	basic ['beɪsɪk]	grundlegend	
	mobility *(no pl)* [məʊ'bɪləti]	Beweglichkeit, Mobilität	
	vote (for) [vəʊt]	wählen; stimmen (für)	
	justice ['dʒʌstɪs]	Gerechtigkeit	
	roll down [rəʊl 'daʊn]	hinunterrollen	
	righteousness *(no pl)* ['raɪtʃəsnəs]	Rechtschaffenheit	
	rise up [raɪz‿'ʌp]	sich auflehnen	
	live out [lɪv‿'aʊt]	*hier:* verwirklichen; erfüllen	
	creed [kriːd]	Überzeugung	
	truth [truːθ]	Wahrheit	*truth* = what is true
	self-evident [ˌself'evɪd(ə)nt]	offensichtlich, selbstverständlich	
	brotherhood ['brʌðəˌhʊd]	Bruderschaft; Brüderlichkeit	
	swelter ['sweltə]	verschmachten, (vor Hitze) umkommen	
	injustice [ɪn'dʒʌstɪs]	Ungerechtigkeit	*injustice* ≠ *justice*
	transform [træns'fɔːm]	verwandeln	
	oasis [əʊ'eɪsɪs]	Oase	
	judge [dʒʌdʒ]	beurteilen, einschätzen	
	content ['kɒntent]	Inhalt; Gehalt	
C5	**appearance** [ə'pɪərəns]	Erscheinen; Aussehen	 John looks after his *appearance*. He has his own *style*.
	style [staɪl]	Stil, Art	
	chorus ['kɔːrəs]	Refrain	
	dreads *(pl)* (= dreadlocks) [dredz]	Dreadlocks	
	crook *(informal)* [krʊk]	Gauner	
	pass sb up with eyes of fire [pɑːs sʌmbədi‿ˌʌp wɪð aɪz‿əv‿'faɪə]	*hier etwa:* an jdm vorbeifahren, ohne ihn/sie mitzunehmen	
	165'er [wʌn sɪks 'faɪvə]	*Bewohner einer verrufenen Gegend in Harlem, New York City*	
	survivor [sə'vaɪvə]	Überlebende/r; Überlebenskünstler/in	*survivor* = someone who survives
	refer to [rɪ'fɜː tə]	hinweisen auf, sich beziehen auf	
	conflict ['kɒnflɪkt]	Konflikt	If you disagree with someone, you might have a *conflict*.
	call sb names [ˌkɔːl sʌmbədi 'neɪmz]	jdn beschimpfen	
	landlord ['lændˌlɔːd]	Hausbesitzer; Vermieter	
L2	definition [ˌdefə'nɪʃn]	Definition, Erklärung	If you explain something exactly, you give a *definition*.

Die Vokabeln aus den OPTIONAL-Teilen findest du im englisch-deutschen Dictionary auf den Seiten 200–227!

Theme 5 – ... and action!

A1	**be fond of sth/doing sth** [bi‿'fɒnd‿əv ˌsʌmθɪŋ/ ˌduːɪŋ ˌsʌmθɪŋ]	etw gerne mögen/machen	*I'm fond of* dogs. = I like dogs. *I'm fond of* playing tennis. = I like playing tennis.
	be hopeless at sth [bi 'həʊpləs‿ət ˌsʌmθɪŋ]	ein hoffnungsloser Fall sein	
	athletics *(no pl)* [æθ'letɪks]	Leichtathletik	
A2	world-champion ['wɜːldˌtʃæmpiən]	weltbeste/r	 She's an *ice-skater.*
	golfer ['gɒlfə]	Golfspieler/in	
	ice-skater ['aɪsˌskeɪtə]	Schlittschuhläufer/in, Eiskunstläufer/in	
	sportswoman ['spɔːtsˌwʊmən]	Sportlerin	These *sportswomen* can be very proud of themselves. They are the *world-champion* runners. 
	sportsman ['spɔːtsmən]	Sportler	
	personality [ˌpɜːsə'næləti]	Persönlichkeit, Charakter	
A3	**more** [mɔː]	noch mehr; weitere(r, s); zusätzliche(r, s)	
	pitcher ['pɪtʃə]	Werfer/in	
	mainly ['meɪnli]	hauptsächlich	
	touchdown *(AE)* ['tʌtʃˌdaʊn]	Versuch	
	field [fiːld]	*hier:* Spielfeld	
	at the same time [æt ðə ˌseɪm 'taɪm]	gleichzeitig	*at the same time* = Two or more things happen together.
	opponent [ə'pəʊnənt]	Opponent/in; Gegner/in	
	goal line ['gəʊl laɪn]	Torlinie	
	kick [kɪk]	treten; schießen	
	crossbar ['krɒsˌbɑː]	Querlatte, Torlatte	
	offensive [ə'fensɪv]	Angriffs-	
	defensive [dɪ'fensɪv]	Verteidigungs-	
	unit ['juːnɪt]	Einheit, Abteilung	
	tackle sb ['tækl ˌsʌmbədi]	jdn angreifen	
	ball carrier ['ɔːl ˌkæriə]	*der-/diejenige, der/die den Ball hat*	
	block [blɒk]	blockieren; *hier:* aufhalten	
	keep away (from) [kiːp ə'weɪ]	fern halten (von)	
	score a touchdown ['skɔːr‿ə ˌtʌtʃdaʊn]	einen Versuch erzielen	
	field goal *(AE)* ['fiːld ˌgəʊl]	Feldtor	
	open play ['əʊpən ˌpleɪ]	ungedecktes Spiel	
	bat and ball game [ˌbæt‿ən 'bɔːl geɪm]	*Spiel mit Schlägern und Ball*	
	pitch [pɪtʃ]	stampfen; *hier:* werfen	
	leather-covered ['leðəˌkʌvəd]	mit Leder bezogen	
	toward(s) [tə'wɔːd(z)]	in Richtung	
	batter ['bætə]	Schlagmann	
	opposing [ə'pəʊzɪŋ]	entgegengesetzt; *hier:* gegnerisch	the *opposing* team = the team which you play against
	score a run ['skɔːr‿ə ˌrʌn]	einen Treffer erzielen	
	pass [pɑːs]	*hier:* überqueren	
	marker ['mɑːkə]	(Kenn)zeichen	
	base [beɪs]	Fuß; *hier:* Mal; Base	
	score a point ['skɔːr‿ə ˌpɔɪnt]	einen Punkt machen	

hoop [huːp]	Reifen	The tiger jumped through the *hoop*. 
pass the ball ['pɑːs ðə ˌbɔːl]	den Ball abgeben, abspielen; zuspielen	
from above [frəm‿ə'bʌv]	von oben	
advance [əd'vɑːns]	voranbringen, weiterbringen	 dribbling = *bouncing* a ball
court [kɔːt]	(Spiel)platz; Court	
bounce [baʊns]	aufspringen lassen	
dribble ['drɪbl]	dribbeln	
teammate ['tiːmˌmeɪt]	Mannschaftskamerad/in, Mitspieler/in	
handle ['hændl]	anfassen; *hier:* umgehen mit	
indoor [ˌɪn'dɔː]	Innen-; *hier:* Hallen-	
variation *(no pl)* [ˌveərɪ'eɪʃn]	Abweichung; Unterschied	There has not been much *variation* in the weather during the past week. It's been raining all the time.
develop [dɪ'veləp]	sich entwickeln; entstehen	
outdoor sport [ˌaʊt'dɔː spɔːt]	Sportart im Freien	Riding is an *outdoor sport*.
surfing ['sɜːfɪŋ]	Surfen, Wellenreiten	
participant [pɑː'tɪsɪpənt]	Teilnehmer/in	
break [breɪk]	sich brechen	
surfboard ['sɜːfˌbɔːd]	Surfbrett	
kneeboard ['niːˌbɔːd]	*eine Art Surfbrett*	
body board ['bɒdi ˌbɔːd]	*eine Art kurzes Surfbrett*	
kayak ['kaɪæk]	Kajak	Whether she's wearing a scarf or not *depends on* the weather. 
do a trick [duː‿ə 'trɪk]	ein Kunststück vorführen	
depend on [dɪ'pend‿ɒn]	abhängen von	
design [dɪ'zaɪn]	Entwurf; Design; *hier:* Konstruktion	
invent [ɪn'vent]	erfinden	
shape [ʃeɪp]	Form; Art	
elements *(pl)* ['elɪmənts]	Elemente, Naturgewalten	*The elements* = the weather, especially wind and rain.
server ['sɜːvə]	der-/diejenige, der/die die Angabe macht *(Volleyball)*	
serve [sɜːv]	*hier:* Angabe haben	
ace [eɪs]	Ass	
pass [pɑːs]	*hier:* zuspielen	
set [set]	*hier:* stellen	
prevent from [prɪ'vent frəm]	an etw hindern, von etw abhalten	
error ['erə]	Fehler; *hier:* Fehlpass	
set [set]	Satz *(Sport)*	
PP4 **play an important part in** [ˌpleɪ‿ən‿ɪmˌpɔːtnt 'pɑːt‿ɪn]	eine wichtige Rolle spielen	Vegetables *play an important part in* a healthy diet.
sporting calendar ['spɔːtɪŋ ˌkælɪndə]	Sportkalender	
opening day ['əʊp(ə)nɪŋ ˌdeɪ]	Eröffnungstag	
World Series [wɜːld 'sɪəriːz]	*jährliches Endspiel zwischen den Gewinnern der beiden großen Baseballligen in den USA*	 Christine would like to work as a *professional* photographer.
professional [prə'feʃnəl]	beruflich; Berufs-; Profi-	

	championship ['tʃæmpiənʃɪp]	Meisterschaft	
	play-off ['pleɪˌɒf]	Play-off; Entscheidungsspiel	
	stadium (*pl* **-s** *or* **-dia**) ['steɪdiəm]	Stadion	A *stadium* is a large building, usually without a roof, where people watch *sporting events.*
	tip-off ['tɪpɒf]	*Start der Basketballsaison*	
	sporting event [ˌspɔːtɪŋ ɪ'vent]	Sportveranstaltung	
	Pennant Races *(AE)* ['penənt ˌreɪsɪz]	*Kampf um die Meisterschaft in einer Regionalliga*	
	bowl *(AE)* [bəʊl]	Stadion; *hier: Meisterschaft im Football*	
	New Year [ˌnjuː 'jɪə]	Neujahrs-	In den USA wird *Thanksgiving,* das amerikanische Erntedankfest, traditionell am vierten Donnerstag im November gefeiert, in Kanada am zweiten Montag im Oktober.
	Thanksgiving Day *(AE)* ['θæŋksˌgɪvɪŋ deɪ]	*hier:* Thanksgiving-	
	YMCA *(no pl)* (= Young Men's Christian Association) [ˌwaɪ em siː 'eɪ]	*christlicher Verein junger Männer*	
	cheer [tʃɪə]	Hurraruf	
	hand-clapping ['hændklæpɪŋ]	Applaudieren	
	marching band ['mɑːtʃɪŋ ˌbænd]	Marschkapelle	A *marching band* is a group of people who play music while marching.
	lacrosse *(no pl)* [lə'krɒs]	Lacrosse *(Ballsportart)*	
	stop short ['stɒp ˌʃɔːt]	*hier:* anhalten	
L1	the movies *(pl)* [ðə 'muːviz]	Kino	
L2	preposition [ˌprepə'zɪʃn]	Verhältniswort, Präposition	"On" and "out" are *prepositions.*
	Mexico ['mæksɪkəʊ]	Mexiko	
	hopeless ['həʊpləs]	hoffnungslos	
B1	**loser** ['luːzə]	Verlierer/in	*loser* ≠ winner
	be a flop [biː‿ə 'flɒp]	eine Niete sein	
	flip out *(informal)* [ˌflɪp‿'aʊt]	ausflippen	to lose → loser to win → winner to play → player to own → owner
	plain [pleɪn]	einfach; *hier:* rein	
	panic *(no pl)* ['pænɪk]	Panik	
	somewhere else [ˌsʌmweər‿'els]	irgendwo anders	
	the couple of times [ðə 'kʌpl‿əv ˌtaɪmz]	die paar/wenigen Male	
	like it was on fire [laɪk‿ɪt ˌwɒz‿ɒn 'faɪə]	als würde es brennen	
	sports [spɔːts]	Sport-	You can get new trainers at the *sports* department. You put your *sports* gear in your *sports* bag.
	someplace *(AE, informal)* ['sʌmpleɪs]	irgendwo	
	be around [biː‿ə'raʊnd]	da sein; in der Nähe sein	
	catch the bus ['kætʃ ðə ˌbʌs]	den Bus kriegen	
	I'd rather be … [aɪd 'rɑːðə biː]	Ich wäre lieber …	
	get a kick out of sth [get‿ə 'kɪk‿aʊt‿əv ˌsʌmθɪŋ]	an etw einen Riesenspaß haben	Das Wort "schedule" wird im britischen Englisch anders ausgesprochen als im amerikanischen Englisch: ['ʃedjuːl] *(BE)* ['skedʒuːl] *(AE)*
	apart from [ə'pɑːt frəm]	abgesehen von	
B2	**schedule** ['ʃedjuːl]	(Zeit-/Fahr)plan; *hier:* Stundenplan	

unusual	≠	usual
unhappy	≠	happy
unfair	≠	fair
unfriendly	≠	friendly
unhealthy	≠	healthy
undrinkable	≠	drinkable

	unusual [ʌn'juːʒʊəl]	ungewöhnlich	
	home room ['həʊm ˌruːm]	*etwa:* Aufenthaltsraum	
	social studies *(AE)* ['səʊʃl ˌstʌdiz]	Gemeinschaftskunde; Sozialkunde	
	P. E. (= physical education) [piː 'iː, ˌfɪzɪkl‿edju'keɪʃn]	Sport(unterricht)	
	elective (subject) [ɪ'lektɪv]	Wahlfach	
	pen friend ['pen ˌfrend]	Brieffreund/in	
B3	lend [lend]	leihen	
	text a message ['tekst‿ə ˌmesɪdʒ]	eine SMS schreiben	You can *text a message* with your cellphone.
B4	IT *(no pl)* (= Information Technology) [aɪ'tiː, ɪnfəˌmeɪʃn tek'nɒlədʒi]	Informationstechnologie	
	assistant [ə'sɪst(ə)nt]	Assistent/in	
	social worker [ˌsəʊʃl 'wɜːkə]	Sozialarbeiter/in	
	office ['ɒfɪs]	Büro-	
	ceramics [sə'ræmɪks]	Keramik; *hier:* Töpfern	
	act [ækt]	handeln; spielen	
B6	**actor/actress** ['æktə, 'æktrəs]	Schauspieler/in	
	technician [tek'nɪʃn]	Techniker/in	
	make-up artist [ˌmeɪkʌp 'ɑːtɪst]	Maskenbildner/in, Visagist/in	
	chess [tʃes]	Schach(spiel)	You don't move a lot when you play *chess*.
	logical ['lɒdʒɪkl]	logisch	
	thinker ['θɪŋkə]	Denker	
	mural designing ['mjʊərəl dɪˌzaɪnɪŋ]	Wandgestaltung	
	drop in *(informal)* [drɒp‿'ɪn]	vorbeischauen, vorbeikommen	
	astronomy *(no pl)* [ə'strɒnəmi]	Astronomie	
	comet ['kɒmɪt]	Komet	With a *telescope*, you can see stars and *comets*.
	telescope ['telɪˌskəʊp]	Teleskop	
PP5	kindergarten ['kɪndəˌgɑːtn]	Vorschule	
	dropout ['drɒpaʊt]	(Studien)abbrecher/in, Schulabgänger/in	
	certificate [sə'tɪfɪkət]	Urkunde, Bescheinigung	A *certificate* is an official sheet of paper.
	in addition to [ˌɪn‿ə'dɪʃn tə]	zusätzlich zu	
	nursery school ['nɜːs(ə)ri ˌskuːl]	Kindergarten	
	optional ['ɒpʃnəl]	*freiwillig*	If something is *optional*, you do not have to do it.
	elementary school [elɪ'ment(ə)ri ˌskuːl]	Grundschule	
	junior high school *(AE)* ['dʒuːniə 'haɪ skuːl]	Junior Highschool *(Aufbauschule)*	
	freshman *(AE, pl -men)* ['freʃmən, 'freʃmən]	Studienanfänger	A *freshman* is someone who has just started studying.
	sophomore *(AE)* ['sɒfəˌmɔː]	*Schüler/in einer Highschool im zweiten Jahr*	

She's a famous *actress*.

	junior *(AE)* ['dʒuːniə]	*Schüler/in einer Highschool im vorletzten Jahr*	
	senior *(AE)* ['siːniə]	*Schüler/in einer Highschool- oder Collegeabgangsklasse*	
L2	timetable ['taɪmteɪbl]	Stundenplan	
	variety [və'raɪəti]	Vielfalt	
C1	**director** [də'rektə]	Direktor/in; *hier:* Regisseur/in	A *director* is someone who is making a film.
	princess [ˌprɪn'ses]	Prinzessin	
	blacksmith ['blækˌsmɪθ]	(Huf)schmied	
	ogre ['əʊgə]	Menschenfresser; *hier:* Scheusal	
	lord [lɔːd]	Lord *(Titel)*	 They *have fallen in love with* each other.
	dragon ['drægən]	Drache	
	fall in love (with) [ˌfɔːl‿ɪn 'lʌv]	sich verlieben (in)	
	flee [fliː]	fliehen, flüchten	
	fairytale ['feəriˌteɪl]	Märchen-	
	donkey ['dɒŋki]	Esel	
	shy [ʃaɪ]	schüchtern	Someone who is nervous in the company of other people is *shy*.
	suit [suːt]	Anzug	
	supernatural [ˌsuːpə'nætʃərəl]	übernatürlich; außergewöhnlich	
	power ['paʊə]	Macht; *hier:* Fähigkeit, Kraft	*power* = control or strength
	superhero ['suːpəˌhɪərəʊ]	Superheld	
	evil ['iːvl]	Übel, das Böse	*evil* = a very bad power
	design [dɪ'zaɪn]	entwerfen, gestalten	
	plot [plɒt]	Handlung, Plot	
C2	fact file ['fækt ˌfaɪl]	Steckbrief	
	date of birth [ˌdeɪt‿əv 'bɜːθ]	Geburtsdatum	
	height [haɪt]	Höhe; (Körper)größe	Das Längenmaß wird in "foot" (ft) und inches angegeben. 1 foot entspricht 12 inches. Ein "foot" wird so dargestellt: 1′ = 1 foot
	television ['telɪˌvɪʒn]	Fernseh-	
	etc (= et cetera) [et 'set(ə)rə]	usw., etc.	
	blockbuster ['blɒkˌbʌstə]	Bestseller; Kassenschlager	
	vegetarian [ˌvedʒə'teəriən]	vegetarisch	I like *vegetarian* food.
	cast sb (in a role) ['kɑːst ˌsʌmbədi]	jdm (eine Rolle) geben	
	series *(pl -)* ['sɪəriːz]	Reihe; Folge; Serie	*series* = similar things that follow each other
	part [pɑːt]	*hier:* Rolle	
	be thrilled [bi 'θrɪld]	außer sich vor Freude sein	to *be thrilled* by something = to like something very much
	bring sth to life ['brɪŋ sʌmθɪŋ tə‿ˌlaɪf]	etw zum Leben erwecken	
	enthusiasm [ɪn'θjuːziˌæzəm]	Enthusiasmus, Begeisterung	
	intensive [ɪn'tensɪv]	intensiv, stark	
	martial arts *(npl)* [ˌmɑːʃl‿'ɑːts]	Kampfsport	
	chef [ʃef]	Koch, Köchin	
	swap [swɒp]	tauschen	

Theme 5

C3	**arrange** [ə'reɪndʒ]	arrangieren
	welcome (to) ['welkəm]	willkommen (in)
	shoot a film/movie [ʃuːt‿ə 'fɪlm/'muːvi]	einen Film drehen
	witness ['wɪtnəs]	beobachten, miterleben
	set [set]	Szenenaufbau; Drehort *(Film)*
	script [skrɪpt]	Drehbuch, Skript
	responsible [rɪ'spɒnsəbl]	verantwortlich, zuständig
	production crew [prə'dʌkʃn kruː]	Produktionsteam
	camera ['kæm(ə)rə]	(Film)kamera
	director of photography [də'rektə‿əv fəˌtɒgrəfi]	Aufnahmeleiter
	shot [ʃɒt]	Aufnahme, Einstellung *(Film)*
	operate ['ɒpəˌreɪt]	bedienen
	clapperboard *(AE)* ['klæppəˌbɔːd]	Klappe *(Film)*
	assistant camera person [ə'sɪst(ə)nt ˌkæmərə pɜːsn]	Kameraassistent/in
	load a film [ˌləʊd‿ə 'fɪlm]	einen Film einlegen
	keep [kiːp]	*hier:* führen
	set [set]	stellen; *hier* einstellen
	gaffer ['gæfə]	Vorarbeiter; *hier:* Oberbeleuchter/in
	best boy [ˌbest 'bɔɪ]	*Assistent des Elektrikers beim Film*
	wire ['waɪə]	Draht; *hier:* Leitung, Kabel
	helper ['helpə]	Helfer/in; Gehilfe/Gehilfin
	though [ðəʊ]	allerdings *(nachgestellt)*
	grip [grɪp]	Bühnenarbeiter *(Film)*
	sound [saʊnd]	*hier:* Ton
	boom operator ['buːm ˌɒpəreɪtə]	Tonassistent/in
	microphone ['maɪkrəˌfəʊn]	Mikrofon
	direct [dɪ'rekt]	leiten, führen; *hier:* anleiten
	sound recordist ['saʊnd ˌrekərdɪst]	Tontechniker/in
	record [rɪ'kɔːd]	aufzeichnen; aufnehmen
	overview of ['əʊvəvjuː‿əv]	Überblick über
	cafeteria [ˌkæfə'tɪəriə]	Cafeteria
	impression [ɪm'preʃn]	Eindruck
	description [dɪ'skrɪpʃn]	Beschreibung
	composer [kəm'pəʊzə]	Komponist/in
	special effect [ˌspeʃl ɪ'fekt]	Spezialeffekt
	compose [kəm'pəʊz]	komponieren
C4	review [rɪ'vjuː]	rezensieren
	review [rɪ'vjuː]	Kritik; Besprechung
	be about [bi‿ə'baʊt]	handeln von
	laboratory [lə'bɒrət(ə)ri]	Labor
	genetically engineered [dʒəˌnetɪkli endʒɪ'nɪəd]	gentechnisch verändert
	leap [liːp]	springen
	secret ['siːkrət]	geheim; *hier:* heimlich

If you see something happen, you *witness* something.

Unregelmäßige Verben
Du weißt ja, dass es viele Verben gibt, die unregelmäßige Formen haben. Diese musst du dir wie neue Wörter einprägen.
Es gibt aber einige Verben, die gleiche Formen haben, z. B.
set – set – set
let – let – let
cut – cut – cut
fit – fit – fit
Versuche doch einmal, die unregelmäßigen Verben rhythmisch zu klatschen oder zu rappen.

A *sound* is something you can hear.

The reporter is holding a *microphone*.

He is writing a *secret* message.

	brilliantly ['brɪljəntli]	brilliant, meisterhaft	
	performance [pə'fɔːməns]	Vorführung; *hier:* Darstellung	His *performance* was very good.
	bad [bæd]	*hier:* böse	
	acting skills ['æktɪŋ skɪlz]	*schauspielerische Fähigkeiten*	
	minor role ['maɪnə ˌrəʊl]	Nebenrolle	
	suspense *(no pl)* [sə'spens]	Spannung	
	deserve [dɪ'zɜːv]	verdienen	
	recommend [ˌrekə'mend]	empfehlen	
	rating *(no pl)* ['reɪtɪŋ]	Einschätzung; *hier:* Bewertung	
C5	movie director ['muːvi dəˌrektə]	Filmregisseur/in	
	horror ['hɒrə]	Entsetzen; *hier:* Horror	*Horror* is a strong feeling of shock or of being afraid.
L1	journalist ['dʒɜːnəlɪst]	Journalist/in	
	identify with [aɪ'dentɪfaɪ ˌwɪð]	sich identifizieren mit	
	murderer ['mɜːdərə]	Mörder/in	
	All the best! [ˌɔːl ðə‿'best]	Alles Gute!	Happy birthday and *all the best*!
L2	curtain ['kɜːtən]	Vorhang, Gardine	
L3	worth [wɜːθ]	(lohnens)wert	

Die Vokabeln aus den OPTIONAL-Teilen findest du im englisch-deutschen Dictionary auf den Seiten 200–227!

Theme 6 – A bite to eat

	a bite to eat [ə 'baɪt‿tə ˌiːt]	eine Kleinigkeit zu essen	
A1	finding ['faɪndɪŋ]	Entdeckung; Ergebnis	
A2	approximately [ə'prɒksɪmətli]	ungefähr, etwa	
	amount [ə'maʊnt]	Menge; *hier:* Betrag	
	absolutely ['æbsəluːtli]	absolut, völlig	
A3	**comment** ['kɒmənt]	Kommentar, Bemerkung	
	be good value (for sb's money) [bi guːd 'væljuː]	sein Geld wert sein	
	anywhere else ['eniweə ˌels]	irgendwo anders	
	spicy ['spaɪsi]	würzig; scharf	
	I wouldn't be caught dead in the place. *(informal)* [aɪ wʊdnt bi kɔːt 'ded‿ɪn ðə‿ˌpleɪs]	*Da würden mich keine zehn Pferde reinbringen.*	
A4	make up one's mind ['meɪk‿ʌp wʌnz 'maɪnd]	sich entscheiden	
	introduction [ˌɪntrə'dʌkʃn]	Vorstellung; Einführung	
	express [ɪk'spres]	ausdrücken	Harry *expressed* his feelings.
A5	assistant manager [ə'sɪst(ə)nt ˌmænɪdʒə]	stellvertretende/r Direktor/in / Filialleiter/in	
	have a bite [ˌhæv‿ə 'baɪt]	*hier:* probieren	
	plastic ['plæstɪk]	Plastik, Kunststoff	
	aluminium foil [ˌæləmɪniəm 'fɔɪl]	Alufolie	
	wrap (up) [ræp]	einwickeln, einpacken	You usually *wrap up* a present.

Theme 5/6

	dishwasher ['dɪʃ,wɒʃə]	Geschirrspülmaschine	
	reduce [rɪ'dju:s]	verringern, reduzieren	A *dishwasher* will *surely reduce* your work at home.
	surely ['ʃɔ:li]	sicher(lich), bestimmt	
	be wrong with [bi 'rɒŋ wɪð]	nicht stimmen mit	
	reported [rɪ'pɔ:tɪd]	indirekt	
A6	nothing but ['nʌθɪŋ bət]	nur, nichts als	
A7	**record** ['rekɔ:d]	*hier:* Protokoll	
L3	spell [spel]	richtig schreiben, buchstabieren	
PP6	**generally** ['dʒen(ə)rəli]	normalerweise, im Allgemeinen	
	spare ribs [,speə 'rɪbz]	Spareribs, Rippchen	They both signed the written *record*.
	turkey ['tɜ:ki]	Truthahn/-henne, Pute(r)	
	clam chowder ['klæm , tʃaʊdə]	*(sämige) Muschelsuppe*	
	baked beans [,beɪkt 'bi:nz]	*Bohnen in Tomatensauce*	
	apple pie ['æpl ,paɪ]	gedeckter Apfelkuchen	
	regional ['ri:dʒn(ə)l]	regional	*Regional* cooking is cooking that is typical of a country or area.
	vary ['veəri]	verschieden sein; sich verändern	
	locally ['ləʊkli]	am/vor Ort	
	cultural ['kʌltʃ(ə)rəl]	kulturell	
	African ['æfrɪkən]	Afrikaner/in; afrikanisch	
	Cajun ['keɪdʒ(ə)n]	Cajun; Cajun-	
	combination [,kɒmbɪ'neɪʃn]	Kombination	Fish and chocolate is a strange *combination.*
	flavouring ['fleɪvərɪŋ]	Aroma, Geschmacksstoff	flavoring *(AE)* = flavouring *(BE)*
	varied ['veərɪd]	unterschiedlich	
	eats *(informal, pl)* [i:ts]	Häppchen	
	pork [,pɔ:k 'rɪbz]	Schwein(efleisch)	
	rack [ræk]	*hier:* Portion	
	jumbo ['dʒʌmbəʊ]	Riesen-	
	chop [tʃɒp]	klein schneiden	to *chop* something
	brisket *(no pl)* ['brɪskɪt]	Bruststück	
	(mixed) pickles *(pl)* ['pɪklz]	Relish; *hier:* Essiggemüse	
	pulled pork [pʊld 'pɔ:k]	*auf besondere Art geräuchertes Schweinefleisch*	
	topped with ['tɒpt wɪð]	überzogen mit	
	creamy ['kri:mi]	cremig, sahnig	
	coleslaw *(no pl)* ['kəʊl,slɔ:]	Krautsalat, Kohlsalat	Somebody is *barbecuing* sausages.
	barbecue ['bɑ:bɪ,kju:]	grillen	
	smoked [sməʊkt]	geräuchert	
	Jalapeno [,hælə'peɪnjəʊ]	grüne oder rote scharfe Paprikaschote	
	chili *(AE)* ['tʃɪli]	Chili, Peperoni	chili *(AE)* = chilli *(BE)*
	fixins' (= fixings) *(AE, informal, pl)* ['fɪksɪŋz]	Beilagen	
	medium ['mi:diəm]	durchschnittlich, mittel	
	rustic ['rʌstɪk]	ländlich, rustikal	
	cheddar *(no pl)* ['tʃedə]	(Cheddar)käse	
	creamed spinach ['kri:md ,spɪnɪdʒ]	Rahmspinat	*Creamed spinach* is spinach with cream.
	mashed potatoes [,mæʃt pə'teɪtəʊz]	Kartoffelbrei	
	gravy ['greɪvi]	Bratensaft; (Braten)soße	
	golden ['gəʊld(ə)n]	aus Gold, golden	

B1	CFC (= chlorofluorocarbon) [ˌsiːef'siː, ˌklɔːrəʊˌflʊərəʊ'kɑːbən]	FCKW (= Fluorchlorkohlenwasserstoff)	
	flyer (= flier) ['flaɪə]	Flugblatt, Handzettel	A *flyer* is a kind of brochure.
	heading ['hedɪŋ]	Überschrift, Titel	
	care for (sb/sth) ['keə fə]	sich um (jdn/etw) kümmern	
	from [frəm]	*hier:* vor	
	explanation [ˌeksplə'neɪʃn]	Erklärung; Erläuterung	
	term [tɜːm]	*hier:* Ausdruck	
	ozone *(no pl)* ['əʊˌzəʊn]	Ozon	
	layer ['leɪə]	Schicht	
	packaging ['pækɪdʒɪŋ]	Verpackung; Verpackungs-	
	spray [spreɪ]	Sprühnebel; *hier:* Spray	
	air conditioner ['eə kən'dɪʃnə]	Klimaanlage	
	foam [fəʊm]	Schaumstoff-	
	ban sth ['bæn ˌsʌmθɪŋ]	etw verbieten; *hier:* herausnehmen aus	
	greatly ['greɪtli]	sehr; *hier:* stark	
	ozone hole ['əʊzəʊn ˌhəʊl]	Ozonloch	
	the Antarctic [ðə æn'tɑːktɪk]	die Antarktis	
	rightly ['raɪtli]	richtig; zu Recht	
	upper ['ʌpə]	obere(r, s)	
	radiation [ˌreɪdi'eɪʃn]	Strahlung	
	protect sb from sth [prə'tekt sʌmbədi frəm ˌsʌmθɪŋ]	jdn vor etw schützen	
	ultraviolet [ˌʌltrə'vaɪələt]	ultraviolett; UV-	
	balance *(no pl)* ['bæləns]	Balance, Gleichgewicht	
	disturb [dɪ'stɜːb]	stören	
	concern [kən'sɜːn]	Anliegen, Sorge	
	specialist ['speʃəlɪst]	Fachmann/Fachfrau, Spezialist/in	
	alternative [ɔːl'tɜːnətɪv]	Alternative	
	be concerned (about) [bi kən'sɜːnd]	beunruhigt sein (wegen)	
B2	**definition** [ˌdefə'nɪʃn]	Definition, Erklärung	
	contain sth [kən'teɪn ˌsʌmθɪŋ]	etw enthalten	
	container [kən'teɪnə]	Behälter	
	chemical ['kemɪkl]	Chemikalie	
	metre ['miːtə]	Meter	
	gas (*pl* **-es** *or* **-ses**) [gæs]	Gas	
	method ['meθəd]	Methode	A *method* is a way of doing something.
B3	**waste** *(no pl)* [weɪst]	Verschwendung; Abfall	
	dustbin ['dʌstbɪn]	Mülleimer	
	household ['haʊsˌhəʊld]	Haushalt	
	printout ['prɪntˌaʊt]	Ausdruck	
	shampoo *(no pl)* [ʃæm'puː]	Shampoo	You need *shampoo* to wash your hair.
	conditioner *(no pl)* [kən'dɪʃnə]	Pflegespülung	
	half-used ['hɑːf ˌjuːzd]	halb verbraucht	

Paul *cares for* his uncle.

Lernen mit Eselsbrücken
Wenn es dir schwer fällt, manche Wörter oder bestimmte grammatische Formen zu behalten, kann es nützlich sein, wenn du dir Eselsbrücken baust. Gut eignen sich z. B. Reime für grammatische Formen:

He, she, it – the 's' must fit.
last + past
Use simple present if you're clever with 'always, often, sometimes, never'!
Like nine before ten, it's 'where' before 'when'.

Für die Rechtschreibung gibt es auch einige Hilfen:

here ≠ hear (ear)
meet ≠ meat (eat)

Du kannst diese Tipps auch in deine Lernkartei aufnehmen.

perfect *balance*

waste

envelope ['envələʊp]	Briefumschlag, Kuvert	The *envelope* is *addressed* to me, but I don't know the *handwriting*. 
address (to) [ə'dres]	adressieren (an)	
handwriting ['hænd,raɪtɪŋ]	Handschrift	
instant coffee [,ɪnstənd 'kɒfi]	Instantkaffee	
candy *(AE)* ['kændi]	Süßigkeit(en)	Before you plant a tree you need to dig a *hole* in the ground. 
bag [bæg]	*hier:* Tüte	
receipt [rɪ'siːt]	Eingang; *hier:* Quittung	
hole [həʊl]	Loch	
food [fuːd]	*hier:* Futter	
hairdresser ['heə,dresə]	Friseur/Friseuse	
tights *(npl)* [taɪts]	Strumpfhose	
sleeping pill ['sliːpɪŋ ,pɪl]	Schlaftablette	
TV guide [tiː,viː 'gaɪd]	Fernsehzeitschrift	
beer *(no pl)* [bɪə]	Bier	 The children played *"hairdresser"* which their mother didn't like at all.
caravan site ['kærə,væn saɪt]	Campingplatz für Wohnwagen	
used [juːzd]	gebraucht	
light bulb ['laɪt ,bʌlb]	Glühbirne	
jar [dʒɑː]	Glas(gefäß)	
bit [bɪt]	*hier:* Scherbe	
coffeepot ['kɒfi,pɒt]	Kaffeekanne	
paint *(no pl)* [peɪnt]	Farbe; Lack	
baby food ['beɪbi ,fuːd]	Babynahrung	
cigarette [,sɪgə'ret]	Zigarette	*Cigarettes* are not good for your health.
tea bag ['tiː ,bæg]	Teebeutel	
tear sth (up) ['teə ,sʌmθɪŋ]	etw zerreißen	
peelings *(pl)* ['piːlɪŋz]	Schalen	
saver Metro ticket ['seɪvə me,trəʊ ,tɪkɪt]	*Sparticket für die U-Bahn*	
cookbook ['kʊk,bʊk]	Kochbuch	There are a lot of recipes in a *cookbook*.
roast [rəʊst]	Braten	
paper bag ['peɪpə bæg]	Papiertüte	
wholegrain ['həʊl,greɪn]	Vollkorn-	
beetroot ['biːtruːt]	Rote Beete	A *beetroot* is a vegetable.
electric [ɪ'lektrɪk]	elektrisch, Elektro-	
bag [bæg]	*hier:* Sack	
rubbish *(no pl)* ['rʌbɪʃ]	Müll	*rubbish* = waste
copy ['kɒpi]	*hier:* abschreiben	
biodegradable [,baɪəʊdɪ'greɪdəbl]	biologisch abbaubar	
B4 **be right** [bi 'raɪt]	Recht haben	
skip sth ['skɪp ,sʌmθɪŋ]	etw überspringen, auslassen	
dairy products *(pl)* ['deəri ,prɒdʌkt]	Molkereierzeugnisse	
on and on [,ɒn‿ənd‿'ɒn]	immer weiter	on and on and on and on and on and on …
complaint [kəm'pleɪnt]	Beschwerde, Klage	
hard [hɑːd]	*hier:* sehr	
innocently ['ɪnəs(ə)ntli]	arglos	
turn off sth [tɜːn‿'ɒf ,sʌmθɪŋ]	etw ausschalten	
PC (= personal computer) [piː'siː]	PC	

	lay the table ['leɪ ðə‿ˌteɪbl]	den Tisch decken	 Who *laid the table*?
	suspicious [sə'spɪʃəs]	verdächtig	
	cereal ['sɪəriəl]	Frühstückszerealien; Frühstücksflocken	
	clever ['klevəli]	klug; geschickt	
	first [fɜːst]	*hier:* zum ersten Mal	
	burn [bɜːn]	verbrennen	
	fuel ['fjuːəl]	Brennstoff; *hier:* Nahrung	 *fuel*
	steady ['stedi]	*hier:* kontinuierlich, gleich bleibend	
	pace [peɪs]	Tempo	
	convert into [kən'vɜːt‿ˌɪntə]	verwandeln in	
	slice [slaɪs]	Scheibe; Stück	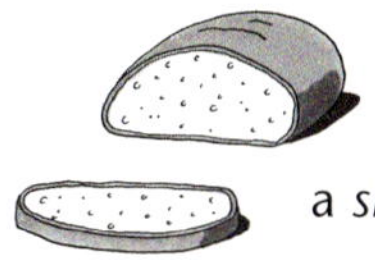 a *slice* of bread
	jelly *(AE)* ['dʒeli]	Gelee	
	lunchbox ['lʌntʃˌbɒks]	Brotdose	
	nut [nʌt]	Nuss	
	brain [breɪn]	Gehirn; Verstand	*brain* 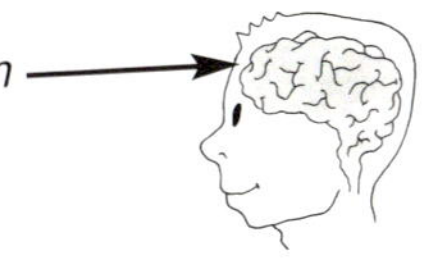
	barley *(no pl)* ['bɑːli]	Gerste	
	reluctant [rɪ'lʌktənt]	widerwillig, widerstrebend	If you do something *reluctantly*, you don't like doing it.
	Me too. [mi 'tuː]	Ich auch.	
	go with ['gəʊ wɪð]	passen zu; *hier:* dazu	
	hopefully ['həʊpfli]	hoffnungsvoll	
	takeaway ['teɪkəˌweɪ]	Imbissbude; *hier:* Essen zum Mitnehmen	
	carefully ['keəfli]	vorsichtig; sorgfältig	
	evidence *(no pl)* ['evɪd(ə)ns]	Beweis(e)	He is looking for *evidence*. 
	clear up [klɪər‿'ʌp]	klären; *hier:* aufräumen	
	knock off [nɒk‿'ɒf]	hinunterstoßen	
	gain weight [geɪn 'weɪt]	zunehmen	
	clue [kluː]	Hinweis	
L3	**adverb** ['ædvɜːb]	Adverb	
	luckily ['lʌkɪli]	glücklicherweise	
	learner ['lɜːnə]	Lernende/r	
L4	rhyme with ['raɪm wɪð]	(sich) reimen auf	*"Rhyme" rhymes with* "crime".
	rhyme [raɪm]	Reim	
C1	match sth ['mætʃ ˌsʌmθɪŋ]	zu etw passen	
	smoothie ['smuːði]	Shake	
	squash *(AE)* [skwɒʃ]	Kürbis	
	hash browns *(pl, AE)* [hʌʃ 'braʊnz]	Rösti	
	made from ['meɪd frəm]	hergestellt/gemacht aus	
	nutshell *(no pl)* ['nʌtˌʃel]	Nussschale	 These nuts all have *nutshells*.
	the big cheese *(AE, informal)* [ðə bɪg 'tʃiːz]	der Boss	
	taste [teɪst]	*hier:* probieren	
C2	translation [træns'leɪʃn]	Übersetzung	
	secondary school ['sekənd(ə)ri ˌskuːl]	weiterführende Schule	
	entrée *(AE)* ['ɒntreɪ]	Hauptgericht	
	BBQ (= barbecue) ['bɑːbɪˌkjuː]	Grill, Bratrost; *hier:* vom Grill	*barbecue* 
	breaded ['bredɪd]	paniert	

croquette [krɒ'ket]	Krokette	*croquette* = a food made from a mixture of fish, meat or vegetables and cooked in oil
stir-fry ['stɜːˌfraɪ]	Chinapfanne	
double-decker *(AE, informal)* [ˌdʌbl'dekə]	*doppeltes Sandwich*	
grilled [grɪld]	gegrillt	
supreme *(no pl)* [sʊ'priːm]	Geschnetzeltes	
macaroni *(no pl)* [ˌmækə'rəʊni]	Makkaroni	*Macaroni* is a type of short pasta.
roast chicken ['rəʊst ˌtʃɪkɪn]	Brathuhn	
roast turkey ['rəʊst ˌtɜːki]	gebratener Truthahn	
spaghetti [spə'geti]	Spaghetti	
stuffed [stʌft]	ausgestopft; *hier:* gefüllt	
shell [ʃel]	*hier:* Muschelschale	
corn [kɔːn]	*hier:* Mais	 *corn*
w/ (= with) [wið]	mit	
topping ['tɒpɪŋ]	Garnierung	
item ['aɪtəm]	*hier:* Gericht	
french fries *(npl)* [ˌfrentʃ 'fraɪz]	Pommes frites	
potato rounds [pə'teɪtəʊ ˌraʊndz]	gebratene Kartoffelscheiben	
waffle fries ['wɒfl ˌfraɪz]	*Pommes in Waffelform*	
dino tots ['daɪnə ˌtɒts]	*Pommes in Dinosaurierform*	
beverage ['bev(ə)rɪdʒ]	Getränk	*beverage* = drink
canned [kænd]	konserviert; Dosen-	This is a *canned* drink. 
iced tea [aɪst 'tiː]	Eistee	
pint [paɪnt]	Pint *(0,568 l)*	
cracker ['krækə]	Kräcker	
soft [sɒft]	weich	*soft* ≠ hard
pretzel ['pretsl]	Brezel	
steamed [stiːmd]	gedämpft, in Dampf gegart	
line [laɪn]	*hier:* Sortiment	
filet (= fillet) ['fɪlɪt]	Filet	
BLT (= bacon, lettuce and tomato) [ˌbiːel'tiː]	*Sandwich mit Schinken, Salat und Tomate*	
sub (= submarine sandwich) [sʌb]	*Sandwich in U-Boot-Form*	
wafer ['weɪfə]	Waffel; *hier:* Scheibe	
baked [beɪkt]	gebacken	*baked* bread
pie [paɪ]	Kuchen; Pastete	
doz. (= dozen) ['dʌzn]	Dutzend	
ea. (= each) [iːtʃ]	jede(r, s)	
gelatin *(AE, informal)* ['dʒelətɪn]	Wackelpudding	*Gelatin* and *pudding* are desserts.
gel [dʒel]	Gel; *hier:* Creme	
pudding *(AE, no pl)* ['pʊdɪŋ]	Pudding	
sundae ['sʌndeɪ]	Eisbecher	
miscellaneous [ˌmɪsə'leɪniəs]	verschiedene(r, s)	*miscellaneous* = of various kinds of people or things
honey ['hʌni]	Honig	
mustard *(no pl)* ['mʌstəd]	Senf	
poptart ['pɒptɑːt]	*mit Früchten oder Schokolade gefülltes flaches Gebäck, das im Toaster erwärmt wird*	

dressing ['dresɪŋ]	(Salat)soße, Dressing	You usually put a *dressing* on your salad.
string cheese ['strɪŋ tʃiːz]	*traditioneller amerik. Käse in Stangenform*	
muffin *(AE)* ['mʌfɪn]	*kleiner, runder, meist süßer Kuchen*	Als *muffin* wird im britischen Englisch oft ein flaches rundes Hefebrötchen, das halbiert getoastet und mit Butter oder auch Marmelade gegessen wird, bezeichnet. Im amerikanischen Englisch ist ein *muffin* ein meist süßer kleiner runder Kuchen aus Rührteig.
patty ['pæti]	Pastetchen	
bun [bʌn]	(rundes) Gebäckstück	
budget ['bʌdʒɪt]	Budget, Etat	
C4 idiom ['ɪdiəm]	(idiomatische) Redewendung	
butter sb up [ˌbʌtə sʌmbədi‿'ʌp]	jdm Honig um den Bart schmieren	
hot potato [ˌhɒt pə'teɪtəʊ]	heißes Eisen *(Politik)*	A *hot potato* is something nobody wants to touch.
spill the beans [ˌspɪl ðə 'biːnz]	aus der Schule plaudern	He's *spilling the beans.* 
use one's noodle [ˌjuːz wʌnz 'nuːdl]	seinen Grips anstrengen	
have a sweet tooth [hæv‿ə ˌswiːt 'tuːθ]	eine Naschkatze sein	If you *have a sweet tooth*, you love to eat sweet things.
cool as a cucumber [kuːl əz‿ə‿'kjuˌkʌmbə]	völlig gelassen; cool	
L3 city centre [ˌsɪti 'sentə]	Innenstadt	
biro ['baɪrəʊ]	Kugelschreiber	
mate [meɪt]	Freund/in, Kumpel	A *mate* is a good friend.
ballpoint pen *(AE)* [ˌbɔːlpɔɪnt 'pen]	Kugelschreiber	
railway(s) ['reɪlweɪ]	Eisenbahn	
truck *(AE)* [trʌk]	Last(kraft)wagen	
meter *(AE)* ['miːtə]	Meter	
postal service ['pəʊstl ˌsɜːvɪs]	Postservice	

Die Vokabeln aus den OPTIONAL-Teilen findest du im englisch-deutschen Dictionary auf den Seiten 200–227!

D Dictionary English – German

A

a/an [ə, ən] ein(e)
be able to [bi‿ˌeɪbl tə] können, imstande sein
about [ə'baʊt] über; ungefähr
* about [ə'baʊt] *hier:* herum 4/O1
be about [bi‿ə'baʊt] handeln von 5/C4
How about ...? [ˌhaʊ‿ə'baʊt] Was ist mit ...?, Wie wäre es mit ...? 1/A3
What about ...? *(informal)* [ˌwɒt‿ə'baʊt] Was ist mit ...?, Wie wäre es mit ...?
above [ə'bʌv] über
absolutely ['æbsəlu:tli] absolut, völlig 6/A2
accent ['æksnt] Akzent; Betonung 3/BL4
* accept [ək'sept] annehmen 1/O
accident ['æksɪd(ə)nt] Unfall
accommodation *(no pl)* [əˌkɒmə'deɪʃn] Unterkunft 2/B4
ace [eɪs] Ass 5/A3
achieve [ə'tʃi:v] erreichen
acorn ['eɪkɔ:n] Eichel 2/B2
acre ['eɪkə] Morgen *(altes Feldmaß)* 2/B2
across [ə'krɒs] über; *hier:* quer durch 4/B1
across [ə'krɒs] *hier:* überall in 4/B4
across from [ə'krɒs frəm] gegenüber 2/C5
* across from sb [ə'crɒs frəm ˌsʌmbədi] jdm gegenüber 1/O2
act [ækt] handeln; spielen 5/B4
act out [ækt‿'aʊt] nachspielen
acting skills ['æktɪŋ skɪlz] *schauspielerische Fähigkeiten* 5/C4
active ['æktɪv] aktiv
activity [æk'tɪvəti] Aktivität
actor/actress ['æktə, 'æktrəs] Schauspieler/in 5/B6
actually ['æktʃuəli] eigentlich; wirklich, tatsächlich
AD (= Anno Domini) [ˌeɪ'di:] n. Chr. (nach Christus) 2/BL1
ad (= advertisement) [æd, əd'vɜ:tɪsmənt] Werbung, Reklame; Anzeige 1/B3
add [æd] hinzufügen
add up [æd‿'ʌp] addieren 1/A2
* addictive [ə'dɪktɪv] Sucht-; *hier:* süchtig machend 1/O2
in addition to [ˌɪn‿ə'dɪʃn tə] zusätzlich zu 5/PP5
address [ə'dres] Adresse
address (to) [ə'dres] adressieren (an) 6/B3
adjective ['ædʒɪktɪv] Adjektiv 4/BL1
admire [əd'maɪə] bewundern 2/B2
admission [əd'mɪʃn] Eintritt 3/A4
* admit [əd'mɪt] *hier:* zulassen 3/O1
* adopt [ə'dɒpt] adoptieren, die Patenschaft übernehmen 1/O
adult ['ædʌlt] Erwachsene/r
advance [əd'vɑ:ns] voranbringen, weiterbringen 5/A3
advanced [əd'vɑ:nst] fortgeschritten
advancement [əd'vɑ:nsmənt] Vorrücken, Vorankommen 4/C3
advantage [əd'vɑ:ntɪdʒ] Vorteil
adventure [əd'ventʃə] Abenteuer, Erlebnis
adventurous [əd'ventʃ(ə)rəs] abenteuerlich; abenteuerlustig 3/A1
adverb ['ædvɜ:b] Adverb 6/BL3
advertising ['ædvəˌtaɪzɪŋ] Werbung, Reklame 1/B3
advice [əd'vaɪs] Rat
afford [ə'fɔ:d] sich leisten 3/B1
be afraid (of) [ˌbi‿ə'freɪd] Angst haben/sich fürchten (vor)
Africa ['æfrɪkə] Afrika 4/C1
African ['æfrɪkən] Afrikaner/in; afrikanisch 6/PP6
African American [ˌæfrɪkən‿ə'merɪkən] Afroamerikaner/in; afroamerikanisch 2/C2
after ['ɑ:ftə] danach; nach; nach(dem)
* after all [ˌɑ:ftər‿'ɔ:l] *hier:* schließlich 5/O1
afternoon [ˌɑ:ftə'nu:n] Nachmittag
in the afternoon [ˌɪn ði:‿ɑ:ftə'nu:n] am Nachmittag
afterwards ['ɑ:ftəwədz] später, danach 3/C5
again [ə'gen] wieder, noch einmal, noch mal
against [ə'genst] gegen
age [eɪdʒ] Alter
at the age of [ˌət ðə‿'eɪdʒ‿əv] im Alter von 1/B3
aggressive [ə'gresɪv] aggressiv
ago [ə'gəʊ] vor
* long ago [lɒŋ ə'gəʊ] vor langer Zeit 4/O1
two weeks ago [ˌtu: wi:ks‿ə'gəʊ] vor zwei Wochen
agree [ə'gri:] zustimmen
agree [ə'gri:] *hier:* vereinbaren 1/C4
* agree [ə'gri:] *hier:* sich einig sein 1/O2
agricultural [ˌægrɪ'kʌltʃ(ə)rəl] landwirtschaftlich 2/A3
ahead [ə'hed] vorn; *hier:* vorwärts 4/PP3
aim (at) [eɪm] zielen (auf) 4/A7
air [eə] Luft
air conditioner ['eə kən'dɪʃnə] Klimaanlage 6/B1
* air-conditioned ['eəkənˌdɪʃnd] klimatisiert 1/O2
airport ['eəˌpɔ:t] Flughafen
aisle [aɪl] Gang, Korridor 2/C5
alarm [ə'lɑ:m] Angst, Beunruhigung 2/C7
alarm clock [ə'lɑ:m ˌklɒk] Wecker
* alas [ə'læs] leider (Gottes) 4/O1
alcohol ['ælkəˌhɒl] Alkohol 4/A4
Algonquian [æl'gɒŋkwiən] Algonkin *(indian. Sprache)* 3/PP2
alive [ə'laɪv] lebendig, lebend 4/B2
all [ɔ:l] alle(s)
all day (long) [ˌɔ:l 'deɪ] den ganzen Tag
all over ['ɔ:l‿ˌəʊvə] überall in/auf
all right [ˌɔ:l 'raɪt] in Ordnung
All the best! [ˌɔ:l ðə‿'best] Alles Gute! 5/CL1
all the time [ˌɔ:l ðə 'taɪm] die ganze Zeit 1/B2
allow [ə'laʊ] erlauben, gestatten; ermöglichen
be allowed to do sth [bi‿əˌlaʊd tə 'du: sʌmθɪŋ] etw tun dürfen
almost ['ɔ:lməʊst] fast, beinahe
alone [ə'ləʊn] allein
along [ə'lɒŋ] entlang
already [ɔ:l'redi] schon
alright [ɔ:l'raɪt] in Ordnung
also ['ɔ:lsəʊ] auch
altar ['ɔ:ltə] Altar 1/B4
alternative [ɔ:l'tɜ:nətɪv] Alternative 6/B1
although [ɔ:l'ðəʊ] obwohl, obgleich
altogether [ˌɔ:ltə'geðə] völlig, ganz; insgesamt
aluminium foil [ˌæləmɪniəm 'fɔɪl] Alufolie 6/A5
always ['ɔ:lweɪz] immer
am (= ante meridiem) [eɪ em] morgens, vormittags *(nur hinter Uhrzeit zwischen Mitternacht und 12 Uhr mittags)* 3/A4
* amazing [ə'meɪzɪŋ] erstaunlich; *hier:* toll 2/O1
America [ə'merɪkə] Amerika 1/PP1
American [ə'merɪkən] Amerikaner/in; amerikanisch
among [ə'mʌŋ] unter 2/B2
amount [ə'maʊnt] Menge; *hier:* Betrag 6/A2
amusing [ə'mju:zɪŋ] amüsant, unterhaltsam 3/C3
anarchist ['ænəkɪst] Anarchist/in 3/B1
ancestor ['ænsestə] Vorfahr(e)/Vorfahrin 2/C2
ancestry ['ænsestri] Abstammung 2/C2
and [ænd] und
angry ['æŋgri] verärgert; zornig; wütend
animal ['ænɪml] Tier
announce [ə'naʊns] bekannt geben
announcement [ə'naʊnsmənt] Bekanntmachung, Mitteilung
annoy [ə'nɔɪ] ärgern, aufregen
annoyed [ə'nɔɪd] verärgert 3/C1
annoying [ə'nɔɪɪŋ] ärgerlich; lästig
* annual ['ænjuəl] jährlich 5/O1
anorak ['ænəˌræk] Anorak
another [ə'nʌðə] noch eine(r, s); ein zweiter/zweites/eine zweite; *hier:* weitere(r, s) 2/A1
answer ['ɑ:nsə] Antwort
answer ['ɑ:nsə] (be)antworten
the Antarctic [ðə æn'tɑ:ktɪk] die Antarktis 6/B1
anxious ['æŋkʃəs] besorgt 3/C1
any ['eni] irgendein(e); jede(r, s)
not any [nɒt‿'eni] (überhaupt) keine
anybody ['eniˌbɒdi] jede(r, s); jemand
not anymore [ˌnɒt‿eni'mɔ:] nicht mehr

anyone ['eni,wʌn] jede(r, s); jemand
anything ['eni,θɪŋ] alles; etwas
not anything [nɒt‿'eniθɪŋ] nichts
anytime ['eni,taɪm] jederzeit 1/C1
anyway ['eni,weɪ] sowieso; jedenfalls
not … anywhere [nɒt 'eni,weə] nirgendwo
not anywhere else [nɒt ,eniweər‿'els] nirgendwo anders (hin) 4/A4
anywhere else ['enɪweə ,els] irgendwo anders 6/A3
apart from [ə'pɑːt frəm] abgesehen von 5/B1
apartment [ə'pɑːtmənt] Wohnung 3/A4
appear [ə'pɪə] erscheinen
appearance [ə'pɪərəns] Erscheinen; Aussehen 4/C5
apple ['æpl] Apfel
apple pie ['æpl ,paɪ] gedeckter Apfelkuchen 6/PP6
apply to [ə'plaɪ tə] gelten für, betreffen 4/C2
appointment [ə'pɔɪntmənt] Ernennung; Termin
approach [ə'prəʊtʃ] Nähern; Ansatz
approach [ə'prəʊtʃ] sich nähern
approximately [ə'prɒksɪmətli] ungefähr, etwa 6/A2
April ['eɪprəl] April
area ['eəriə] Gebiet, Region; Viertel, Gegend; *hier:* Fläche 2/A5
argument ['ɑːgjʊmənt] Wortwechsel; *hier:* Streit; Argument 4/B1
argumentation *(no pl)* [,ɑːgjʊmen'teɪʃ(ə)n] Argumentation 3/C7
arithmetic *(no pl)* [ə'rɪθmətɪk] Arithmetik 2/C5
arm [ɑːm] Arm
army ['ɑːmi] Armee
around [ə'raʊnd] um; im; um … herum
be around [biː‿ə'raʊnd] da sein; in der Nähe sein 5/B1
walk/go around [,wɔːk/,gəʊ‿ə'raʊnd] herumlaufen; arrangieren 5/C3
arrest [ə'rest] verhaften
arrive [ə'raɪv] ankommen
art [ɑːt] Kunst
article ['ɑːtɪkl] Artikel
as [æz] als; wie; da; während
as … as … [æz] (genau)so … wie …
as well [æz 'wel] auch
as you please [,æz‿jə 'pliːz] wie es dir/Ihnen gefällt 3/A4
Asian ['eɪʃn] Asiat/in; asiatisch
ask [ɑːsk] fragen; bitten
ask (for) [ɑːsk] bitten (um), fragen (nach)
ask questions [ɑːsk‿'kwestʃnz] Fragen stellen
* fall asleep [,fɔːl‿ə'sliːp] einschlafen 1/O2
aspect ['æspekt] Aspekt, Gesichtspunkt
assistant [ə'sɪst(ə)nt] Assistent/in 5/B4

assistant camera person [ə'sɪst(ə)nt ,kæmərə pɜːsn] Kameraassistent/in 5/C3
assistant manager [ə'sɪst(ə)nt ,mænɪdʒə] stellvertretende/r Direktor/in / Filialleiter/in 6/A5
astonished [ə'stɒnɪʃt] erstaunt 1/C4
astronaut ['æstrə,nɔːt] Astronaut/in
astronomy *(no pl)* [ə'strɒnəmi] Astronomie 5/B6
at [æt] auf, an, in, bei; um
not at all [,nɒt‿ət‿'ɔːl] überhaupt nicht
at home [æt 'həʊm] zu Hause
at last [ət 'lɑːst] zu guter Letzt, endlich
at least [ət 'liːst] mindestens, wenigstens
at night [ət 'naɪt] am Abend, in der Nacht
at once [æt 'wʌns] auf einmal; sofort
at the age of [,ət ðə‿'eɪdʒ‿əv] im Alter von 1/B3
at the back [,æt ðə 'bæk] hinten
at the beginning [ət ðə bɪ'gɪnɪŋ] am Anfang, zu Beginn 2/A1
at the moment [,æt ðə 'məʊmənt] im Augenblick, momentan
at the same time [æt ðə ,seɪm 'taɪm] gleichzeitig 5/A3
athletics *(no pl)* [æθ'letɪks] Leichtathletik 5/A1
the Atlantic (Ocean) *(no pl)* [ði‿ət'læntɪk] der Atlantik 2/A3
atmosphere ['ætməs,fɪə] Atmosphäre; Stimmung 4/B1
attack [ə'tæk] angreifen 3/C4
attempt [ə'tempt] Versuch 1/B3
attend [ə'tend] teilnehmen (an) 2/B2
attic ['ætɪk] Dachboden, Speicher 3/B4
attract [ə'trækt] anziehen 4/A4
attraction [ə'trækʃn] Anziehung(skraft); Attraktion 2/A6
August ['ɔːgəst] August
aunt [ɑːnt] Tante
Austria ['ɒstriə] Österreich 3/B3
the authorities *(pl)* [ði‿ɔː'θɒrətiz] die Behörden
automatic [,ɔːtə'mætɪk] automatisch
autumn ['ɔːtəm] Herbst
available [ə'veɪləbl] verfügbar; erhältlich
avarice *(no pl)* ['ævərɪs] (Hab)gier, Habsucht 4/A1
average ['æv(ə)rɪdʒ] Durchschnitt 4/A4
avoid [ə'vɔɪd] (ver)meiden 4/A7
awake [ə'weɪk] wach 3/C3
award [ə'wɔːd] Preis, Auszeichnung
award [ə'wɔːd] verleihen 3/B3
make sb aware of sth ['meɪk sʌmbədi‿ə,weər‿əv ,sʌmθɪŋ] jdm etw bewusst machen 4/A6
away [ə'weɪ] weg
* awful ['ɔːfl] furchtbar, schrecklich 2/O1

B

baby food ['beɪbi ,fuːd] Babynahrung 6/B3
babysit ['beɪbi,sɪt] babysitten; aufpassen auf
back [bæk] Rücken
at the back [,æt ðə 'bæk] hinten
back [bæk] zurück
talk back [tɔːk 'bæk] eine freche Antwort geben 3/C1
back in (+ *Jahreszahl*) ['bæk‿ɪn] schon … 2/C7
background ['bæk,graʊnd] Hintergrund
bacon ['beɪkən] (Schinken)speck
bad [bæd] schlecht; schlimm; *hier:* böse 5/C4
* too bad ['tuː bæd] wirklich schade 1/O2
bag [bæg] Tasche; *hier:* Tüte, Sack 6/B3
* bake [beɪk] backen 6/O1
baked [beɪkt] gebacken 6/C2
baked beans [,beɪkt 'biːnz] *Bohnen in Tomatensauce* 6/PP6
baked potatoes *(pl)* [,beɪkt pə'teɪtəʊz] Ofenkartoffeln 1/A3
baker ['beɪkə] Bäcker/in
(at the) baker's ['beɪkəz] (in der) Bäckerei
bakery ['beɪkəri] Bäckerei
baking powder ['beɪkɪŋ ,paʊdə] Backpulver 1/B5
balance *(no pl)* ['bæləns] Balance, Gleichgewicht 6/B1
* bald [bɔːld] glatzköpfig, kahl 5/O1
bald eagle [bɔːld 'iːgl] weißköpfiger Seeadler 2/A5
ball [bɔːl] Ball
ball carrier ['ɔːl ,kæriə] *der-/diejenige, der/die den Ball hat* 5/A3
balloon [bə'luːn] (Luft)ballon
ballpoint pen *(AE)* [,bɔːlpɔɪnt 'pen] Kugelschreiber 6/CL3
ban sth ['bæn ,sʌmθɪŋ] etw verbieten; *hier:* herausnehmen aus 6/B1
banana [bə'nɑːnə] Banane
bandage ['bændɪdʒ] Verband
bank [bæŋk] Ufer 2/A1
bank [bæŋk] Bank *(Geld)* 3/C1
Baptist ['bæptɪst] Baptisten- 4/PP3
bar [bɑː] Stange; Riegel
barbecue ['bɑːbɪ,kjuː] grillen 6/PP6
* bark *(no pl)* [bɑːk] (Baum)rinde, Borke 1/O2
bark-covered ['bɑːk,kʌvəd] mit Rinde gedeckt 2/A1
barley *(no pl)* ['bɑːli] Gerste 6/B4
base [beɪs] Fuß; *hier:* Mal; Base 5/A3
be based on [bi 'beɪst‿ɒn] basieren/beruhen auf
basic ['beɪsɪk] grundlegend 4/PP3
basket ['bɑːskɪt] Korb 1/B5
basketball ['bɑːskɪt,bɔːl] Basketball 1/A2
bat [bæt] Schläger, Schlagholz 1/C1
bat and ball game [,bæt‿ən 'bɔːl geɪm] *Spiel mit Schlägern und Ball* 5/A3

bath [bɑːθ] (Bade)wanne; Bad
have a bath [ˌhæv‿ə 'bɑːθ] baden
bathroom ['bɑːθˌruːm] Bad(ezimmer)
batter ['bætə] Schlagmann 5/A3
battle ['bætl] Kampf, Gefecht, Schlacht
Bavaria [bə'veəriə] Bayern 1/PP1
BBQ (= barbecue) ['bɑːbɪˌkjuː] Grill, Bratrost; *hier:* vom Grill 6/C2
BC (= before Christ) [ˌbiː'siː] v. Chr. (vor Christus) 2/BL1
be [biː] sein
beach [biːtʃ] Strand
bean [biːn] Bohne
bear [beə] Bär 2/A1
* bear fruit [beə 'fruːt] Früchte tragen 4/O1
beard [bɪəd] Bart 3/B1
beat [biːt] schlagen; rühren
beautiful ['bjuːtəfl] schön
beauty ['bjuːti] Schönheit 2/A3
because [bɪ'kɒz] weil
because of [bɪ'kɒz‿əv] wegen
become [bɪ'kʌm] werden
bed [bed] Bett
bedpost ['bedˌpəʊst] Bettpfosten 1/B4
bedroom ['bedruːm] Schlafzimmer
beef [biːf] Rindfleisch
* beep [biːp] Piep(s)ton 1/O2
beer *(no pl)* [bɪə] Bier 6/B3
beetroot ['biːtruːt] Rote Beete 6/B3
before [bɪ'fɔː] bevor; vor; vorher 1/C4
begin [bɪ'gɪn] anfangen, beginnen
beginner [bɪ'gɪnə] Anfänger/in
beginning [bɪ'gɪnɪŋ] Anfang
at the beginning [ət ðə bɪ'gɪnɪŋ] am Anfang, zu Beginn 2/A1
behave [bɪ'heɪv] sich verhalten 2/B6
behind [bɪ'haɪnd] hinten; hinter
belief [bɪ'liːf] Glaube; Überzeugung 4/A2
believe [bɪ'liːv] glauben
bell [bel] Glocke; Klingel
belly ['beli] Bauch
belong [bɪ'lɒŋ tə] gehören
below [bɪ'ləʊ] unten; unter; unterhalb 2/A5
belt [belt] Gürtel 3/C1
bench [bentʃ] Bank
beneath [bɪ'niːθ] unter 1/B4
* berry ['beri] Beere 6/O1
beside [bɪ'saɪd] neben 3/C1
best [best] beste(r, s)
best [best] am meisten/liebsten
best boy [ˌbest 'bɔɪ] *Assistent des Elektrikers beim Film* 5/C3
bet [bet] setzen, wetten 4/B2
between [bɪ'twiːn] zwischen
beverage ['bev(ə)rɪdʒ] Getränk 6/C2
bicycle ['baɪsɪkl] Fahrrad
big [bɪg] groß
The Big Apple *(informal)* [ðə‿bɪg‿'æpl] New York 3/A3
the big cheese *(AE, informal)* [ðə bɪg 'tʃiːz] der Boss 6/C1
bighorn sheep ['bɪghɔːn ˌʃiːp] Dickhornschaf 2/B2

bike [baɪk] (Fahr)rad
bike ride ['baɪk raɪd] Radtour
bill [bɪl] Rechnung
billion ['bɪljən] Milliarde 2/A1
biodegradable [ˌbaɪəʊdɪ'greɪdəbl] biologisch abbaubar 6/B3
biography [baɪ'ɒgrəfi] Biografie 1/B5
bird [bɜːd] Vogel
biro ['baɪrəʊ] Kugelschreiber 6/CL3
birthday ['bɜːθdeɪ] Geburtstag
Happy birthday (to you)! [ˌhæpi 'bɜːθdeɪ] Alles Gute zum Geburtstag! 1/C4
biscuit ['bɪskɪt] Keks
bit [bɪt] Stück
bit [bɪt] *hier:* Scherbe 6/B3
a bit [ə 'bɪt] ein bisschen
bite [baɪt] beißen 1/B4
have a bite [ˌhæv‿ə 'baɪt] *hier:* probieren 6/A5
a bite to eat [ə 'baɪt‿tə ˌiːt] eine Kleinigkeit zu essen 6/I
* bitter ['bɪtə] bitter 1/O2
black [blæk] schwarz
black widow [blæk 'wɪdəʊ] schwarze Witwe 2/B2
blackboard ['blækˌbɔːd] Tafel
blacksmith ['blækˌsmɪθ] (Huf)schmied 5/C1
blame (sb for sth) ['bleɪm ˌsʌmbədi fə ˌsʌmθɪŋ] (jdm) die Schuld (an etw) geben 4/A7
blanket ['blæŋkɪt] (Bett)decke
blazer ['bleɪzə] Blazer; Jacke der Schuluniform
* blessing ['blesɪŋ] Segen 3/O1
blind [blaɪnd] blind
* blob [blɒb] Klecks; *hier:* Klumpen 5/O1
block [blɒk] Block; *hier:* Häuserblock 3/C1
block [blɒk] blockieren; *hier:* aufhalten 5/A3
blockbuster ['blɒkˌbʌstə] Bestseller; Kassenschlager 5/C2
blow [bləʊ] wehen, blasen
BLT (= bacon, lettuce and tomato) [ˌbiːel'tiː] *Sandwich mit Schinken, Salat und Tomate* 6/C2
blue [bluː] blau
little town blues ['lɪtl taʊn ˌbluːz] *hier etwa: kleinstädtischer Frust* 3/A1
blush [blʌʃ] erröten, rot werden 1/B4
Blvd (= boulevard) ['buːləˌvɑːd] Boulevard, Prachtstraße 3/C1
board [bɔːd] Brett; Tafel
on board [ɒn bɔːd] an Bord 3/A4
board a ship [ˌbɔːd‿ə 'ʃɪp] ein Schiff besteigen 2/C4
boat [bəʊt] Boot; Schiff
body ['bɒdi] Körper
body board ['bɒdi ˌbɔːd] *eine Art kurzes Surfbrett* 5/A3
bone [bəʊn] Knochen
boob *(AE, informal)* [buːb] Trottel 1/B4
book [bʊk] Buch
boom operator ['buːm ˌɒpəreɪtə] Tonassistent/in 5/C3

boot [buːt] Stiefel 3/A1
border ['bɔːdə] Grenze
be bored [bi 'bɔːd] sich langweilen
boring ['bɔːrɪŋ] langweilig
* born [bɔːn] geboren; *hier:* gebürtige(r, s) 3/O1
be born [bi 'bɔːn] geboren werden
borough ['bʌrə] Verwaltungsbezirk 3/A3
bossy ['bɒsi] herrschsüchtig, herrisch
both [bəʊθ] beide
both … and ['bəʊθ ˌənd] sowohl … als auch … 3/A3
bottle ['bɒtl] Flasche
bottom ['bɒtəm] Boden; unteres Ende
bounce [baʊns] aufspringen lassen 5/A3
bowl [bəʊl] Schüssel; Schale 4/B6
bowl *(AE)* [bəʊl] Stadion; *hier: Meisterschaft im Football* 5/PP4
box [bɒks] Schachtel; Kasten
box office ['bɒks‿ˌɒfɪs] Kasse *(im Kino, Theater)* 4/C2
boy [bɔɪ] Junge
boycott ['bɔɪˌkɒt] Boykott 4/C3
boyfriend ['bɔɪˌfrend] Freund
brain [breɪn] Gehirn; Verstand 6/B4
brains *(pl)* [breɪnz] Intelligenz, Grips 3/B1
brake [breɪk] Bremse
branch [brɑːntʃ] Zweig; Ast
brand [brænd] Marke 1/B3
brand-new [brændnjuː] brandneu 3/A1
* brave [breɪv] mutig, unerschrocken 4/O1
bread [bred] Brot
breadbasket ['bredˌbɑːskɪt] Brotkorb; Kornkammer 2/A3
breaded ['bredɪd] paniert 6/C2
break [breɪk] Pause
have/take a break [hæv/teɪk‿ə 'breɪk] eine Pause machen 2/C7
break [breɪk] (zer)brechen
break [breɪk] sich brechen 5/A3
break into [breɪk‿'ɪntə] einbrechen in
break out [breɪk‿'aʊt] ausbrechen 4/A7
break up [breɪk‿'ʌp] beenden; sich trennen; scheitern, in die Brüche gehen
breakfast ['brekfəst] Frühstück
have breakfast [hæv 'brekfəst] frühstücken
* take a deep breath [ˌteɪk‿ə diːp 'breθ] tief Luft holen 1/O2
* breathe [briːð] atmen 2/O1
* breeze [briːz] Brise 1/O2
bride [braɪd] Braut 1/B4
bridegroom ['braɪdˌgruːm] Bräutigam 1/B4
bridge [brɪdʒ] Brücke
bright [braɪt] hell; farbenfroh
bright [braɪt] *hier:* strahlend 1/B6
* bright [braɪt] *hier:* leuchtend 1/O2
Brilliant! *(BE, informal)* ['brɪljənt] Toll!, Klasse!

brilliantly ['brɪljəntli] brilliant, meisterhaft 5/C4
bring [brɪŋ] (mit)bringen
bring in [brɪŋ‿'ɪn] (herein)bringen
bring sth to life ['brɪŋ sʌmθɪŋ tə‿ˌlaɪf] etw zum Leben erwecken 5/C2
bring up [brɪŋ‿'ʌp] heraufbringen; großziehen
brisket *(no pl)* ['brɪskɪt] Bruststück 6/PP6
Britain ['brɪtn] Großbritannien 1/A4
British ['brɪtɪʃ] britisch 1/A3
the British *(pl)* [ðə 'brɪtɪʃ] die Briten 3/A3
bro (= brother, *AE informal*) [brəʊ, 'brʌðə] Bruder 3/C1
brochure ['brəʊʃə] Broschüre
brother ['brʌðə] Bruder
brotherhood ['brʌðəˌhʊd] Bruderschaft; Brüderlichkeit 4/PP3
brown [braʊn] braun
* brush *(pl -es)* [brʌʃ] Pinsel 4/O1
bubble ['bʌbl] Blase 1/B1
buddy *(AE, informal)* ['bʌdi] Kumpel 1/A3
budget ['bʌdʒɪt] Budget, Etat 6/C2
build [bɪld] bauen
building ['bɪldɪŋ] Gebäude, Bau
bun [bʌn] (rundes) Gebäckstück 6/C2
burger (= hamburger) ['bɜːgə, 'hæmˌbɜːgə] (Ham)burger
burger-flipper *(AE, informal)* ['bɜːgəˌflɪpə] *jd, der in einem Fast-food-Restaurant arbeitet* 1/A3
burglar ['bɜːglə] Einbrecher/in
burglary ['bɜːgləri] Einbruch
burn [bɜːn] brennen; *hier:* anbrennen lassen; verbrennen 6/B4
* burst [bɜːst] platzen 4/O1
bury ['beri] be-/vergraben
bus [bʌs] Bus
bush [bʊʃ] Busch
business *(no pl)* ['bɪznəs] Handel; Geschäft; Angelegenheit
businessman *(pl -men)* ['bɪznəsmæn, 'bɪznəsmen] Geschäftsmann 2/C4
busy ['bɪzi] beschäftigt; arbeitsreich; *hier:* gut besucht 1/A3
* busy ['bɪzi] *hier:* stark befahren 2/O1
but [bət] aber
(at the) butcher's ['bʊtʃəz] (in der) Metzgerei, Fleischerei
butter ['bʌtə] Butter
butter sb up [ˌbʌtə sʌmbədi‿'ʌp] jdm Honig um den Bart schmieren 6/C4
button ['bʌtn] Knopf 1/B4
buy [baɪ] kaufen
by [baɪ] bei, in der Nähe; mit; *hier:* von 3/B1
by [baɪ] *hier:* indem 4/A2
* by [baɪ] *hier:* (spätestens) bis 1/O2
by heart [baɪ 'hɑːt] auswendig
by plane [baɪ 'pleɪn] mit dem Flugzeug
by the way [ˌbaɪ ðə 'weɪ] übrigens 1/B3
bye *(informal)* [baɪ] tschüss

C

cab *(AE)* [kæb] Taxi 4/C5
café ['kæfeɪ] Café
cafeteria [ˌkæfə'tɪəriə] Cafeteria 5/C3
Cajun ['keɪdʒ(ə)n] Cajun; Cajun- 6/PP6
cake [keɪk] Kuchen
Californian [ˌkælɪ'fɔːniən] Kalifornier/in; kalifornisch 1/PP1
call [kɔːl] Anruf; Ruf
call [kɔːl] anrufen; nennen
call sb names [ˌkɔːl sʌmbədi 'neɪmz] jdn beschimpfen 4/C5
calm down [kɑːm 'daʊn] sich beruhigen
camera ['kæm(ə)rə] Kamera, Fotoapparat; *hier:* Aufnahme 3/A4; Filmkamera 5/C3
can [kæn] Dose; Büchse 1/B5; *hier:* Mülleimer 2/B5
can [kæn] können
candle ['kændl] Kerze
candy *(AE)* ['kændi] Süßigkeit(en) 6/B3
canned [kænd] konserviert; Dosen- 6/C2
canvas *(no pl)* ['kænvəs] Segeltuch; Leinwand 1/PP1
cap [kæp] Mütze, Kappe 1/C1
capital (city) ['kæpɪtl] Hauptstadt
captain ['kæptɪn] Kapitän/in
car [kɑː] Auto
car park ['kɑː ˌpɑːk] Parkplatz
caravan site ['kærəˌvæn saɪt] Campingplatz für Wohnwagen 6/B3
card [kɑːd] Karte; Pappe, Karton
care for (sb/sth) ['keə fə] sich um (jdn/etw) kümmern 6/B1
career [kə'rɪə] Beruf; Karriere
careful ['keəfl] vorsichtig; genau
carefully ['keəfli] vorsichtig; sorgfältig 6/B4
caress [kə'res] streicheln 3/B1
Caribbean [ˌkærɪ'biːən] karibisch 3/PP2
carrot ['kærət] Möhre, Karotte, Mohrrübe
carry ['kæri] tragen; übertragen
carry ['kæri] *hier:* mitnehmen 2/B5
case [keɪs] Fall 4/C3
cash *(no pl)* [kæʃ] Bargeld
cash register ['kæʃ ˌredʒɪstə] Registrierkasse 1/C4
casino [kə'siːnəʊ] (Spiel)kasino 2/A1
* cast [kɑːst] werfen 4/O1
cast sb (in a role) ['kɑːst ˌsʌmbədi] jdm (eine Rolle) geben 5/C2
castle [kɑːsl] Burg; Schloss
cat [kæt] Katze
catch [kætʃ] fangen
catch a cold [ˌkætʃ‿ə 'kəʊld] sich erkälten
catch the bus ['kætʃ ðə ˌbʌs] den Bus kriegen 5/B1
* catechism ['kætəˌkɪz(ə)m] Fragenkatalog 3/O1

cause [kɔːz] verursachen, hervorrufen
'cause (= because) [kəz, bɪ'kɒz] weil, da
CD [ˌsiː 'diː] CD 1/A3
celebrate ['seləbreɪt] feiern
* celebration [ˌselə'breɪʃn] Feier 6/O1
cellphone ['selˌfəʊn] Mobiltelefon, Handy 1/A2
center *(AE = centre BE)* ['sentə] Zentrum, Mitte 2/A1
central ['sentrəl] zentral; Mittel-
centre ['sentə] Zentrum, Mitte
century ['sentʃəri] Jahrhundert
ceramics [sə'ræmɪks] Keramik; *hier:* Töpfern 5/B4
cereal ['sɪəriəl] Frühstückszerealien; Frühstücksflocken 6/B4
cereal *(no pl)* ['sɪəriəl] Getreide 2/A3
ceremony ['serəməni] Zeremonie, Feier 3/B3
certainly ['sɜːtnli] sicher(lich); bestimmt
certificate [sə'tɪfɪkət] Urkunde, Bescheinigung 5/PP5
CFC (= chlorofluorocarbon) [ˌsiːef'siː, ˌklɔːrəʊˌflʊərəʊ'kɑːbən] FCKW (= Fluorchlorkohlenwasserstoff) 6/B1
chain [tʃeɪn] Kette
chair [tʃeə] Stuhl
chalk [tʃɔːk] Kalkstein; Kreide 3/B1
chalk [tʃɔːk] mit Kreide schreiben 3/B1
challenge ['tʃælɪndʒ] Herausforderung, schwierige Aufgabe
championship ['tʃæmpiənʃɪp] Meisterschaft 5/PP4
chance [tʃɑːns] Glück; Möglichkeit
change [tʃeɪndʒ] (Ver)änderung
change [tʃeɪndʒ] (ver)ändern; tauschen; sich ändern; *hier:* (aus)wechseln 4/B6
change [tʃeɪndʒ] *hier:* umsteigen 2/C4
change trains [ˌtʃeɪndʒ 'treɪnz] umsteigen
character ['kærɪktə] Charakter; Figur
charity ['tʃærəti] Barmherzigkeit; Wohltätigkeitsorganisation
* chart [tʃɑːt] Diagramm, Grafik 5/O1
cheap [tʃiːp] billig, preiswert
* cheat [tʃiːt] täuschen, betrügen 4/O1
check [tʃek] überprüfen, kontrollieren
check out sth *(AE)* ['tʃek‿aʊt ˌsʌmθɪŋ] sich etw ansehen 1/A3
cheddar *(no pl)* ['tʃedə] (Cheddar)käse 6/PP6
cheek [tʃiːk] Wange, Backe 3/B1
cheer [tʃɪə] Hurraruf 5/PP4
cheerfully ['tʃɪəf(ə)li] fröhlich, vergnügt 3/C1
cheerleading ['tʃɪəˌliːdɪŋ] *Cheerleaden* 1/A4
cheese [tʃiːz] Käse
chef [ʃef] Koch, Köchin 5/C2
chemical ['kemɪkl] Chemikalie 6/B2
chess [tʃes] Schach(spiel) 5/B6
chest [tʃest] Brust(korb)

chew [tʃuː] kauen
chew on sth ['tʃuː‿ɒn ˌsʌmθɪŋ] auf etw herumkauen; sich etw gründlich durch den Kopf gehen lassen 1/B3
*chew over sth ['tʃuː sʌmθɪŋ 'əʊvə] sich etw gründlich überlegen 1/O2
chewing ['tʃuːɪŋ] Kau- 1/B2
chewing gum *(no pl)* ['tʃuːɪŋ ˌgʌm] Kaugummi 1/A3
chicken ['tʃɪkɪn] Huhn
chief [tʃiːf] Leiter/in; Oberhaupt
child (*pl* **children**) [tʃaɪld, 'tʃɪldrən] Kind
chili (*AE* = chilli *BE*) ['tʃɪli] Chili, Peperoni 6/PP6
chimpanzee [ˌtʃɪmpæn'ziː] Schimpanse
Chinese [ˌtʃaɪ'niːz] Chinese/Chinesin; chinesisch 1/A2
chips *(pl)* [tʃɪps] Pommes frites
chocolate *(no pl)* ['tʃɒklət] Schokolade
choice [tʃɔɪs] Wahl
choir [kwaɪə] Chor 1/B4
choose [tʃuːz] auswählen
chop [tʃɒp] klein schneiden 6/PP6
chorus ['kɔːrəs] Refrain 4/C5
Christian ['krɪstʃən] Christ/in; christlich
Christmas ['krɪsməs] Weihnachten
*Christmas Day [ˌkrɪsməs 'deɪ] der erste Weihnachtsfeiertag 6/O1
church [tʃɜːtʃ] Kirche
cigarette [ˌsɪgə'ret] Zigarette 6/B3
cinema ['sɪnəmə] Kino
circle ['sɜːkl] Kreis
circumstance ['sɜːkəmstəns] Umstand 4/PP3
citizen ['sɪtɪzn] (Staats)bürger/in 4/C3
citizenship ['sɪtɪznʃɪp] Staatsbürgerschaft 3/B3
city ['sɪti] (Groß)stadt
city centre [ˌsɪti 'sentə] Innenstadt 6/CL3
*city limit ['sɪti ˌlɪmɪt] Stadtgrenze 1/O
civil rights *(pl)* [ˌsɪvl 'raɪts] Bürgerrechte 4/PP3
civil rights movement [ˌsɪvl ˌraɪts 'muːvmənt] Bürgerrechtsbewegung 4/C4
civil war [ˌsɪvl 'wɔː] Bürgerkrieg 4/C1
claim [kleɪm] *Anteil an einem Goldgräberunternehmen* 4/B2
clam chowder ['klæm ˌ tʃaʊdə] *(sämige) Muschelsuppe* 6/PP6
clap one's hands [ˌklæp wʌnz 'hændz] in die Hände klatschen 2/B5
clapperboard *(AE)* ['klæppəˌbɔːd] Klappe *(Film)* 5/C3
class [klɑːs] (Schul)klasse; Unterricht(sstunde)
classic ['klæsɪk] klassisch 3/A4
classmate ['klɑːsˌmeɪt] Klassenkamerad/in, Mitschüler/in
classroom ['klɑːsˌruːm] Klassenzimmer
clean [kliːn] sauber machen, reinigen, putzen
clean [kliːn] sauber
*clear ['klɪə] klar, deutlich 1/O2
clear up [klɪər‿'ʌp] klären; *hier:* aufräumen 6/B4
clever ['klevəli] klug; geschickt 6/B4
cliff [klɪf] Klippe, Kliff 2/B2
climate ['klaɪmət] Klima 2/B2
climb [klaɪm] (hinauf)steigen; klettern
climber ['klaɪmə] Bergsteiger/in 2/AL1
climbing *(no pl)* ['klaɪmɪŋ] Bergsteigen; Klettern 2/B2
*clip [klɪp] *hier:* klappern 3/O1
clock [klɒk] Uhr
close [kləʊz] schließen, zumachen
close [kləʊs] nah(e)
be close to sb [bi‿'kləʊs tə‿ˌsʌmbədi] jdm (sehr) nahestehen 3/C5
closed [kləʊzd] geschlossen, zu 3/C3
cloth [klɒθ] Tuch, Stoff 1/PP1
clothes *(npl)* [kləʊðz] Kleider, Kleidung
make clothes [meɪk 'kləʊðz] Kleider nähen 1/PP1
clothing company ['kləʊðɪŋ ˌkʌmp(ə)ni] Bekleidungsfirma 1/PP1
*cloud [klaʊd] Wolke 4/O1
club [klʌb] Klub, Verein
clue [kluː] Hinweis 6/B4
Co. = company [kəʊ, 'kʌmp(ə)ni] Firma, Unternehmen 1/PP1
coach [kəʊtʃ] (Omni)bus, Reisebus
coast [kəʊst] Küste
coat [kəʊt] Mantel
code [kəʊd] Kode; Gesetzbuch; *hier:* Gesetz 4/C1
coffee ['kɒfi] Kaffee
coffeepot ['kɒfiˌpɒt] Kaffeekanne 6/B3
coin [kɔɪn] Münze, Geldstück 3/B3
cold [kəʊld] Kälte; Erkältung
catch a cold [ˌkætʃ‿ə 'kəʊld] sich erkälten
cold [kəʊld] kalt
coleslaw *(no pl)* ['kəʊlˌslɔː] Krautsalat, Kohlsalat 6/PP6
collage ['kɒlɑːʒ] Collage 2/C6
collapse [kə'læps] zusammenbrechen 3/B1
collar ['kɒlə] Kragen 1/B4
colleague ['kɒliːg] (Arbeits)kollege/-kollegin; *hier:* Mitarbeiter/in 3/BL3
collect [kə'lekt] sammeln; einsammeln
collection [kə'lekʃn] Sammlung
college ['kɒlɪdʒ] *Bildungseinrichtung; hier:* Hochschule 2/A3
Colonel ['kɜːnl] (Herr) Oberst 3/B3
color (*AE* = colour *BE*) ['kʌlə] Farbe 1/C2
colored *(AE)* (= coloured *BE*) ['kʌləd] farbig 2/C5
coloring (*AE* = colouring *BE*) *(no pl)* ['kʌlərɪŋ] Farbstoff 1/B3
colour ['kʌlə] Farbe
column ['kɒləm] Säule; Spalte
combination [ˌkɒmbɪ'neɪʃn] Kombination 6/PP6
come [kʌm] kommen
come in [kʌm‿'ɪn] hereinkommen
come in [kʌm‿'ɪn] *hier:* eintreffen 1/PP1
Come on! [kʌm‿'ɒn] Komm(t) jetzt!, Mach(t) schon! 1/C4
come out [kʌm‿'aʊt] herauskommen
come over [ˌkʌm‿'əʊvə] herüberkommen; vorbeischauen 1/A3
comet ['kɒmɪt] Komet 5/B6
comfortable ['kʌmftəbl] bequem
commemorate [kə'meməˌreɪt] gedenken 2/A1
*commence [kə'mens] beginnen, anfangen 3/O1
comment ['kɒmənt] Kommentar, Bemerkung 6/A3
*comment ['kɒmənt] sich äußern, einen Kommentar abgeben 1/O2
have sth in common with [hæv ˌsʌmθɪŋ ɪn 'kɒmən wɪð] etw gemein(sam) haben mit 1/A2
communication [kəˌmjuːnɪ'keɪʃn] Kommunikation, Verständigung 4/B4
communications *(pl)* [kəˌmjuːnɪ'keɪʃns] Fernmeldewesen 2/A3
community [kə'mjuːnəti] Gemeinde; Gemeinschaft
community spirit [kə'mjuːnəti ˌspɪrɪt] Gemeinschaftsgeist 3/C5
*companion [kəm'pænjən] Begleiter/in 1/O2
company ['kʌmp(ə)ni] Firma; Gesellschaft
compare [kəm'peə] vergleichen
competition [ˌkɒmpə'tɪʃn] Wettbewerb
competition [ˌkɒmpə'tɪʃn] *hier:* Konkurrenz 1/B5
*complain [kəm'pleɪn] klagen, sich beklagen 1/O2
complaint [kəm'pleɪnt] Beschwerde, Klage 6/B4
complete [kəm'pliːt] vervollständigen
complete [kəm'pliːt] vollständig, komplett
completely [kəm'pliːtli] völlig 4/PP3
compose [kəm'pəʊz] komponieren 5/C3
composer [kəm'pəʊzə] Komponist/in 5/C3
concentrate ['kɒnsnˌtreɪt] (sich) konzentrieren
concern [kən'sɜːn] Anliegen, Sorge 6/B1
be concerned (about) [bi kən'sɜːnd] beunruhigt sein (wegen) 6/B1
concert ['kɒnsət] Konzert
conditioner *(no pl)* [kən'dɪʃnə] Pflegespülung 6/B3
conditions *(pl)* [kən'dɪʃnz] Bedingungen, Verhältnisse
conductor *(AE)* [kən'dʌktə] Zugführer/in 4/C1

conflict ['kɒnflɪkt] Konflikt 4/C5
conquer ['kɒŋkə] erobern; besiegen 3/A3
constant ['kɒnstənt] dauernd, ständig 1/PP1
constitution [ˌkɒnstɪ'tjuːʃn] Verfassung 4/C3
constitutional [ˌkɒnstɪ'tjuːʃn(ə)l] konstitutionell 2/A5
contact ['kɒntækt] Kontakt 4/A7
contain sth [kən'teɪn ˌsʌmθɪŋ] etw enthalten 6/B2
container [kən'teɪnə] Behälter 6/B2
content ['kɒntent] Inhalt; Gehalt 4/PP3
continent ['kɒntɪnənt] Kontinent, Erdteil 1/B4
continental [ˌkɒntɪ'nentl] Kontinental- 2/A5
continue [kən'tɪnjuː] fortführen; fortsetzen 3/A4
in contrast (to) [ɪn 'kɒntrɑːst] im Gegensatz (zu) 4/C1
control [kən'trəʊl] kontrollieren 3/C4
take control of sth [teɪk kən'trəʊl‿əv ˌsʌmθɪŋ] die Gewalt über etw übernehmen 4/A7
conversation [ˌkɒnvə'seɪʃn] Gespräch, Unterhaltung
convert into [kən'vɜːt‿ˌɪntə] verwandeln in 6/B4
cook [kʊk] kochen
cookbook ['kʊkˌbʊk] Kochbuch 6/B3
cookie ['kʊki] Keks, Plätzchen 1/B3
cooking ['kʊkɪŋ] Kochen 1/A3
cool as a cucumber [kuːl əz‿ə‿'kjuˌkʌmbə] völlig gelassen; cool 6/C4
cope (with) [kəʊp] zurechtkommen, fertig werden mit 4/B2
copper ['kɒpə] Kupfer 1/PP1
copy ['kɒpi] Kopie; Exemplar
copy ['kɒpi] *hier:* abschreiben 6/B3
copy into ['kɒpi‿ˌɪntə] abschreiben in 2/BL1
copy out [ˌkɒpi‿'aʊt] abschreiben
corn [kɔːn] Getreide, Korn 2/A3; *hier:* Mais 6/C2
corner ['kɔːnə] Ecke
correct [kə'rekt] korrigieren
correct [kə'rekt] richtig, korrekt
cost [kɒst] Preis, Kosten
cost [kɒst] kosten
costume ['kɒstjuːm] Tracht; Kostüm
cotton ['kɒtn] Baumwolle 2/C7
cough [kɒf] husten 3/B1
could [kʊd] könnte(n)/könntest/könntet
count [kaʊnt] zählen
country ['kʌntri] Land
countryside ['kʌntriˌsaɪd] Land(schaft)
couple ['kʌpl] Paar
the couple of times [ðə 'kʌpl‿əv ˌtaɪmz] die paar/wenigen Male 5/B1
of course [əv 'kɔːs] natürlich
court [kɔːt] Gericht 4/C3; (Spiel)platz; Court 5/A3

cousin ['kʌzn] Cousin/e
cover ['kʌvə] Buchdeckel 2/AL2
cover ['kʌvə] bedecken; abdecken
cover ['kʌvə] *hier:* sich erstrecken über 2/A1
be covered in/with sweat [bi 'kʌvəd ɪn/wɪð ˌswet] in Schweiß gebadet sein 2/C7
cow [kaʊ] Kuh
coyote [kɔɪ'əʊti] Kojote 2/B2
cracker ['krækə] Kräcker 6/C2
crazy ['kreɪzi] verrückt
go crazy [gəʊ 'kreɪzi] verrückt werden 1/B4
cream [kriːm] Sahne
creamed spinach ['kriːmd ˌspɪnɪdʒ] Rahmspinat 6/PP6
creamy ['kriːmi] cremig, sahnig 6/PP6
create [kri'eɪt] erschaffen; *hier:* gestalten 1/B6
creative [kri'eɪtɪv] kreativ, schöpferisch 1/B6
* creature ['kriːtʃə] Kreatur, Lebewesen 4/O1
creed [kriːd] Überzeugung 4/PP3
* creep [kriːp] kriechen 1/O2
crime [kraɪm] Verbrechen; Kriminalität 3/C5
crisis ['kraɪsɪs] Krise 2/C4
crisps *(npl)* [krɪsps] Chips
crocodile ['krɒkədaɪl] Krokodil
crook *(informal)* [krʊk] Gauner 4/C5
-crooked ['krʊkɪd] krumm 3/B1
crop [krɒp] Feldfrucht; Ernte 2/A3
croquette [krɒ'ket] Krokette 6/C2
cross [krɒs] Kreuz
cross [krɒs] durchqueren; überqueren
cross out [krɒs‿'aʊt] aus-, durchstreichen 2/C7
crossbar ['krɒsˌbɑː] Querlatte, Torlatte 5/A3
* crossing ['krɒsɪŋ] *Übergang* 1/O
crown [kraʊn] Krone
cruel ['kruːəl] grausam; gemein
cruise [kruːz] Kreuzfahrt 3/A4
cry [kraɪ] weinen; schreien
cucumber ['kjuːˌkʌmbə] (Salat)gurke
cultural ['kʌltʃ(ə)rəl] kulturell 6/PP6
culture ['kʌltʃə] Kultur 1/A1
cup [kʌp] Tasse
cupboard ['kʌbəd] Schrank
curious ['kjʊəriəs] neugierig 3/A1
currency [kʌrənsi] Währung
curtain ['kɜːtən] Vorhang, Gardine 5/CL2
custom ['kʌstəm] Brauch, Sitte
customer ['kʌstəmə] Kunde/Kundin
cut [kʌt] schneiden
* cut down [kʌt 'daʊn] umhauen, fällen 6/O1
cut out [kʌt‿'aʊt] herausschneiden
the Czech Republic [tʃek rɪ'pʌblɪk] die Tschechische Republik 3/BL3

D

dad *(informal)* [dæd] Papa, Vati
daily ['deɪli] täglich

dairy products *(pl)* ['deəri ˌprɒdʌkt] Molkereierzeugnisse 6/B4
Dakota [de'kəʊtə] *(indian. Sprache)* 3/PP2
damage ['dæmɪdʒ] Schaden
damage ['dæmɪdʒ] schaden; (be)schädigen
dance [dɑːns] Tanz
dance [dɑːns] tanzen
dancer ['dɑːnsə] Tänzer/in
danger ['deɪndʒə] (Lebens)gefahr
dangerous ['deɪndʒərəs] gefährlich
Danish ['deɪnɪʃ] Dänisch 2/A2
dark [dɑːk] Dunkelheit
dark [dɑːk] dunkel
darling ['dɑːlɪŋ] Liebling, Schatz 3/B4
database ['deɪtəˌbeɪs] Datenbank 3/B1
date [deɪt] Datum
date of birth [ˌdeɪt‿əv 'bɜːθ] Geburtsdatum 5/C2
daughter ['dɔːtə] Tochter
day [deɪ] Tag
one day [wʌn 'deɪ] eines Tages 4/A4
all day (long) [ˌɔːl 'deɪ] den ganzen Tag
dead [ded] tot
deaf [def] taub; schwerhörig
* deal [diːl] Geschäft, Handel 1/O2
dear [dɪə] lieb, teuer
Dear … [dɪə] *in Briefen:* Liebe(r) …; Sehr geehrte(r) …
death [deθ] Tod
decay [dɪ'keɪ] verfallen 3/A3
December [dɪ'sembə] Dezember
decide [dɪ'saɪd] sich entscheiden; beschließen; entscheiden; bestimmen 2/A1
decision [dɪ'sɪʒn] Entscheidung
the Declaration of Independence [ðə dekləˌreɪʃn‿əv‿ɪndɪ'pendəns] *die Unabhängigkeitserklärung der USA* 2/A1
declare [dɪ'kleə] verkünden, bekannt machen 4/C1
decorate ['dekəˌreɪt] schmücken
decoration [ˌdekə'reɪʃn] Dekoration
deep [diːp] tief
* deer *(no pl)* [dɪə] Hirsch 6/O1
defeat sb [dɪ'fiːt ˌsʌmbədi] jdn besiegen 4/C1
defensive [dɪ'fensɪv] Verteidigungs- 5/A3
definition [ˌdefə'nɪʃn] Definition, Erklärung 6/B2
degree [dɪ'griː] Grad; Maß 2/C7
delicious [dɪ'lɪʃəs] köstlich, lecker
deliver [dɪ'lɪvə] liefern; zustellen
demonstration [ˌdemən'streɪʃn] Demonstration 4/C3
denim® ['denɪm] Denim; blauer Jeansstoff 1/PP1
denims *(pl)* ['denɪmz] Jeans 1/PP1
dentist ['dentɪst] Zahnarzt/ärztin 3/C5
deny [dɪ'naɪ] abstreiten; *hier:* verweigern 3/B2
department manager [dɪ'pɑːtmənt ˌmænɪdʒə] Abteilungsleiter/in 1/C1

depend on [dɪ'pend‿ɒn] abhängen von 5/A3
deport [dɪ'pɔːt] ausweisen 3/B3
depressive [dɪ'presɪv] depressiv 4/A4
describe [dɪ'skraɪb] beschreiben
description [dɪ'skrɪpʃn] Beschreibung 5/C3
* desert ['dezət] Wüste 2/O1
deserve [dɪ'zɜːv] verdienen 5/C4
design [dɪ'zaɪn] Entwurf; Design; *hier:* Konstruktion 5/A3
design [dɪ'zaɪn] entwerfen, gestalten 5/C1
desk [desk] Schreibtisch
* desperately ['desp(ə)rətli] verzweifelt 4/O1
despite [dɪ'spaɪt] trotz 4/A4
dessert [dɪ'zɜːt] Nachtisch, Dessert
destination [ˌdestɪ'neɪʃn] (Reise)ziel, Bestimmungsort 2/C4; *hier:* Schauplatz 3/A4
destroy [dɪ'strɔɪ] zerstören
detail ['diːteɪl] Detail, Einzelheit
develop [dɪ'veləp] sich entwickeln; entstehen 5/A3
development [dɪ'veləpmənt] Entwicklung; Wachstum
devote oneself to sth [dɪ'vəʊt wʌnˌself tə ˌsʌmθɪŋ] sich etw widmen 2/A3
devotee [ˌdevəʊ'tiː] Verehrer/in; Anhänger/in 4/PP3
dialogue ['daɪə'lɒg] Gespräch, Dialog
diary ['daɪəri] Tagebuch
roll a dice [ˌrəʊl‿ə 'daɪs] würfeln
dictionary ['dɪkʃən(ə)ri] Wörterbuch; Wörterverzeichnis
die [daɪ] sterben
diet ['daɪət] Nahrung, Ernährung; Diät
differ (from sth) ['dɪfə] sich (von etw) unterscheiden 2/A3
difference ['dɪfrəns] Unterschied
different ['dɪfrənt] anders, andere(r, s); verschieden
difficult ['dɪfɪklt] schwierig, schwer
* difficulty ['dɪfɪklti] Mühe; Schwierigkeit 1/O2
dig (for) [dɪg] graben (nach); *hier:* schürfen 4/B2
(gold) digger ['dɪgə] Goldgräber 4/B2
dinner ['dɪnə] Abendessen; Mittagessen
dino tots ['daɪnə ˌtɒts] *Pommes in Dinosaurierform* 6/C2
direct [dɪ'rekt] leiten, führen; *hier:* anleiten 5/C3
direct [dɪ'rekt] direkt
* direction [dɪ'rekʃn] Richtung 4/O1
director [də'rektə] Direktor/in; *hier:* Regisseur/in 5/C1
director of photography [də'rektə‿əv fəˌtɒgrəfi] Aufnahmeleiter 5/C3
dirty ['dɜːti] dreckig, schmutzig
disadvantage [ˌdɪsəd'vɑːntɪdʒ] Nachteil
disagree [ˌdɪsə'griː] nicht übereinstimmen; nicht einverstanden sein; nicht zustimmen
disappear [ˌdɪsə'pɪə] verschwinden
disappointed [ˌdɪsə'pɔɪntɪd] enttäuscht
disco (= discotheque) ['dɪskəʊ] Disko(thek)
discover [dɪ'skʌvə] herausfinden, entdecken
discovery [dɪ'skʌv(ə)ri] Entdeckung 2/B2
discrimination [dɪˌskrɪmɪ'neɪʃn] Diskriminierung, Benachteiligung 4/C1
discuss [dɪ'skʌs] besprechen, diskutieren
disease [dɪ'ziːz] Krankheit
dish [dɪʃ] Schale; Gericht
the dishes *(pl)* [ðə ''dɪʃɪz] das Geschirr
dishwasher ['dɪʃˌwɒʃə] Geschirrspülmaschine 6/A5
distance ['dɪstəns] Strecke; Entfernung
district ['dɪstrɪkt] Gebiet; Bezirk 2/A1
disturb [dɪ'stɜːb] stören 6/B1
* dive [daɪv] einen Kopfsprung machen; tauchen 4/O1
divide [dɪ'vaɪd] (auf)teilen 2/AL1
is divided into [ɪz dɪ'vaɪdɪd ˌɪntə] ist aufgeteilt in 2/A3
do [duː] machen, tun
do a paper round [ˌduː‿ə 'peɪpə ˌraʊnd] Zeitungen austragen
do a trick [duː‿ə 'trɪk] ein Kunststück vorführen 5/A3
do the shopping [ˌduː ðə 'ʃɒpɪŋ] einkaufen (gehen)
do the washing up [ˌduː ðə ˌwɒʃɪŋ‿'ʌp] abspülen
doctor ['dɒktə] Arzt/Ärztin
doctorate ['dɒkt(ə)rət] Doktor, Doktortitel 3/B3
dog [dɒg] Hund
walk the dog [ˌwɔːk ðə 'dɒg] den Hund ausführen
donkey ['dɒŋki] Esel 5/C1
door [dɔː] Tür
double ['dʌbl] doppelt; zweimal
double-decker *(AE, informal)* [ˌdʌbl'dekə] *doppeltes Sandwich* 6/C2
double-decker bus [ˌdʌbldekə 'bʌs] Doppeldecker(bus) 3/A4
dough *(AE, informal)* [dəʊ] Kohle, Knete 1/B4
down [daʊn] hinunter, hinab
downtown [ˌdaʊn'taʊn] Innenstadt- 3/A4
doz. (= dozen) ['dʌzn] Dutzend 6/C2
dozen ['dʌzn] Dutzend 4/B5
dragon ['drægən] Drache 5/C1
drama ['drɑːmə] Schauspielerei; Theater
draw [drɔː] zeichnen
drawer ['drɔːə] Schublade
dreads *(pl)* (= dreadlocks) [dredz] Dreadlocks 4/C5
dream [driːm] Traum
dream [driːm] träumen
dress [dres] Kleid
dress [dres] (sich) anziehen
dress up [dres‿'ʌp] sich herausputzen; sich verkleiden
dressed [drest] angezogen; gekleidet 2/C7
dressing ['dresɪŋ] (Salat)soße, Dressing 6/C2
dressing room ['dresɪŋ ˌruːm] Ankleideraum, Umkleidekabine 1/C1
dribble ['drɪbl] dribbeln 5/A3
drink [drɪŋk] Getränk
drink [drɪŋk] trinken
drinkable ['drɪŋkəbl] trinkbar
* drip [drɪp] tropfen, tröpfeln 1/O2
drive [draɪv] fahren
driver ['draɪvə] Fahrer/in
drop [drɒp] fallen lassen
drop [drɒp] (herunter)fallen 1/C4
drop in *(informal)* [drɒp‿'ɪn] vorbeischauen, vorbeikommen 5/B6
dropout ['drɒpaʊt] (Studien)abbrecher/in, Schulabgänger/in 5/PP5
drug [drʌg] Medikament; Droge
dry [draɪ] trocken
duck [dʌk] Ente
dude *(informal)* [duːd] *feiner Pinkel; Typ* 3/C1
during ['djʊərɪŋ] während
dust *(no pl)* [dʌst] Staub 2/C7
dustbin ['dʌstbɪn] Mülleimer 6/B3
Dutch [dʌtʃ] holländisch, niederländisch 4/A7
the Dutch *(pl)* [ðə 'dʌtʃ] die Holländer/Niederländer 4/A7

E

e. g. [ˌiː'dʒiː] z. B. (zum Beispiel) 2/C4
ea. (= each) [iːtʃ] jede(r, s) 6/C2
each [iːtʃ] jede(r, s)
each other [ˌiːtʃ‿'ʌðə] einander
eagle ['iːgl] Adler 2/B2
ear [ɪə] Ohr
early ['ɜːli] früh
earn [ɜːn] verdienen
earring ['ɪərɪŋ] Ohrring
earth [ɜːθ] Erde
east [iːst] Osten
in the east (of) [ɪn ðiˌ'iːst] im Osten (von) 2/B1
easy ['iːzi] einfach
feel easy [fiːl‿'iːzi] sich behaglich fühlen 1/B6
eat [iːt] essen
eatable ['iːtəbl] essbar, genießbar
eats *(informal, pl)* [iːts] Häppchen 6/PP6
economy [ɪ'kɒnəmi] Wirtschaft
edge [edʒ] *hier:* sich langsam bewegen 1/C4
education [ˌedjʊ'keɪʃn] (Aus)bildung 2/C4
* effort ['efət] Mühe, Anstrengung 4/O1
egg [eg] Ei
eight [eɪt] acht
elderly ['eldəli] ältere(r, s)
elect [ɪ'lekt] wählen 3/B3

elective (subject) [ɪ'lektɪv] Wahlfach 5/B2
electric [ɪ'lektrɪk] elektrisch, Elektro- 6/B3
electricity [ɪˌlek'trɪsəti] Elektrizität, Strom
elementary school [elɪ'ment(ə)ri ˌsku:l] Grundschule 5/PP5
elements *(pl)* ['elɪmənts] Elemente, Naturgewalten 5/A3
elephant ['elɪfənt] Elefant
eleven [ɪ'levn] elf
else [els] andernfalls, sonst
anywhere else ['enɪweə ˌels] irgendwo anders 6/A3
somebody else [ˌsʌmbədi‿'els] jemand anders
something else [ˌsʌmθɪŋ‿'els] noch etwas
somewhere else [ˌsʌmweər‿'els] irgendwo anders 5/B1
what else [wɒt‿'els] was noch, was sonst
emigrate (to) ['emɪgreɪt] auswandern (nach) 1/PP1
employer [ɪm'plɔɪə] Arbeitgeber/in 4/C1
empty ['empti] leer
encyclopaedia [ɪnˌsaɪklə'pi:diə] Lexikon, Enzyklopädie 2/A2
end [end] Ende
in the end [ɪn ði‿'end] letzten Endes; schließlich 3/C5
end [end] beenden, zu Ende bringen; enden
ending ['endɪŋ] Ende, Schluss 3/C2
England ['ɪŋglənd] England
English ['ɪŋglɪʃ] Engländer/in; englisch
* Englishman ['ɪŋglɪʃmən, 'ɪŋglɪʃmən] Engländer 3/O1
enjoy [ɪn'dʒɔɪ] genießen
enjoyable [ɪn'dʒɔɪəbl] angenehm, nett
enough [ɪ'nʌf] genug, genügend, ausreichend
ensure [ɪn'ʃɔ:] sicherstellen, garantieren 4/C3
enter ['entə] hineingehen (in); betreten
entertainment [ˌentə'teɪnmənt] Unterhaltung, Unterhaltungs- 2/A1
enthusiasm [ɪn'θju:ziˌæzəm] Enthusiasmus, Begeisterung 5/C2
entrance ['entrəns] Eingang; Einfahrt; Eintritt
entrance fee ['entrəns ˌfi:] Eintritt(sgeld) 4/C2
entrée *(AE)* ['ɒntreɪ] Hauptgericht 6/C2
entry ['entri] Eintritt; Eintrag
entry ['entri] *hier:* Einreise 3/B1
envelope ['envələʊp] Briefumschlag, Kuvert 6/B3
environment [ɪn'vaɪrənmənt] Umgebung; Umwelt 4/A2
equal ['i:kwəl] gleich; *hier:* gleichberechtigt 4/C2
equipment [ɪ'kwɪpmənt] Ausrüstung, Ausstattung

eraser [ɪ'reɪzə] Radiergummi
error ['erə] Fehler; *hier:* Fehlpass 5/A3
escape [ɪ'skeɪp] (ent)fliehen; entkommen
especially [ɪ'speʃli] besonders
* establish [ɪ'stæblɪʃ] gründen; *hier:* durchsetzen 3/O1
was established [wɒz‿ɪ'stæblɪʃt] wurde gegründet 2/B2
etc (= et cetera) [et 'set(ə)rə] usw., etc. 5/C2
ethnic ['eθnɪk] ethnisch 4/C4
Europe ['jʊərəp] Europa
European [ˌjʊərə'pi:ən] Europäer/in, europäisch 3/PP2
even ['i:vn] selbst; sogar; *hier:* noch
not even [nɒt‿'i:vn] (noch) nicht einmal
evening ['i:vnɪŋ] Abend
in the evening [ˌɪn ði‿'i:vnɪŋ] am Abend
ever ['evə] jemals
ever since [ˌevə 'sɪns] seitdem
ever so *(informal)* ['evə səʊ] wahnsinnig *(als Verstärkung)* 2/C7
every ['evri] jede(r, s)
every few … *(informal)* ['evri‿fju: …] alle paar … 3/C5
everybody ['evriˌbɒdi] jede/r
everyone ['evriwʌn] jede/r; alle
everything ['evriθɪŋ] alles
everywhere ['evriweə] überall
evidence *(no pl)* ['evɪd(ə)ns] Beweis(e) 6/B4
evil ['i:vl] Übel, das Böse 5/C1
exact [ɪg'zækt] genau
exam (= examination) [ɪg'zæm, ɪgˌzæmɪ'neɪʃn] Prüfung
examine [ɪg'zæmɪn] prüfen; untersuchen
example [ɪg'zɑ:mpl] Beispiel
for example [ˌfər‿ɪg'zɑ:mpl] zum Beispiel
excellent ['eksələnt] ausgezeichnet
* exchange [ɪks'tʃeɪndʒ] austauschen 6/O1
excited [ɪk'saɪtɪd] aufgeregt
exciting [ɪk'saɪtɪŋ] aufregend; spannend
Excuse me! [ɪk'skju:z ˌmi] Entschuldigen Sie bitte!, Entschuldigung!
exercise ['eksəˌsaɪz] Übung
exercise book ['eksəsaɪz ˌbʊk] Heft
exist [ɪg'zɪst] existieren, bestehen 4/A7
expect [ɪk'spekt] erwarten
expense [ɪk'spens] (Geld)ausgabe; Kosten
expensive [ɪk'spensɪv] teuer
experience [ɪk'spɪəriəns] Erfahrung
experience [ɪk'spɪəriəns] erleben; kennen lernen 3/A4
explain [ɪk'spleɪn] erklären
explanation [ˌeksplə'neɪʃn] Erklärung; Erläuterung 6/B1
explore [ɪk'splɔ:] erforschen, erkunden 3/A4
express [ɪk'spres] ausdrücken 6/A4

expression [ɪk'spreʃn] Ausdruck, Äußerung 3/A1
extra ['ekstrə] zusätzlich
extract ['ekstrækt] Auszug, Exzerpt 4/PP3
extremely [ɪk'stri:mli] äußerst 1/C4
eye [aɪ] Auge
* eye contact *(no pl)* ['aɪ ˌkɒntækt] Blickkontakt 5/O1
eye-catching ['aɪˌkætʃɪŋ] auffällig 1/B6
eyewitness ['aɪˌwɪtnəs] Augenzeuge/-zeugin 3/B1

F

F (= Fahrenheit) ['færənhaɪt] Fahrenheit *(Maßeinheit für Temperatur)* 2/B2
face [feɪs] Gesicht
face down [ˌfeɪs 'daʊn] mit dem Gesicht nach unten; *hier:* mit dem Text nach unten 3/B6
face sb ['feɪs ˌsʌmbədi] sich jdm zuwenden, zu jdm blicken 2/C7
facilities *(pl)* [fə'sɪlətiz] Einrichtungen, Anlagen 2/B4
fact [fækt] Wirklichkeit; Tatsache; tatsächlich 3/C1
in fact [ɪn 'fækt] tatsächlich 3/C1
fact file ['fækt ˌfaɪl] Steckbrief 5/C2
factory ['fæktri] Fabrik; Werk
facts (on/about) *(pl)* [fækts] Fakten (über) 2/A5
Fahrenheit ['færənhaɪt] Fahrenheit *(Maßeinheit für Temperatur)* 2/B2
* fail [feɪl] versagen, scheitern 4/O1
fair [feə] *hier:* angemessen 1/C1
fairytale ['feəriˌteɪl] Märchen- 5/C1
faith [feɪθ] Vertrauen; Glaube
* faithful ['feɪθfl] treu 4/O1
falcon ['fɔ:lkən] Falke 2/B2
fall *(AE)* [fɔ:l] Herbst 2/B1
fall [fɔ:l] fallen
* fall asleep [ˌfɔ:l‿ə'sli:p] einschlafen 1/O2
fall down [fɔ:l 'daʊn] hinfallen, umfallen
fall in love (with) [ˌfɔ:l‿ɪn 'lʌv] sich verlieben (in) 5/C1
false [fɔ:ls] falsch 3/A4
familiar [fə'mɪliə] vertraut; bekannt
family ['fæmli] Familie
famous ['feɪməs] berühmt
fantastic *(informal)* [fæn'tæstɪk] fantastisch
* fantastically *(informal)* [fæn'tæstɪkli] unwahrscheinlich, unglaublich 5/O1
far [fɑ:] von weit her; weit
as far as [əz 'fɑ:r‿əz] soweit 3/B4
fare [feə] Fahrpreis 3/C3
farm [fɑ:m] Bauernhof
farmer ['fɑ:mə] Bauer, Farmer
farming ['fɑ:mɪŋ] Ackerbau und Viehzucht 2/A3
fascinated ['fæsɪneɪtɪd] fasziniert 4/B6
fashion ['fæʃn] Mode
fast [fɑ:st] schnell
fat [fæt] dick

father ['fɑːθə] Vater
fatigue *(no pl)* [fə'tiːg] Ermüdung; Anstrengung, Strapaze 4/PP3
favorite (*AE* = favourite *BE*) ['feɪv(ə)rət] Lieblings- 1/B4
favourite ['feɪv(ə)rət] Liebling; Favorit/in
favourite ['feɪv(ə)rət] Lieblings-
*feast [fiːst] schlemmen 6/O1
*feather ['feðə] Feder 1/O2
February ['februəri] Februar
federal ['fed(ə)rəl] föderativ 2/A5
fee [fiː] Gebühr
feed [fiːd] zu essen geben, füttern
feel [fiːl] (sich) fühlen; sich anfühlen
feel uneasy [fiːl 'ʌn'iːzi] sich unbehaglich fühlen 3/C1
feeling ['fiːlɪŋ] Gefühl
ferry ['feri] Fähre
festival ['festɪvl] Fest
few [fjuː] einige; wenige
a few [ə 'fjuː] einige
field [fiːld] Wiese; Feld; *hier:* Spielfeld 5/A3
field goal *(AE)* ['fiːld ˌgəʊl] Feldtor 5/A3
field hockey ['fiːld ˌhɒki] (Feld)hockey 1/A2
field trip ['fiːld trɪp] Exkursion 2/B1
fifth [fɪfθ] fünfte(r, s)
fight [faɪt] Kampf; Streit
fight [faɪt] kämpfen
figure ['fɪgə] Gestalt
figures ['fɪgəz] *hier:* Zahlen 2/C2
figure ['fɪgə] *hier:* ausrechnen 2/C7
file [faɪl] (Akten)hefter; Datei
filet (= fillet) ['fɪlɪt] Filet 6/C2
fill [fɪl] füllen
fill in [fɪl‿'ɪn] ausfüllen; eintragen
film [fɪlm] Film
shoot a film [ʃuːt‿ə 'fɪlm] einen Film drehen 5/C3
film [fɪlm] filmen, drehen 3/A4
final ['faɪnl] letzte(r, s) 3/C1
finally ['faɪn(ə)li] schließlich; endlich
finances *(pl)* ['faɪnænsɪz] Finanzen 2/A3
financial district [faɪ'nænʃl ˌdɪstrɪkt] Finanzbezirk 3/A4
find [faɪnd] finden
find out [faɪnd‿'aʊt] herausfinden
Find out what each paragraph is about. [faɪnd‿'aʊt wɒt‿iːtʃ ˌpærəgrɑːf ɪz‿əˌbaʊt] Finde heraus, worum es in jedem Abschnitt geht. 2/B2
find out about [ˌfaɪnd‿'aʊt‿əˌbaʊt] sich informieren über
finding [faɪndɪŋ] Entdeckung; Ergebnis 6/A1
fine [faɪn] in Ordnung, gut; fein
finger ['fɪŋgə] Finger
finish ['fɪnɪʃ] beenden, aufhören; aufessen; fertig stellen
*finishing line ['fɪnɪʃɪŋ ˌlaɪn] Ziellinie 5/O1
fire [faɪə] Feuer
like it was on fire [laɪk‿ɪt ˌwɒz‿ɒn 'faɪə] als würde es brennen 5/B1
firefighter ['faɪəˌfaɪtə] Feuerwehrmann/-frau
fireplace ['faɪəˌpleɪs] Kamin
first [fɜːst] erste(r, s)
first [fɜːst] zuerst; als Erstes
first [fɜːst] *hier:* zum ersten Mal 6/B4
firstly ['fɜːstli] erstens 3/C5
fish (*pl* **fish** *or* **fishes**) [fɪʃ] Fisch
fish and chips [ˌfɪʃ‿ən 'tʃɪps] Fisch und Chips 1/A4
fisherman (*pl* -men) ['fɪʃəmən] Fischer; Angler 4/A2
fishing ['fɪʃɪŋ] Fischerei, Fischen 2/A3
(at the) fishmonger's ['fɪʃˌmɒŋgəz] (im/in der) Fischgeschäft, Fischhandlung
fit [fɪt] sich eignen; passen (zu)
five [faɪv] fünf
fix [fɪks] festmachen; reparieren
fixins' (= fixings) *(AE, informal, pl)* ['fɪksɪŋz] Beilagen 6/PP6
flag [flæg] Fahne; Flagge
flame [fleɪm] Flamme
*flap [flæp] flattern 5/O1
flash by [flæʃ 'baɪ] vorbeirasen 3/C1
flat [flæt] (Etagen)wohnung, Mietwohnung
flat [flæt] flach; platt
flavor (*AE* = flavour *BE*) ['fleɪvə] Geschmack, Aroma 1/B3
flavouring ['fleɪvərɪŋ] Aroma, Geschmacksstoff 6/PP6
flee [fliː] fliehen, flüchten 5/C1
flight [flaɪt] Fliegen; Flug
flip out *(informal)* [ˌflɪp‿'aʊt] ausflippen 5/B1
*flip-flop *(informal)* ['flɪpˌflɒp] *schlappen, schlenkern* 5/O1
*float [fləʊt] schwimmen; *hier:* schweben 1/O2
floor [flɔː] Boden; *hier:* Stock(werk) 1/C1
be a flop [biː‿ə 'flɒp] eine Niete sein 5/B1
flower ['flaʊə] Blume; Blüte
fly [flaɪ] fliegen
flyer (= flier) ['flaɪə] Flugblatt, Handzettel 6/B1
foam [fəʊm] Schaumstoff- 6/B1
follow ['fɒləʊ] (be)folgen
following ['fɒləʊɪŋ] folgende(r, s)
be fond of sth/doing sth [bi‿'fɒnd‿əv ˌsʌmθɪŋ/ˌduːɪŋ ˌsʌmθɪŋ] etw gerne mögen/machen 5/A1
food *(no pl)* [fuːd] Essen
food [fuːd] *hier:* Futter 6/B3
*food stamp *(AE)* ['fuːd ˌstæmp] *eine Art Berechtigungsschein zum Erwerb von Lebensmitteln* 1/O
on foot [ɒn 'fʊt] zu Fuß
foot (*pl* **feet**) [fʊt, fiːt] Fuß
foot (ft) (*pl* **feet**) [fʊt, fiːt] Fuß; Längenmaß = 30,48 Zentimeter 2/A1
football ['fʊtbɔːl] Fußball
footballer ['fʊtbɔːlə] Fußballspieler/in
footpath ['fʊtˌpɑːθ] Fußweg 4/A7
for [fɔː] für; wegen, aus
for (+ *Zeitspanne*) [fə] seit ...; ... lang 4/A4
for all [fə‿'ɔːl] *hier:* die ganzen 1/C1
for example [ˌfər‿ɪg'zɑːmpl] zum Beispiel
for free *(informal)* [fə 'friː] gratis, umsonst 1/B5
for the first time [fə ðə‿'fɜːst‿ˌtaɪm] zum ersten Mal 1/A3
for years [fə‿'jɪəz] seit Jahren; jahrelang 2/B2
force sb (to do sth) ['fɔːs ˌsʌmbədi] jdn zwingen (etw zu tun) 3/B4
foreign [ˌfɒrɪn] ausländisch, fremd
forest ['fɒrɪst] Wald
forever [fər'evə] ewig 1/A3
forget [fə'get] vergessen
fork [fɔːk] Gabel
form [fɔːm] Form 2/BL2
form [fɔːm] bilden, formen; gründen
former ['fɔːmə] ehemalige(r, s), frühere(r, s) 4/C2
forward(s) ['fɔːwəd] nach vorn(e)
look forward to doing sth [lʊk 'fɔːwəd tə ˌduːɪŋ sʌmθɪŋ] sich auf etw freuen 2/B3
found [faʊnd] gründen
foundation [faʊn'deɪʃn] Fundament 2/A1
was founded [wɒz 'faʊndɪd] wurde gegründet 2/A3
four [fɔː] vier
fragment ['frægmənt] Splitter; Brocken 3/B1
France [frɑːnts] Frankreich 1/PP1
Franco- [fræŋkəʊ] französisch- *(in Komposita)* 2/A1
*frantically ['fræntɪkli] wie wild, verzweifelt 4/O1
free [friː] frei; gratis
free time [friː 'taɪm] Freizeit
freedom ['friːdəm] Freiheit, Unabhängigkeit
French [frentʃ] französisch 2/C2; Französisch 3/PP2
french fries *(npl)* [ˌfrentʃ 'fraɪz] Pommes frites 6/C2
frequency *(no pl)* ['friːkwənsi] Häufigkeit
fresh [freʃ] neu; frisch
freshman (*AE*, *pl* -men) ['freʃmən, 'freʃmən] Studienanfänger 5/PP5
Friday ['fraɪdeɪ] Freitag
fridge *(informal)* [frɪdʒ] Kühlschrank
fried [fraɪd] gebraten 1/A3
friend [frend] Freund/in
friendly ['frendli] freundlich
friendship ['frendʃɪp] Freundschaft
fries *(AE, pl)* [fraɪz] Pommes Frites 1/A3
frightened ['fraɪtnd] verängstigt
*frightening ['fraɪtnɪŋ] Furcht erregend 1/O2
frog [frɒg] Frosch
from [frəm] von, aus
from [frəm] wegen, aufgrund von 4/A7

from [frəm] *hier:* vor 6/B1
from above [frəm‿ə'bʌv] von oben 5/A3
in front [ɪn 'frʌnt] vorn(e)
in front of [ɪn 'frʌnt‿əv] vor
* frost [frɒst] Frost 6/O1
fruit [fru:t] Frucht; Obst
frying pan ['fraɪɪŋ ˌpæn] Bratpfanne
fuel ['fju:əl] Brennstoff; *hier:* Nahrung 6/B4
fulfill (*AE* = fulfil *BE*) [fʊl'fɪl] erfüllen 3/B1
full [fʊl] voll(ständig)
fun *(no pl)* [fʌn] Spaß
be fun [bi 'fʌn] Spaß machen
* funds *(pl)* [fʌndz] (finanzielle) Mittel 3/O1
funny ['fʌni] lustig, witzig, komisch
further ['fɜ:ðə] weiter (entfernt), ferner
future ['fju:tʃə] Zukunft

G

Gaelic ['geɪlɪk] gälisch 3/B4
gaffer ['gæfə] Vorarbeiter; *hier:* Oberbeleuchter/in 5/C3
gain [geɪn] bekommen 4/A4
gain weight [geɪn 'weɪt] zunehmen 6/B4
gamble ['gæmbl] Risiko, Wagnis 4/B2
gamble ['gæmbl] (um Geld) spielen 4/B2
gambling ['gæmblɪŋ] Glücksspiel 2/A1
game [geɪm] Spiel
gape [geɪp] starren; *hier:* offen stehen 2/B2
garage ['gærɑ:ʒ] Garage 2/C7
garbage *(no pl)* ['gɑ:bɪdʒ] Müll, Abfall 1/C1
garden ['gɑ:dn] Garten
gardening *(no pl)* ['gɑ:dnɪŋ] Gartenarbeit, Gärtnern 1/A4
gas (*pl* **-es or -ses**) [gæs] Gas 6/B2
gate [geɪt] Tor
gather ['gæðə] sammeln 2/B2
* gather ['gæðə] *hier:* einbringen, ernten 6/O1
gear [gɪə] Ausrüstung, Sachen; Gang(schaltung)
gel [dʒel] Gel; *hier:* Creme 6/C2
gelatin *(AE, informal)* ['dʒelətɪn] Wackelpudding 6/C2
general ['dʒen(ə)rəl] allgemein; verbreitet
generally ['dʒen(ə)rəli] normalerweise, im Allgemeinen 6/PP6
generation [ˌdʒenə'reɪʃn] Generation 4/A4
genetically engineered [dʒəˌnetɪkli endʒɪ'nɪəd] gentechnisch verändert 5/C4
gentleman (*pl* **gentlemen**) ['dʒentlmən, 'dʒentlmən] Gentleman; Herr
geography [dʒi:'ɒgrəfi] Erdkunde, Geografie
German ['dʒɜ:mən] Deutsche/r; deutsch
Germany ['dʒɜ:məni] Deutschland
get [get] erhalten, bekommen; werden; kaufen; (an)kommen
get a kick out of sth [get‿ə 'kɪk‿aʊt‿əv ˌsʌmθɪŋ] an etw einen Riesenspaß haben 5/B1
get by (with) [get 'baɪ] auskommen (mit) 3/C5
* get down to sth [get 'daʊn tə ˌsʌmθɪŋ] sich an etw machen, mit etw beginnen 1/O2
get in [get‿'ɪn] hineingehen; hereinkommen
get in touch with [get‿ɪn 'tʌtʃ wɪð] in Kontakt treten mit 4/A6
get into sth [get‿'ɪntə ˌsʌmθɪŋ] in etw (ein)steigen 3/C1
get in(to) trouble [ˌget‿ɪn 'trʌbl] in Schwierigkeiten geraten 2/C7
get lost [get 'lɒst] sich verirren; sich verlaufen haben
get off [get‿'ɒf] aussteigen (aus)
get on [get‿'ɒn] sich verstehen; einsteigen
get out of [get‿'aʊt‿əv] hinauskommen aus
get up [get‿'ʌp] aufstehen
Get well soon! [ˌget wel 'su:n] Gute Besserung!
ghost [gəʊst] Geist
giant ['dʒaɪənt] riesig 2/B2
giraffe [dʒə'rɑ:f] Giraffe
girl [gɜ:l] Mädchen
girlfriend ['gɜ:lˌfrend] Freundin 4/B6
give [gɪv] geben
give a speech [ˌgɪv‿ə 'spi:tʃ] eine Rede halten 4/C4
give an opinion (on sth) [gɪv‿ən‿ə'pɪnjən] seine Meinung (zu etw) äußern 3/CL1
* give thanks [gɪv 'θæŋks] danken 6/O1
give up [gɪv‿'ʌp] aufgeben; überlassen 2/B2
glad [glæd] glücklich
glass [glɑ:s] Glas
glasses *(npl)* ['glɑ:sɪz] Brille
glove [glʌv] Handschuh
glue *(no pl)* [glu:] Klebstoff
glue stick ['glu: ˌstɪk] Klebestift
go [gəʊ] gehen; fahren
go around [ˌgəʊ‿ə'raʊnd] herumlaufen
go crazy [gəʊ 'kreɪzi] verrückt werden 1/B4
go for a walk [ˌgəʊ fər‿ə 'wɔ:k] spazieren gehen
go for sth ['gəʊ‿fə ˌsʌmθɪŋ] etw holen; *hier:* mögen 1/A3
go on [gəʊ‿'ɒn] weitermachen
go out [gəʊ‿'aʊt] (hinaus)gehen; ausgehen
go through [gəʊ 'θru:] durchgehen 2/A1
go with ['gəʊ wɪð] passen zu; *hier:* dazu 6/B4
goal [gəʊl] Tor; Ziel
* set oneself a goal [set wʌnˌself‿ə 'gəʊl] sich ein Ziel setzen 2/O1
goal line ['gəʊl laɪn] Torlinie 5/A3
goat [gəʊt] Ziege
* gobble [gɒbl] kollern 6/O1
God [gɒd] Gott 2/A5
gold [gəʊld] Gold
gold nugget ['gəʊld nʌgɪt] Goldnugget 4/B1
gold rush ['gəʊld ˌrʌʃ] Goldrausch 1/PP1
golden ['gəʊld(ə)n] aus Gold, golden 6/PP6
goldfield ['gəʊldˌfi:ld] Goldfeld 4/B2
goldmine ['gəʊldˌmaɪn] Goldmine 1/PP1
golfer ['gɒlfə] Golfspieler/in 5/A2
gonna (*AE, informal* = going to) ['gɒnə] werden 1/C1
good [gʊd] gut
be good at sth [bi 'gʊd‿ət ˌsʌmθɪŋ] gut in etw sein
Goodbye. [ˌgʊd'baɪ] Auf Wiedersehen.
* goose (*pl* geese) [gu:s, gi:s] Gans 6/O1
gorilla [gə'rɪlə] Gorilla
government ['gʌvnmənt] Regierung
Governor ['gʌv(ə)nə] Gouverneur 3/B3
grab sth ['græb ˌsʌmθɪŋ] sich etw schnappen 1/C4
grade [greɪd] Klasse 2/B1
grader ['greɪdə] *hier:* -klässler 2/C4
graduation [ˌgrædʒu'eɪʃn] Abschluss 2/C5
grandma *(informal)* ['grænˌmɑ:] Oma, Omi
grandmother ['grænˌmʌðə] Großmutter
grandpa *(informal)* ['grænˌpɑ:] Opa, Opi
grandparents *(pl)* ['grænˌpeərənts] Großeltern
grandson ['grænˌsʌn] Enkel 4/C2
grant [grɑ:nt] gewähren 3/B3
grape [greɪp] (Wein)traube
pick grapes [pɪk 'greɪpz] Trauben lesen 2/C7
* grasp at sth ['grɑ:sp‿ət ˌsʌmθɪŋ] nach etw greifen 4/O1
grass [grɑ:s] Gras
gravy ['greɪvi] Bratensaft; (Braten)soße 6/PP6
greasy ['gri:si] fettig; schmierig; fett
great [greɪt] groß, riesig; großartig, wunderbar
great-grandfather [ˌgreɪt'grænˌfɑ:ðə] Urgroßvater 3/B5
great-grandma *(informal)* [ˌgreɪt'grænmɑ] Uroma 3/B4
great-grandpa *(informal)* [ˌgreɪt'grænpɑ:] Uropa 3/B4
greatly ['greɪtli] sehr; *hier:* stark 6/B1
Grecian ['gri:ʃn] griechisch 2/C5
green [gri:n] grün
(at the) greengrocer's ['gri:ngrəʊsəz] (im) Obst- und Gemüseladen
greetings *(pl)* ['gri:tɪŋz] Grüße 1/C1

grey [greɪ] grau
grid [grɪd] Gitter; *hier:* Tabelle 2/CL4
grilled [grɪld] gegrillt 6/C2
grin [grɪn] grinsen 3/C1
grip [grɪp] Bühnenarbeiter *(Film)* 5/C3
* grocery ['grəʊsəri] Lebensmittelgeschäft 1/O
* groovy *(informal)* ['gru:vi] doll, klasse 1/O2
ground *(no pl)* [graʊnd] (Erd)boden, Erde
grounds *(npl)* [graʊndz] Anlagen 3/A4
ground squirrel ['graʊnd ˌskwɪrəl] Erdhörnchen 2/B2
group [gru:p] Gruppe
grow [grəʊ] wachsen
grow apart [grəʊ ə'pɑ:t] sich auseinander leben; *hier:* sich voneinander entfernen 3/PP2
* grow sth ['grəʊ ˌsʌmθɪŋ] etw anbauen 6/O1
grow up [grəʊ‿'ʌp] erwachsen werden
guard [gɑ:d] Wache, Wach(t)posten
* guess [ges] Vermutung, Annahme 6/O1
guess [ges] (er)raten; denken; annehmen 1/A3
Guess what! [ges 'wɒt] Stell dir vor! 1/C1
guest [gest] Gast
guide [gaɪd] Führer/in
guided tour ['gaɪdəd tʊə] Führung 2/B2
guilty ['gɪlti] schuldig 4/A7
guitar [gɪ'tɑ:] Gitarre
gum [gʌm] (Kau)gummi 1/A4
gun [gʌn] (Schuss)waffe, Pistole 3/B4
guy [gaɪ] Kerl, Typ

H

habit ['hæbɪt] Gewohnheit
hair *(no pl)* [heə] Haar(e)
hairdresser ['heəˌdresə] Friseur/Friseuse 6/B3
half (*pl* **halves**) [hɑ:f, hɑ:vz] Hälfte
half [hɑ:f] halb
half an hour [ˌhɑ:f‿ən‿'aʊə] eine halbe Stunde 1/A3
half-used ['hɑ:f ˌju:zd] halb verbraucht 6/B3
hall [hɔ:l] Korridor; Halle
* Hall of Fame *(AE)* [ˌhɔ:l‿əv 'feɪm] Ruhmeshalle 2/O1
Hallelujah! [ˌhælɪ'lu:jə] Halleluja!, Gott sei Dank! 1/B4
ham [hæm] Schinken
hand [hænd] Hand
be out of hand [bi‿ˌaʊt‿ɒf 'hænd] außer Kontrolle sein 4/B2
hand sth to sb ['hænd sʌmθɪŋ tə‿ˌsʌmbədi] jdm etw übergeben 1/C4
hand-clapping ['hændklæpɪŋ] Applaudieren 5/PP4
* handful ['hændfʊl] Handvoll 4/O1
handkerchief ['hæŋkəˌtʃɪf] Taschentuch 2/C7
handle ['hændl] anfassen; *hier:* umgehen mit 5/A3
handlebars *(npl)* ['hændlˌbɑ:z] Lenkstange, Lenker
handsome ['hæns(ə)m] gut aussehend; attraktiv
handwriting ['hændˌraɪtɪŋ] Handschrift 6/B3
hang (up) [hæŋ] (auf)hängen
happen ['hæpən] geschehen, passieren
happy ['hæpi] glücklich; zufrieden; fröhlich
Happy birthday (to you)! [ˌhæpi 'bɜ:θdeɪ] Alles Gute zum Geburtstag! 1/C4
harbor (*AE* = harbour *BE*) ['hɑ:bə] Hafen 3/A4
hard [hɑ:d] hart; schwierig
hard [hɑ:d] *hier:* sehr 6/B4
hardly ['hɑ:dli] kaum
* harmful ['hɑ:mfl] schädlich 1/O2
* harvest ['hɑ:vɪst] Ernte 6/O1
harvest ['hɑ:vɪst] ernten 2/A3
hash browns *(pl, AE)* [hʌʃ 'braʊnz] Rösti 6/C1
hat [hæt] Hut
hate [heɪt] hassen, nicht ausstehen können
have [hæv] haben; essen
I'll have [aɪl 'hæv] Ich hätte gern
have a bath [ˌhæv‿ə 'bɑ:θ] baden
have a bite [ˌhæv‿ə 'baɪt] *hier:* probieren 6/A5
have a break [hæv‿ə 'breɪk] eine Pause machen 2/C7
have a good time [ˌhæv‿ə gʊd 'taɪm] sich amüsieren
have a great time [ˌhæv‿ə ˌgreɪt‿'taɪm] sich sehr gut amüsieren
have a look (at) [ˌhæv‿ə 'lʊk] sich ansehen
have a rest [ˌhæv‿ə 'rest] eine Pause machen/einlegen
have a ride *(AE, informal)* [ˌhæv‿ə 'raɪd] mitgenommen werden 3/C1
have a sweet tooth [hæv‿ə ˌswi:t 'tu:θ] eine Naschkatze sein 6/C4
have a try at [hæv‿ə 'traɪ‿ət] versuchen 3/B1
have breakfast [hæv 'brekfəst] frühstücken
have got [hæv 'gɒt] haben
have sth in common with [hæv ˌsʌmθɪŋ ɪn 'kɒmən wɪð] etw gemein(sam) haben mit 1/A2
have to ['hæv tə] müssen
he [hi] er
head [hed] Kopf
shake one's head ['ʃeɪk wʌnz ˌhed] den Kopf schütteln 1/C4
keep one's head down ['ki:p wʌnz ˌhed‿daʊn] den Kopf einziehen 2/C7
head for ['hed fə] zusteuern auf 2/C7
headache ['hedeɪk] Kopfschmerzen, Kopfweh
heading ['hedɪŋ] Überschrift, Titel 6/B1
headline ['hedˌlaɪn] Schlagzeile 4/C1
heal [hi:l] heilen
health [helθ] Gesundheit
healthcare *(no pl)* ['helθˌkeə] Gesundheitsfürsorge 3/C5
healthy ['helθi] gesund
hear [hɪə] hören
heart [hɑ:t] Herz
by heart [baɪ 'hɑ:t] auswendig
heat [hi:t] Wärme; Hitze
* heater ['hi:tə] Heizkörper 5/O1
heavy ['hevi] schwer; stark
* heel [hi:l] Ferse; *hier:* Absatz 3/O1
height [haɪt] Höhe; (Körper)größe 5/C2
helicopter ['helɪˌkɒptə] Hubschrauber 3/A4
hello [he'ləʊ] hallo
help [help] Hilfe
help [help] helfen
help out [help‿'aʊt] (aus)helfen, unterstützen
helper ['helpə] Helfer/in; Gehilfe/Gehilfin 5/C3
helpful ['helpfl] hilfsbereit; hilfreich, nützlich
her [hɜ:] sie; ihr(e, n)
here [hɪə] hier; hierher
Here you are! [ˌhɪə ju:‿'ɑ:] Hier, bitte!, Bitte schön!
herself [hə'self] sich
hide [haɪd] (sich) verstecken
hiding place ['haɪdɪŋ ˌpleɪs] Versteck 4/C1
high [haɪ] hoch
hike [haɪk] wandern 2/B5
hiking ['haɪkɪŋ] Wandern 1/A4
go hiking [gəʊ 'haɪkɪŋ] wandern gehen 1/A4
hill [hɪl] Hügel
him [hɪm] ihm, ihn
himself [hɪm'self] sich; selbst
hippo (= hippopotamus) ['hɪpəʊ, ˌhɪpə'pɒtəməs] Nilpferd
hire ['haɪə] mieten; ausleihen
hire sb ['haɪə ˌsʌmbədi] jdn einstellen 1/PP1
his [hɪs] sein(e, r)
historic [hɪ'stɒrɪk] historisch 3/A4
* historical [hɪ'stɒrɪkl] geschichtlich, historisch 2/O1
history ['hɪst(ə)ri] Geschichte
hit [hɪt] schlagen; anfahren; treffen
hold [həʊld] (fest)halten
hold a position ['həʊld‿ə pəˌzɪʃn] einen Posten innehaben 4/C4
* hold on to sb/sth [həʊld‿'ɒn tə ˌsʌmbədi/ˌsʌmθɪŋ] jdn/etw festhalten 4/O1
* hold out [həʊld‿'aʊt] ausstrecken 1/O2
hole [həʊl] Loch 6/B3
holiday(s) *(npl)* ['hɒlɪdeɪ(z)] Ferien, Urlaub
home [həʊm] Zuhause
at home [æt 'həʊm] zu Hause

home [həʊm] zu Hause; nach Hause
home country [həʊm 'kʌntri] Heimatland 2/C3
home room ['həʊm ˌruːm] *etwa:* Aufenthaltsraum 5/B2
home state [həʊm 'steɪt] Heimat(bundes)staat 2/A6
home town [ˌhəʊm 'taʊn] Heimatstadt
homework *(no pl)* ['həʊmˌwɜːk] Hausaufgaben
honey ['hʌni] Honig 6/C2
honor (*AE* = honour *BE*) ['ɒnə] in Ehren halten 4/PP3
* in honor of [ɪn 'ɒnə‿ˌəv] zu Ehren 4/O1
* hooked [hʊkt] abhängig 1/O2
play hooky *(informal)* [pleɪ 'hʊki] die Schule schwänzen 3/C1
hoop [huːp] Reifen 5/A3
hop off [hɒp‿'ɒf] schnell aussteigen 3/A4
hop on [hɒp‿'ɒn] schnell einsteigen 3/A4
hope [həʊp] Hoffnung 2/A1
hope [həʊp] hoffen
hopeful ['həʊpfl] zuversichtlich 1/AL1
hopefully ['həʊpfli] hoffnungsvoll 6/B4
hopeless ['həʊpləs] hoffnungslos 5/AL2
be hopeless at sth [bi 'həʊpləs‿ət ˌsʌmθɪŋ] ein hoffnungsloser Fall sein 5/A1
horrible ['hɒrəbl] schrecklich
horror ['hɒrə] Entsetzen; *hier:* Horror 5/C5
horse [hɔːs] Pferd
hospital ['hɒspɪtl] Krankenhaus
hostler (= ostler) ['ɒslə] Stallknecht, Stallbursche *(historisch)* 4/B5
hot [hɒt] heiß; scharf
hot potato [ˌhɒt pə'teɪtəʊ] heißes Eisen *(Politik)* 6/C4
hotel [həʊ'tel] Hotel
hour [aʊə] Stunde
house [haʊs] Haus
household ['haʊsˌhəʊld] Haushalt 6/B3
housemaid ['haʊsˌmeɪd] Hausmädchen 4/C2
housing *(no pl)* ['haʊzɪŋ] Wohnungen 3/C7
how [haʊ] wie
How about …? [ˌhaʊ‿ə'baʊt] Was ist mit …?, Wie wäre es mit …? 1/A3
How are things going? *(informal)* [ˌhaʊ‿ɑː θɪŋz 'gəʊɪŋ] Wie geht's? 1/C1
How are you? [haʊ‿'ɑː ˌjʊ] Wie geht es dir/Ihnen/euch?
How much is/are …? [ˌhaʊ mʌtʃ‿'ɪz/ɑː] Was kostet/kosten …?
how to ['haʊ‿tə] wie man 1/B3
however [haʊ'evə] egal wie; jedoch
* howling ['haʊlɪŋ] Gebrüll; *hier:* Heulen 6/O1
huge [hjuːdʒ] riesig, riesengroß
hum [hʌm] brummen; *hier:* summen 1/C4
* human ['hjuːmən] menschlich 1/O2
hundred ['hʌndrəd] hundert
hundreds of thousands of [ˌhʌndrədz‿əv 'θaʊzndz‿əv] Hunderttausende von 4/B1
hungry ['hʌŋgri] hungrig
* hunt [hʌnt] jagen 6/O1
hunter ['hʌntə] Jäger/in 4/A2
hunting ['hʌntɪŋ] Jagen, Jagd 2/B2
hurry ['hʌri] sich beeilen; hetzen
hurt [hɜːt] wehtun; verletzen
husband ['hʌzbənd] Ehemann

I

I [aɪ] ich
I would like (to) … [ˌaɪ wʊd 'laɪk tə] Ich hätte/würde gern …
I wouldn't be caught dead in the place. *(informal)* [aɪ wʊdnt bi kɔːt 'ded‿ɪn ðə‿ˌpleɪs] *Da würden mich keine zehn Pferde reinbringen.* 6/A3
I'd rather be … [aɪd 'rɑːðə biː] Ich wäre lieber … 5/B1
I'll have [aɪl 'hæv] Ich hätte gern
ice [aɪs] Eis
ice cream ['aɪs ˌkriːm] Eiskreme
ice-skater ['aɪsˌskeɪtə] Schlittschuhläufer/in, Eiskunstläufer/in 5/A2
iced tea [aɪst 'tiː] Eistee 6/C2
* ID (= identification) [ˌaɪ'diː] Ausweis 1/O
idea [aɪ'dɪə] Idee
ideal [aɪ'dɪəl] ideal
identify with [aɪ'dentɪfaɪ ˌwɪð] sich identifizieren mit 5/CL1
idiom ['ɪdiəm] (idiomatische) Redewendung 6/C4
* idiot ['ɪdiət] Idiot 5/O1
if [ɪf] wenn, falls; ob
igloo ['ɪgluː] Iglu 3/PP2
ignore [ɪg'nɔː] ignorieren 1/C4
ill [ɪl] krank
illustrate ['ɪləˌstreɪt] illustrieren, bebildern
imagine [ɪ'mædʒɪn] sich vorstellen
immediately [ɪ'miːdiətli] sofort, gleich
immigrant ['ɪmɪgrənt] Einwanderer/in 2/A1
immigrate ['ɪmɪˌgreɪt] einwandern 2/C3
immigration [ˌɪmɪ'greɪʃn] Einwanderung 3/A4
* immigration bureau [ɪmɪ'greɪʃn ˌbjʊərəʊ] Einwanderungsbehörde 3/O1
important [ɪm'pɔːtnt] wichtig
impression [ɪm'preʃn] Eindruck 5/C3
improve [ɪm'pruːv] verbessern
improve [ɪm'pruːv] besser werden; sich verbessern 4/A4
in [ɪn] in; an
in English [ɪn‿'ɪŋglɪʃ] auf Englisch 3/PP2
in fact [ɪn 'fækt] genau genommen 1/B3; tatsächlich 3/C1
in front [ɪn 'frʌnt] vorn(e)
in front of [ɪn 'frʌnt‿əv] vor
in German [ɪn 'dʒɜːmən] auf Deutsch
in my opinion [ɪn ˌmaɪ ə'pɪnjən] meiner Meinung nach
in order to [ɪn‿'ɔːdə tə] um zu 2/B2
in other words [ɪn‿'ʌðər ˌwɜːdz] mit anderen Worten 3/B2
in pairs [ɪn 'peəz] paarweise
in short [ɪn 'ʃɔːt] kurz gesagt 2/A5
in silence [ɪn‿'saɪlənz] still 1/C1
in spite of [ɪn 'spaɪt‿əv] trotz
in the afternoon [ˌɪn ðiː‿ɑːftə'nuːn] am Nachmittag
in the end [ɪn ði‿'end] letzten Endes; schließlich 3/C5
in the evening [ˌɪn ði‿'iːvnɪŋ] am Abend
in the morning [ˌɪn ðə 'mɔːnɪŋ] am Morgen
in time [ɪn 'taɪm] rechtzeitig 1/C1
inch [ɪntʃ] Zoll (2,54 cm) 4/A7
include [ɪn'kluːd] beinhalten, einschließen; beifügen
including [ɪn'kluːdɪŋ] einschließlich
income ['ɪnkʌm] Einkommen
increase [ɪn'kriːs] erhöhen, verstärken 1/B3
* indeed [ɪn'diːd] in der Tat, wirklich 1/O2
independence *(no pl)* [ˌɪndɪ'pendəns] Unabhängigkeit, Selbstständigkeit 2/A5
Indian ['ɪndiən] Inder/in; indisch
Indian ['ɪndiən] Indianer/in; indianisch 4/A2
* indigo ['ɪndɪgəʊ] indigoblau 4/O1
indoor [ˌɪn'dɔː] Innen-; *hier:* Hallen- 5/A3
industry ['ɪndəstri] Industrie
infant [ˌɪnfənt] Säugling 4/A4
infertile [ɪn'fɜːtaɪl] unfruchtbar 4/A2
inflation [ɪn'fleɪʃn] Inflation, Preisauftrieb 2/C4
have influence on [ˌhæv‿'ɪnfluəns‿ɒn] Einfluss haben auf 1/A1
information *(no pl)* [ˌɪnfə'meɪʃn] Information(en); Auskunft
information center (*AE* = centre *BE*) [ɪnfə'meɪʃn ˌsentə] Informationsstelle 2/B4
ingredient [ɪn'griːdiənt] Zutat 1/B3
inhabit [ɪn'hæbɪt] bewohnen 2/B2
inhabitant [ɪn'hæbɪtənt] Einwohner/in; Bewohner/in 2/A3
injection [ɪn'dʒekʃn] Injektion, Spritze
injury ['ɪndʒəri] Verletzung
injustice [ɪn'dʒʌstɪs] Ungerechtigkeit 4/PP3
innocence *(no pl)* ['ɪnəs(ə)ns] Unschuld, Arglosigkeit 4/A1
innocently ['ɪnəs(ə)ntli] arglos 6/B4
insanity *(no pl)* [ɪn'sænəti] Wahnsinn, Geisteskrankheit 3/B1
insect ['ɪnsekt] Insekt 2/C7
inside ['ɪnˌsaɪd] innen; hinein; im Inneren

inspect [ɪn'spekt] untersuchen; kontrollieren 3/B1
inspector [ɪn'spektə] Inspektor/in 3/B1
instant coffee [ˌɪnstənd 'kɒfi] Instantkaffee 6/B3
instead [ɪn'sted] stattdessen 1/PP1
instead of [ɪn'sted‿əv] (an)statt 1/B3
institution [ˌɪnstɪ'tjuːʃn] Institution
instruct [ɪn'strʌkt] anweisen 3/B4
instrument ['ɪnstrʊment] Instrument
intend [ɪn'tend] beabsichtigen 1/PP1
intensive [ɪn'tensɪv] intensiv, stark 5/C2
interest ['ɪntrəst] Interesse
interest ['ɪntrəst] interessieren
interested ['ɪntrəstɪd] interessiert
interesting ['ɪntrəstɪŋ] interessant
international [ˌɪntə'næʃn(ə)l] international
search (on) the Internet [ˌsɜːtʃ ði‿'ɪntənet] im Internet suchen 3/B4
interrupt [ˌɪntə'rʌpt] unterbrechen
interview ['ɪntəˌvjuː] befragen
* interviewer ['ɪntəˌvjuːə] Interviewer/in 1/O2
into ['ɪntʊ] in
introduce [ˌɪntrə'djuːs] vorstellen
introduce (to) [ˌɪntrə'djuːs] einführen (in) 1/B5
introduction [ˌɪntrə'dʌkʃn] Vorstellung; Einführung 6/A4
invent [ɪn'vent] erfinden 5/A3
invention [ɪn'venʃn] Erfindung; Fantasie 1/A1
invitation [ˌɪnvɪ'teɪʃn] Einladung
invite [ɪn'vaɪt] einladen
involve [ɪn'vɒlv] beinhalten; betreffen 1/B4
Ireland ['aɪələnd] Irland 3/A3
Irish ['aɪrɪʃ] irisch 2/C5
Irishman (*pl* -men) ['aɪriʃmæn, 'aɪriʃmen] Ire 4/B2
iron ['aɪən] Eisen 2/A3
the Iroquois [ðə‿'ɪrəkwɔɪz] die Irokesen *(Indianer)* 2/A1
island ['aɪlənd] Insel
it [ɪt] es
IT *(no pl)* (= Information Technology) [aɪ'tiː, ɪnfəˌmeɪʃn tek'nɒlədʒi] Informationstechnologie 5/B4
It sure is a change from … *(AE, informal)* [ɪt ˌʃɔː‿ɪz‿ə 'tʃeɪndʒ frəm] Das ist echt eine Abwechslung vom … 1/C1
It's got me on the go. *(informal)* [ɪts ˌgɒt me ən ðə 'gəʊ] Es macht mich noch wahnsinnig. 1/B4
Italian [ɪ'tæliən] Italiener/in; italienisch 1/A2
Italy ['ɪtəli] Italien 3/A3
item ['aɪtəm] Punkt; Artikel
item ['aɪtəm] *hier:* Gericht 6/C2
its [ɪts] sein(e), ihr(e)
itself [ɪt'self] sich (selbst); selbst

J

jacket ['dʒækɪt] Jacke
jail [dʒeɪl] Gefängnis
Jalapeno [ˌhælə'peɪnjəʊ] grüne oder rote scharfe Paprikaschote 6/PP6
jam [dʒæm] Marmelade
January ['dʒænjuəri] Januar
jar [dʒɑː] Glas(gefäß) 6/B3
jelly *(AE)* ['dʒeli] Gelee 6/B4
jewellery *(no pl)* ['dʒuːəlri] Schmuck
Jewish ['dʒuːɪʃ] jüdisch
job [dʒɒb] Arbeit, Stelle, Tätigkeit, Aufgabe
join [dʒɔɪn] verbinden; sich zu jdm gesellen
join in [dʒɔɪn‿'ɪn] teilnehmen, mitmachen
* joke [dʒəʊk] Spaß; Witz 5/O1
joke [dʒəʊk] scherzen
journalist ['dʒɜːnəlɪst] Journalist/in 5/CL1
journey ['dʒɜːni] Reise
judge [dʒʌdʒ] Richter/in; Schiedsrichter/in
judge [dʒʌdʒ] beurteilen, einschätzen 4/PP3
judo ['dʒuːdəʊ] Judo 3/C1
juice [dʒuːs] Saft
July [dʒʊ'laɪ] Juli
jumbo ['dʒʌmbəʊ] Riesen- 6/PP6
jump [dʒʌmp] springen
jumper ['dʒʌmpə] Pullover, Pulli
June [dʒuːn] Juni
junior *(AE)* ['dʒuːniə] *Schüler/in einer Highschool im vorletzten Jahr* 5/PP5
junior high school *(AE)* ['dʒuːniə 'haɪ skuːl] Junior Highschool *(Aufbauschule)* 5/PP5
just [dʒʌst] gleich; nur; einfach; gerade; genau
justice ['dʒʌstɪs] Gerechtigkeit 4/PP3

K

kangaroo [ˌkæŋgə'ruː] Känguru
kayak ['kaɪæk] Kajak 5/A3
be keen on doing sth [bi 'kiːn‿ɒn ˌduːɪŋ sʌmθɪŋ] etw mit Begeisterung tun 2/B3
keep [kiːp] (be)halten; bleiben; aufbewahren
keep [kiːp] *hier:* führen 5/C3
keep (on) doing sth [kiːp 'duːɪŋ ˌsʌmθɪŋ] etw weiter(hin) tun 1/C4
* keep a promise [ˌkiːp‿ə 'prɒmɪs] ein Versprechen halten 4/O1
keep away (from) [kiːp ə'weɪ] fern halten (von) 5/A3
keep one's head down ['kiːp wʌnz ˌhed‿daʊn] den Kopf einziehen 2/C7
keep one's mouth shut ['kiːp wʌnz ˌmaʊθ ʃʌt] den Mund halten 3/C1
keep up [kiːp‿'ʌp] hoch halten; *hier:* erhalten 3/C5
keyword ['kiːˌwɜːd] Schlüssel(wort), Stichwort 1/B5
kick [kɪk] treten; schießen 5/A3
get a kick out of sth [get‿ə 'kɪk‿aʊt‿əv ˌsʌmθɪŋ] an etw einen Riesenspaß haben 5/B1
kidnap ['kɪdnæp] entführen 3/C1
kill [kɪl] töten
kilometre [kɪ'ləˌmiːtə] Kilometer
kind [kaɪnd] Art, Sorte
kind [kaɪnd] nett, freundlich, liebenswürdig
kindergarten ['kɪndəˌgɑːtn] Vorschule 5/PP5
king [kɪŋ] König
kiss [kɪs] küssen
kitchen ['kɪtʃən] Küche
knee [niː] Knie
kneeboard ['niːˌbɔːd] *eine Art Surfbrett* 5/A3
knife (*pl* **knives**) [naɪf, naɪvz] Messer
knock off [nɒk‿'ɒf] hinunterstoßen 6/B4
know [nəʊ] wissen; kennen
knowledge *(no pl)* ['nɒlɪdʒ] Kenntnisse; Wissen 2/A2
known [nəʊn] bekannt 4/C1

L

labor (*AE* = labour *BE*) ['leɪbə] Arbeit 2/CL4
labor camp *(AE)* (= labour camp *BE*) ['leɪbə kæmp] Arbeitslager 2/C7
laboratory [lə'bɒrət(ə)ri] Labor 5/C4
lacrosse *(no pl)* [lə'krɒs] Lacrosse *(Ballsportart)* 5/PP4
lady ['leɪdi] Frau; Dame
lake [leɪk] See
lame [leɪm] lahm 3/B1
lameness *(no pl)* ['leɪmnes] Lähmung 3/B1
lamp [læmp] Lampe
land [lænd] (Fest)land
land [lænd] landen
landlord ['lændˌlɔːd] Hausbesitzer; Vermieter 4/C5
* landscape ['lændˌskeɪp] Landschaft 2/O1
language ['læŋgwɪdʒ] Sprache
large [lɑːdʒ] groß
* large [lɑːdʒ] *hier:* korpulent 1/O2
lasso (*pl* -s *or* -es) [lə'suː] Lasso 3/PP2
last [lɑːst] (an)dauern; halten 1/PP1
last [lɑːst] letzte(r, s)
last [lɑːst] zuletzt
at last [ət 'lɑːst] zu guter Letzt, endlich
last but not least [ˌlɑːst bət nɒt 'liːst] nicht zu vergessen 2/B5
late [leɪt] (zu) spät
later ['leɪtə] später 1/A3
laugh [lɑːf] lachen
laugh at sb ['lɑːf‿ət ˌsʌmbədi] jdn auslachen
laugh out (loud) [lɑːf‿'aʊt laʊd] (laut) auflachen 1/C1
law [lɔː] Gesetz; Jura, Jura- 4/A5
lawn [lɔːn] Rasen 1/C1
* lawnmower ['lɔːnˌməʊə] Rasenmäher 2/O1

lawyer ['lɔːjə] Rechtsanwalt/-anwältin 2/C4
lay the table ['leɪ ðə‿ˌteɪbl] den Tisch decken 6/B4
layer ['leɪə] Schicht 6/B1
lazy ['leɪzi] faul; träge
lead [liːd] führen
leader ['liːdə] Leiter/in, Führer/in 4/A7
leaf (*pl* **leaves**) [liːf, liːvz] Blatt
leaflet ['liːflət] Prospekt 2/B6
* lean [liːn] sich beugen 4/O1
leap [liːp] springen 5/C4
learn [lɜːn] lernen
learn about [ˌlɜːn‿ə'baʊt] erfahren von/über 2/A3
learner ['lɜːnə] Lernende/r 6/BL3
at least [ət 'liːst] mindestens, wenigstens
leather-covered ['leðəˌkʌvəd] mit Leder bezogen 5/A3
leave [liːv] verlassen; dalassen; abfahren, aufbrechen; zurücklassen
leave [liːv] *hier:* weggehen 1/C3
leave behind [liːv bɪ'haɪnd] zurücklassen 2/C7
left [left] übrig; (nach) links
left [left] linke(r, s) 3/C1
on the left [ˌɒn ðə 'left] links, auf der linken Seite
leg [leg] Bein
legal ['liːgl] legal, gesetzlich zulässig 2/A1
* legend ['ledʒ(ə)nd] Sage, Legende 4/O1
leisure culture ['leʒə ˌkʌltʃə] Freizeitkultur 1/A1
lemonade [ˌlemə'neɪd] Limonade
lend [lend] leihen 5/B3
less [les] weniger
lesson ['lesn] Stunde *(Schule)*
let [let] lassen
let out [let‿'aʊt] herauslassen
* let through [let 'θruː] durchlassen 3/O1
let's (= let us) [lets, 'let‿əs] lass(t) uns
letter ['letə] Brief; Buchstabe
liberty ['lɪbəti] Freiheit 3/B1
library ['laɪbrəri] Bibliothek, Bücherei
lie [laɪ] liegen; lügen 4/B2
life (*pl* **lives**) [laɪf, laɪvz] Leben
bring sth to life ['brɪŋ sʌmθɪŋ tə‿ˌlaɪf] etw zum Leben erwecken 5/C2
life expectancy [ˌlaɪf ɪk'spektənsi] Lebenserwartung 4/A4
light [laɪt] Licht; Lampe
light [laɪt] erhellen; beleuchten; anzünden
light [laɪt] leicht
light bulb ['laɪt ˌbʌlb] Glühbirne 6/B3
lighthouse ['laɪtˌhaʊs] Leuchtturm 1/B4
like [laɪk] mögen
I would like (to) ... [ˌaɪ wʊd 'laɪk tə] Ich hätte/würde gern ...
like [laɪk] wie
like it was on fire [laɪk‿ɪt ˌwɒz‿ɒn 'faɪə] als würde es brennen 5/B1
like this [laɪk 'ðɪs] so

What's ... like? [wɒts laɪk] Wie ist ...?
* likely ['laɪkli] wahrscheinlich 3/O1
likes and dislikes *(pl)* [ˌlaɪkz‿ən dɪs'laɪkz] Vorlieben und Abneigungen 1/A3
limit ['lɪmɪt] einschränken 4/C1
limousine [ˌlɪmə'ziːn] (Luxus)limousine; Kleinbus 3/C1
line [laɪn] Linie; Reihe; Zeile
line [laɪn] *hier:* Sortiment 6/C2
stand in line *(AE)* [stænd‿ɪn 'laɪn] anstehen 1/A3
lion ['laɪən] Löwe
lipstick ['lɪpstɪk] Lippenstift
list [lɪst] Liste
list [lɪst] auflisten
listen to ['lɪsn tə] zuhören
* literacy *(no pl)* ['lɪt(ə)rəsi] Lese- und Schreibfähigkeit 3/O1
* litter removal ['lɪtə rɪˌmuːvl] Müllbeseitigung 1/O
little ['lɪtl] klein; wenig
a little [ə 'lɪtl] ein bisschen
live [lɪv] leben, wohnen
live off ['lɪv‿ɒf] leben von
live out [lɪv‿'aʊt] *hier:* verwirklichen; erfüllen 4/PP3
living room ['lɪvɪŋ ˌruːm] Wohnzimmer
lizard ['lɪzəd] Eidechse, Echse 2/B2
load a film [ˌləʊd‿ə 'fɪlm] einen Film einlegen 5/C3
* lobster *(no pl)* ['lɒbstə] Hummer(fleisch) 2/O1
local ['ləʊkl] hiesig, örtlich
locally ['ləʊkli] am/vor Ort 6/PP6
be located [bi ləʊ'keɪtəd] sich befinden 2/A1
location [ləʊ'keɪʃn] Lage; Standort 2/B6
lock [lɒk] abschließen; einsperren
locker ['lɒkə] Schließfach 2/B5
lodging ['lɒdʒɪŋ] Unterkunft 4/PP3
logical ['lɒdʒɪkl] logisch 5/B6
lonely ['ləʊnli] einsam
long [lɒŋ] lang
long (to/for) [lɒŋ] sich sehnen (nach) 3/A1
* long ago [lɒŋ ə'gəʊ] vor langer Zeit 4/O1
look [lʊk] Blick
have/take a look (at) [ˌhæv/ˌteɪk‿ə 'lʊk] sich ansehen
look [lʊk] sehen, schauen; aussehen
look after [lʊk‿'ɑːftə] sich kümmern um
look around [ˌlʊk‿ə'raʊnd] sich umsehen 1/C4
look at ['lʊk‿æt] (sich) ansehen/anschauen
look for ['lʊk fə] suchen nach
look forward to doing sth [lʊk 'fɔːwəd tə ˌduːɪŋ sʌmθɪŋ] sich auf etw freuen 2/B3
look up [lʊk‿'ʌp] nach oben sehen 2/C7
lord [lɔːd] Lord *(Titel)* 5/C1
lorry ['lɒri] Last(kraft)wagen, LKW

lose [luːz] verlieren
lose *(weight)* [luːz] abnehmen 1/B3
loser ['luːzə] Verlierer/in 5/B1
* loss [lɒs] Verlust 3/O1
be lost [bi 'lɒst] sich verirrt haben
get lost [get 'lɒst] sich verirren; sich verlaufen haben
a lot [ə 'lɒt] sehr
a lot (of) [ə 'lɒt (əv)] viel(e)
lots (= a lot) [lɒts] viel; sehr; oft 2/A1
lots of ['lɒts‿əv] viel, jede Menge
loud [laʊd] laut
love *(no pl)* [lʌv] Liebe; herzliche Grüße
love [lʌv] lieben; sehr gern mögen
fall in love (with) [ˌfɔːl‿ɪn 'lʌv] sich verlieben (in) 5/C1
lovely ['lʌvli] schön, hübsch; nett, liebenswürdig
low [ləʊ] niedrig 2/A5
Lower Saxony [ˌləʊə 'sæksəni] Niedersachsen 2/C4
luck [lʌk] Glück
be in luck [ˌbi‿ɪn 'lʌk] Glück haben
luckily ['lʌkɪli] glücklicherweise 6/BL3
lucky ['lʌki] glücklich; glückbringend, Glücks-
be lucky [bi 'lʌki] Glück haben
luggage ['lʌgɪdʒ] (Reise)gepäck
* lump [lʌmp] Klumpen 1/O2
lunch [lʌntʃ] Mittagessen
lunchbox ['lʌntʃˌbɒks] Brotdose 6/B4
lunchtime ['lʌntʃˌtaɪm] Mittagszeit; Mittagspause
lung [lʌŋ] Lungenflügel 3/B1
* the lungs *(pl)* [ðə‿'lʌŋz] die Lunge 4/O1
lyrics *(pl)* ['lɪrɪks] (Lied)text 3/A1

M

macaroni *(no pl)* [ˌmækə'rəʊni] Makkaroni 6/C2
mad [mæd] wahnsinnig, verrückt
made in ['meɪd ɪn] hergestellt in 1/I
made from ['meɪd frəm] hergestellt/gemacht aus 6/C1
magazine [ˌmægə'ziːn] Zeitschrift, Magazin
magnificent [mæg'nɪfɪsnt] wunderbar, großartig 3/A4
maid [meɪd] Magd
mail *(AE, no pl)* [meɪl] Post 4/B4
main [meɪn] Haupt-
mainly ['meɪnli] hauptsächlich 5/A3
major ['meɪdʒə] bedeutend, wichtig
make [meɪk] machen; lassen
make [meɪk] *hier:* gewinnen 4/B2
make a comparison [ˌmeɪk‿ə kəm'pærɪsn] einen Vergleich anstellen 2/C2
make a living *(no pl)* [meɪk‿ə 'lɪvɪŋ] seinen Lebensunterhalt verdienen 2/C7
make a move *(informal)* [ˌmeɪk‿ə 'muːv] sich auf den Weg machen 1/A3
make a pledge ['meɪk‿ə ˌpledʒ] geloben 4/PP3

make a try at [meɪk‿ə 'traɪ‿ət] versuchen 3/B1
make clothes [meɪk 'kləʊðz] Kleider nähen 1/PP1
make friends [meɪk 'frendz] sich anfreunden
make it *(informal)* ['meɪk‿ˌɪt] es schaffen 3/A1
make notes [meɪk 'nəʊts] (sich) Notizen machen
make one's way [meɪk wʌnz 'weɪ] sich auf den Weg machen 4/B1
make sb do sth [ˌmeɪk sʌmbədi 'duː sʌmθɪŋ] jdn dazu bringen, etw zu tun 3/B4
make sure [ˌmeɪk 'ʃɔː] sich versichern, darauf achten
make up [meɪk‿'ʌp] erfinden, (sich) ausdenken
make up one's mind ['meɪk‿ʌp wʌnz 'maɪnd] sich entscheiden 6/A4
make-up artist [ˌmeɪkʌp 'ɑːtɪst] Maskenbildner/in, Visagist/in 5/B6
maker ['meɪkə] Hersteller/in, Produzent/in 1/B5
what makes sb tick [wɒt meɪks ˌsʌmbədi 'tɪk] was jdn bewegt 2/C5
(shopping) mall [mɔːl] *überdachtes Einkaufszentrum* 1/C1
man (*pl* **men**) [mæn, men] Mann; Mensch
man [mæn] Mensch!, Mann! 3/C1
manage ['mænɪdʒ] leiten, führen; es schaffen
management of *(no pl)* ['mænɪdʒmənt‿əv] Umgang mit 4/B5
mango (*pl* **-s or** -es) ['mæŋgəʊ] Mango
manner ['mænə] Weise, Art
many ['meni] viele
map [mæp] (Land)karte
maple syrup *(no pl)* [ˌmeɪpl 'sɪrəp] Ahornsirup 1/A2
* marathon ['mærəθ(ə)n] Marathon(lauf) 5/O1
March [mɑːtʃ] März
march [mɑːtʃ] Marsch 4/C3
march [mɑːtʃ] marschieren 4/A7
marching band ['mɑːtʃɪŋ ˌbænd] Marschkapelle 5/PP4
marine [mə'riːn] Marinesoldat/in 3/C1
mark [mɑːk] schmutzig machen; markieren
* On your marks, get set, go! [ɒn jə mɑːks get set 'gəʊ] Auf die Plätze, fertig, los! 5/O1
marker ['mɑːkə] (Kenn)zeichen 5/A3
market ['mɑːkɪt] Markt
marriage ['mærɪdʒ] Heirat; Ehe
marry ['mæri] heiraten
martial arts *(npl)* [ˌmɑːʃl‿'ɑːts] Kampfsport 5/C2
mashed potatoes [ˌmæʃt pə'teɪtəʊz] Kartoffelbrei 6/PP6
mass [mæs] Masse
match (*pl* **-es**) [mætʃ, 'mætʃɪz] Streichholz
match (with) [mætʃ] zuordnen
match sth ['mætʃ ˌsʌmθɪŋ] zu etw passen 6/C1
mate [meɪt] Freund/in, Kumpel 6/CL3
material [mə'tɪəriəl] Material
math (*AE* = maths *BE*, *informal* = mathematics) [mæθ(s), ˌmæθə'mætɪks] Mathe 2/C6
as a matter of fact [əz‿ə ˌmætər‿əv 'fækt] übrigens; *hier:* ehrlich gesagt 1/C4
May [meɪ] Mai
may [meɪ] können; dürfen
maybe ['meɪbi] vielleicht
me *(1st pers. sing)* [miː] mir, mich
Me too. [mi 'tuː] Ich auch. 6/B4
meal [miːl] Mahlzeit, Essen
mean [miːn] bedeuten; meinen
meaning ['miːnɪŋ] Bedeutung
means of transport [ˌmiːnz‿əv 'trænspɔːt] Transportmittel 3/A4
meanwhile ['miːnˌwaɪl] inzwischen, unterdessen
meat *(no pl)* [miːt] Fleisch
meat loaf ['miːt ˌləʊf] Hackbraten 1/A3
the media *(pl)* [ðə 'miːdɪə] die Medien 1/A1
mediate ['miːdieɪt] vermitteln; *hier:* übersetzen 1/C3
medical ['medɪkl] medizinisch; ärztlich 3/B1
medicine *(no pl)* [medsn] Medizin, Medikament(e)
medium ['miːdiəm] durchschnittlich, mittel 6/PP6
meet [miːt] (sich) treffen
meet up ['miːt‿ʌp] sich treffen 1/C4
meeting ['miːtɪŋ] Versammlung; Treffen; Veranstaltung
melt (away) [melt] (dahin)schmelzen 3/A1
member ['membə] Angehörige/r; Mitglied 4/A4
memory ['mem(ə)ri] Gedächtnis; Erinnerung
mental ['mentl] geistig; *hier:* verrückt 3/B1
mention ['menʃn] erwähnen
menu ['menjuː] Speisekarte
mess [mes] Unordnung, Durcheinander
message ['mesɪdʒ] Nachricht
metal ['metl] Metall
metal detector ['metl dɪˌtektə] Metalldetektor 3/C5
meter (*AE* = metre *BE*) ['miːtə] Meter 6/CL3
method ['meθəd] Methode 6/B2
metre ['miːtə] Meter 6/B2
Mexican ['meksikæn] Mexikaner/in, mexikanisch 2/A3
Mexico ['mæksɪkəʊ] Mexiko 5/AL2
microphone ['maɪkrəˌfəʊn] Mikrofon 5/C3
mid- [mɪd] Mitte *(in Komposita)* 2/A3
middle ['mɪdl] Mitte
the Midwest [ðə ˌmɪd'west] der Mittelwesten 2/A3
might [maɪt] könnte
mighty ['maɪti] gewaltig; mächtig 1/B4
migrant ['maɪgrənt] Wanderarbeiter- 2/C7
mile [maɪl] Meile
milk [mɪlk] Milch
million ['mɪljən] Million
millionaire [ˌmɪljə'neə] Millionär 1/B3
mind [maɪnd] Geist, Verstand
to my mind [tə maɪ 'maɪnd] meiner Meinung nach 3/C3
not mind sth [ˌnɒt 'maɪnd sʌmθɪŋ] nichts gegen etw einzuwenden haben 1/A3
mine [maɪn] meine(r, s)
mineral water ['mɪn(ə)rəl ˌwɔːtə] Mineralwasser
miniskirt ['mɪniˌskɜːt] Minirock
minor role ['maɪnə ˌrəʊl] Nebenrolle 5/C4
minority [maɪ'nɒrəti] Minderheit, Minderheiten- 4/A4
* mint sauce [mɪnt 'sɔːs] Minzsoße 1/O2
minute ['mɪnɪt] Minute
mirror ['mɪrə] Spiegel
miscellaneous [ˌmɪsə'leɪniəs] verschiedene(r, s) 6/C2
Miss [mɪs] Fräulein *(Anrede)*; Frau Lehrerin
miss [mɪs] vermissen; fehlen; verpassen
be missing [bi 'mɪsɪŋ] fehlen
* Missis *(informal)* ['mɪsɪz] gnä' Frau; *hier:* Frau 3/O1
* miss out on sth [mɪs‿'aʊt‿ɒn ˌsʌmθɪŋ] sich etw entgehen lassen 2/O1
* mist *(no pl)* [mɪst] (leichter) Nebel, Dunst 1/O2
* mister ['mɪstə] Herr 3/O1
mix [mɪks] (ver)mischen, (ver)rühren
mixture ['mɪkstʃə] Mischung
mobile (phone) ['məʊˌbaɪl] Handy
mobility *(no pl)* [məʊ'bɪləti] Beweglichkeit, Mobilität 4/PP3
moccasin ['mɒkəsɪn] Mokassin 3/PP2
model ['mɒdl] Modell
modern ['mɒdn] modern
mom (*AE* = mum *BE*) [mɒm] Mama 1/A3
moment ['məʊmənt] Moment, Augenblick
at the moment [ˌæt ðə 'məʊmənt] im Augenblick, momentan
Monday ['mʌndeɪ] Montag
money ['mʌni] Geld
monkey ['mʌŋki] Affe
monster ['mɒnstə] Monster
month [mʌnθ] Monat
mood [muːd] Laune, Stimmung 1/C1
more [mɔː] mehr; noch mehr; weitere(r, s); zusätzliche(r, s) 5/A3
more and more [mɔːr‿ən 'mɔː] mehr und mehr, immer mehr 1/B3

morning ['mɔːnɪŋ] Morgen
in the morning [ˌɪn ðə 'mɔːnɪŋ] am Morgen
mortality rate [mɔː'tæləti reɪt] Sterblichkeitsrate 4/A4
(the) most [məʊst] am/die meisten
mostly ['məʊstli] meistens; größtenteils 4/A2
mother ['mʌðə] Mutter
motorbike *(informal)* ['məʊtəˌbaɪk] Motorrad
motto (*pl* -s *or* -es) ['mɒtəʊ] Motto, Wahlspruch 1/C1
mountain ['maʊntɪn] Berg
mountain lion ['maʊntɪn ˌlaɪən] Puma 2/B2
mouse (*pl* **mice**) [maʊs, maɪs] Maus
moustly ['məʊstli] meistens; größtenteils 4/A2
mouth [maʊθ] Mund
move [muːv] (sich) bewegen; einen Spielzug machen; schieben; umziehen (nach)
make a move *(informal)* [ˌmeɪk‿ə 'muːv] sich auf den Weg machen 1/A3
be on the move [bi‿ɒn ðə 'muːv] unterwegs sein; sich im Umbruch befinden 4/I
move around [muːv‿ə'raʊnd] herumgehen; umherreisen 2/C7
move away [ˌmuːv‿ə'weɪ] weggehen, -fahren; wegziehen
Move it! *(informal)* ['muːv‿ɪt] Beweg dich! 3/C1
movement ['muːvmənt] Bewegung
movie ['muːvi] (Kino)film 1/A2
shoot a movie [ʃuːt‿ə 'muːvi] einen Film drehen 5/C3
movie *(AE)* ['muːvi] Kino-, Film- 3/A4
movie director ['muːvi dəˌrektə] Filmregisseur/in 5/C5
the movies *(pl)* [ðə 'muːviz] Kino 5/AL1
mow [məʊ] mähen 1/C1
* mph (= miles per hour) [ˌempiːˌeɪtʃ, 'maɪlz pə‿ˌaʊə] Meilen in der/pro Stunde 2/O1
Mr ['mɪstə] Herr *(Anrede)*
Mrs ['mɪsɪz] Frau *(Anrede)*
Mt (= Mount) *(no pl)* [maʊnt] *erster Teil eines Bergnamens* 2/A5
much [mʌtʃ] viel; sehr
How much is/are ...? [ˌhaʊ mʌtʃ‿'ɪz/ɑː] Was kostet/kosten ...?
* mud *(no pl)* [mʌd] Schlamm, Matsch 5/O1
muesli ['mjuːzli] Müsli
muffin *(AE)* ['mʌfɪn] *kleiner, runder, meist süßer Kuchen* 6/C2
mule deer ['mjuːl ˌdɪə] Maultierhirsch 2/B2
mum *(informal)* [mʌm] Mama, Mutti
mural designing ['mjʊərəl dɪˌzaɪnɪŋ] Wandgestaltung 5/B6
murder ['mɜːdə] Mord 4/PP3
murder ['mɜːdə] ermorden, umbringen 4/B2
murderer ['mɜːdərə] Mörder/in 5/CL1
museum [mjuː'ziːəm] Museum
mushroom ['mʌʃruːm] Pilz
music ['mjuːzɪk] Musik
musical instrument [ˌmjuːzɪkl‿'ɪnstrʊmənt] Musikinstrument
musician [mjʊ'zɪʃn] Musiker/in
* muskrat ['mʌskræt] Moschusratte 4/O1
Muslim ['mʊzləm] Moslem/in; mohammedanisch
must [mʌst] müssen
must not [mʌst 'nɒt] nicht dürfen
mustard *(no pl)* ['mʌstəd] Senf 6/C2
my [maɪ] mein(e)
myself [maɪ'self] mir, mich; selbst

N

name [neɪm] Name
name [neɪm] nennen
was named after [wɒz 'neɪm ˌɑːftə] wurde nach ... benannt 2/A3
name [neɪm] *hier:* ernennen 3/B3
call sb names [ˌkɔːl sʌmbədi 'neɪmz] jdn beschimpfen 4/C5
narrow ['nærəʊ] eng, schmal
nation ['neɪʃn] Nation, Land; *hier:* Stamm 2/A1
national ['næʃn(ə)l] national; National-
national anthem [ˌnæʃn(ə)l 'ænθəm] Nationalhymne 2/A5
national holiday *(AE)* [ˌnæʃn(ə)l 'hɒlɪdeɪ] gesetzlicher Feiertag; Nationalfeiertag 4/PP3
nationality [ˌnæʃə'nælɪti] Nationalität; Staatsangehörigkeit 2/C5
Native American [ˌneɪtɪv‿ə'merɪkən] amerikanische/r Ureinwohner/in 2/A1
Native Rights [neɪtɪv 'raɪts] *hier:* Rechte der amerik. Ureinwohner/innen 4/A4
native speaker [ˌneɪtɪv 'spiːkə] Muttersprachler/in 3/B4
natural ['nætʃ(ə)rəl] natürlich 4/A2
near [nɪə] nahe
nearby [ˌnɪə'baɪ] in der Nähe gelegen 3/C1
nearly ['nɪəli] fast, beinahe
neat [niːt] ordentlich, sauber 2/C7
necessary ['nesəs(ə)ri] nötig, notwendig, erforderlich
neck [nek] Hals; Nacken
need [niːd] brauchen
need to ['niːd tə] müssen
negative ['negətɪv] negativ
Negro ['niːgrəʊ] Neger 4/PP3
neighbor (*AE* = neighbour *BE*) ['neɪbə] Nachbar/in 3/C5
neighborhood (*AE* = neighbourhood *BE*) ['neɪbəˌhʊd] Viertel; Nachbarschaft 1/C1
neighboring *(AE)* (= neighbouring *BE*) ['neɪbərɪŋ] benachbart, Nachbar- 2/A5
neighbour ['neɪbə] Nachbar/in
neighbourhood ['neɪbəˌhʊd] Viertel; Nachbarschaft
neither ['naɪðə] keine(r, s) von beiden
neither ... nor [ˌnaɪðə 'nɔː] weder ... noch ... 1/A4
nervous ['nɜːvəs] nervös
net [net] Netz
never ['nevə] nie(mals)
new [njuː] neu
the New World [ðə 'njuː ˌwɜːld] die Neue Welt (*veraltet für* Amerika) 4/C1
New Year [ˌnjuː 'jɪə] Neujahrs- 5/PP4
news *(no pl)* [njuːz] Neuigkeit; Nachrichten
(at the) newsagent's ['njuːzˌeɪdʒ(ə)ntz] (im) Zeitschriftengeschäft
newspaper ['njuːzˌpeɪpə] Zeitung
next [nekst] nächste(r, s)
next [nekst] dann, gleich darauf; als Nächstes
next to ['nekst‿tə] neben
* the Niagara Falls *(pl)* [ðə naɪ'ægrə ˌfɔːlz] die Niagarafälle 2/O1
nice [naɪs] schön, angenehm; nett, freundlich
nickname ['nɪkˌneɪm] Spitzname; Kosename 2/A6
night [naɪt] Nacht; Abend
at night [ət 'naɪt] am Abend, in der Nacht
nine [naɪn] neun
no [nəʊ] kein(e)
no [nəʊ] nein
no matter where ... from [nəʊ 'mætə weə frəm] ganz gleich woher ... 3/A3
no one ['nəʊ ˌwʌn] keiner, niemand
Noah's ark [ˌnəʊəz‿'ɑːk] die Arche Noah 2/C5
Nobel Peace Prize [nəʊˌbel piːs 'praɪz] Friedensnobelpreis 4/PP3
Nobel Prize [nəʊˌbel 'praɪz] Nobelpreis 3/B3
nobody ['nəʊbɒdi] niemand
noise [nɔɪz] Lärm, Krach; Geräusch
noisy ['nɔɪzi] laut
non-profit [ˌnɒn'prɒfɪt] gemeinnützig 3/AL3
nonreligious [nɒnrə'lɪdʒəs] *ohne Glaubenszugehörigkeit* 2/A5
normal ['nɔːml] normal, üblich
normally ['nɔːm(ə)li] normalerweise
north [nɔːθ] Norden 2/A5
north [nɔːθ] nördlich; Nord-
in the north (of) [ɪn ðə‿'nɔːθ] im Norden (von) 2/B1
northern ['nɔːð(ə)n] nördlich 4/C1
northwest [ˌnɔːθ'west] (nach) Nordwesten 2/A1
nose [nəʊs] Nase
not [nɒt] nicht
not ... anywhere [nɒt 'eniˌweə] nirgendwo
not any [nɒt‿'eni] (überhaupt) keine
not anymore [ˌnɒt‿eni'mɔː] nicht mehr
not at all [ˌnɒt‿ət‿'ɔːl] überhaupt nicht

not even [nɒt‿ˈiːvn] (noch) nicht einmal
not yet [nɒt ˈjet] noch nicht
note [nəʊt] Notiz
* note [nəʊt] *hier:* Schein 3/O1
note down [nəʊt ˈdaʊn] (sich) notieren 3/BL4
take/make notes [teɪk/meɪk ˈnəʊts] (sich) Notizen machen
nothing [ˈnʌθɪŋ] nichts
nothing but [ˈnʌθɪŋ bət] nur, nichts als 6/A6
Nothing one could do about it! [ˈnʌθɪŋ wʌn kəd duː‿əˌbaʊt‿ɪt] Nichts zu machen! 1/C4
Nothing ventured, nothing gained. [nʌθɪŋ ˌventʃəd nʌθɪŋ ˈgeɪnd] Wer wagt, gewinnt., Frisch gewagt ist halb gewonnen. 4/B2
notice [ˈnəʊtɪs] bemerken
noun [naʊn] Hauptwort, Substantiv 4/BL1
novel [ˈnɒvl] Roman 3/B1
November [nəʊˈvembə] November
now [naʊ] jetzt; *hier:* heute 4/A3
nowadays [ˈnaʊəˌdeɪz] heutzutage 3/C5
* nowhere [ˈnəʊweə] nirgends, nirgendwo 5/O1
number [ˈnʌmbə] Zahl; Ziffer; Nummer; *hier:* Anzahl 2/C7
figure [ˈfɪgə] *hier:* ausrechnen 2/C7
nurse [nɜːs] (Kranken)schwester/(Kranken)pfleger
nursery school [ˈnɜːs(ə)ri ˌskuːl] Kindergarten 5/PP5
nut [nʌt] Nuss 6/B4
nutshell *(no pl)* [ˈnʌtˌʃel] Nussschale 6/C1

O

(one) o'clock [(wʌn) əˈklɒk] (ein) Uhr
oasis [əʊˈeɪsɪs] Oase 4/PP3
oats *(pl)* [əʊts] Haferkörner 2/A3
object [ˈɒbdʒɪkt] Objekt; Gegenstand
* ocean [ˈəʊʃn] Ozean, (Welt)meer 6/O1
October [ɒkˈtəʊbə] Oktober
the odd one out [ðiˌɒd wʌn‿ˈaʊt] das fünfte Rad am Wagen; *hier: das Wort, das nicht zu den anderen passt* 3/CL4
of [əv] von
off [ɒf] (weg) von; vor
offensive [əˈfensɪv] Angriffs- 5/A3
offer [ˈɒfə] Angebot 3/A4
offer [ˈɒfə] (an)bieten
office [ˈɒfɪs] Büro
office [ˈɒfɪs] Büro- 5/B4
* officer [ˈɒfɪsə] Beamtin/Beamter 3/O1
official [əˈfɪʃl] offiziell, amtlich
often [ˈɒfn] oft, häufig
ogre [ˈəʊgə] Menschenfresser; *hier:* Scheusal 5/C1
oil [ɔɪl] Öl
old [əʊld] alt
old-fashioned [ˌəʊldˈfæʃnd] altmodisch

olive [ˈɒlɪv] Olive 1/A3
on [ɒn] auf; am, an; in
on and on [ˌɒn‿ənd‿ˈɒn] immer weiter 6/B4
on foot [ɒn ˈfʊt] zu Fuß
on one's own [ˌɒn wʌnz‿ˈəʊn] (für sich) allein(e)
It's got me on the go. *(informal)* [ɪts ˌgɒt me ən ðə ˈgəʊ] Es macht mich noch wahnsinnig. 1/B4
on the left [ˌɒn ðə ˈleft] links, auf der linken Seite
on the one hand [ən ðə ˈwʌn ˌhænd] einerseits 1/C1
on the other hand [ən ði‿ˈʌðər ˌhænd] andererseits 1/C1
on the right [ˌɒn ðə ˈraɪt] rechts, auf der rechten Seite
on time [ɒn ˈtaɪm] pünktlich; rechtzeitig
once [wʌns] einmal
once [wʌns] *hier:* früher, einst 4/A7
at once [æt ˈwʌns] auf einmal; sofort
one [wʌn] eins; ein(e, er, es)
one day [wʌn ˈdeɪ] eines Tages 4/A4
165'er [wʌn sɪks ˈfaɪvə] *Bewohner einer verrufenen Gegend in Harlem, New York City* 4/C5
onion [ˈʌnjən] Zwiebel
only [ˈəʊnli] einzige(r, s)
only [ˈəʊnli] nur; noch
only child [ˌəʊnli ˈtʃaɪld] Einzelkind
onto [ˈɒntə] auf
open [ˈəʊp(ə)n] öffnen; (sich) öffnen; eröffnen
open [ˈəʊp(ə)n] offen, geöffnet
* open [ˈəʊpən] *hier:* frei 2/O1
open play [ˈəʊpən ˌpleɪ] ungedecktes Spiel 5/A3
opening day [ˈəʊp(ə)nɪŋ ˌdeɪ] Eröffnungstag 5/PP4
opening times *(pl)* [ˈəʊp(ə)nɪŋ ˌtaɪmz] Öffnungszeiten
operate [ˈɒpəˌreɪt] bedienen 5/C3
opinion [əˈpɪnjən] Meinung, Ansicht
in my opinion [ɪn ˌmaɪ əˈpɪnjən] meiner Meinung nach
give an opinion (on sth) [gɪv‿ən‿əˈpɪnjən] seine Meinung (zu etw) äußern 3/CL1
opponent [əˈpəʊnənt] Opponent/in; Gegner/in 5/A3
opportunity [ˌɒpəˈtjuːnəti] Gelegenheit 4/A6
opposing [əˈpəʊzɪŋ] entgegengesetzt; *hier:* gegnerisch 5/A3
opposite [ˈɒpəzɪt] Gegenteil
opposite [ˈɒpəzɪt] gegenüber(liegend) 3/C1
oppression *(no pl)* [əˈpreʃn] Unterdrückung 4/A1
optional [ˈɒpʃnəl] *freiwillig* 5/PP5
or [ɔː] oder
orange [ˈɒrɪndʒ] Orange, Apfelsine
orange [ˈɒrɪndʒ] orange(farben)
* ordain [ɔːˈdeɪn] ordinieren; *hier:* bestimmen, verfügen 3/O1

order [ˈɔːdə] Ordnung; Reihenfolge; Befehl, Anweisung; *hier:* Bestellung 1/PP1
order [ˈɔːdə] bestellen; anordnen, befehlen 4/C2
* organ transplant [ˈɔːgən ˌtrænsplɑːnt] Organtransplantation 2/O1
organization [ˌɔːgənaɪˈzeɪʃn] Organisation 3/AL3
organize [ˈɔːgəˌnaɪz] organisieren
organized crime *(no pl)* [ˌɔːgənaɪzd ˈkraɪm] organisiertes Verbrechen 3/B3
origin [ˈɒrɪdʒɪn] Ursprung; Herkunft 2/A3
original [əˈrɪdʒn(ə)l] ursprünglich; originell, außergewöhnlich
other [ˈʌðə] andere(r, s)
our [aʊə] unser(e)
ourselves [aʊəˈselvz] uns; selbst
out (of) [aʊt] aus
be out of hand [biˌaʊt‿ɒf ˈhænd] außer Kontrolle sein 4/B2
* outdoor [ˌaʊtˈdɔː] im Freien, draußen 6/O1
outdoor sport [ˌaʊtˈdɔː spɔːt] Sportart im Freien 5/A3
* outline [ˈaʊtlaɪn] Übersicht; *hier:* Umriss 2/O1
outside [ˌaʊtˈsaɪd] außen, außerhalb; im Freien, draußen
* oven [ˈʌvn] (Back)ofen 6/O1
over [ˈəʊvə] über; hinüber; herüber
come over [ˌkʌm‿ˈəʊvə] herüberkommen; vorbeischauen 1/A3
be over [bi‿ˈəʊvə] vorbei sein 2/C7
over the years [ˌəʊvə‿ðə‿ˈjɪəz] mit den Jahren, im Laufe der Jahre 2/B2
over there [ˌəʊvə ˈðeə] dort drüben; dorthin
overalls *(pl, AE)* [ˈəʊvərˌɔːlz] Latzhose 1/PP1
overhear [ˌəʊvəˈhɪə] zufällig mithören 4/A8
overland [ˈəʊvəˌlænd] Überland-, Land- 4/B5
overnight [ˌəʊvəˈnaɪt] in der Nacht, über Nacht 1/B3
* overtake [əʊvəˈteɪk] überholen 5/O1
overview of [ˈəʊvəvjuː‿əv] Überblick über 5/C3
own [əʊn] besitzen 4/C1
own [əʊn] eigene(r, s)
on one's own [ˌɒn wʌnz‿ˈəʊn] (für sich) allein(e)
owner [ˈəʊnə] Besitzer/in, Eigentümer/in
ozone *(no pl)* [ˈəʊˌzəʊn] Ozon 6/B1
ozone hole [ˈəʊzəʊn ˌhəʊl] Ozonloch 6/B1

P

pace [peɪs] Tempo 6/B4
pack [pæk] Packung 1/B5
pack [pæk] packen; einpacken
pack up (sth) [pæk‿ˈʌp] (etw) zusammenpacken 1/PP1

* package ['pækɪdʒ] Paket 1/O2
packaging ['pækɪdʒɪŋ] Verpackung; Verpackungs- 6/B1
* packet ['pækɪt] Packung, Schachtel 1/O2
page [peɪdʒ] Seite
pain [peɪn] Schmerz(en)
paint *(no pl)* [peɪnt] Farbe; Lack 6/B3
paint [peɪnt] malen; anstreichen
painting ['peɪntɪŋ] Bild, Gemälde
pair [peə] Paar
in pairs [ɪn 'peəz] paarweise
pan for gold [pæn fə 'gəʊld] nach Gold schürfen 4/B1
pancake ['pæn,keɪk] Pfannkuchen, Omelette 1/A2
panic *(no pl)* ['pænɪk] Panik 5/B1
pants *(AE)* [pænts] (lange) Hose 1/C1
paper ['peɪpə] Papier
paper bag ['peɪpə bæg] Papiertüte 6/B3
do a paper round [ˌduː‿ə 'peɪpə ˌraʊnd] Zeitungen austragen
* papers *(pl)* ['peɪpəz] (Ausweis)papiere 3/O1
paragraph ['pærəˌgrɑːf] Absatz, Abschnitt 2/B2
Find out what each paragraph is about. [faɪnd‿'aʊt wɒt‿iːtʃ ˌpærəgrɑːf ɪz‿əˌbaʊt] Finde heraus, worum es in jedem Abschnitt geht. 2/B2
parcel ['pɑːsl] Paket; Päckchen
parents ['peərənts] Eltern
park [pɑːk] Park
parliament *(no pl)* ['pɑːləmənt] Parlament
part [pɑːt] Teil
part [pɑːt] *hier:* Rolle 5/C2
take part (in) [teɪk 'pɑːt] teilnehmen (an)
play an important part in [ˌpleɪ‿ən‿ɪmˌpɔːtnt 'pɑːt‿ɪn] eine wichtige Rolle spielen 5/PP4
part-time [ˌpɑːt'taɪm] Teilzeit-
participant [pɑː'tɪsɪpənt] Teilnehmer/in 5/A3
participate [pɑː'tɪsɪˌpeɪt] teilnehmen, sich beteiligen
partner ['pɑːtnə] Partner/in
pass [pɑːs] vorbeikommen (an); verabschieden; *hier:* überqueren 5/A3
pass [pɑːs] *hier:* zuspielen 5/A3
pass on [pɑːs‿'ɒn] fortfahren; übertragen
* pass sth to sb ['pɑːs‿sʌmθɪŋ tə ˌsʌmbədi] jdm etw geben 1/O2
pass sb up with lights of fire [pɑːs sʌmbədi‿ˌʌp wɪð laɪts‿əv‿'faɪə] *hier etwa:* an jdm vorbeifahren, ohne ihn/sie mitzunehmen 4/C5
pass the ball ['pɑːs ðə ˌbɔːl] den Ball abgeben, abspielen; zuspielen 5/A3
pass through [pɑːs 'θruː] durchlaufen; *hier:* passieren 3/B1; *hier:* durchkommen 4/A7
passenger ['pæsɪndʒə] Fahrgast; *hier:* Beifahrer 3/C1
passenger seat ['pæsɪndʒə siːt] Beifahrersitz 3/C1
passive ['pæsɪv] Passiv 3/BL3
passport ['pɑːspɔːt] Pass
past [pɑːst] Vergangenheit
past [pɑːst] vergangen
past [pɑːst] nach; vorbei an
pasta *(no pl)* ['pæstə] Nudeln, Teigwaren
paste [peɪst] kleben; einfügen 1/B4
pastor ['pɑːstə] Pfarrer, Pastor 4/PP3
* pat sb on the back ['pæt sʌmbədi‿ɒn ðə ˌbæk] jdm auf die Schulter klopfen 5/O1
patent ['peɪtnt] sich patentieren lassen 1/PP1
path [pɑːθ] Weg, Pfad 4/A7
patient ['peɪʃnt] Patient/in
patient ['peɪʃntli] geduldig 1/C1
* pattern ['pæt(ə)n] Muster 4/O1
patty ['pæti] Pastetchen 6/C2
pause [pɔːz] eine (kurze) Pause machen, innehalten 3/C1
pavement ['peɪvmənt] Gehsteig, Bürgersteig 3/CL4
* paw *(informal)* [pɔː] betatschen, begrapschen 3/O1
pay *(no pl)* [peɪ] Lohn, Gehalt 1/C1
pay [peɪ] bezahlen
PC (= personal computer) [piː'siː] PC 6/B4
P. E. (= physical education) [piː 'iː, ˌfɪzɪkl‿edju'keɪʃn] Sport(unterricht) 5/B2
pea [piː] Erbse
peace [piːs] Frieden
peace conference ['piːs ˌkɒnf(ə)rəns] Friedenskonferenz 4/A7
peaceful ['piːsfl] friedlich; friedfertig
peach [piːtʃ] Pfirsich
peanut ['piːnʌt] Erdnuss 1/A4
pear [peə] Birne
peculiar [pɪ'kjuːliə] seltsam, merkwürdig 1/B4
pedal ['pedl] Pedal
pedestrian [pə'destriən] Fußgänger/in 2/AL1
peel [piːl] schälen
peelings *(pl)* ['piːlɪŋz] Schalen 6/B3
pen [pen] Stift
pen friend ['pen ˌfrend] Brieffreund/in 5/B2
pencil ['pensl] Bleistift
pencil case ['pensl ˌkeɪs] Federmäppchen
penguin ['peŋgwɪn] Pinguin
penknife *(pl* **-knives)** ['penˌnaɪf, 'penˌnaɪvz] Taschenmesser
Pennant Races *(AE)* ['penənt ˌreɪsɪz] *Kampf um die Meisterschaft in einer Regionalliga* 5/PP4
people *(pl)* ['piːpl] Leute, Menschen
* peoples *(pl)* ['piːplz] Völker 6/O1
pepper ['pepə] Pfeffer; Paprika
per [pə] pro
* perceive sth [pə'siːv ˌsʌmθɪŋ] etw wahrnehmen, empfinden 4/O1
percent *(AE* = per cent *BE)* [pə 'sent] Prozent 3/B1
perfect ['pɜːfɪkt] vollkommen, perfekt
performance [pə'fɔːməns] Vorführung; *hier:* Darstellung 5/C4
perhaps [pə'hæps] vielleicht
period ['pɪəriəd] Zeitspanne, Zeitraum 4/B1
permission [pə'mɪʃn] Erlaubnis, Genehmigung 4/C1
person ['pɜːsn] Person, Mensch
personal ['pɜːsnəl] persönlich; privat
personality [ˌpɜːsə'næləti] Persönlichkeit, Charakter 5/A2
persuade [pə'sweɪd] überreden; überzeugen 2/C4
pet [pet] Haustier
pharmaceuticals *(pl)* [ˌfɑːmə'sjuːtɪklz] Pharmaka 2/A3
phone (= telephone) [fəʊn, 'telɪˌfəʊn] Telefon
phone [fəʊn] anrufen
photo ['fəʊtəʊ] Foto
take a photo [ˌteɪk‿ə 'fəʊtəʊ] fotografieren, ein Foto machen 3/A2
photograph ['fəʊtəˌgrɑːf] Foto(grafie)
phrase [freɪz] Satz; Ausdruck, (Rede)wendung
physical ['fɪzɪkl] körperlich, physisch
physics ['fɪzɪks] Physik 3/B3
pick [pɪk] aussuchen; pflücken
pick grapes [pɪk 'greɪpz] Trauben lesen 2/C7
pick pockets [pɪk 'pɒkɪts] Taschendiebstahl begehen
pick up [pɪk‿'ʌp] aufheben; abholen; mitnehmen
(mixed) pickles *(pl)* ['pɪklz] Relish; *hier:* Essiggemüse 6/PP6
picnic ['pɪknɪk] Picknick
picture ['pɪktʃə] Bild
pie [paɪ] Kuchen; Pastete 6/C2
pie chart ['paɪ ˌtʃɑːt] Tortendiagramm 2/C2
piece [piːs] Stück
piece of information [ˌpiːs‿əv‿ɪnfə'meɪʃn] Information
piece of paper [ˌpiːs‿əv 'peɪpə] Blatt Papier
pier [pɪə] Pier, Hafendamm; Landungsbrücke 3/A4
pig [pɪg] Schwein
pilgrim ['pɪlgrɪm] Pilger/in 2/A2
pillow ['pɪləʊ] (Kopf)kissen
pilot ['paɪlət] Pilot/in
pin (on/to) [pɪn] befestigen (an) 4/B5
pineapple ['paɪnˌæpl] Ananas
pink [pɪŋk] rosa, pink
pint [paɪnt] Pint *(0,568 l)* 6/C2
pioneer [ˌpaɪə'nɪə] Pionier/in, Wegbereiter/in 1/B3
pitch [pɪtʃ] stampfen; *hier:* werfen 5/A3
pitcher ['pɪtʃə] Werfer/in 5/A3

be a pity [ˌbiˍə ˈpɪti] schade/bedauerlich sein
pizza [ˈpiːtsə] Pizza
place [pleɪs] Ort; Platz
place of birth [ˌpleɪsˍəv ˈbɜːθ] Geburtsort 3/B6
* plain [pleɪn] Ebene 2/O1
plain [pleɪn] einfach; *hier:* rein 5/B1
plan [plæn] Plan
plan [plæn] planen
plane [pleɪn] Fläche; Flugzeug
plant [plɑːnt] Pflanze
plant [plɑːnt] pflanzen
plantation [plɑːnˈteɪʃn] Plantage, Pflanzung 4/C1
plaster [ˈplɑːstə] (Ver)putz; Gips(verband)
plastic [ˈplæstɪk] Plastik, Kunststoff 6/A5
plate [pleɪt] Teller
play [pleɪ] Spiel; (Theater)stück
play [pleɪ] spielen
play an important part in [ˌpleɪˍənˍɪmˌpɔːtnt ˈpɑːtˍɪn] eine wichtige Rolle spielen 5/PP4
play hooky *(informal)* [pleɪ ˈhʊki] die Schule schwänzen 3/C1
play-off [ˈpleɪˌɒf] Play-off; Entscheidungsspiel 5/PP4
player [ˈpleɪə] Spieler/in
* pleasant [ˈpleznt] angenehm 1/O2
please [pliːz] bitte
as you please [ˌæzˍjə ˈpliːz] wie es dir/Ihnen gefällt 3/A4
pleasure *(no pl)* [ˈpleʒə] Freude, Vergnügen
plenty [ˈplenti] genug
plot [plɒt] Handlung, Plot 5/C1
plum [plʌm] Pflaume, Zwetschge
pm (= post meridiem) [ˌpiːˈem, ˈpəʊst məˌrɪdɪəm] nachmittags, abends *(nur hinter Uhrzeit zwischen 12 Uhr mittags und Mitternacht)* 3/A4
pocket [ˈpɒkɪt] Tasche
pocket money [ˈpɒkɪt ˌmʌni] Taschengeld
pick pockets [pɪk ˈpɒkɪts] Taschendiebstahl begehen
poem [ˈpəʊɪm] Gedicht
poet [ˈpəʊɪt] Dichter 2/C5
point [pɔɪnt] Spitze; Punkt
point (to) [pɔɪnt] deuten/zeigen (auf)
point of view [ˌpɔɪntˍəv ˈvjuː] Gesichtspunkt, Standpunkt 1/C4
Poland [ˈpəʊlənd] Polen 3/BL3
the police *(npl)* [ðə pəˈliːs] die Polizei
police officer [pəˈliːs ˌɒfɪsə] Polizeibeamter/-beamtin
police station [pəˈliːsˍˌsteɪʃn] Polizeiwache
policeman *(pl* **-men)** [pəˈliːsmən, pəˈliːsmən] Polizist
policewoman *(pl* **-women)** [pəˈliːsˌwʊmən, pəˈliːsˌwɪmɪn] Polizistin
Polish [ˈpɒlɪʃ] polnisch 2/C5
polite [pəˈlaɪt] höflich 1/C1
political [pəˈlɪtɪkl] politisch
poor [pɔː] arm
* pop *(informal* = population) [pɒp] Einwohnerzahl 1/O
poptart [ˈpɒptɑːt] *mit Früchten oder Schokolade gefülltes flaches Gebäck, das im Toaster erwärmt wird* 6/C2
popular [ˈpɒpjʊlə] beliebt
populated [ˈpɒpjʊˌleɪtɪd] bevölkert 4/B4
population [ˌpɒpjʊˈleɪʃn] Bevölkerung
populous [ˈpɒpjʊləs] bevölkerungsreich, dicht besiedelt 2/A3
pork [ˌpɔːk ˈrɪbz] Schwein(efleisch) 6/PP6
porridge [ˈpɒrɪdʒ] Porridge, Haferbrei
port [pɔːt] Hafen 4/B1
portfolio [pɔːtˈfəʊliəʊ] (Akten)mappe 1/AL3
position [pəˈzɪʃn] Platz, Stelle, Lage 4/C3
positive [ˈpɒzətɪv] sicher; positiv
possible [ˈpɒsəbl] möglich
possibly [ˈpɒsəbli] möglicherweise, vielleicht 3/PP2
post [pəʊst] per Post schicken; durch Aushang bekannt geben 4/C2
post office [ˈpəʊstˍɒfɪs] Post(amt)
postal service [ˈpəʊstl ˌsɜːvɪs] Postservice 6/CL3
postcard [ˈpəʊstˌkɑːd] Postkarte
poster [ˈpəʊstə] Poster
* posterity *(no pl)* [pɒˈsterəti] Nachwelt 3/O1
postman *(pl* **-men)** [ˈpəʊstmən, ˈpəʊstmən] Postbote, Briefträger
potato *(pl* **potatoes)** [pəˈteɪtəʊ, pəˈteɪtəʊz] Kartoffel
potato chip [pəˈteɪtəʊ ˌtʃɪp] Kartoffelchip 1/B3
potato rounds [pəˈteɪtəʊ ˌraʊndz] gebratene Kartoffelscheiben 6/C2
pound [paʊnd] Pfund
* pour [pɔː] gießen; schütten 4/O1
poverty [ˈpɒvəti] Armut 2/C7
power [ˈpaʊə] Macht; *hier:* Fähigkeit, Kraft 5/C1
* powerful [ˈpaʊəfl] mächtig, einflussreich 4/O1
practice [ˈpræktɪs] Übung(sstunde) 3/C1
practice *(AE* = practise *BE)* [ˈpræktɪs] üben 3/C1
practise [ˈpræktɪs] üben; trainieren
* prayer [ˈpreə] Gebet 6/O1
prefer [prɪˈfɜː] vorziehen, bevorzugen
pregnancy [ˈpregnənsi] Schwangerschaft 4/A4
prejudice [ˈpredʒʊdɪs] Vorurteil 3/C5
prepare [prɪˈpeə] vorbereiten; zubereiten
preposition [ˌprepəˈzɪʃn] Verhältniswort, Präposition 5/AL2
prescription [prɪˈskrɪpʃən] Rezept
present [ˈpreznt] Geschenk
present [prɪˈzent] bieten; überreichen; präsentieren
present perfect [ˌpreznt ˈpɜːfɪkt] Perfekt 3/AL3
present progressive [ˌpreznt prəʊˈgresɪv] Verlaufsform (des) Präsens 3/AL1
presentation [ˌpreznˈteɪʃn] Präsentation
president [ˈprezɪdənt] Präsident/in; Vorsitzende/r
* press [pres] drücken 3/O1
pretend [prɪˈtend] vorgeben, vortäuschen 3/C1
pretty [ˈprɪti] hübsch
pretty *(informal)* [ˈprɪti] ziemlich 1/C1
pretzel [ˈpretsl] Brezel 6/C2
prevent [prɪˈvent] verhindern; vorbeugen
prevent from [prɪˈvent frəm] an etw hindern, von etw abhalten 5/A3
price [praɪs] Preis
princess [ˌprɪnˈses] Prinzessin 5/C1
printout [ˈprɪntˌaʊt] Ausdruck 6/B3
prize [praɪz] Preis; Gewinn
probably [ˈprɒbəbli] wahrscheinlich
problem [ˈprɒbləm] Schwierigkeit; Problem
process sb [ˈprəʊses ˌsʌmbədi] jdn abfertigen 3/B1
produce [prəˈdjuːs] herstellen, produzieren 1/B3
producer [prəˈdjuːsə] Hersteller/in; Produzent/in 1/B3
product [ˈprɒdʌkt] Produkt, Erzeugnis
production crew [prəˈdʌkʃn kruː] Produktionsteam 5/C3
professional [prəˈfeʃnəl] beruflich; Berufs-; Profi- 5/PP4
professor [prəˈfesə] Professor/in 3/B3
profile [ˈprəʊfaɪl] Profil; Porträt 3/B3
programme [ˈprəʊgræm] Programm, Spielplan
project [ˈprɒdʒekt] Projekt, Vorhaben
* keep a promise [ˌkiːpˍə ˈprɒmɪs] ein Versprechen halten 4/O1
promise [ˈprɒmɪs] versprechen
prompt [prɒmpt] Stichwort 2/A3
pronounce [prəˈnaʊns] aussprechen 1/PP1
-proof [pruːf] -sicher 2/B5
proper [ˈprɒpə] echt, richtig
the pros and cons [ðə ˌprəʊzˍənd ˈkɒnz] das Für und Wider, das Pro und Kontra 1/C1
protect [prəˈtekt] schützen 2/B5
protect sb from sth [prəˈtekt sʌmbədi frəm ˌsʌmθɪŋ] jdn vor etw schützen 6/B1
protection [prəˈtekʃn] Schutz
protest [ˈprəʊtest] Protest
protest (against) [prəˈtest] protestieren (gegen) 4/C4
Protestant [ˈprɒtɪstənt] Protestant/in, protestantisch 2/A3
proud [praʊd] stolz

pub *(informal)* [pʌb] Kneipe
public ['pʌblɪk] öffentlich
public school *(AE)* [ˌpʌblik 'sku:l] staatliche Schule 2/C5
public transport(ation) *(no pl)* [ˌpʌblɪk ˌtrænspɔ:'teɪʃn] öffentliche Verkehrsmittel 4/C3
pudding *(AE, no pl)* ['pʊdɪŋ] Pudding 6/C2
* puddle ['pʌdl] Pfütze 5/O1
* puff (at) a cigar *(informal)* [pʌf‿ə sɪ'gɑ:] eine Zigarre paffen 1/O2
pull [pʊl] ziehen
pull out [pʊl‿'aʊt] (heraus)ziehen; *hier:* auseinanderziehen 1/B4
pull over [pʊl‿'əʊvə] zur Seite fahren 3/C1
pulled pork [pʊld 'pɔ:k] *auf besondere Art geräuchertes Schweinefleisch* 6/PP6
pump [pʌmp] Pumpe
* pumpkin ['pʌmpkɪn] Kürbis 6/O1
punchbag ['pʌntʃˌbæg] Sandsack
pupil ['pju:pl] Schüler/in
purple ['pɜ:pl] violett, lila
push [pʊʃ] schieben 3/B1
* push sb back [ˌpʊʃ sʌmbədi 'bæk] jdn zurückdrängen 3/O1
push into sth ['pʊʃ ˌɪntə sʌmθɪŋ] sich Zugang zu etw verschaffen 4/A2
put [pʊt] setzen, legen, stellen
put on [pʊt‿'ɒn] anziehen; auftragen
put on [pʊt‿'ɒn] *hier:* stecken an 1/B4
put on weight [ˌpʊt‿ɒn 'weɪt] zunehmen
put sb right *(informal)* [pʊt ˌsʌmbədi 'raɪt] jdn eines Besseren belehren 1/B4
put up [pʊt‿'ʌp] aufhängen; aufstellen
put up with [pʊt‿'ʌp wɪð] sich abfinden mit 3/C5
* pyjamas *(npl)* [pə'dʒɑ:məz] Pyjama, Schlafanzug 1/O2

Q

quality ['kwɒləti] Qualität 1/PP1
quarter ['kwɔ:tə] Viertel(stunde)
queen [kwi:n] Königin
question ['kwestʃn] Frage
ask questions [ɑ:sk‿'kwestʃnz] Fragen stellen
queue [kju:] Schlange, Reihe
queue [kju:] anstehen, Schlange stehen 1/A3
quick [kwɪk] schnell
quiet ['kwaɪət] leise, ruhig
quite [kwaɪt] ziemlich; ganz
quiz [kwɪz] Quiz, Ratespiel 2/A2
quote [kwəʊt] zitieren; nennen 3/B1

R

rabbit ['ræbɪt] Kaninchen
raccoon [rə'ku:n] Waschbär/in 3/PP2
race [reɪs] Rennen; Rasse 2/C5
racial ['reɪʃl] rassisch, Rassen- 4/C3
racism *(no pl)* ['reɪˌsɪz(ə)m] Rassismus 4/C4
racist ['reɪsɪst] rassistisch 4/C3
rack [ræk] *hier:* Portion 6/PP6
radiation [ˌreɪdi'eɪʃn] Strahlung 6/B1
radio ['reɪdiəʊ] Radio
rail [reɪl] Bahn
railroad *(AE)* ['reɪlˌrəʊd] Schienen; (Eisen)bahn 4/C1
railway(s) ['reɪlweɪ] Eisenbahn 6/CL3
rain [reɪn] Regen
rain [reɪn] regnen
* rainbow ['reɪnˌbəʊ] Regenbogen 4/O1
raincoat ['reɪnˌkəʊt] Regenmantel
raise [reɪz] heben; aufziehen
* raise [reɪz] *hier:* Spenden sammeln 2/O1
raise money [reɪz 'mʌni] Geld aufbringen/auftreiben
ranger ['reɪndʒə] Aufseher/in, Ranger/in 2/B5
rather ['rɑ:ðə] ziemlich 1/C4
rating *(no pl)* ['reɪtɪŋ] Einschätzung; *hier:* Bewertung 5/C4
rattlesnake ['rætlˌsneɪk] Klapperschlange 2/B2
raven ['reɪvn] Rabe 2/B2
reach [ri:tʃ] erreichen
react [rɪ'ækt] reagieren 1/C4
read [ri:d] lesen
read along [ˌri:d‿ə'lɒŋ] mitlesen 1/B4
read out [ri:d‿'aʊt] laut vorlesen
read sth to sb ['ri:d ˌsʌmθɪŋ tə ˌsʌmbədi] jdm etw vorlesen
ready ['redi] fertig; bereit
real [rɪəl] wirklich; echt
realize sth ['rɪəlaɪz ˌsʌmθɪŋ] sich einer Sache bewusst sein/werden; bemerken
really ['rɪəli] wirklich
reason ['ri:zn] Grund
rebellion [rɪ'beljən] Rebellion; Aufstand 3/B4
recapture sth [ri:'kæptʃə ˌsʌmθɪŋ] *hier:* etw wieder lebendig werden lassen 4/A7
receipt [rɪ'si:t] Eingang; *hier:* Quittung 6/B3
receive [rɪ'si:v] erhalten 1/C4
recent ['ri:snt] kürzlich; neueste(r, s); jüngste(r, s); letzte(r, s) 2/B2
recently ['ri:sntli] kürzlich, vor kurzem, neulich
recipe ['resɪpi] Rezept
recognize ['rekəgˌnaɪz] erkennen
recommend [ˌrekə'mend] empfehlen 5/C4
record ['rekɔ:d] Aufzeichnungen; Rekord; *hier:* Protokoll 6/A7
* set a record [ˌset‿ə 'rekɔ:d] einen Rekord aufstellen 2/O1
record [rɪ'kɔ:d] aufzeichnen; aufnehmen 5/C3
red [red] rot
reduce [rɪ'dju:s] verringern, reduzieren 6/A5
refer to [rɪ'fɜ: tə] hinweisen auf, sich beziehen auf 4/C5
reflector [rɪ'flektə] Reflektor; Rückstrahler
* refreshing [rɪ'freʃɪŋ] erfrischend; *hier:* wohltuend 1/O2
refuse [rɪ'fju:z] ablehnen; verweigern 3/B1; *hier:* sich weigern 4/C3
region ['ri:dʒ(ə)n] Region, Bezirk 2/A3
regional ['ri:dʒn(ə)l] regional 6/PP6
* registration [ˌredʒɪ'streɪʃn] Anmeldung 3/O1
regret [rɪ'gret] bedauern 3/B1
regular ['regjʊlə] regelmäßig; geregelt
relationship [rɪ'leɪʃnʃɪp] Beziehung
relative ['relətɪv] Verwandte/r, Angehörige/r
relatively ['relətɪvli] relativ
relax [rɪ'læks] sich entspannen
release [rɪ'li:s] freilassen; entlassen 3/B3
religion [rɪ'lɪdʒ(ə)n] Religion; Glaube
reluctant [rɪ'lʌktənt] widerwillig, widerstrebend 6/B4
remain [rɪ'meɪn] bleiben
remaining [rɪ'meɪnɪŋ] übrig, restlich 2/A4
remember [rɪ'membə] sich erinnern (an)
remind [rɪ'maɪnd] erinnern
repair [rɪ'peə] reparieren
repeat [rɪ'pi:t] wiederholen 2/AL4
replace [rɪ'pleɪs] ersetzen
reply [rɪ'plaɪ] antworten, erwidern 3/C1
report [rɪ'pɔ:t] Meldung; Bericht
report [rɪ'pɔ:t] berichten
report back to [rɪˌpɔ:t 'bæk tə] jdm Bericht erstatten 1/B2
reported [rɪ'pɔ:tɪd] indirekt 6/A5
reporter [rɪ'pɔ:tə] Reporter/in
represent [ˌreprɪ'zent] vertreten; symbolisieren 2/A2
republic [rɪ'pʌblɪk] Republik 2/A5
reputation [ˌrepjʊ'teɪʃn] Ruf 3/C5
rescue ['reskju:] retten
reservation [ˌrezə'veɪʃn] Reservat 4/A2
residence ['rezɪd(ə)ns] Wohnsitz 2/A1
resident ['rezɪd(ə)nt] Bewohner/in 2/B2
resin *(no pl)* ['rezɪn] Harz 1/B3
in response to [ɪn rɪ'spɒns tə] in Erwiderung auf 4/C3
responsible [rɪ'spɒnsəbl] verantwortlich, zuständig 5/C3
rest [rest] Rest; (Ruhe)pause
have a rest [ˌhæv‿ə 'rest] eine Pause machen/einlegen
rest [rest] (sich) ausruhen 1/C5
restaurant ['rest(ə)rɒnt] Restaurant
result [rɪ'zʌlt] Folge; Ergebnis
* retrieve [rɪ'tri:v] wiederfinden; *hier:* herausholen 4/O1
return [rɪ'tɜ:n] Rückkehr 4/A1
return [rɪ'tɜ:n] zurückkehren
review [rɪ'vju:] Kritik; Besprechung 5/C4

review [rɪ'vjuː] rezensieren 5/C4
revolution [ˌrevə'luːʃn] Revolution
the Rhine *(no pl)* [ðə ˌraɪn] der Rhein 3/A4
rhyme [raɪm] Reim 6/BL4
rhyme with ['raɪm wɪð] (sich) reimen auf 6/BL4
* rhythm ['rɪðəm] Rhythmus, Takt 5/O1
rice [raɪs] Reis
rich [rɪtʃ] reich
rich [rɪtʃ] *hier:* vielfältig 3/C5
ride [raɪd] Fahrt
ride [raɪd] *hier:* Mitfahrgelegenheit 3/C1
ride [raɪd] Fahrt; *hier:* Ritt 4/B6
ride *(AE, informal)* [raɪd] fahrbarer Untersatz 3/C1
have a ride *(AE, informal)* [ˌhæv‿ə 'raɪd] mitgenommen werden 3/C1
bike ride ['baɪk raɪd] Radtour
ride [raɪd] fahren; reiten
ride off [raɪd‿'ɒf] *hier:* weiterreiten 4/B6
rider ['raɪdə] Reiter/in 4/B4
right [raɪt] Recht
right [raɪt] (nach) rechts
on the right [ˌɒn ðə 'raɪt] rechts, auf der rechten Seite
right [raɪt] richtig
right [raɪt] völlig; *hier:* genau, direkt 3/C1
right through the very heart ['raɪt θruː ðə ˌveri hɑːt] genau mitten durch 3/A1
be right [bi 'raɪt] Recht haben 6/B4
put sb right *(informal)* [pʊt ˌsʌmbədi 'raɪt] jdn eines Besseren belehren 1/B4
right at his/her side ['raɪt‿ət‿ɪz/hə ˌsaɪd] direkt neben ihm/ihr 1/B4
right now [raɪt 'naʊ] jetzt, sofort, gleich
righteousness *(no pl)* ['raɪtʃəsnəs] Rechtschaffenheit 4/PP3
rightly ['raɪtli] richtig; zu Recht 6/B1
* rim [rɪm] Rand 5/O1
ring [rɪŋ] Ring
ring [rɪŋ] klingeln, läuten
ringlet ['rɪŋlət] Locke 3/B1
rioting ['raɪətɪŋ] Randalieren, Krawalle 4/PP3
rise [raɪz] steigen; sich erheben
rise up [raɪz‿'ʌp] sich auflehnen 4/PP3
river ['rɪvə] Fluss
riverbank ['rɪvəˌbæŋk] Flussufer 4/B2
rivet ['rɪvɪt] Niete 1/PP1
road [rəʊd] Straße
roast [rəʊst] Braten 6/B3
roast chicken ['rəʊst ˌtʃɪkɪn] Brathuhn 6/C2
roast turkey ['rəʊst ˌtɜːki] gebratener Truthahn 6/C2
* roast [rəʊst] rösten; braten 6/O1
rob [rɒb] bestehlen; (aus)rauben 3/C1
rock [rɒk] Stein
rock [rɒk] *hier:* Fels(en) 2/B2
role [rəʊl] Rolle
roll [rəʊl] Rolle; Brötchen
roll a dice [ˌrəʊl‿ə 'daɪs] würfeln
roll down [rəʊl 'daʊn] hinunterrollen 4/PP3
roof *(pl* **roofs** *or* **rooves)** [ruːf, ruːfs, ruːvz] Dach
room [ruːm] Zimmer
room [ruːm] Platz; Raum 4/C1
* root [ruːt] Wurzel 4/O1
rose [rəʊz] Rose
rough [rʌf] rau; hart, schwer
round [raʊnd] rund
route [ruːt] Strecke, Route
row [rəʊ] Reihe 2/C7
royal ['rɔɪəl] königlich
rub [rʌb] reiben 3/B1
rubber ['rʌbə] Gummi; Radiergummi 1/B4
* rubber stamp [ˌrʌbə 'stæmp] Stempel 3/O1
rubbish *(no pl)* ['rʌbɪʃ] Müll 6/B3
rule [ruːl] Regel
rule [ruːl] regieren; *hier:* entscheiden 4/C3
ruler ['ruːlə] Lineal
score a run ['skɔːr‿ə ˌrʌn] einen Treffer erzielen 5/A3
run [rʌn] laufen, rennen; fahren, verkehren
run off [rʌn‿'ɒf] abhauen
run through sth [rʌn 'θruː ˌsʌmθɪŋ] durchgehen; *hier:* durch etw durchfahren 3/B1
run-down [ˌrʌn'daʊn] heruntergekommen 3/C5
* runner ['rʌnə] Läufer/in 5/O1
* running shoe ['rʌnɪŋ ʃuː] Laufschuh 5/O1
Russian ['rʌʃn] Russe/Russin; russisch 2/C5
rustic ['rʌstɪk] ländlich, rustikal 6/PP6

S

* sacred ['seɪkrɪd] heilig; geheiligt 4/O1
sad [sæd] traurig
saddle ['sædl] Sattel
sadly ['sædli] bedauerlicherweise, leider 3/C5
safe [seɪf] sicher
safety ['seɪfti] Sicherheit
sail [seɪl] *(mit dem Schiff)* fahren; segeln 3/A4
* set sail [set 'seɪl] in See stechen 6/O1
sailor ['seɪlə] Matrose, Seemann 4/B1
salad ['sæləd] Salat
sale [seɪl] (Aus)verkauf
sales *(pl)* [seɪlz] Absatz; Umsatz 1/B3
* sales figures *(pl)* ['seɪlz ˌfɪgəz] Verkaufszahlen 1/O2
* salesman ['seɪlzmən] Verkäufer, Handelsvertreter 3/O1
salsa ['sælsə] Salsasoße 1/A3
salt [sɔːlt] Salz
the same [ðə 'seɪm] der-/die-/dasselbe
sand dune ['sænd ˌdjuːn] Sanddüne 2/B2
* sandal ['sændl] Sandale 5/O1
satisfied ['sætɪsˌfaɪd] zufrieden 1/C1
Saturday ['sætədeɪ] Samstag
Saturdays ['sætədeɪz] samstags 3/A4
sauce [sɔːs] Soße, Sauce
sausage ['sɒsɪdʒ] Wurst, Würstchen
save [seɪv] sparen
saver Metro ticket ['seɪvə meˌtrəʊ ˌtɪkɪt] *Sparticket für die U-Bahn* 6/B3
say [seɪ] sagen
scare away [ˌskeər‿ə'weɪ] verscheuchen, abschrecken 2/B5
scarf *(pl* **-s** *or* **scarves)** [skɑːf, skɑːvz] Schal
scene [siːn] Szene
scenic ['siːnɪk] landschaftlich (schön) 2/A3
schedule ['ʃedjuːl] (Zeit-/Fahr)plan; *hier:* Stundenplan 5/B2
school [skuːl] Schule
science *(no pl)* ['saɪəns] (Natur)wissenschaft
(pair of) scissors *(npl)* ['sɪzəz] Schere
* scoop up sth [skuːp‿'ʌp ˌsʌmθɪŋ] etw hochheben 4/O1
score [skɔː] Punktestand
score a point ['skɔːr‿ə ˌpɔɪnt] einen Punkt machen 5/A3
score a run ['skɔːr‿ə ˌrʌn] einen Treffer erzielen 5/A3
score a touchdown ['skɔːr‿ə ˌtʌtʃdaʊn] einen Versuch erzielen 5/A3
scorpion ['skɔːpiən] Skorpion 2/B2
Scottish ['skɒtɪʃ] schottisch 2/C2
scream [skriːm] schreien; kreischen
screen [skriːn] Leinwand; Bildschirm 3/A4
script [skrɪpt] Drehbuch, Skript 5/C3
scurvy *(no pl)* ['skɜːvi] Skorbut *(Krankheit)* 4/B2
sea [siː] Meer
sea level ['siː ˌlevl] Meeresspiegel 2/A5
seaport ['siːˌpɔːt] Seehafen 3/A4
search for ['sɜːtʃ fə] suchen nach 1/PP1
search (on) the Internet [ˌsɜːtʃ ði‿'ɪntənet] im Internet suchen 3/B4
seasick ['siːˌsɪk] seekrank
* seaside resort ['siːsaɪd rɪˌzɔːt] Seebad 2/O1
season ['siːzn] Jahreszeit
seat [siːt] (Sitz)platz; Sitz
second ['sekənd] Sekunde 3/C1
second ['sekənd] zweite(r, s)
* second ['sekənd] zweitens 5/O1
be second to none [bi ˌsekənd tə 'nʌn] unvergleichlich sein 3/C5
secondary school ['sekənd(ə)ri ˌskuːl] weiterführende Schule 6/C2
secondly ['sekəndli] zweitens 3/C5
secret ['siːkrət] Geheimnis
secret ['siːkrət] geheim; *hier:* heimlich 5/C4
secretary ['sekrətri] Sekretär/in

*secretly ['siːkrətli] heimlich 1/O2
section ['sekʃn] Teil
*secure sth [sɪ'kjʊə ˌsʌmθɪŋ] etw sichern/garantieren 3/O1
see [siː] sehen; treffen; besuchen; *hier:* ansehen, besichtigen 3/A4
See you (soon)! *(informal)* [ˌsiː jə 'suːn] Bis bald! 1/A3
be seen as [biː 'siːn‿əs] angesehen werden als 4/A2
seed [siːd] Same(n)
seem [siːm] scheinen
segregate ['segrɪˌgeɪt] absondern; trennen 4/C3
segregated ['segrɪˌgeɪtɪd] nur für Weiße oder Schwarze 4/C3
segregation *(no pl)* [ˌsegrɪ'geɪʃn] Trennung 4/C2
self-evident [ˌself'evɪd(ə)nt] offensichtlich, selbstverständlich 4/PP3
selfish ['selfɪʃ] selbstsüchtig
sell [sel] verkaufen
seminar ['semɪˌnɑː] Seminar 4/A4
send [send] (zu)schicken
*send word [send 'wɜːd] eine Mitteilung machen *(förmlich)* 6/O1
senior *(AE)* ['siːniə] *Schüler/in einer Highschool- oder Collegeabgangsklasse* 5/PP5
senior citizens *(pl)* [ˌsiːniə 'sɪtɪznz] ältere Menschen 3/A4
sense of community [sens‿əv kə'mjuːnəti] Gemeinschaftsgefühl 3/C5
sensible ['sensəbl] vernünftig, angemessen, passend
sentence ['sentəns] Satz
sentence sb to sth ['sentəns ˌsʌmbədi tə ˌsʌmθɪŋ] jdn zu etw verurteilen 3/B3
separate ['sepəˌreɪt] (sich) trennen
separate ['sep(ə)rət] getrennt, separat 4/A2
September [sep'tembə] September
sequoia (tree) [sɪ'kwɔɪə] Sequoia, Mammutbaum 2/B2
series *(pl -)* ['sɪəriːz] Reihe; Folge; Serie 5/C2
be serious [bi 'sɪəriəs] es ernst meinen
serious ['sɪəriəs] ernst 1/C1
serve [sɜːv] servieren
serve [sɜːv] *hier:* Angabe haben 5/A3
serve sb ['sɜːv ˌsʌmbədi] jdn bedienen 1/C1
server ['sɜːvə] der-/diejenige, der/die die Angabe macht *(Volleyball)* 5/A3
set [set] Szenenaufbau; Drehort *(Film)* 5/C3
set [set] Satz *(Sport)* 5/A3
set [set] stellen; *hier* einstellen 5/C3
*set [set] bereit, fertig 5/O1
*On your marks, get set, go! [ɒn jə mɑːks get set 'gəʊ] Auf die Plätze, fertig, los! 5/O1
*set a record [ˌset‿ə 'rekɔːd] einen Rekord aufstellen 2/O1
*set oneself a goal [set wʌnˌself‿ə 'gəʊl] sich ein Ziel setzen 2/O1
*set sail [set 'seɪl] in See stechen 6/O1
set up [set‿'ʌp] aufschlagen; aufbauen
setting ['setɪŋ] Lage; Schauplatz 3/A4
settle ['setl] (be)siedeln 2/A1
settlement ['setlmənt] Siedlung 4/A7
settler ['setlə] Siedler/in 3/PP2
seven ['sevn] sieben
several ['sev(ə)rəl] einige; verschiedene; *hier:* mehrere 1/C1
shadow ['ʃædəʊ] Schatten 2/C7
*shake [ʃeɪk] schütteln; *hier:* erschüttern 3/O1
shake one's head ['ʃeɪk wʌnz ˌhed] den Kopf schütteln 1/C4
we shall [wiː 'ʃæl] wir werden/sollen
shampoo *(no pl)* [ʃæm'puː] Shampoo 6/B3
shape [ʃeɪp] Form; Art 5/A3
be in bad shape [bi‿ɪn 'bæd ˌʃeɪp] in schlechtem Zustand sein 3/C5
share [ʃeə] teilen
be the sharpest knife in the drawer *(informal)* [bi ðə ˌʃɑːpəst naɪf ɪn ðə 'drɔːə] *etwa: der/die Hellste sein* 3/C1
shave [ʃeɪv] sich rasieren 3/B1
she [ʃɪ] sie
sheep *(pl -)* [ʃiːp] Schaf
sheet [ʃiːt] Laken; Blatt, Bogen
shelf *(pl* **shelves***)* [ʃelf, ʃelvz] Regal
shell [ʃel] *hier:* Muschelschale 6/C2
shift [ʃɪft] Wechsel, Änderung; Schicht
shine [ʃaɪn] scheinen; glänzen, leuchten
ship [ʃɪp] Schiff
shirt [ʃɜːt] Hemd
shock [ʃɒk] Schock
shocking ['ʃɒkɪŋ] schockierend; völlig überraschend 3/C3
shoe [ʃuː] Schuh
shoot [ʃuːt] (er-, an-)schießen
shoot a film/movie [ʃuːt‿ə 'fɪlm/'muːvi] einen Film drehen 5/C3
shop [ʃɒp] Geschäft, Laden
shop [ʃɒp] einkaufen
shop assistant ['ʃɒp‿əˌsɪst(ə)nt] Verkäufer/in 1/C2
shoplifting *(no pl)* ['ʃɒpˌlɪftɪŋ] Ladendiebstahl 3/B3
shopping ['ʃɒpɪŋ] Einkaufen; Einkaufs-
do the shopping [ˌduː ðə 'ʃɒpɪŋ] einkaufen (gehen)
shore [ʃɔː] Küste; Ufer; Strand 3/A4
short [ʃɔːt] kurz
in short [ɪn 'ʃɔːt] kurz gesagt 2/A5
shot [ʃɒt] Aufnahme, Einstellung *(Film)* 5/C3
should [ʃʊd] sollte/müsste
shoulder ['ʃəʊldə] Schulter
shout [ʃaʊt] schreien
shout at sb ['ʃaʊt‿æt ˌsʌmbədi] jdn anschreien 3/C1
show [ʃəʊ] zeigen
show sb around [ˌʃəʊ sʌmbədi‿ə'raʊnd] jdn herumführen
shower ['ʃaʊə] Schauer; Dusche
take a shower [teɪk‿ə 'ʃaʊə] duschen 2/C7
*shrug [ʃrʌg] die Achseln zucken 3/O1
shut [ʃʌt] schließen, *hier:* abstellen 3/C1
keep one's mouth shut ['kiːp wʌnz ˌmaʊθ ʃʌt] den Mund halten 3/C1
shy [ʃaɪ] schüchtern 5/C1
Sicily ['sɪsɪli] Sizilien 3/B3
sick [sɪk] krank
side [saɪd] Seite
right at his/her side ['raɪt‿ət‿ɪz/hə ˌsaɪd] direkt neben ihm/ihr 1/B4
sidewalk *(AE)* ['saɪdˌwɔːk] Bürgersteig 3/C1
sight [saɪt] Sehleistung; Sicht; Sehenswürdigkeit
sight [saɪt] *hier:* Anblick 3/B1
be in sight [biː‿ɪn saɪt] in Sichtweite sein 1/B4
sign [saɪn] Zeichen; (Straßen-/Verkehrs)schild
sign [saɪn] unterschreiben 4/C4
silence ['saɪləns] Stille
*silently ['saɪləntli] lautlos 1/O2
Silesia [saɪ'liːziə] Schlesien 3/B3
silly ['sɪli] albern, dumm
similar ['sɪmɪlə] ähnlich
*similarity [ˌsɪmə'lærəti] Ähnlichkeit 1/O
simple ['sɪmpl] einfach 4/A2
simple past [ˌsɪmpl 'pɑːst] einfache Form der Vergangenheit 1/CL3
simple present [ˌsɪmpl 'preznt] Präsens, einfache Gegenwart 1/CL3
simply ['sɪmpli] einfach
since [sɪns] seit; da, weil
sing [sɪŋ] singen
singer ['sɪŋə] Sänger/in
single ['sɪŋgl] einzige(r, s); einzelne(r, s)
single decker [ˌsɪŋgl 'dekə] Bus *(mit einem Deck)* 3/A4
Sioux [suː] *(indian. Sprache)* 3/PP2
*sip sth ['sɪp ˌsʌmθɪŋ] an etw nippen 5/O1
Sir [sə] (mein) Herr *(Anrede)* 3/B1
sister ['sɪstə] Schwester
sit [sɪt] sitzen
sit down [sɪt 'daʊn] sich (hin)setzen
site [saɪt] Stelle, Platz 3/A4
situation [ˌsɪtʃu'eɪʃn] Situation, Lage
six [sɪks] sechs
size [saɪz] Größe
ski [skiː] Schi
ski [skiː] Schi fahren/laufen
skier ['skiːə] Schifahrer/in
*skiing ['skiːɪŋ] Ski- 2/O1
skill [skɪl] Geschick; Fähigkeit, Fertigkeit
skin [skɪn] Haut
skip sth ['skɪp ˌsʌmθɪŋ] etw überspringen, auslassen 6/B4
skirt [skɜːt] Rock
sky [skaɪ] Himmel

skyscraper ['skaɪˌskreɪpə] Wolkenkratzer 1/B5
slap [slæp] schlagen; ohrfeigen 3/C3
slave [sleɪv] Sklave/Sklavin 4/C1
slavery ['sleɪvəri] Sklaverei 4/C1
sleep [sli:p] Schlaf
sleep [sli:p] schlafen
sleeping pill ['sli:pɪŋ ˌpɪl] Schlaftablette 6/B3
* sleepy ['sli:pɪ] schläfrig 1/O2
slice [slaɪs] Scheibe; Stück 6/B4
slide [slaɪd] rutschen; gleiten 1/C4
slip [slɪp] ausrutschen
slow [sləʊ] langsam
small [smɔ:l] klein
* smart [smɑ:t] schick 1/O2
smell [smel] Geruch
smell [smel] riechen
smelly ['smeli] stinkend, übel riechend
smile [smaɪl] Lächeln
smile [smaɪl] lächeln
smoke [sməʊk] Rauch
smoke [sməʊk] rauchen
smoked [sməʊkt] geräuchert 6/PP6
smoothie ['smu:ði] Shake 6/C1
smuggle ['smʌgl] schmuggeln 3/BL3
snake [sneɪk] Schlange
snap back [snæp 'bæk] zurückschnellen 1/B4
sneaker ['sni:kə] Turnschuh 1/C1
snow [snəʊ] Schnee
so [səʊ] also, so
* So far, so easy. [səʊ ˌfɑ: səʊ‿'i:zi] So weit, so gut. 3/O1
so-called ['səʊ kɔ:ld] so genannt 4/C2
* be soaked *(informal)* [bi 'səʊkt] pitschnass sein 5/O1
soap [səʊp] Seife 1/B5
soccer *(AE)* ['sɒkə] Fußball 1/A4
social ['səʊʃl] Gesellschafts-, gesellschaftlich
social studies *(AE)* ['səʊʃl ˌstʌdiz] Gemeinschaftskunde; Sozialkunde 5/B2
social worker [ˌsəʊʃl 'wɜ:kə] Sozialarbeiter/in 5/B4
society [sə'saɪəti] Gesellschaft
sock [sɒk] Socke
* soda *(no pl)* ['səʊdə] Sodawasser 5/O1
soft [sɒft] weich 6/C2
soft toy [ˌsɒft‿'tɔɪ] Plüschtier, Kuscheltier
* softly ['sɒftli] sanft 1/O2
solve [sɒlv] lösen
some [sʌm] einige; etwas
somebody ['sʌmbədi] jemand
somebody else [ˌsʌmbədi‿'els] jemand anders
someday (= some day) ['sʌmˌdeɪ] eines Tages, irgendwann (einmal) 1/C1
somehow ['sʌmhaʊ] irgendwie 3/C1
someone ['sʌmwʌn] jemand
someplace *(AE, informal)* ['sʌmpleɪs] irgendwo 5/B1
something ['sʌmθɪŋ] etwas
something else [ˌsʌmθɪŋ‿'els] noch etwas
sometime ['sʌmtaɪm] irgendwann 2/C7
sometimes ['sʌmtaɪmz] manchmal
somewhere ['sʌmweə] irgendwo
somewhere else [ˌsʌmweər‿'els] irgendwo anders 5/B1
son [sʌn] Sohn
song [sɒŋ] Lied
soon [su:n] bald
sophomore *(AE)* ['sɒfəˌmɔ:] *Schüler/in einer Highschool im zweiten Jahr* 5/PP5
sore throat [sɔ: 'θrəʊt] Halsschmerzen
Sorry! ['sɒri] Verzeihung!, Entschuldigung!; Wie bitte?
I'm sorry. [aɪm 'sɒri] Es tut mir leid.
sort [sɔ:t] Sorte, Art
sort out [sɔ:t‿'aʊt] ordnen, sortieren
sound [saʊnd] Geräusch; Laut; *hier:* Ton 5/C3
sound [saʊnd] (er)klingen
sound recordist ['saʊnd ˌrekərdɪst] Tontechniker/in 5/C3
soup [su:p] Suppe
(the) south [saʊθ] (der) Süden 2/A3
in the south (of) [ɪn ðə 'saʊθ] im Süden (von) 2/B1
southeast *(no pl)* [ˌsaʊθ'i:st] Südosten 2/B1
southern ['sʌðən] südlich, Süd- 3/C5
the Southwest [ðə ˌsaʊθ'west] der Südwesten 2/A3
souvenir [ˌsu:və'nɪə] Andenken, Souvenir
space [speɪs] Raum; Feld
spaghetti [spə'geti] Spaghetti 6/C2
Spanish ['spænɪʃ] spanisch 2/A2
spare ribs [ˌspea 'rɪbz] Spareribs, Rippchen 6/PP6
sparkle ['spɑ:kl] funkeln, glitzern 2/C7
sparkling ['spɑ:klɪŋ] glänzend; mit Kohlensäure
speak [spi:k] sprechen, reden
speaker ['spi:kə] Redner/in
special ['speʃl] besondere(r, s)
special effect [ˌspeʃl ɪ'fekt] Spezialeffekt 5/C3
special offer [ˌspeʃl 'ɒfə] Sonderangebot 3/A4
specialist ['speʃəlɪst] Fachmann/Fachfrau, Spezialist/in 6/B1
* speciality [ˌspeʃi'æləti] Spezialität 2/O1
spectator [spek'teɪtə] Zuschauer/in
speech [spi:tʃ] Sprache; Rede 4/C4
give a speech [ˌgɪv‿ə 'spi:tʃ] eine Rede halten 4/C4
speech bubble ['spi:tʃ ˌbʌbl] Sprechblase 4/C2
speed [spi:d] Geschwindigkeit, Tempo
* speed limit ['spi:d ˌlɪmɪt] Geschwindigkeitsbegrenzung 1/O
be spelt [bi: 'spelt] geschrieben/buchstabiert werden 1/BL2
spell [spel] richtig schreiben, buchstabieren 6/AL3
spelling ['spelɪŋ] Rechtschreibung 2/CL4
spend [spend] ausgeben *(Geld)*; verbringen *(Zeit)*
spicy ['spaɪsi] würzig; scharf 6/A3
spider ['spaɪdə] Spinne
spill the beans [ˌspɪl ðə 'bi:nz] aus der Schule plaudern 6/C4
* spirit ['spɪrɪt] Geist 4/O1
in spite of [ɪn 'spaɪt‿əv] trotz
spoon [spu:n] Löffel
sport [spɔ:t] Sport; Sportart
sporting calendar ['spɔ:tɪŋ ˌkælɪndə] Sportkalender 5/PP4
sporting event [ˌspɔ:tɪŋ ɪ'vent] Sportveranstaltung 5/PP4
sports [spɔ:ts] Sport- 5/B1
sports *(AE)* [spɔ:ts] Sport; Sportart 1/A1
sports department ['spɔ:ts dɪˌpɑ:tmənt] Sportabteilung 1/C1
sportsman ['spɔ:tsmən] Sportler 5/A2
sportswoman ['spɔ:tsˌwʊmən] Sportlerin 5/A2
* sporty ['spɔ:ti] sportlich 5/O1
spot [spɒt] Fleck; Stelle; Pickel
spot [spɒt] entdecken 3/C1
* spotlight ['spɒtˌlaɪt] Scheinwerfer 1/O2
spray [spreɪ] Sprühnebel; *hier:* Spray 6/B1
spread [spred] (sich) ausbreiten; (sich) verbreiten
spring [sprɪŋ] Frühling
sq mi (= square mile) [skweə 'maɪl] Quadratmeile 2/A1
square [skweə] Quadrat; Platz; Spielfeld
squash *(AE)* [skwɒʃ] Kürbis 6/C1
squirrel ['skwɪrəl] Eichhörnchen 2/B2
SS (= steamship) [ˌes'es] Dampfschiff 3/B3
stable ['steɪbl] Stall, Box 2/C7
stadium *(pl* **-s or** -dia) ['steɪdiəm] Stadion 5/PP4
stage [steɪdʒ] Etappe, Station 1/B5
stairs *(npl)* [steəz] Treppe
not (be able to) stand sth [nɒt 'stænd ˌsʌmθɪŋ] etw nicht ertragen/leiden (können) 1/A3
stand in line *(AE)* [stænd‿ɪn 'laɪn] anstehen, Schlange stehen 1/A3
stand up [stænd‿'ʌp] aufstehen
star [stɑ:] Stern 2/A2
the Star-Spangled Banner [ðə ˌstɑ: ˌspæŋgld 'bænə] das Sternenbanner *(Nationalflagge und Nationalhymne der USA)* 2/A5
stare [steə] starren
start [stɑ:t] Anfang, Beginn; Start
start [stɑ:t] anfangen; losfahren
start up [start‿'ʌp] gründen; *hier:* aufmachen 4/A4
starter ['stɑ:tə] Vorspeise

be starving *(informal)* [bi‿'stɑːvɪŋ] ausgehungert sein, vor Hunger sterben 1/A3
state [steɪt] Zustand; körperliche Verfassung 4/B2; *hier:* (Bundes)staat 2/A1
state school ['steɪt ˌskuːl] staatliche Schule 2/CL4
statement ['steɪtmənt] Äußerung
the States *(informal)* [ðə 'steɪts] die Staaten *(Amerika)* 1/A3
station ['steɪʃn] Bahnhof; Station
statue ['stætʃuː] Statue, Standbild 2/A1
Statue of Liberty [ˌstætʃuː‿əv 'lɪbəti] Freiheitsstatue 2/A1
stay [steɪ] bleiben; untergebracht sein, wohnen
steady ['stedi] fest, stabil 1/B4; *hier:* kontinuierlich, gleich bleibend 6/B4
steal [stiːl] stehlen
steamed [stiːmd] gedämpft, in Dampf gegart 6/C2
steel [stiːl] Stahl 2/A3
step [step] Schritt; *hier:* Stufe 3/A3
step out [step‿'aʊt] weggehen; *hier:* aussteigen 3/C1
stereo (*pl* **-os**) ['steriəʊ, 'steriəʊz] Stereo(anlage)
sth is up *(informal)* [ˌsʌmθɪŋ‿ɪz‿'ʌp] hier stimmt etw nicht 3/C1
stick in [stɪk‿'ɪn] einkleben
stick out [stɪk‿'aʊt] (her)ausstrecken 2/C7
stick together ['stɪk təˌgeðə] zusammenhalten 3/C5
sticky ['stɪki] klebrig 1/B3
still [stɪl] ruhig, friedlich; ohne Kohlensäure
still [stɪl] (immer) noch, noch immer; trotzdem
* sting [stɪŋ] stechen; schmerzen 3/O1
stir [stɜː] rühren
stir-fry ['stɜːˌfraɪ] Chinapfanne 6/C2
stone [stəʊn] Stein
stop [stɒp] Halt(estelle)
stop [stɒp] aufhören, beenden; anhalten
stop [stɒp] *hier:* abhalten 4/B2
stop short ['stɒp ˌʃɔːt] *hier:* anhalten 5/PP4
store *(AE)* [stɔː] Laden; Geschäft 1/A3
(department) store ['stɔː] Kaufhaus 1/C1
* stormy ['stɔːmi] stürmisch 6/O1
story ['stɔːri] Geschichte; Erzählung
straight [streɪt] gerade; direkt
straight on [streɪt‿'ɒn] gerade(aus)
straighten ['streɪtn] gerade machen 3/B1
strange [streɪndʒ] sonderbar, merkwürdig
strawberry ['strɔːb(ə)ri] Erdbeere
stray [streɪ] streunen; umherstreifen 3/A1
stream [striːm] Bach 4/B2
street [striːt] Straße
strength *(no pl)* [streŋθ] Kraft, Stärke 4/A7
strengthen ['streŋθ(ə)n] kräftigen, (ver)stärken 1/PP1
stress [stres] Stress; *hier:* Betonung 2/BL4
stretch [stretʃ] (sich) dehnen; strecken
* stretch out ['stretʃ‿aʊt] sich ausstrecken 4/O1
strike it rich *(informal)* ['straɪk‿ɪt rɪtʃ] *einen Glückstreffer landen und reich werden* 4/B2
string [strɪŋ] Schnur
string cheese ['strɪŋ tʃiːz] *traditioneller amerik. Käse in Stangenform* 6/C2
stripe [straɪp] Streifen 2/A2
* stroll [strəʊl] schlendern, bummeln 3/O1
strong [strɒŋ] stark; *hier:* robust, stabil 1/PP1
student ['stjuːdnt] Student/in; Schüler/in
* studio ['stjuːdiəʊ] Atelier, Studio 1/O2
study ['stʌdi] studieren, sich befassen mit
stuff *(informal)* [stʌf] Zeug
stuffed [stʌft] ausgestopft; *hier:* gefüllt 6/C2
stumble ['stʌmbl] stolpern, straucheln 3/C1
stupid ['stjuːpɪd] dumm, blöd
style [staɪl] Stil, Art 4/C5
sub (= submarine sandwich) [sʌb] *Sandwich in U-Boot-Form* 6/C2
subject ['sʌbdʒɪkt] Thema; (Schul)fach; Subjekt, Satzgegenstand
subway *(AE)* ['sʌbˌweɪ] Unterführung, U-Bahn 3/AL3
succeed [sək'siːd] Erfolg haben, erfolgreich sein 3/A1
success [sək'ses] Erfolg
successful [sək'sesfl] erfolgreich
such [sʌtʃ] solch(er, es); so
such as ['sʌtʃ‿əz] wie (zum Beispiel)
sudden ['sʌdn] plötzlich, jäh
suddenly ['sʌdnli] plötzlich, auf einmal
suffer from ['sʌfə frəm] leiden an/unter 3/C5
* sufficient [sə'fɪʃnt] genug, ausreichend 3/O1
sugar ['ʃʊgə] Zucker
suggest [sə'dʒest] vorschlagen
suicide rate ['suːɪsaɪd ˌreɪt] Selbstmordrate 4/A4
suit [suːt] Anzug 5/C1
suitcase ['suːtˌkeɪs] Koffer
sum up [ˌsʌm‿'ʌp] zusammenfassen 3/C5
summary ['sʌməri] Zusammenfassung 1/C2
summer ['sʌmə] Sommer
sun [sʌn] Sonne
* sunburned ['sʌnˌbɜːnt] sonnengebräunt 2/O1
sundae ['sʌndeɪ] Eisbecher 6/C2
Sunday ['sʌndeɪ] Sonntag
(pair of) sunglasses *(npl)* ['sʌnˌglɑːsɪz] Sonnenbrille
sunny ['sʌni] sonnig
* sunshine ['sʌnʃaɪn] Sonnenschein 3/O1
superhero ['suːpəˌhɪərəʊ] Superheld 5/C1
supermarket ['suːpəˌmɑːkɪt] Supermarkt
supernatural [ˌsuːpə'nætʃərəl] übernatürlich; außergewöhnlich 5/C1
supper ['sʌpə] Abendessen
* supply sth [sə'plaɪ ˌsʌmθɪŋ] für etw sorgen, etw bereitstellen 1/O2
support [sə'pɔːt] unterstützen
* support [sə'pɔːt] *hier:* sich seinen Lebenssunterhalt verdienen 3/O1
support oneself [sə'pɔːt wʌnˌself] seinen Lebensunterhalt bestreiten 3/B1
be supposed to [bi sə'pəʊzd tə] sollen
supreme *(no pl)* [sʊ'priːm] Geschnetzeltes 6/C2
Supreme Court [sʊˌpriːm 'kɔːt] oberstes Bundesgericht (in den USA) 4/C3
sure [ʃɔː] sicher
make sure [ˌmeɪk 'ʃɔː] sich versichern, darauf achten
sure *(AE, informal)* [ʃʊə] echt 3/C1
surely ['ʃɔːli] sicher(lich), bestimmt 6/A5
* surface ['sɜːfɪs] Oberfläche 4/O1
surfboard ['sɜːfˌbɔːd] Surfbrett 5/A3
surfing ['sɜːfɪŋ] Surfen, Wellenreiten 5/A3
* Surgeon General *(AE)* [ˌsɜːdʒ(ə)n 'dʒen(ə)rəl] Gesundheitsminister/in 1/O2
surprise [sə'praɪz] Überraschung
surprised [sə'praɪzd] überrascht
surprising [sə'praɪzɪŋ] überraschend
surprisingly [sə'praɪzɪŋli] überraschenderweise 1/B3
* surround [sə'raʊnd] umgeben 1/O2
survey ['sɜːveɪ] Untersuchung, Umfrage
survive [sə'vaɪv] überleben 3/PP2
survivor [sə'vaɪvə] Überlebende/r; Überlebenskünstler/in 4/C5
suspense *(no pl)* [sə'spens] Spannung 5/C4
suspicious [sə'spɪʃəs] verdächtig 6/B4
* sustain sb [sə'steɪn ˌsʌmbədi] jdn (am Leben) erhalten, versorgen 3/O1
swap [swɒp] tauschen 5/C2
* sweaty ['sweti] verschwitzt 5/O1
sweet(s) [swiːt] Süßigkeit(en)
sweet [swiːt] süß
have a sweet tooth [hæv‿ə ˌswiːt 'tuːθ] eine Naschkatze sein 6/C4
swelter ['sweltə] verschmachten, (vor Hitze) umkommen 4/PP3
swim [swɪm] schwimmen
swimming ['swɪmɪŋ] Schwimmen

* switch on/off [swɪtʃ‿'ɒn/ɒf] ein-/ausschalten 1/O2
switchboard ['swɪtʃˌbɔːd] Satzschalttafel 1/AL2
swollen ['swəʊlən] geschwollen
syllable ['sɪləbl] Silbe 2/BL4
symbol ['sɪmbl] Symbol, Zeichen
synonym ['sɪnənɪm] Synonym 2/CL2
system ['sɪstəm] System

T

table ['teɪbl] Tisch; Tabelle
tackle sb ['tækl ˌsʌmbədi] jdn angreifen 5/A3
tailor ['teɪlə] Schneider/in 1/PP1
take [teɪk] (mit)nehmen; machen; dauern; bringen
take a break [teɪk‿ə 'breɪk] eine Pause machen 2/C7
* take a deep breath [ˌteɪk‿ə diːp 'breθ] tief Luft holen 1/O2
take a look (at) [ˌteɪk‿ə 'lʊk] sich ansehen
take a photo [ˌteɪk‿ə 'fəʊtəʊ] fotografieren, ein Foto machen 3/A2
take a shower [teɪk‿ə 'ʃaʊə] duschen 2/C7
take care of [teɪk‿'keər‿əv] sich kümmern um, versorgen
take control of sth [teɪk kən'trəʊl‿əv ˌsʌmθɪŋ] die Gewalt über etw übernehmen 4/A7
take notes [teɪk 'nəʊts] (sich) Notizen machen
take off [teɪk‿'ɒf] abnehmen; ausziehen
take on [teɪk‿'ɒn] auf sich nehmen; annehmen
take out [teɪk‿'aʊt] herausnehmen, hinausbringen; ausführen
take over [teɪk‿'əʊvə] übernehmen 4/A7
take part (in) [teɪk 'pɑːt] teilnehmen (an)
take place [teɪk 'pleɪs] stattfinden
take sb for a walk [ˌteɪk sʌmbədi fər‿ə 'wɔːk] mit jdm einen Spaziergang machen
take steps [teɪk 'steps] Schritte unternehmen 4/C1
takeaway ['teɪkəˌweɪ] Imbissbude; *hier:* Essen zum Mitnehmen 6/B4
It takes (sb) … [ɪt‿'teɪks] Es dauert …
talk [tɔːk] Gespräch; Unterhaltung; Vortrag
talk (to) [tɔːk] sprechen/reden (mit)
talk back [tɔːk 'bæk] eine freche Antwort geben 3/C1
tall [tɔːl] hoch; groß
task [tɑːsk] Aufgabe
taste [teɪst] Geschmack 1/B3
taste [teɪst] schmecken; *hier:* probieren 6/C1
tasty ['teɪsti] schmackhaft, lecker
* tax [tæks] Abgabe 1/O2
taxi ['tæksi] Taxi
tea [tiː] Tee
tea bag ['tiː ˌbæg] Teebeutel 6/B3
teach [tiːtʃ] unterrichten; lehren
teacher ['tiːtʃə] Lehrer/in
teammate ['tiːmˌmeɪt] Mannschaftskamerad/in, Mitspieler/in 5/A3
tear [tɪə] Träne 2/A1
tear sth (up) ['teə ˌsʌmθɪŋ] etw zerreißen 6/B3
technician [tek'nɪʃn] Techniker/in 5/B6
tee [tiː] Tee, Abschlagstelle *(Golf)* 1/C1
teenage ['tiːnˌeɪdʒ] jugendlich, im Teenageralter 1/C4
teens *(pl)* [tiːnz] Jugendjahre 1/B5
telephone ['telɪˌfəʊn] Telefon
telescope ['telɪˌskəʊp] Teleskop 5/B6
television ['telɪˌvɪʒn] Fernseh- 5/C2
watch television [ˌwɒtʃ 'telɪvɪʒn] fernsehen
tell [tel] erzählen; sagen
temperature ['temprɪˌtʃə] Temperatur; Fieber
ten [ten] zehn
tense [tens] Zeitform, Tempus 1/CL1
tent [tent] Zelt 1/PP1
tepee ['tiːpiː] Indianerzelt 3/PP2
term [tɜːm] Semester; Schuljahresabschnitt
term [tɜːm] *hier:* Ausdruck 6/B1
terrible ['terəbl] schrecklich, furchtbar
territory ['terətri] Gebiet, Territorium 4/A2
test [test] prüfen, testen
text a message ['tekst‿ə ˌmesɪdʒ] eine SMS schreiben 5/B3
text message ['tekst ˌmesɪdʒ] SMS
textbook ['tekstˌbʊk] Lehrbuch
than [ðæn] als
thank [θæŋk] danken
thank you ['θæŋk ˌjə] danke
* thankful ['θæŋkfl] froh; dankbar 4/O1
thanks [θæŋks] danke
* give thanks [gɪv 'θæŋks] danken 6/O1
* thanksgiving *(no pl)* ['θæŋksˌgɪvɪŋ] Dankbarkeit 6/O1
Thanksgiving Day *(AE)* ['θæŋksˌgɪvɪŋ deɪ] *hier:* Thanksgiving- 5/PP4
that [ðæt] das; der/die/das
that [ðæt] dass 1/A3
the [ðə] der/die/das
* the … the … [ðə ðə] je … desto … 1/O2
The lights went out. *(informal)* [ðə ˌlaɪts went‿'aʊt] *hier:* Ich kippte um. 3/C1
theater *(AE* = **theatre** *BE)* ['θɪətə] Theater 3/A3
theatre ['θɪətə] Theater
their [ðeə] ihr(e)
them [ðem] sie, ihnen
theme [θiːm] Thema; Lektion, Kapitel
themselves [ðem'selvz] sich; (sie) selbst
then [ðen] damals; dann
theoretical [ˌθɪə'retɪkl] theoretisch 3/B3
there [ðeə] dort(hin)
there are [ðeər‿'ɑː] es gibt, da sind
there is [ðeər‿'ɪz] es gibt
There you are. [ˌðeə jʊ‿'ɑː] Hier, bitte!
these *(pl of* this) [ðiːz] diese
they [ðeɪ] sie
thick [θɪk] dick
thin [θɪn] dünn
thing [θɪŋ] Ding, Gegenstand
think [θɪŋk] denken, glauben, meinen; überlegen; nachdenken
think of ['θɪŋk‿əv] denken an; sich vorstellen
think over [θɪŋk‿'əʊvə] sich überlegen, überdenken
thinker ['θɪŋkə] Denker 5/B6
third [θɜːd] dritte(r, s)
one third [wʌn 'θɜːd] ein Drittel 4/A4
Third World [ˌθɜːd 'wɜːld] Dritte Welt 4/A4
this [ðɪs] diese(r, s); das
This being the States, … [ðɪs 'biːɪŋ ðə ˌsteɪts] Da wir in den Staaten sind, … 1/C1
those *(pl of* that) [ðəʊz] diese
though [θəʊ] obwohl; (je)doch
though [ðəʊ] allerdings *(nachgestellt)* 5/C3
thought [θɔːt] Gedanke 1/B1
thousand ['θaʊznd] tausend
thousands *(pl)* ['θaʊzndz] Tausende
threads *(informal)* [θreds] Zeug 3/C1
three [θriː] drei
be thrilled [bi 'θrɪld] außer sich vor Freude sein 5/C2
through [θruː] durch
through *(AE)* [θruː] *hier:* bis 3/A4
throw [θrəʊ] werfen
thumb lock ['θʌm ˌlɒk] *Technik beim Judo* 3/C1
Thursday ['θɜːzdeɪ] Donnerstag
* thus [ðʌs] folglich; so, auf diese Weise 4/O1
tidy ['taɪdi] aufräumen
tidy up [ˌtaɪdi‿'ʌp] aufräumen
tie [taɪ] Krawatte
* tie [taɪ] binden 5/O1
tiger ['taɪgə] Tiger
tights *(npl)* [taɪts] Strumpfhose 6/B3
* tile [taɪl] Fliese 3/O1
till [tɪl] bis
time [taɪm] Zeit; Mal
for the first time [fə ðə‿'fɜːst‿ˌtaɪm] zum ersten Mal 1/A3
the couple of times [ðə 'kʌpl‿əv ˌtaɪmz] die paar/wenigen Male 5/B1
all the time [ˌɔːl ðə 'taɪm] die ganze Zeit 1/B2
at that time [ˌæt ðæt 'taɪm] zu diesem Zeitpunkt 4/C1
at the same time [æt ðə ˌseɪm 'taɪm] gleichzeitig 5/A3
in time [ɪn 'taɪm] rechtzeitig 1/C1
on time [ɒn 'taɪm] pünktlich; rechtzeitig
what time [wɒt‿'taɪm] (um) wie viel Uhr

have a good time [ˌhæv‿ə gʊd 'taɪm] sich amüsieren
have a great time [ˌhæv‿ə ˌgreɪt‿'taɪm] sich sehr gut amüsieren
timetable ['taɪmteɪbl] Stundenplan 5/BL2
timid ['tɪmɪd] ängstlich, schüchtern 3/A1
tin [tɪn] Zinn; Büchse, Dose
tip-off ['tɪpɒf] *Start der Basketballsaison* 5/PP4
tired ['taɪəd] müde
title ['taɪtl] Titel
to [tə] in, nach, zu, an; bis
toast [təʊst] Toast
tobacco *(no pl)* [tə'bækəʊ] Tabak 3/PP2
today [tə'deɪ] heute
together [tə'geðə] zusammen; gemeinsam
toilet ['tɔɪlət] Toilette, Klo
tomato *(pl* **-es**) [tə'mɑːtəʊ, tə'mɑːtəʊz] Tomate
tomorrow [tə'mɒrəʊ] morgen
ton [tʌn] Tonne 1/B3
tonight [tə'naɪt] heute Abend
tons *(informal)* [tʌnz] jede Menge 3/C5
too [tuː] zu; auch
* too bad ['tuː bæd] wirklich schade 1/O2
tooth (*pl* **teeth**) [tuːθ, tiːθ] Zahn
toothache ['tuːθeɪk] Zahnschmerzen 3/C5
top [tɒp] oberes Ende, Spitze
* top [tɒp] *hier:* Gipfel 2/O1
be (at the) top of the heap [biː 'tɒp‿əv ðə ˌhiːp] zu den Gewinnern zählen 3/A1
topic ['tɒpɪk] Thema
topped with ['tɒpt wɪð] überzogen mit 6/PP6
topping ['tɒpɪŋ] Garnierung 6/C2
torch [tɔːtʃ] Taschenlampe
total ['təʊtl] gesamt; völlig
totally ['təʊtli] völlig, total 4/A7
touch [tʌtʃ] berühren
get in touch with [get‿ɪn 'tʌtʃ wɪð] in Kontakt treten mit 4/A6
touchdown *(AE)* ['tʌtʃˌdaʊn] Versuch 5/A3
tough [tʌf] robust, zäh; *hier:* schwierig, hart 1/C1
touring ['tuːrɪŋ] Reisen 3/A4
tourist ['tʊərɪst] Tourist/in
toward(s) [tə'wɔːd(z)] in Richtung 5/A3
towel ['taʊəl] Handtuch
tower ['taʊə] Turm
town [taʊn] Stadt
toy [tɔɪ] Spielzeug
* track [træk] Weg; Pfad 3/O1
trader ['treɪdə] Händler/in 4/A7
tradition [trə'dɪʃn] Tradition
traditional [trə'dɪʃn(ə)l] traditionell
traditionally [trə'dɪʃn(ə)li] traditionell; üblicherweise 2/B1
traffic ['træfɪk] Verkehr
traffic light ['træfɪk ˌlaɪt] Ampel
trail [treɪl] Weg, Pfad 2/B5
train [treɪn] Zug
change trains [ˌtʃeɪndʒ 'treɪnz] umsteigen
trainer ['treɪnə] Trainer/in; Turnschuh
transform [træns'fɔːm] verwandeln 4/PP3
translation [træns'leɪʃn] Übersetzung 6/C2
transport ['trænspɔːt] Transport; Verkehrsmittel 3/A6
travel ['trævl] Reisen
travel ['trævl] reisen
travel ['trævl] Reise-
traveling *(AE)* (= travelling *BE*) ['trævliŋ] Reisen 2/C4
tray [treɪ] Tablett 1/A3
* treat [triːt] (Extra)vergnügen 2/O1
treatment ['triːtmənt] Behandlung 3/C5
tree [triː] Baum
tribe [traɪb] Stamm; Sippe 2/A1
trip [trɪp] Ausflug
trip [trɪp] *hier:* Reise, Fahrt 4/C1
trophy ['trəʊfi] Trophäe, Preis
tropical rainforest [ˌtrɒpɪkl 'reɪnˌfɒrɪst] tropischer Regenwald 1/B3
trouble ['trʌbl] Schwierigkeiten, Ärger
get in(to) trouble [ˌget‿ɪn 'trʌbl] in Schwierigkeiten geraten 2/C7
trousers *(npl)* ['traʊzəz] Hose
truck *(AE)* [trʌk] Last(kraft)wagen 6/CL3
true [truː] wahr
trust in (sb/sth) ['trʌst‿ɪn] vertrauen auf (jdn/etw) 2/A5
truth [truːθ] Wahrheit 4/PP3
make/have a try at [meɪk/hæv‿ə 'traɪ‿ət] versuchen 3/B1
try [traɪ] versuchen; probieren
try on [traɪ‿'ɒn] anprobieren
try out [traɪ‿'aʊt] ausprobieren 1/C1
Tuesday ['tjuːzdeɪ] Dienstag
tunnel ['tʌnl] Tunnel
turkey ['tɜːki] Truthahn/-henne, Pute(r) 6/PP6
turmoil ['tɜːmɔɪl] Tumult, Aufruhr 2/C4
be one's turn [ˌbi wʌnz 'tɜːn] an der Reihe sein, dran sein
turn [tɜːn] sich (um)drehen; werden; abbiegen; umblättern
turn back [ˌtɜːn 'bæk] umkehren, zurückgehen 4/PP3
turn back sb [ˌtɜːn 'bæk sʌmbədi] jdn zurückschicken, zurückweisen 3/B4
turn off sth [tɜːn‿'ɒf ˌsʌmθɪŋ] etw ausschalten 6/B4
turn pale [tɜːn 'peɪl] blass werden 2/C7
take (it in) turns [teɪk 'tɜːnz] sich abwechseln
* turtle (*pl* -, *or* -s) ['tɜːtl] Schildkröte 4/O1
TV (= television) [ˌtiː'viː, 'telɪˌvɪʒn] Fernseher; Fernsehen
watch TV [ˌwɒtʃ tiː'viː] fernsehen
TV guide [tiːˌviː 'gaɪd] Fernsehzeitschrift 6/B3
twenty ['twenti] zwanzig
twice [twaɪs] zweimal
twin [twɪn] Zwilling
two [tuː] zwei
type [taɪp] Art; Typ; Sorte
typical ['tɪpɪkl] typisch
tyre ['taɪə] Reifen

U

* ultramodern [ʌltrə'mɒd(ə)n] hypermodern 1/O2
ultraviolet [ˌʌltrə'vaɪələt] ultraviolett; UV- 6/B1
umbrella [ʌm'brelə] Regenschirm
unbelievable [ˌʌnbɪ'liːvəbl] unglaublich
uncle ['ʌŋkl] Onkel
under ['ʌndə] unter
underground *(no pl)* ['ʌndəˌgraʊnd] U-Bahn
underground ['ʌndəˌgraʊnd] unterirdisch; Untergrund- 4/C1
underneath [ˌʌndə'niːθ] unter 2/C7
the undersigned [ðə 'ʌndəˌsaɪnd] der/die Unterzeichnete *(förmlich)* 4/B5
understand [ˌʌndə'stænd] verstehen
undeveloped [ˌʌndɪ'veləpt] unerschlossen, unbebaut 2/A3
undrinkable [ʌn'drɪŋkəbl] nicht trinkbar
feel uneasy [fiːl 'ʌn'iːzi] sich unbehaglich fühlen 3/C1
uneatable [ʌn'iːtəbl] ungenießbar
unemployed [ˌʌnɪm'plɔɪd] arbeitslos
unemployment *(no pl)* [ˌʌnɪm'plɔɪmənt] Arbeitslosigkeit 3/C5
unexpected [ˌʌnɪk'spektɪd] unerwartet 1/C4
unfair [ʌn'feə] unfair
unfortunate [ʌn'fɔːtʃ(ə)nət] unglücklich; bedauerlich 3/B1
unfortunately [ʌn'fɔːtʃ(ə)nətli] unglücklicherweise
unfriendly [ʌn'frendli] unfreundlich
unhappy [ʌn'hæpi] unglücklich
unhealthy [ʌn'helθi] kränklich; ungesund
uniform ['juːnɪˌfɔːm] Uniform
* uninteresting [ʌn'ɪntrəstɪŋ] uninteressant 4/O1
union ['juːnjən] Union, Staatenbund 2/A1
the Union [ði‿'juːnjən] die Nation 4/B1
unit ['juːnɪt] Einheit, Abteilung 5/A3
the United States [ði‿juː'naɪtɪd ˌsteɪts] die Vereinigten Staaten 2/A1
universe ['juːnɪˌvɜːs] Universum 3/B3
university [ˌjuːnɪ'vɜːsəti] Universität 2/A3

* *unknown [ʌn'nəʊn] unbekannt 1/O2
* *unmarried [ʌn'mærid] unverheiratet, ledig 3/O1
* **unpack** [ʌn'pæk] auspacken
* **unthinkable** [ʌn'θɪŋkəbl] undenkbar, nicht vorstellbar
* **untidy** [ʌn'taɪdi] unordentlich; ungepflegt
* **until** [ən'tɪl] bis
* **unusual** [ʌn'ju:ʒʊəl] ungewöhnlich 5/B2
* unveil [ʌn'veɪl] enthüllen 3/B3
* **up** [ʌp] (nach) oben, hinauf
* **up to** ['ʌp tə] bis
* be up to sb/sth [bi:‿'ʌp tə ˌsʌmbədi, sʌmθɪŋ] von jdm/etw abhängen 3/A1
* *upon [ə'pɒn] auf 4/O1
* **upper** ['ʌpə] obere(r, s) 6/B1
* *uproot [ʌp'ru:t] herausreißen, entwurzeln 4/O1
* **us** [ʌs] uns
* (the) US (= United States) [ˌju:'es, ju:n'aɪtɪd steɪts] die USA 2/A2
* **the USA (= United States of America)** [ði‿ju:es'eɪ, ju:ˌnaɪtɪd ˌsteɪts‿əv‿ə'merɪkə] die USA (= Vereinigte Staaten von Amerika) 1/A1
* **use** [ju:z] Benutzung; Verwendung 4/C4
* **use** [ju:z] benutzen
* use one's noodle [ˌju:z wʌnz 'nu:dl] seinen Grips anstrengen 6/C4
* used [ju:zd] gebraucht 6/B3
* **used to …** (+ *infinitive*) ['ju:sd tə] früher … 3/B4
* **used to be** ['ju:zd tə ˌbi] früher gewesen sein
* **be used to sth** [bi: 'ju:zd tə ˌsʌmθɪŋ] etw gewohnt sein 1/A3
* get used to sth [get 'ju:sd tə ˌsʌmθɪŋ] sich an etw gewöhnen 4/B6
* **useful** ['ju:sfl] nützlich, praktisch
* **usual** ['ju:ʒʊəl] gewöhnlich, üblich, normal
* **usually** ['ju:ʒʊəli] gewöhnlich, normalerweise

V

* vacation *(AE)* [və'keɪʃn] Ferien, Urlaub 1/C1
* vagabond ['vægəˌbɒnd] Vagabunden- 3/A1
* be good value (for sb's money) [bi gu:d 'vælju:] sein Geld wert sein 6/A3
* van *(AE)* [væn] Kleinbus, Minibus 2/C7
* vanish ['vænɪʃ] verschwinden; verloren gehen 4/A1
* **variation** *(no pl)* [ˌveərɪ'eɪʃn] Abweichung; Unterschied 5/A3
* varied ['veərɪd] unterschiedlich 6/PP6
* variety [və'raɪəti] Vielfalt 5/BL2
* **a variety of** [ə və'raɪəti‿əv] verschiedene 2/B2
* **various** ['veəriəs] verschiedene(r, s) 2/B2
* **vary** ['veəri] verschieden sein; sich verändern 6/PP6
* vast [vɑ:st] gewaltig, riesig 2/A3
* **vegetable** ['vedʒtəbl] Gemüse
* **vegetarian** [ˌvedʒə'teəriən] vegetarisch 5/C2
* **vehicle** ['vi:ɪkl] Fahrzeug 2/A1
* verb [vɜ:b] Verb 1/BL3
* verse [vɜ:s] Dichtung; Strophe 1/B4
* **very** ['veri] sehr
* **via** ['vaɪə] über 4/B5
* **victim** ['vɪktɪm] Opfer
* **video** ['vɪdiəʊ] Video
* **view** [vju:] Sicht; Ansicht
* **village** ['vɪlɪdʒ] Dorf
* vineyard ['vɪnjəd] Weinberg 2/C7
* *violet ['vaɪələt] violett 4/O1
* **visit** ['vɪzɪt] Besuch
* **visit** ['vɪzɪt] besuchen
* visit ['vɪzɪt] *hier:* besichtigen 2/A4
* **visitor** ['vɪzɪtə] Besucher/in
* **vitamin** ['vɪtəmɪn] Vitamin
* **voice** [vɔɪs] Stimme 3/C1
* volleyball ['vɒliˌbɔ:l] Volleyball 1/A2
* **vote (for)** [vəʊt] wählen; stimmen (für) 4/PP3
* voting *(no pl)* ['vəʊtɪŋ] Wählen, Wahl 4/C4

W

* w/ (= with) [wið] mit 6/C2
* wafer ['weɪfə] Waffel; *hier:* Scheibe 6/C2
* waffle fries ['wɒfl ˌfraɪz] *Pommes in Waffelform* 6/C2
* wag(g)on ['wægən] Wagen; Karren 1/B5
* wagon train ['wægən ˌtreɪn] Wagenkolonne 4/B1
* **wage(s)** [weɪdʒ(ɪz)] Lohn 4/B5
* *waist [weɪst] Taille 5/O1
* **wait** [weɪt] warten
* **wait for** ['weɪt fə] warten auf 4/B6
* **waiter/waitress** ['weɪtə, 'weɪtrəs] Bedienung, Kellner/in
* **wake up** [weɪk‿'ʌp] aufwachen 2/C7
* **walk** [wɔ:k] Gehen; Spaziergang
* **go for a walk** [ˌgəʊ fər‿ə 'wɔ:k] spazieren gehen
* **take sb for a walk** [ˌteɪk sʌmbədi fər‿ə 'wɔ:k] mit jdm einen Spaziergang machen
* **walk** [wɔ:k] (zu Fuß) gehen
* **walk around** [ˌwɔ:k‿ə'raʊnd] herumlaufen
* **walk the dog** [ˌwɔ:k ðə 'dɒg] den Hund ausführen
* walk up to sb ['wɔ:k‿ʌp tə ˌsʌmbədi] auf jdn zugehen 1/C4
* **wall** [wɔ:l] Wand
* walnut tree ['wɔ:lnʌt tri:] Walnussbaum 2/C7
* wander around ['wɒndə əˌraʊnd] umherstreifen 1/C1
* wanna *(informal)* (= want to) ['wɒnə] wollen 1/C1
* **want** [wɒnt] wünschen; wollen
* wanted ['wɒntɪd] erwünscht; gesucht 4/B5
* **war** [wɔ:] Krieg
* **wardrobe** ['wɔ:drəʊb] (Kleider)schrank
* warehouse ['weəˌhaʊs] Lagerhaus, Lagerhalle 1/PP1
* **warm** [wɔ:m] warm
* **warn about** [ˌwɔ:n‿ə'baʊt] warnen vor
* *warning ['wɔ:nɪŋ] Warnung 1/O2
* warrior ['wɒriə] Krieger 4/A2
* was invented [ɪn'vent] wurde erfunden 1/PP1
* **wash** [wɒʃ] (sich) waschen; abwaschen
* *wash [wɒʃ] *hier:* spülen 6/O1
* **do the washing up** [ˌdu: ðə ˌwɒʃɪŋ‿'ʌp] abspülen
* **waste** *(no pl)* [weɪst] Verschwendung; Abfall 6/B3
* **waste** [weɪst] verschwenden
* **watch** [wɒtʃ] beobachten; zusehen, zuschauen; ansehen
* **watch out (for)** [wɒtʃ‿'aʊt] Ausschau halten (nach); aufpassen (auf)
* **watch television** [ˌwɒtʃ 'telɪvɪʒn] fernsehen
* **watch TV** [ˌwɒtʃ ti:'vi:] fernsehen
* **water** ['wɔ:tə] Wasser
* water hose ['wɔ:tə həʊz] Wasserschlauch 2/C7
* waterfall ['wɔ:təˌfɔ:l] Wasserfall 2/B2
* **wave** [weɪv] Welle 4/B2
* **way** [weɪ] Weg; Art und Weise
* make one's way [meɪk wʌnz 'weɪ] sich auf den Weg machen 4/B1
* **we** [wi:] wir
* **weak** [wi:k] schwach
* **wealthy** ['welθi] reich, wohlhabend, vermögend
* **wear** [weə] tragen
* **weather** ['weðə] Wetter
* **Wednesday** ['wenzdeɪ] Mittwoch
* **week** [wi:k] Woche
* **weekend** [ˌwi:k'end] Wochenende
* **weight** [weɪt] Gewicht
* **put on weight** [ˌpʊt‿ɒn 'weɪt] zunehmen
* **welcome (in)** ['welkəm] willkommen heißen
* welcome (to) ['welkəm] willkommen (in) 5/C3
* **You're welcome.** [jə 'welkəm] Nichts zu danken., Keine Ursache.
* **well** [wel] gut
* **Well done!** [ˌwel 'dʌn] Gut gemacht!
* **Get well soon!** [ˌget wel 'su:n] Gute Besserung!
* **well** [wel] nun (ja), tja
* **well-known** [ˌwel'nəʊn] (allgemein) bekannt; berühmt
* **west** [west] Westen
* west [west] westwärts, nach Westen 4/B1
* in the west (of) [ɪn ðə‿'west] im Westen (von) 2/B1
* **wet** [wet] nass

* wharf (*pl* wharves *or* -s) [wɔ:f] Kai 3/O1
what [wɒt] was; welche(r, s)
what … [wɒt] was für … 2/A6
What about …? *(informal)* [ˌwɒt‿ə'baʊt] Was ist mit …?, Wie wäre es mit …?
what else [wɒt‿'els] was noch, was sonst
what for? ['wɒt fɔ:] wofür?, warum? 1/A2
what time [wɒt‿'taɪm] (um) wie viel Uhr
What's … like? [wɒts laɪk] Wie ist …?
whatever [wɒt'evə] was (auch immer)
wheat *(no pl)* [wi:t] Weizen 2/A3
wheel [wi:l] Rad
wheezy ['wi:zi] keuchend 3/B1
when [wen] wann; wenn; als
whenever [wen'evə] jedes Mal, wenn … 2/C7
where [weə] wo(hin)
no matter where … from [nəʊ 'mætə weə frəm] ganz gleich woher … 3/A3
Where to? ['weə tʊ] Wohin?
wherever [wer'evə] wo(hin) auch immer 4/C2
whether ['weðə] ob
which [wɪtʃ] welche(r, s); *hier:* was 4/A7
while [waɪl] Weile
while [waɪl] während
whisper ['wɪspə] flüstern 2/C7
whistle [wɪsl] pfeifen 1/C4
white [waɪt] weiß
the White House [ðə 'waɪt ˌhaʊs] das Weiße Haus 1/B4
who [hu:] wer; *hier:* der/die/das 3/B3
who with? ['hu: wɪð] mit wem? 1/A2
whole [həʊl] ganz
wholegrain ['həʊlˌgreɪn] Vollkorn- 6/B3
whose [hu:z] wessen; dessen, deren
why [waɪ] warum
wide [waɪd] breit; groß
widen ['waɪdn] verbreitern; erweitern 4/A7
widespread ['waɪdˌspred] weit verbreitet 2/A3
wife (*pl* **wives**) [waɪf, waɪvz] Ehefrau
wild [waɪld] wild
wild flower ['waɪld ˌflaʊə] wild wachsende Blume 2/B2
wilderness ['wɪldənəs] Wildnis 2/B2

willingly ['wɪlɪŋli] gern(e); freiwillig 1/C1
win [wɪn] gewinnen
wind [wɪnd] Wind
window ['wɪndəʊ] Fenster
windy ['wɪndi] windig
winner ['wɪnə] Gewinner/in; Sieger/in
winter ['wɪntə] Winter
wipe [waɪp] abwischen, abputzen 1/C1
wipe out [waɪp‿'aʊt] auswischen; auslöschen 4/A7
wire ['waɪə] Draht; *hier:* Leitung, Kabel 5/C3
* wish [wɪʃ] Wunsch 2/O1
wish [wɪʃ] (sich) wünschen
with [wɪð] mit
with [wɪð] *hier:* bei, dabei 1/A3
within [wɪð'ɪn] innerhalb 2/C7
without [wɪð'aʊt] ohne
witness ['wɪtnəs] beobachten, miterleben 5/C3
* wolf (*pl* wolves) [wʊlf, wʊlvz] Wolf 6/O1
woman (*pl* **women**) ['wʊmən, 'wɪmɪn] Frau
wonder ['wʌndə] sich fragen
wonderful ['wʌndəfl] wunderbar, wundervoll
* wood [wʊd] Holz 6/O1
wooden ['wʊdn] Holz-, hölzern
word [wɜ:d] Wort
word web ['wɜ:d ˌweb] Wortnetz 1/A1
work [wɜ:k] Arbeit; Werk
work [wɜ:k] arbeiten; funktionieren
work out ['wɜ:k‿aʊt] ausrechnen; ausarbeiten; verstehen, begreifen
worker ['wɜ:kə] Arbeiter/in 4/B1
world [wɜ:ld] Welt
World Series [wɜ:ld 'sɪəri:z] *jährliches Endspiel zwischen den Gewinnern der beiden großen Baseballligen in den USA* 5/PP4
world-champion ['wɜ:ldˌtʃæmpiən] weltbeste/r 5/A2
be worried [bi 'wʌrɪd] sich Sorgen machen
worry ['wʌri] sich Sorgen machen
* worship ['wɜ:ʃɪp] anbeten 6/O1
worth [wɜ:θ] (lohnens)wert 5/CL3
be worth it [bi: 'wɜ:θ‿ɪt] die Mühe wert sein 1/A3
would [wʊd] würde(st/n/t) 1/B4
wrap (up) [ræp] einwickeln, einpacken 6/A5

* wrapper ['ræpə] Verpackung; *hier:* Papier 1/O2
write [raɪt] schreiben
write down [ˌraɪt 'daʊn] aufschreiben
* writer ['raɪtə] Verfasser/in; Autor/in 3/O1
wrong [rɒŋ] falsch
be wrong with [bi 'rɒŋ wɪð] nicht stimmen mit 6/A5

X

* X-ing (= crossing) ['krɒsɪŋ] Übergang 1/O

Y

yeah *(informal)* [jeə] ja(wohl) 4/B2
year [jɪə] Jahr
year [jɪə] *hier:* Klasse 2/CL4
year after year [jɪə‿ˌɑ:ftə‿'jɪə] Jahr für Jahr 2/C7
year of birth [ˌjɪər‿əv 'bɜ:θ] Geburtsjahr 3/B6
for years [fə‿'jɪəz] seit Jahren; jahrelang 2/B2
over the years [ˌəʊvə‿ðə‿'jɪəz] mit den Jahren, im Laufe der Jahre 2/B2
yell [jel] (laut/gellend) schreien 2/B5
yellow ['jeləʊ] gelb
yes [jes] ja; doch
yesterday ['jestədeɪ] gestern
yet [jet] bis jetzt; schon
not yet [nɒt 'jet] noch nicht
YMCA *(no pl)* (= Young Men's Christian Association) [ˌwaɪ em si: 'eɪ] *christlicher Verein junger Männer* 5/PP4
yoghurt ['jɒgət] Jogurt
you [jʊ] du, dich, dir, Sie, Ihnen; ihr, euch
you guys *(AE, informal)* [jə 'gaɪz] ihr 1/A3
You're welcome. [jə 'welkəm] Nichts zu danken., Keine Ursache.
young [jʌŋ] jung
your [jɔ:] dein(e); euer/eure; Ihr(e)
yours truly ['jɔ:z 'tru:li] mit freundlichen Grüßen *(in Briefen)* 4/C2
yourself (*pl* **yourselves**) [jə'self, jə'selvz] dich, dir; selbst

Z

zero ['zɪərəʊ] Null
zone [zəʊn] Zone, Region 2/A2
zoo [zu:] Zoo

D Dictionary German – English

A

abbiegen turn
am **Abend** in the evening, at night
heute **Abend** tonight
Abendessen dinner, supper
abends *(nur hinter Uhrzeit)* pm
Abenteuer adventure
aber but
abgesehen von apart from
abhängen von depend on
abholen pick up
abnehmen take off, lose *(Gewicht)*
Absatz paragraph
Abschnitt paragraph
abschreiben copy out
absolut absolutely
abspülen do the washing up
abwaschen wash
sich **abwechseln** take it in turns
acht eight
Adresse address
Adverb adverb
Affe monkey
aggressiv aggressive
ähnlich similar
aktiv active
Aktivität activity
albern silly
alle(s) all
alle everyone
allein alone
alles anything, everything
als when, as, than *(Vergleich)*
als Erstes first
als Nächstes next
also so
alt old
Alter age
im **Alter von** at the age of
altmodisch old-fashioned
am on
am Abend in the evening, at night
am Morgen in the morning
am Nachmittag in the afternoon
Amerika America
Amerikaner/in American
Ampel traffic light
an at, to; on; in
Ananas pineapple
anbieten offer
andere(r, s) different, other
andererseits on the other hand
(sich) **ändern** change
anders different
jemand **anders** somebody else
am **Anfang** at the beginning
anfangen begin, start
Anfänger/in beginner
sich **anfreunden** make friends
Angebot offer
Angehörige/r relative *(Verwandte/r)*, member *(Mitglied)*
angenehm nice, enjoyable
Angst haben (vor) be afraid (of)
anhalten stop
ankommen arrive
anprobieren try on
Anruf call
anrufen call, phone
(sich) **anschauen** look at, have/take a look (at)
jdn **anschreien** shout at sb
anstatt instead of
Antwort answer
antworten answer, reply
Anzeige ad (= advertisement)
anziehen put on *(Kleidung)*, attract
(sich) **anziehen** dress
Anzug suit
Apfel apple
Apfelsine orange
April April
Arbeit work, job
arbeiten work
Arbeiter/in worker
Arbeitgeber/in employer
Arbeitskollege/-kollegin colleague
arbeitslos unemployed
Ärger trouble
ärgerlich annoying
ärgern annoy
Argument argument
Arm arm
arm poor
Art kind, sort, type, manner *(Weise)*, style *(Stil)*, shape *(Form)*
Art und Weise way
Artikel article, item *(Ware)*
Arzt/Ärztin doctor
Asiat/in, asiatisch Asian
Ast branch
attraktiv handsome
auch too, also, as well
auf at, on, onto
auf der linken Seite on the left
auf der rechten Seite on the right
auf Deutsch in German
auf einmal suddenly, at once
Auf Wiedersehen. Goodbye.
Aufgabe job, task
aufgeben give up
aufgeregt excited
aufhängen hang (up), put up
aufheben pick up
aufhören finish, stop
aufnehmen *(auf Datenträger)* record
aufräumen tidy (up)
aufregend exciting
aufschreiben write down
aufstehen get up, stand up
aufstellen put up
aufwachen wake up
Auge eye
Augenblick moment
im **Augenblick** at the moment
August August
aus from, out (of)
(sich) **ausdenken** make up
ausdrücken express
Ausflug trip
ausfüllen fill in
ausgeben *(Geld)* spend
ausgehen go out
aushalten stand
jdn **auslachen** laugh at sb
ausländisch foreign
ausleihen hire
Ausrüstung gear, equipment
etw **ausschalten** turn off sth
aussehen look
außen outside
außerhalb outside
äußerst extremely
Äußerung statement, expression
aussprechen pronounce
nicht **ausstehen können** hate
aussteigen (aus) get off
auswählen choose
auswandern (nach) emigrate (to)
auswendig by heart
ausziehen *(Kleidung)* take off
Auto car

B

Bäcker baker
Bäckerei bakery
(in der) **Bäckerei** (at the) baker's
Bad(ezimmer) bathroom
baden have a bath
Bad(ewanne) bath
Bahnhof station
bald soon
Banane banana
Bank bench, bank *(Geld)*
Bargeld cash *(no pl)*
Bart beard
Bau building
Bauch belly
bauen build
Bauer farmer
Bauernhof farm
Baum tree
bedeuten mean
Bedeutung meaning
Bedingungen conditions *(pl)*
sich **beeilen** hurry
beenden finish, stop, end, break up
zu **Beginn** at the beginning
beginnen begin
behalten keep
bei at, by
beide both
keine(r, s) von **beiden** neither
Bein leg
beinahe almost, nearly
zum **Beispiel** for example
(allgemein) **bekannt** well-known
bekommen get, gain
beliebt popular
Benachteiligung discrimination
benutzen use
beobachten watch
bequem comfortable
bereit ready
Berg mountain
Bericht report
berichten report
berühmt famous, well-known
berühren touch
beschäftigt busy
beschließen decide
beschreiben describe
besitzen own
besondere(r, s) special

besonders especially
besprechen discuss
beste(r, s) best
bestellen order
Bestellung order
bestimmen decide
bestimmt certainly, surely
Besuch visit
besuchen visit
Besucher/in visitor
Bett bed
bevor before
bevorzugen prefer
(sich) **bewegen** move
bezahlen pay
Beziehung relationship
Bibliothek library
Bier beer *(no pl)*
Bild picture, painting
bilden form
Bildschirm screen
billig cheap
Birne pear
bis till, until, up to *(bei Zahlenangaben)*
bis (*auch:* **in, nach, zu, an**) to
Bis bald! See you (soon)! *(informal)*
ein **bisschen** a bit, a little
bitte please
Bitte schön! Here you are!
bitten (um) ask (for)
blasen blow
Blatt leaf (*pl* leaves), sheet *(Papier)*, piece of paper
blau blue
bleiben stay, remain
Bleistift pencil
blind blind
blöd stupid
Blume flower
Boden bottom *(unteres Ende)*, floor, ground *(no pl)*
Bohne bean
Boot boat
böse bad
brauchen need
braun brown
(zer)**brechen** break
breit wide
Bremse brake
Brief letter
Brieffreund/in pen friend
Briefträger postman (*pl* -men)
Briefumschlag envelope
Brille glasses
bringen bring (in)
die **Briten** the British *(pl)*
britisch British
Broschüre brochure
Brot bread
Brötchen roll
Brotdose lunchbox
Brücke bridge
Bruder brother
Brust(korb) chest
Buch book
Bücherei library
Buchstabe letter
Burg castle
Büro office
Bus bus, coach *(Reisebus)*
Busch bush
Butter butter

C

Charakter character, personality
Chips crisps *(npl)*
Christ/in; christlich Christian
Cousin/e cousin

D

da *(weil)* as, because, since
da sind there are
Dach roof (*pl* roofs *or* rooves)
Dame lady
danach after, afterwards
danke thanks, thank you
danken thank
dann then
das the *(Artikel)*, that, this
dass that
dasselbe the same
Datum date
(Bett)**decke** blanket
(sich) **dehnen** stretch
denken (an) think (of)
der the, that *(der da)*
der/die/das who
deren whose
derselbe the same
dessen whose
deuten (auf) point (to)
Deutsche/r; deutsch German
Deutschland Germany
Dezember December
Dialog dialogue
Diät diet
dick fat, thick
die the, that *(die da)*
Dienstag Tuesday
diese(r, s) this
diese these, those
Ding thing
dir you, yourself (*pl* yourselves)
diskutieren discuss
(je)**doch** though
Donnerstag Thursday
doppelt double
Dorf village
dort(hin) there
dort drüben, dorthin over there
draußen outside
dreckig dirty
drei three
dritte(r, s) third
Droge drug
du you
dumm stupid, silly
dunkel dark
Dunkelheit dark
dünn thin
durch through
Durchschnitt average
dürfen may
nicht **dürfen** must not
etw tun **dürfen** be allowed to do sth
Dusche shower

E

Ecke corner
Ehefrau wife (*pl* wives)
Ehemann husband
Ei egg
eigene(r, s) own
ein(e) a/an
noch **eine(r, s)** another
ein bisschen a bit, a little
einander each other
Eindruck impression
einerseits on the one hand
einfach easy, simply, simple
Einfluss influence
Einführung introduction
Eingang entrance
einige some, (a) few
einige several
einkaufen shop
einkaufen (gehen) do the shopping
einkleben stick in
einladen invite
Einladung invitation
einmal once
einpacken wrap (up)
eins one
einsam lonely
einsammeln collect
einsteigen get on
Eintritt entrance, entry, admission
Einwanderer/in immigrant
einwandern immigrate
Einwanderung immigration
einwickeln wrap (up)
Einzelheit detail
Einzelkind only child
einzelne(r, s) single
einzige(r, s) single, only
Eis ice
Eiskreme ice cream
Elefant elephant
elektrisch electric
Elemente elements *(pl)*
elf eleven
Eltern parents
Ende end
endlich finally, at last
eng narrow
England England
Engländer/in; englisch English
etw **enthalten** contain sth
entlang along
sich **entscheiden** decide
Entscheidung decision
Entschuldigung! Sorry!, Excuse me!
sich **entspannen** relax
enttäuscht disappointed
Entwicklung development
er he
Erbse pea
Erdbeere strawberry
Erdboden ground *(no pl)*
Erde ground *(no pl) (Boden)*, earth
Erdkunde geography
Ereignis event
Erfahrung experience
erfinden make up, invent
Erfolg success

erfolgreich successful
Ergebnis result
erhalten get, receive
erinnern remind
sich **erinnern (an)** remember
sich **erkälten** catch a cold
erkennen recognize
erklären explain
Erklärung explanation, definition
erleben experience
Erlebnis adventure
es **ernst meinen** be serious
erraten guess
erste(r, s) first
als **Erstes** first
ertragen stand
erwachsen werden grow up
Erwachsene/r adult
erwähnen mention
erwarten expect
erwidern reply
erzählen tell
Erzählung story
es gibt there are, there is
Es tut mir leid. I'm sorry.
Essen food *(no pl)*, meal *(Mahlzeit)*
essen eat; have
etwas some, something
Europa Europe
Europäer/in, europäisch European

F

Fabrik factory
(Schul)**fach** subject
Fähre ferry
fahren go, ride, drive
Fahrer/in driver
Fahrrad bike, bicycle
Fahrt ride
Fakten (über) facts (on/about) *(pl)*
fallen fall
fallen lassen drop
falls if
falsch wrong, false
Familie family
fangen catch
Farbe colour, color *(AE)*, paint *(no pl)*
fast almost, nearly
faul lazy
Februar February
Federmäppchen pencil case
Feld field; space
Fenster window
Ferien holiday(s)
fernsehen watch TV
fertig ready
Feuer fire
Feuerwehrmann/-frau firefighter
Fieber temperature
Film film; movie
finden find
Finger finger
Firma company, Co. = company
Fisch fish (*pl* fish *or* fishes)
flach flat
Flasche bottle
Fleisch meat *(no pl)*
fliegen fly
Flug flight
Flughafen airport
Flugzeug plane
mit dem **Flugzeug** by plane
Fluss river
flüstern whisper
folgende(r, s) following
Foto(grafie) photo(graph)
Fotoapparat camera
fotografieren take a photo
Frage question
sich **fragen** wonder
fragen (nach) ask (for)
Fragen stellen ask questions
Frau woman (*pl* women), lady
Frau *(Anrede)* Mrs
frei free
Freiheit freedom, liberty
Freitag Friday
Freizeit free time
fremd foreign
sich auf etw **freuen** look forward to (doing) sth
Freund boyfriend
Freund/in friend
Freundin girlfriend
freundlich friendly, nice, kind
Freundschaft friendship
Frieden peace
friedlich peaceful, still
frisch fresh
Friseur/Friseuse hairdresser
fröhlich happy
Frucht fruit
früh early
frühere(r, s) former
Frühling spring
Frühstück breakfast
frühstücken have breakfast
(sich) **fühlen** feel
füllen fill
fünf five
fünfte(r, s) fifth
funktionieren work
für for
das **Für und Wider** the pros and cons
furchtbar terrible
sich **fürchten (vor)** be afraid (of)
Fuß foot (*pl* feet)
zu **Fuß** on foot
zu **Fuß gehen** walk
Fußball football
Fußballspieler/in footballer
füttern feed

G

Gabel fork
Garten garden
Gast guest
Gebäude building
geben give
Gebiet area
geboren werden be born
Geburtsdatum date of birth
Geburtsort place of birth
Geburtstag birthday
Gedächtnis memory
Gedanke thought
Gedicht poem
Sehr **geehrte(r)** Dear …
gefährlich dangerous
Gefängnis jail
Gefühl feeling
gegen against
Gegend area
Gegenteil opposite
gegenüber(liegend) opposite
Geheimnis secret
gehen go
(zu Fuß) **gehen** walk
(hinaus)**gehen** go out
Wie **geht es dir/Ihnen/euch?** How are you?
gehören belong
gelb yellow
Geld money
Geld aufbringen/auftreiben raise money
gemein cruel
gemeinsam together
Gemüse vegetable
genießen enjoy
genug enough, plenty
Geografie geography
(Reise)**gepäck** luggage
gerade(aus) straight (on)
Geräusch noise, sound
Ich hätte **gern …** I'll have …, I would like (to) …
Ich würde **gern …** I would like (to) …
Geschäft shop *(Laden)*, store *(AE)*, business *(no pl)*
Geschenk present
Geschichte history, story *(Erzählung)*
das **Geschirr** the dishes *(pl)*
Geschirrspülmaschine dishwasher
Geschmack taste
Geschwindigkeit speed
Gesellschaft company *(Firma)*, society
Gesetz law
Gesicht face
Gesichtspunkt aspect, point of view
Gespräch talk, conversation, dialogue
gestern yesterday
gesund healthy
Gesundheit health
Getränk drink
Gewicht weight
Gewinn prize
gewinnen win
Gewinner/in winner
Gewohnheit habit
etw **gewohnt sein** be used to sth
es **gibt** there are, there is
Gitarre guitar
glänzen shine
Glas glass
Glaube religion, faith, belief
glauben think, believe
gleichzeitig at the same time
Glück haben be lucky
glücklich glad, happy, lucky
Gold gold
Grad degree
Gras grass

gratis free
grau grey
Grenze border
groß big, great, tall, large, wide
großartig great
Großbritannien Britain
Größe size, height
Großeltern grandparents *(pl)*
Großmutter grandmother
Großstadt city
grün green
Grund *(Ursache)* reason
Grundschule elementary school
Gruppe group
mit freundlichen **Grüßen** *(in Briefen)* yours truly
(Salat)**gurke** cucumber
Gürtel belt
gut good, fine, well *(adv)*
Gut gemacht! Well done!
gut in etw sein be good at sth
Gute Besserung! Get well soon!

H

Haar(e) hair *(no pl)*
haben have, have got
halb half
Hälfte half (*pl* halves)
Hals neck
Halsschmerzen sore throat
Hand hand
Handschuh glove
Handtuch towel
Handy mobile (phone)
(auf)**hängen** hang (up)
hart hard
hassen hate
Ich **hätte gern** … I'll have …, I would like (to) …
häufig often
Hauptstadt capital (city)
Haus house
Hausaufgaben homework
zu/nach **Hause** (at) home
Haushalt household
Haustier pet
Haut skin
Heft exercise book
heiraten marry
heiß hot
helfen help
Hemd shirt
herausfinden discover, find out
herauskommen come out
herausnehmen take out
herausschneiden cut out
herausziehen pull out
Herbst autumn, fall *(AE)*
hereinbringen bring in
hereinkommen come in
Herr Mr *(Anrede)*, gentleman (*pl* gentlemen)
herumlaufen walk/go around
Herz heart
herzliche Grüße love *(no pl)*
heute today
heute Abend tonight
hier, hierher here
Hier, bitte! Here/There you are!
hilfsbereit helpful
Himmel sky
hinab down
hinauf up
hinausbringen take out
hinausgehen go out
hinauskommen aus get out of
hinein inside
hinfallen fall down
sich **hinsetzen** sit down
hinten behind, at the back
hinter behind
Hintergrund background
hinunter down
hinzufügen add
Hitze heat
hoch high, tall
hoffen hope
Hoffnung hope
hören hear
Hose trousers *(npl)*
Hotel hotel
hübsch pretty, lovely
Hubschrauber helicopter
Hügel hill
den **Hund ausführen** walk the dog
hundert hundred
hungrig hungry
Hut hat

I

ich I
Ich hätte gern … I'll have …, I would like (to) …
Ich würde gern … I would like (to) …
Idee idea
ihr(e, n) her
im Augenblick at the moment
immer always
immer noch still
in in, at, into, to
in Ordnung all right, alright, fine
Information(en) information *(no pl)*, piece of information
Inhalt content
innen inside
im **Inneren** inside
insgesamt altogether
Instrument instrument
interessant interesting
interessiert interested
international international
im **Internet suchen** search the Internet
irgendein(e) any
irgendwann sometime
irgendwann (einmal) someday (= some day)
irgendwie somehow
irgendwo (anders) somewhere (else)

J

ja yes
Jacke jacket
Jahr year
seit **Jahren** for years
Jahreszeit season
Jahrhundert century
Januar January
jede/r anybody, everybody
jede(r, s) any, each, every
jederzeit anytime
jedoch however, though
jemand anders somebody else
jetzt now, right now
jüdisch Jewish
Juli July
jung young
Junge boy
jüngste(r, s) recent
Juni June

K

Kaffee coffee
kalt cold
Kälte cold
Kamera camera
Kapitel theme
Karotte carrot
Karte card
(Land)**karte** map
Kartoffel potato (*pl* potatoes)
Käse cheese
Kasten box
kauen chew
kaufen buy
Kaugummi chewing gum *(no pl)*
kaum hardly
kein(e) no
keine(r, s) von beiden neither
keiner no one
Kellner/in waiter/waitress
kennen know
Kerze candle
Kilometer kilometre
Kind child (*pl* children)
Kino cinema
Kirche church
(Kopf)**kissen** pillow
Klasse class
Klassenkamerad/in classmate
Klassenzimmer classroom
Klebestift glue stick
Kleid dress
Kleider, Kleidung clothes
Kleiderschrank wardrobe
klein little, small
klettern climb
klingeln ring
Kneipe pub *(informal)*
Knie knee
Knochen bone
Knopf button
kochen cook
Koffer suitcase
komisch funny
kommen come
können can, be able to, may
könnte might, could
kontrollieren check
(sich) **konzentrieren** concentrate
Konzert concert
Kopf head
Kopfschmerzen, Kopfweh headache
Kopie copy

Korb basket
Körper body
korrigieren correct
kosten cost
Was **kostet/kosten ...?** How much is/are ...?
Krach noise
krank ill, sick
Krankenhaus hospital
Krankenschwester/Krankenpfleger nurse
Krankheit disease
Krieg war
Küche kitchen
Kuchen cake
Kühlschrank fridge *(informal)*
Kultur culture
sich um (jdn/etw) **kümmern** care for (sb/sth), take care of (sb/sth), look after
Kunde/Kundin customer
Kunst art
kurz short
Kuscheltier soft toy
küssen kiss

L

lächeln smile
lachen laugh
Laden shop, store *(AE)*
Lampe light, lamp
Land country, nation
Land(schaft) countryside
landen land
Landkarte map
lang long
langsam slow
langweilig boring
Lärm noise
lass(t) uns let's (= let us)
laufen run
laut loud, noisy
laut vorlesen read out
Leben life (*pl* lives)
leben live
lecker delicious, tasty
leer empty
legen put
lehren teach
Lehrer/in teacher
leicht light
Es tut mir **leid.** I'm sorry.
leiden an/unter suffer from
leise quiet *(adj)*
Lektion theme
lernen learn
lesen read
letzte(r, s) last, recent
Leute people *(pl)*
Licht light
lieb dear
Liebe love *(no pl)*
Liebe(r) ... Dear ...
lieben love
Lieblings- favourite
Lied song
liegen lie
lila purple
Lineal ruler
Linie line
linke(r, s) left
(nach) **links** left
links, auf der linken Seite on the left
Liste list
Loch hole
Löffel spoon
Luft air
lügen lie
lustig funny

M

machen do, make
Mädchen girl
Mahlzeit meal
Mai May
malen paint
Mama mum *(informal)*
manchmal sometimes
Mann man (*pl* men)
Mantel coat
Markt market
Marmelade jam
März March
Material material
Mathe math *(AE)*, maths *(BE)*
Medikament drug, medicine *(no pl)*
Meer sea
mehr more
mehr und mehr more and more
meinen mean, think
meiner **Meinung nach** in my opinion
am/die **meisten** (the) most
jede **Menge** lots of
Mensch person, man (*pl* men)
Menschen people *(pl)*
merkwürdig strange
Messer knife (*pl* knives)
mieten hire
Mietwohnung flat
Milch milk
mindestens at least
Minirock miniskirt
Minute minute
mit with; by
mitbringen bring
Mitglied member
mitnehmen take
Mitschüler/in classmate
Mittagessen lunch, dinner
Mitte middle, centre, center *(AE)*
Mittwoch Wednesday
Mode fashion
modern modern
mögen like
sehr gern **mögen** love
mohammedanisch Muslim
Möhre, Mohrrübe carrot
Monat month
Montag Monday
morgen tomorrow
am **Morgen** in the morning
morgens *(nur hinter Uhrzeit)* am
Moslem/in Muslim
Motorrad motorbike *(informal)*
müde tired
Müll rubbish *(no pl)*
Mülleimer dustbin
Mund mouth
Museum museum
Musik music
Musiker/in musician
Müsli muesli
müssen must, have to, need to
Mutter mother

N

nach after, to *(Richtung)*, past *(Uhrzeit)*
nach Hause home
nach(dem) after
Nachbar/in neighbour, neighbor *(AE)*
am **Nachmittag** in the afternoon
nachmittags *(nur hinter Uhrzeit)* pm
Nachrichten news *(no pl)*
nächste(r, s) next
Nacht night
in der **Nacht** at night
Nachteil disadvantage
Nachtisch dessert
Nacken neck
Name name
Nase nose
nass wet
Nationalität nationality
Naturwissenschaft science *(no pl)*
neben next to, beside
negativ negative
nehmen take
nein no
nett nice, enjoyable, kind
neu new, fresh
neueste(r, s) recent
neugierig curious
neun nine
nicht not
nicht ausstehen können hate
nicht dürfen must not
(noch) **nicht einmal** not even
nicht mehr not anymore
nichts not anything, nothing
Nichts zu danken. You're welcome.
nie(mals) never
niemand nobody, no one
Nilpferd hippo (= hippopotamus)
nirgendwo not ... anywhere
(immer) **noch** still
noch (ein)mal again
noch etwas something else
noch immer still
noch nicht not yet
Nord-; nördlich north
Norden north
normalerweise normally, usually
nötig necessary
November November
Null zero
Nummer number
nur only, just
nützlich useful, helpful

O

ob if, whether
(nach) **oben** up
obgleich although

Obst fruit
obwohl although, though
oder or
offen open
(sich) **öffnen** open
oft often, lots (= a lot)
ohne without
Ohr ear
Ohrring earring
Oktober October
Oma; Omi grandma
Onkel uncle
Opa; Opi grandpa
Orange orange
orange(farben) orange
in **Ordnung** all right, alright, fine
organisieren organize
Ort place
Osten east

P

paarweise in pairs
Päckchen parcel
(ein)**packen** pack
Papier paper
Pappe card
Paprika pepper
Park park
Pass passport
passieren happen
Patient/in patient
Pause break
perfekt perfect
Person person
Persönlichkeit personality
Pfeffer pepper
Pferd horse
Pfirsich peach
Pflanze plant
Pflaume plum
Pickel spot
Pilot/in pilot
Pilz mushroom
pink pink
Plan plan
(Zeit-/Fahr)**plan** schedule
planen plan
platt flat
plötzlich suddenly
die **Polizei** the police *(npl)*
Polizist policeman (*pl* -men)
Polizistin policewoman (*pl* -women)
Pommes frites chips *(pl)*
positiv positive
Post(amt) post office
Postbote postman (*pl* -men)
Postkarte postcard
das **Pro und Kontra** the pros and cons
probieren try; taste
Problem problem
Produkt product
Projekt project
Prozent percent *(AE)*, per cent *(BE)*
prüfen test, examine
Prüfung exam (= examination)
Pullover, Pulli jumper
Punkt item
einen Punkt machen score a point
pünktlich on time
putzen clean

Q

Qualität quality
Quittung receipt

R

Rad wheel, bike *(Fahrrad)*
Radiergummi eraser, rubber
Radio radio
raten guess
rauchen smoke
Rechnung bill
Recht haben be right
(nach) **rechts** right
rechts, auf der rechten Seite on the right
reden speak
reden (mit) talk (to)
Regal shelf (*pl* shelves)
Regel rule
regelmäßig regular *(adj)*
Regen rain
Regenschirm umbrella
Regierung government
regnen rain
reich rich, wealthy
Reifen tyre
an der **Reihe sein** be one's turn
Reihenfolge order
Reis rice
reisen travel
reiten ride
Religion religion
rennen run
reparieren repair; fix
Reporter/in reporter
Rezept prescription, recipe *(Kochen)*
Richter/in judge
richtig correct, proper, right
riechen smell
riesig great, huge
Rindfleisch beef
Ring ring
Rock skirt
rosa pink
rot red
Rücken back
ruhig quiet, still
(ver)**rühren** mix, stir
rund round

S

Saft juice
sagen say, tell
Sahne cream
Salat salad
Salz salt
sammeln collect
Sammlung collection
Samstag Saturday
Sänger/in singer
Satz phrase, sentence
sauber clean
sauber machen clean
Schachtel box
Schal scarf (*pl* scarves)
scharf hot
Schauspieler/in actor/actress
Scheibe slice
scheinen shine *(Licht)*, seem
Schere (pair of) scissors *(npl)*
schicken send
schieben push
Schiff boat, ship
(Straßen-/Verkehrs)**schild** sign
Schinken ham
Schlaf sleep
schlafen sleep
Schlafzimmer bedroom
schlagen hit, beat
Schlange queue *(Warteschlange)*
schlecht bad
schließen close, shut
schließlich finally
schlimm bad
schmecken taste
Schmerz(en) pain
schmutzig dirty
Schnee snow
schneiden cut
schnell fast, quick *(adj)*, quickly *(adv)*
Schokolade chocolate *(no pl)*
schon already, yet
schön beautiful, nice, lovely
Schrank cupboard, wardrobe
schrecklich terrible, horrible
schreiben write
eine SMS **schreiben** text a message
Schreibtisch desk
schüchtern shy
Schuh shoe
Schule school
Schüler/in pupil, student
Schulfach subject
Schulter shoulder
schwach weak
schwarz black
schwer heavy *(Gewicht)*, difficult
schwerhörig deaf
Schwester sister
schwierig difficult; hard; tough
schwimmen swim
sechs six
See lake
sehen look, see
Sehenswürdigkeit sight
sehr much, very, lots (= a lot)
Sehr geehrte(r) … Dear …
Seife soap
sein be
seit since (+ *Zeitpunkt*), for (+ *Zeitspanne*)
Seite page *(Buch)*, side
Sekunde second
selbst, sogar even
September September
sich (hin)**setzen** sit down
sicher(lich) certainly, surely
sieben seven
singen sing
Sitz(platz) seat
sitzen sit

SMS text message
so so, like this, such *(adj)*
(genau)**so ... wie ...** as ... as ...
Socke sock
sofort right now, at once
sogar even
Sohn son
solch(er, es) such
sollen be supposed to
sollte should
Sommer summer
Sonne sun
Sonnenbrille (pair of) sunglasses
sonnig sunny
Sonntag Sunday
sich **Sorgen machen** worry, be worried
Sorte kind, sort, type
sowohl ... als auch ... both ... and
spannend exciting
sparen save
Spaß machen be fun
(zu) **spät** late
später later, afterwards
spazieren gehen go for a walk
Speisekarte menu
Spiegel mirror
Spiel play, game
spielen play
Spieler/in player
Spielzeug toy
Sport(art) sport
Sprache language, speech
sprechen (mit) talk (to), speak
Staatsangehörigkeit nationality
Stadt city, town
Standpunkt point of view
Start start
(an)**statt** instead of
stattfinden take place
stehen stand
stehlen steal
Stein stone, rock
stellen put, stand
sterben die
Stiefel boot
Stift pen
Stimme voice
Stock(werk) floor
stolz proud
stören disturb
Strand beach, shore
Straße street, road
Strom electricity
Stück bit, piece, slice
studieren study
Stuhl chair
Stunde hour, lesson *(Schule)*
eine halbe **Stunde** half an hour
Stundenplan schedule
Subjekt subject
suchen nach look for, search for
(der) **Süden** (the) south
südlich, Süd- southern
Supermarkt supermarket
Suppe soup
süß sweet
Süßigkeit(en) sweet(s)

T

Tabelle table
Tafel board, blackboard
Tag day
den ganzen **Tag** all day (long)
Tagebuch diary
Tante aunt
Tanz dance
tanzen dance
Tänzer/in dancer
Tasche bag, pocket *(Kleidung)*
Taschengeld pocket money
Taschenlampe torch
Taschenmesser penknife (*pl* -knives)
Tasse cup
Tatsache fact
taub deaf
tauschen change
tausend thousand
Tee tea
teilen share
teilnehmen (an) take part (in), attend
Teilzeit- part-time
Telefon phone, telephone
Teller plate
Temperatur temperature
testen test
teuer expensive *(Preis)*, dear
Theater theatre, theater *(AE)*
Thema subject, theme, topic
tief deep
Tier animal
Tiger tiger
Tisch table
den **Tisch decken** lay the table
Tochter daughter
Toilette toilet
Tomate tomato
Tor gate, goal *(Fußball)*
tragen carry, wear *(Kleidung)*
Trainer/in trainer
Träne tear
Traube grape
Traum dream
träumen dream
traurig sad
Treffen meeting
(sich) **treffen** meet
Treppe stairs *(npl)*
treten kick
trinken drink
trocken dry
trotzdem still
tschüss bye *(informal)*
tun do
Tür door
Turnschuh trainer
typisch typical

U

U-Bahn underground *(no pl)*
üben practise, practice *(AE)*
über about, over, across, above, via
überall everywhere
überhaupt keine not any
überhaupt nicht not at all
überleben survive
überprüfen check
überrascht surprised
überreden persuade
Überschrift heading
übrig left
Übung exercise
Ufer shore
Uhr clock
(ein) **Uhr** (one) o'clock
(um) wie viel **Uhr** what time
um around
um *(Uhrzeit)* at
um ... herum around
um zu in order to
umblättern turn
sich **umdrehen** turn
umfallen fall down
Umfrage survey
umsteigen change trains
umziehen (nach) move
und and
Unfall accident
unfreundlich unfriendly
ungefähr about
ungesund unhealthy
Universität university
unordentlich untidy
uns us, ourselves
unser(e) our
unten below
unter under, beneath, below
unterrichten teach
Unterschied difference, variation *(no pl)*
unterschreiben sign
untersuchen examine
Urlaub holiday(s)
die **USA (= Vereinigte Staaten von Amerika)** the USA (= United States of America)
usw. etc (= et cetera)

V

Vater father
vegetarisch vegetarian
verantwortlich responsible
verärgert angry, annoyed
verbessern improve
Verbrechen crime
verbringen *(Zeit)* spend
verdienen earn
Verein club
die **Vereinigten Staaten** the United States
Vergangenheit past
vergessen forget
vergleichen compare
verhaften arrest
Verkauf sale
verkaufen sell
Verkäufer/in shop assistant
Verkehr traffic
sich **verkleiden** dress up
verlassen leave
verletzen hurt
Verletzung injury
sich **verlieben (in)** fall in love (with)
verlieren lose

vermissen miss
vernünftig sensible
verrückt crazy, mad
verschieden different
versprechen promise
(sich) **verstecken** hide
verstehen understand
sich **verstehen** get on
versuchen try
Verwandte/r relative
viel much, lots of, lots (= a lot)
viele many, a lot (of)
vielleicht maybe, perhaps, possibly
vier four
Viertel(stunde) quarter
Vogel bird
voll full
völlig altogether *(adv)*, total *(adj)*, totally *(adv)*, completely, absolutely
von from, of
vor in front of *(örtlich)*, before *(zeitlich)*
vor (zwei Wochen) (two weeks) ago
vorbereiten prepare
vorher before
jdm etw **vorlesen** read sth to sb
laut **vorlesen** read out
vormittags *(nur hinter Uhrzeit)* am
vorn(e) in front
nach **vorn(e)** forward(s)
vorschlagen suggest
vorstellen introduce
Vorteil advantage
Vorurteil prejudice

W

wachsen grow
Wahl choice
wählen elect, vote (for)
wahr true
während during, while, as
Wahrheit truth
wahrscheinlich probably
Wald forest
Wand wall
wann when
(Bade)**wanne** bath
warm warm
Wärme heat
warten auf wait for
warum why
was what
Was kostet/kosten ...? How much is/are ...?
(sich) **waschen** wash
Wasser water
Wecker alarm clock
weder ... noch ... neither ... nor
Weg way, path
weg away
wegen because of, for
wegziehen move away
wehtun hurt
weich soft
Weihnachten Christmas
weil because, since
Weile while
Weinbeere, -traube grape
weinen cry
weiß white
weit far
weitermachen go on
welche(r, s) which, what
Welt world
wenig little
wenige few
weniger less
wenigstens at least
wenn when, if *(falls)*
wer who
Werbung ad (= advertisement)
werden become
werfen throw
wessen whose
Westen west
Wettbewerb competition
Wetter weather
wichtig important, major
wie how, like, as, such as
Wie bitte? Sorry?
Wie geht es dir/Ihnen/euch? How are you?
Wie ist ...? What's ... like?
(um) **wie viel Uhr** what time
wieder again
wild wild
Wind wind
windig windy
Winter winter
wir we
wirklich real *(adj)*, really *(adv)*, actually
Wissen knowledge *(no pl)*
wissen know
(Natur)**wissenschaft** science *(no pl)*
witzig funny
wo(hin) where
Woche week
Wochenende weekend
Wohin? Where to?
wohnen live
Wohnung apartment, flat
Wohnzimmer living room
wollen want
Wort word
Wörterbuch, -verzeichnis dictionary
wunderbar wonderful
wünschen want
(sich) **wünschen** wish
Ich **würde gern ...** I would like (to) ...
würfeln roll a dice
Wurst, Würstchen sausage
wütend angry

Z

Zahl number
zählen count
Zahn tooth (*pl* teeth)
Zahnarzt/ärztin dentist
zehn ten
Zeichen sign, symbol
zeichnen draw
zeigen show, point (to)
Zeile line
Zeit time
die ganze **Zeit** all the time
Zeitschrift magazine
Zeitung newspaper
Zeitungen austragen do a paper round
Zelt tent
Zentrum centre, center *(AE)*
zerstören destroy
ziehen pull
Ziel goal
Zigarette cigarette
Zimmer room
Zoo zoo
zu to, too *(allzu)*
zu Fuß on foot
zu Hause (at) home
zu spät late
Zucker sugar
zuerst first
zufrieden happy
Zug train
zuhören listen to
Zukunft future
zuletzt last
zum Beispiel for example, such as
z. B. (zum Beispiel) e. g.
zumachen close
zuordnen match (with)
zurück back
zurückkehren return
zusammen together
Zusammenfassung summary
zuschauen watch
Zuschauer/in spectator
zustimmen agree
zwanzig twenty
zwei two
zweimal twice
zweite(r, s) second
ein **zweiter/zweites/eine zweite** another
Zwetschge plum
Zwiebel onion
zwischen between
zwölf twelve

N Names

Girls/Women
Alexa ['ælɪksə]
Amy ['eɪmi]
Ann [æn]
Ashley ['æʃli]
Betty ['beti]
Carolina [ˌkærl'aɪnə]
Cathleen [kæθ'li:n]
Cathy ['kæθi]
Deborah ['debrə]
Derya ['dɜ:rjə]
Elif ['i:lɪf]
Elisabeth [ɪ'lɪzəbəθ]
Emily ['emɪli]
Erin ['erɪn]
Fiona [fɪ'əʊnə]
Ina ['i:nə]
Jane [dʒeɪn]
Jasmin ['dʒæzmɪn]
Jennifer ['dʒenɪfə]
Jenny ['dʒeni]
Kim [kɪm]
Linda ['lɪndə]
Liz [liz]
Lucy ['lu:si]
Madison ['mædɪs(ə)n]
Mary ['meəri]
Mary Jane [ˌmeəri 'dʒeɪn]
Maude [mɔ:d]
Monica ['mɒnɪkə]
Pat [pæt]
Rachel ['reɪtʃl]
Rosa ['rəʊzə]
Rosemary ['rəʊzməri]
Sabrina [sə'bri:nə]
Sarah ['seərə]
Shannaw ['ʃænɔ:]
Tami ['tæmi]
Vanessa [və'nesə]
Whitnie ['wɪtni]

Boys/Men
Antonio [æn'təʊniəʊ]
Ben [ben]
Bill [bɪl]
Billy ['bɪli]
Chandler ['tʃɑ:ndlə]
Chris [krɪs]
Curtis ['kɜ:tɪs]
Danny ['dæni]
David ['deɪvɪd]
Elvis ['elvɪs]
Emre ['emrə]
Fergus ['fɜ:gəs]
George [dʒɔ:dʒ]
Greg [greg]
Guiseppe [dʒɪ'səp]
Harry ['hæri]
Henry ['henri]
Hugh [hju:]
Jack [dʒæk]
James [dʒeɪmz]
Joe [dʒəʊ]
John [dʒɒn]
Johnny ['dʒɒni]
José [həʊ'zeɪ]
Josh [dʒɒʃ]
Leroy ['li:rɔɪ]
Liam ['li:əm]
Logan ['ləʊgən]
Mark [mɑ:k]
Matt [mæt]
Ned [ned]
Neil [ni:l]
Panchito [pæn'ʃɪtəʊ]
Patrick ['pætrɪk]
Peter ['pi:tə]
Phil [fɪl]
Roberto [rəʊ'bɜ:təʊ]
Ryan ['raɪən]
Sam [sæm]
Simon ['saɪmən]
Squanto ['skwɒntəʊ]
Steven ['sti:vən]
Thomas ['tɒməs]
Tobias [təʊ'baɪəs]
Tom [tɒm]
Tommy ['tɒmi]
Tony ['təʊni]
Victor ['vɪktə]
Vincent ['vɪntsənt]
Will [wɪl]
Zachary ['zækəri]

Families
Baker ['beɪkə]
Billington ['bɪlɪŋtən]
Bradford ['brædfəd]
Brown [braʊn]
Castano [kæs'tɑ:nəʊ]
Chapman ['tʃæpmən]
Deermount ['dɪəmaʊnt]
Drake [dreɪk]
Duong ['dju:əʊŋ]
Farquaad ['fɑ:kwɔ:d]
Flynn [flɪn]
Gibbons ['gɪbənz]
Grigley ['grɪgli]
Harris ['hærɪs]
Johnson ['dʒɒnsən]
Jones [dʒəʊnz]
Letterman ['letəmən]
Marshall ['mɑ:ʃl]
Mason ['meɪsn]
Miller ['mɪlə]
O'Shea [əʊ'ʃeɪ]
Parker ['pɑ:kə]
Parks [pɑ:ks]
Pender ['pendə]
Perkins ['pɜ:kɪnz]
Raimi ['reɪmi]
Raleigh ['ræli]
Seymour ['si:mɔ:]
Sliwa ['slɪwə]
Smart [smɑ:t]
Sparrow ['spærəʊ]
Sullivan ['sʌlɪv(ə)n]
Swann [swɒn]
Tripp [trɪp]
Turner ['tɜ:nə]
Vargas ['vɒgəs]
Watson ['wɒtsn]
Whitney ['wɪtni]
Wrigley ['rɪgli]

Other Names
Abraham Lincoln [ˌeɪbrəhæm 'lɪŋkən]
Abraham Lincoln High School [ˌeɪbrəhæm ˌlɪŋkən 'haɪ ˌsku:l]
Ahwahnee [ə'wɔ:ni:]
the Ahwahneechee [ði‿ə'wɔ:nətʃi:]
Alexander Graham Bell [ælɪgˌzɑ:ndə ˌgreɪəm 'bel]
Algonquian [æl'gɒŋkwiən]
American Football *(no pl)* [əˌmerɪkən 'fʊtbɔ:l]
American Pie [əˌmerɪkən 'paɪ]
Annie Moore [ˌæni 'mɔ:]
Barbarossa [ˌbɑ:bər'ɒsə]
Bayou ['baɪ(j)u:]
Bill Cosby [bɪl 'kɒzbi]
Blocksberg ['blɒksbɜ:g]
Burgerland ['bɜ:gəlænd]
Capitol Hill [ˌkæpɪtl 'hɪl]
Capri Sun [kæp'ri: sʌn]
Carcachita [kaka'ʃɪtə]
Chickasaw ['tʃɪkəsɔ:]
chicle ['tʃɪkl]
Chief Massasoit [tʃi:f mæsə'sɔɪt]
Chief Tecumseh [tʃi:f tekɒm'zi:]
Curls [kɜ:lz]
David Lee [ˌdeɪvɪd 'li:]
Debi Thomas [ˌdebɪ 'tɒməs]
Delaware ['deləweə]
Desperate Houswives [ˌdesp(ə)rət 'haʊswaɪvz]
Destiny's Child [ˌdestəniz 'tʃaɪld]
Disneyland ['dɪznilænd]
Domino ['dɒmɪnəʊ]
Doritos ['dɒrɪtəs]
Doublemint ['dʌblmɪnt]
El Capitan [el 'kæpɪtæn]
El Dorado [ˌel də'rɑ:dəʊ]
Ellis Island Immigrant Station ['elɪs‿aɪlənd ˌɪmɪgrənt ˌsteɪʃn]
Elvis Presley [ˌelvɪs 'prezlɪ]
Emergency Room [ɪ'mɜ:dʒ(ə)nsi ˌru:m]
Empire State Building Observatory [empaɪə ˌsteɪt bɪldɪŋ əb'zɜ:vətri]
Enigma [ɪ'nɪgmə]
Federal Hall ['fedrəl ˌhɔ:l]
Field Museum [ˌfi:ld mju:'zi:əm]
Foot Locker ['fʊt ˌlɒkə]
Francisco Jimenéz [frænˌsɪskəʊ dʒɪmə'ni:z]
Frank Sinatra [fræŋk sɪ'nɑ:trə]
Frankenstein ['fræŋkənstaɪn]
Fred Ebb [fred‿'eb]
Friends [frendz]
Gap [gæp]
George Bush [dʒɔ:dʒ 'bʊʃ]
George Clooney [dʒɔ:dʒ 'klu:ni]
George Washington [dʒɔ:dʒ 'wɒʃɪŋtən]
Ghostbusters [gəʊst'bʌstəz]
The Guardian Angels [ðə ˌgɑ:diən 'eɪndʒ(ə)lz]
halloween [ˌhæləʊ'i:n]
Harvard ['hɑ:vəd]
Henry Ford [ˌhenri 'fɔ:d]
Hitch [hɪtʃ]
Inuit (*pl* -s *or* -) ['ɪnuɪt]
the Iroquois [ði‿'ɪrəkwɔɪz]
Jacob Davis [ˌdʒeɪkəb 'deɪvɪs]

James Naismith [dʒeɪmz naɪ'smɪθ]
JFK Airport [dʒeɪ ef 'keɪ‿eə,pɔːt]
John Harvey Kellogg [dʒɒn ,hɑːvi 'kelɒg]
John Kander [dʒɒn 'kændə]
John Stith Pemberton [dʒɒn stɪð 'pembətən]
John Weber [dʒɒn 'webə]
Juicy Fruit [,dʒuːsi 'fruːt]
Kickapoo ['kɪkəpuː]
Kirsten Dunst [,kɜːstn 'dʌnst]
Langston Hughes [,læŋstən 'hjuːdʒəz]
Lenny Kravitz [,leni 'krævɪts]
Lenox ['lenəks]
Leonardo di Caprio [liːə,nɑːdəʊ dɪ 'kæprɪəʊ]
Levi Strauss [,liːvaɪ 'straʊs]
Lord of the Rings [,lɔːd‿əv ðə 'rɪŋz]
Lucky Luciano [,lʌki luːsi'ɑːnəʊ]
Lyndon B. Johnson [,lɪndən biː 'dʒɒnsən]
Macy's Department Store [,meɪsiz 'dɪpɑːtmənt stɔː]
Madonna [mə'dɒnə]
the March on Washington [ðə ,mɑːtʃ‿ɒn 'wɒʃɪŋtən]
Maria Goeppert Mayer [mə,riːə ,gɜːpət 'meɪə]
Mariposa Grove [,mæri'pəʊsə grəʊv]
Martin Luther King [,mɑːtɪn ,luːθə 'kɪŋ]
Martin Luther King Junior [,mɑːtɪn ,luːθə kɪŋ 'dʒuːniə]
Mary Robinson [,meəri 'rɒbɪnsən]
Matrix ['meɪtrɪks]
Maurice McDonald [,mɒrɪs mək'dɒnəld]
the Mayflower [ðə 'meɪflaʊə]
McComet [mə'kɒmɪt]
McDonald's [mək'dɒnəldz]
McKinley [mə'kɪnli]
Men in Black [,men‿ɪn 'blæk]
Michael Jordan [,maɪkl 'dʒɔːrdn]
Minton's Playhouse [,mɪntənz 'pleɪ,haʊs]
Miwok [maɪwək]
the Mohawks [ðə 'məʊhɔːkz]
Muhammad Ali [,mʊhæməd 'ɑlɪ]
NAACP (= National Association for the Advancement of Colored People) ['næʃn(ə)l ə,səʊʃi,eɪʃn fə ðə əd,vɑːnsmənt‿əv ,kʌləd 'piːpl, en,ei,ei,siː'piː]
Nebraska University [nə,bræskə juːnɪ'vɜːsəti]
New York Times [njuː ,jɔːk 'taɪmz]
Ouray ['aʊreɪ]
Patty ['pæti]
Penn Manor [,pen 'mænə]
Pirates of the Caribbean [,paɪrətz‿əv ðə ,kærɪ'biːən]
Pittsburg Post ['pɪtsbɜːg ,pəʊst]
Pleasantville ['plezntvɪl]
the Pocumtucks [ðə 'pɒkəmtəks]
Pony Express ['pəʊni ɪk,spres]
power bar ['paʊə ,bɑː]
Red Hot Chilli Peppers [red hɒt ,tʃɪli 'pepəz]
REM [,ɑːriː'em]
Richard McDonald [,rɪtʃəd mək'dɒnəld]
Roddy Doyle [,rɒdi 'dɔɪl]
Roseanne [rəʊ'zæn]
Seminole ['semɪnəʊl]
Serena Williams [sɜː,riːnə 'wɪljəmz]
Shakespeare ['ʃeɪkspɪə]
Shawnee [ʃɔː'niː]
Sim City [,sɪm 'sɪti]
Skyland ['skaɪlænd]
Spider-Man ['spaɪdəmæn]
SS Nevada [es,es nə'vɑːdə]
St. George Hotel [seɪnt ,dʒɔːdʒ həʊ'tel]
Starbucks ['stɑːrbʌkz]
Subway ['sʌb,weɪ]
Super Bowl ['suːpə ,bəʊl]
SuperChew ['suːpə,tʃuː]
Tennessee Williams [tenə,siː 'wɪljəmz]
The Cider House Rules [ðə 'saɪdə haʊs ruːlz]
The Late Night Show [ðə 'leɪt naɪt ,ʃəʊ]
The Simple Life [ðə 'sɪmpl laɪf]
The Simpsons [ðə 'sɪmpsnz]
Theodore Roosevelt ['θiːədɔː ,rəʊzəvelt]
Tobey Maguire [,təʊbi mə'gwaɪə]
Trinity Church [,trɪnəti 'tʃɜːtʃ]
Turkey Hill ['tɜːki ,hɪl]
Uintah ['juːɪntɑː]
Universal Studios [juːnɪ'vɜːsl ,stjuːdiəʊz]
Walt Disney [wɒlt 'dɪzni]
the White Man [ðə ,waɪt 'mæn]
Will & Grace [,wɪl‿ənd 'greɪs]
Willem Dafoe [,wɪləm də'fəʊ]
William Wrigley Jr. [,wɪljəm 'rɪglɪ ,dʒuːniə]
Woolworth ['wʊlwəθ]
Wrigley Building ['rɪgli ,bɪldɪŋ]
Wrigley's Spearmint [,rɪglɪs‿'spɪə,mɪnt]
Yale [jeɪl]

Geographical Names

Alabama [,ælə'bæmə]
Alaska [ə'læskə]
Ankara ['æŋkərə]
the Appalachian (Mountains) [ði‿æpə,leɪʃən 'maʊntɪnz]
Arizona [,ærɪ'zəʊnə]
Australia [ɒ'streɪliə]
Battery Park ['bætəri ,pɑːk]
Bismarck ['bɪzmɑːk]
Black Hills [blæk 'hɪlz]
Boston ['bɒstən]
Broadway ['brɔːd,weɪ]
the Bronx [ðə brɒŋks]
Brooklyn ['brʊklɪn]
California [,kælɪ'fɔːniə]
Cambridge ['keɪmbrɪdʒ]
Canada ['kænədə]
Cape Cod [,keɪp 'kɒd]
Central Park ['sentrəl pɑːk]
Chicago [ʃɪ'kɑːgəʊ]
Chinatown ['tʃaɪnə,taʊn]
City Hall Park [,sɪti 'hɔːl pɑːk]
Colorado [,kɒlər'ɑːdəʊ]
Connecticut [kə'netɪkət]
Connecticut River [kə'netɪkət ,rɪvə]
Dallas ['dæləs]
Dante's View [,dæntiz 'vjuː]
DC *(no pl)* (= District of Columbia) [,diː'siː, ,dɪstrɪkt‿əv kə'lʌmbiə]
Death Valley [,deθ 'væli]
Deerfield ['dɪəfiːld]
Delaware ['deləweə]
Denver ['denvə]
Dublin ['dʌblin]
The East River [ði‿'iːst ,rɪvə]
Ellis Island ['elɪs‿,aɪlənd]
Empire State Building [,empaɪə 'steɪt ,bɪldɪŋ]
Fairbury ['feəbəri]
Fifth Avenue [fɪfθ 'ævə,njuː]
Florida ['flɒrɪdə]
Frankfort ['fræŋkfɜːt]
Galway ['gɔːlweɪ]
Genoa ['dʒenəʊə]
Georgia ['dʒɔːdʒə]
Gibraltar [dʒɪ'brɔːltə]
Golden Gate Bridge [,gəʊld(ə)n 'geɪt brɪdʒ]
Great Britain [,greɪt 'brɪtn]
Green Mountain [griːn 'maʊntɪn]
Guadalajara [,gwɑːdələ'hɑːrə]
Harlem ['hɑːləm]
Harney Peak ['hɑːni piːk]
Harrisburg ['hærɪsbɜːg]
Hawaii [hə'waɪiː]
Hollywood ['hɒliwʊd]
Hong Kong [,hɒŋ'kɒŋ]
Hudson River ['hʌds(ə)n ,rɪvə]
Illinois [,ɪlɪ'nɔɪ]
Indiana [ɪndi'ænə]
Iowa ['aɪəʊə]
Jamaica [dʒə'meɪkə]
Jamestown ['dʒeɪmztaʊn]
Kansas ['kænzəs]
Kansas City [,kænzəs 'sɪti]
Katowice [,kætəʊ'vɪtseɪ]
Kentucky [ken'tʌki]
La Guardia Airport [la 'gɑːdiə‿eə,pɔːt]
Lake Erie [leɪk 'ɪəri]
Lake Michigan [leɪk 'mɪʃɪgən]
Las Vegas [,læs 'veɪgəs]
Limburg ['lɪmbɜːg]
Lincoln Memorial [,lɪŋkən mə'mɔːriəl]
London ['lʌndən]
Los Angeles [lɒs 'ændʒɪliːz]
Louisville ['luːivɪl]
Lower Manhattan [,ləʊə mæn'hæt(ə)n]
Maine [meɪn]
Manhattan [mæn'hæt(ə)n]
Maryland ['meərilænd]
Massachusetts [,mæsə'tʃuːsɪts]
Memphis ['mempfɪs]
Mexiko ['meksɪ,kəʊ]
Miami [maɪ'æmi]
the Mississippi [ðə ,mɪsɪ'sɪpɪ]
Mississippi [,mɪsɪ'sɪpɪ]
Mississippi-Missouri [mɪsɪ,sɪpɪ mɪ'zʊri]
Missouri [mɪ'zʊəri]
Montgomery [mənt'gʌməri]
Mount McKinley [,maʊnt mə'kɪnli]
Nebraska [nɪ'bræskə]
Nevada [nə'vɑːdə]
New Amsterdam [njuː 'æmstədæm]
New England [ŋeuengland]

Names

New Hampshire [ˌnjuː ˈhæmpʃə]
New Jersey [ˌnjuː ˈdʒɜːzi]
New Orleans [ˌnjuː ˈɔːliənz]
New York [ˌnjuː ˈjɔːk]
New York City [ˌnjuː jɔːk ˈsɪti]
Newburyport [ˈnjuːbərɪpɔːt]
Nimes [niːm]
North Dakota [ˌnɔːθ dəˈkəʊtə]
North Michigan Avenue [nɔːθ ˌmɪʃɪgən ˈævəˌnjuː]
Ohio [əʊˈhaɪəʊ]
Oklahoma [ˌəʊkləˈhəʊmə]
Ontario [ɒnˈteəriəʊ]
Pennsylvania [ˌpensɪlˈveɪniə]
Peru [pəˈruː]
Philadelphia [ˌfɪləˈdelfiə]
Plymouth [ˈplɪməθ]
Plymouth Rock [ˈplɪməθ rɒk]
Polynesia [ˌpɒlɪˈniːʒə]
Queens [kwiːnz]
Rhode Island [ˌrəʊd‿ˈaɪlənd]
Richmond [ˈrɪtʃmənd]
Rio Grande [ˌriːəʊ ˈgrænd]
the Rocky Mountains [ðə ˌrɒki ˈmaʊntɪnz]
Sacramento [ˌsækrəˈmentəʊ]
Salt Lake City [ˌsɔːlt leɪk ˈsɪti]
San Francisco [ˌsæn frənˈsɪskəʊ]
Santa Monica [ˌsæntə ˈmɒnɪkə]
the Sears Tower [ðə ˈsɪəz ˌtaʊə]
Seattle [siˈætl]
Selbitz [ˈselbɪts]
Sierra Nevada [siˌerə nəˈvɑːdə]
South America [ˌsaʊθ‿əˈmerɪkə]
South Street [saʊθ ˈstriːt]
the Southern States [ðə ˌsʌðn ˈsteɪts]
Springfield [ˈsprɪŋfiːld]
St. Joseph [seɪnt ˈdʒəʊzɪf]
St. Louis [sənt ˈluːɪs]
Staten Island [ˈsteɪtən‿ˌaɪlənd]
Strivers Row [ˈstraɪvəs rəʊ]
Telescope Peak [ˈtelɪskəʊp piːk]
Tennessee [ˌtenəˈsiː]
Texas [ˈteksəs]
Topeka [təʊˈpiːkə]
Turkey [ˈtɜːki]
Utah [ˈjuːtɑː]
Vermont [vəˈmɒnt]
Vietnam [ˌvjetˈnæm]
Virginia [vəˈdʒɪnjə]
Wall Street [ˈwɔːl ˌstriːt]
Washington DC [ˌwɒʃɪŋtən ˌdiːˈsiː]
Wyoming [waɪˈəʊmɪŋ]
Yosemite [jəʊˈsemɪti]
Yosemite National Park [jəʊˌsemɪti ˈnæʃn(ə)l pɑːk]
Zabriskie Point [zæˈbrɪski pɔɪnt]

Irregular verbs

infinitive	simple past	past participle	
to be [biː]	was/were [wɒz/wɜː]	been [biːn]	sein
to beat [biːt]	beat [biːt]	beaten [ˈbiːt(ə)n]	schlagen
to become [bɪˈkʌm]	became [bɪˈkeɪm]	become [bɪˈkʌm]	werden
to begin [bɪˈgɪn]	began [bɪˈgæn]	begun [bɪˈgʌn]	anfangen, beginnen
to bet [bet]	bet/betted [bet/ˈbetɪd]	bet/betted [bet/ˈbetɪd]	setzen, wetten
to bite [baɪt]	bit [bɪt]	bit/bitten [bɪt/ˈbɪtn]	beißen
to blow [bləʊ]	blew [bluː]	blown [bləʊn]	wehen, blasen
to break [breɪk]	broke [brəʊk]	broken [ˈbrəʊkən]	(zer)brechen
to bring [brɪŋ]	brought [brɔːt]	brought [brɔːt]	(mit)bringen
to build [bɪld]	built [bɪlt]	built [bɪlt]	bauen
to burn [bɜːn]	burnt/burned [bɜːnt/bɜːnd]	burnt/burned [bɜːnt/bɜːnd]	(ver)brennen
to buy [baɪ]	bought [bɔːt]	bought [bɔːt]	kaufen
to cast [kɑːst]	cast [kɑːst]	cast [kɑːst]	eine Rolle *(Film etc.)* besetzen
to catch [kætʃ]	caught [kɔːt]	caught [kɔːt]	fangen
to choose [tʃuːz]	chose [tʃəʊz]	chosen [ˈtʃəʊzn]	auswählen
to come [kʌm]	came [keɪm]	come [kʌm]	kommen
to cost [kɒst]	cost [kɒst]	cost [kɒst]	kosten
to cut [kʌt]	cut [kʌt]	cut [kʌt]	schneiden
to dig [dɪg]	dug [dʌg]	dug [dʌg]	graben
to do [duː]	did [dɪd]	done [dʌn]	machen, tun
to draw [drɔː]	drew [druː]	drawn [drɔːn]	zeichnen
to dream [driːm]	dreamt/dreamed [dremt/driːmd]	dreamt/dreamed [dremt/driːmd]	träumen
to drink [drɪŋk]	drank [dræŋk]	drunk [drʌŋk]	trinken
to drive [draɪv]	drove [drəʊv]	driven [ˈdrɪvn]	fahren
to eat [iːt]	ate [eɪt]	eaten [ˈiːtn]	essen
to fall [fɔːl]	fell [fel]	fallen [ˈfɔːlən]	fallen
to feed [fiːd]	fed [fed]	fed [fed]	zu essen geben, füttern
to feel [fiːl]	felt [felt]	felt [felt]	(sich) fühlen
to fight [faɪt]	fought [fɔːt]	fought [fɔːt]	kämpfen
to find [faɪnd]	found [faʊnd]	found [faʊnd]	finden
to fit [fɪt]	fit/fitted [fɪt/ˈfɪtɪd]	fit/fitted [fɪt/ˈfɪtɪd]	sich eignen, passen (zu)
to flee [fliː]	fled [fled]	fled [fled]	fliehen, flüchten
to fly [flaɪ]	flew [fluː]	flown [fləʊn]	fliegen
to forget [fəˈget]	forgot [fəˈgɒt]	forgotten [fəˈgɒtn]	vergessen
to get [get]	got [gɒt]	got [gɒt]	erhalten; werden
to give [gɪv]	gave [geɪv]	given [ˈgɪvn]	geben
to go [gəʊ]	went [went]	gone [gɒn]	gehen; fahren
to grow [grəʊ]	grew [gruː]	grown [grəʊn]	wachsen
to hang [hæŋ]	hung [hʌŋ]	hung [hʌŋ]	hängen
to have [hæv]	had [hæd]	had [hæd]	haben; essen

infinitive	simple past	past participle	
to hear [hɪə]	heard [hɜːd]	heard [hɜːd]	hören
to hide [haɪd]	hid [hɪd]	hidden ['hɪdn]	(sich) verstecken
to hit [hɪt]	hit [hɪt]	hit [hɪt]	schlagen; treffen
to hold [həʊld]	held [held]	held [held]	(fest)halten
to hurt [hɜːt]	hurt [hɜːt]	hurt [hɜːt]	wehtun, verletzen
to keep [kiːp]	kept [kept]	kept [kept]	(be)halten; bleiben
to know [nəʊ]	knew [njuː]	known [nəʊn]	wissen, kennen
to lay [leɪ]	laid [leɪd]	laid [leɪd]	legen
to lead [liːd]	led [led]	led [led]	führen
to leap [liːp]	leapt/leaped [lept/liːpt]	leapt/leaped [lept/liːpt]	springen
to learn [lɜːn]	learnt/learned [lɜːnt/lɜːnd]	learnt/learned [lɜːnt/lɜːnd]	lernen
to leave [liːv]	left [left]	left [left]	verlassen; zurücklassen; abfahren
to lend [lend]	lent [lent]	lent [lent]	leihen
to let [let]	let [let]	let [let]	lassen
to lie [laɪ]	lay [leɪ]	lain [leɪn]	liegen
to light [laɪt]	lit [lɪt]	lit [lɪt]	beleuchten; anzünden
to lose [luːz]	lost [lɒst]	lost [lɒst]	verlieren
to make [meɪk]	made [meɪd]	made [meɪd]	machen
to mean [miːn]	meant [ment]	meant [ment]	bedeuten; meinen
to meet [miːt]	met [met]	met [met]	(sich) treffen
to mow [məʊ]	mowed [məʊd]	mown [məʊn]	mähen
to pay [peɪ]	paid [peɪd]	paid [peɪd]	bezahlen
to put [pʊt]	put [pʊt]	put [pʊt]	setzen, stellen, legen
to read [riːd]	read [red]	read [red]	lesen
to ride [raɪd]	rode [rəʊd]	ridden ['rɪdn]	fahren; reiten
to ring [rɪŋ]	rang [ræŋ]	rung [rʌŋ]	klingeln, läuten
to rise [raɪz]	rose [rəʊz]	risen ['rɪzn]	steigen; sich erheben
to run [rʌn]	ran [ræn]	run [rʌn]	laufen, rennen
to say [seɪ]	said [sed]	said [sed]	sagen
to see [siː]	saw [sɔː]	seen [siːn]	sehen; treffen; besuchen; besichtigen
to sell [sel]	sold [səʊld]	sold [səʊld]	verkaufen
to send [send]	sent [sent]	sent [sent]	(zu)schicken
to set [set]	set [set]	set [set]	stellen
to shine [ʃaɪn]	shone [ʃɒn]	shone [ʃɒn]	scheinen; glänzen, leuchten
to shoot [ʃuːt]	shot [ʃɒt]	shot [ʃɒt]	(er-, an-)schießen
to show [ʃəʊ]	showed [ʃəʊd]	shown [ʃəʊn]	zeigen
to shut [ʃʌt]	shut [ʃʌt]	shut [ʃʌt]	schließen
to sing [sɪŋ]	sang [sæŋ]	sung [sʌŋ]	singen
to sit [sɪt]	sat [sæt]	sat [sæt]	sitzen
to sleep [sliːp]	slept [slept]	slept [slept]	schlafen
to slide [slaɪd]	slid [slɪd]	slid [slɪd]	rutschen; gleiten
to smell [smel]	smelt/smelled [smelt/smeld]	smelt/smelled [smelt/smeld]	riechen
to speak [spiːk]	spoke [spəʊk]	spoken ['spəʊkən]	sprechen, reden
to spell [spel]	spelt/spelled [spelt/speld]	spelt/spelled [spelt/speld]	richtig schreiben; buchstabieren
to spend [spend]	spent [spent]	spent [spent]	ausgeben (Geld); verbringen (Zeit)
to spread [spred]	spread [spred]	spread [spred]	(sich) ausbreiten; (sich) verbreiten
to stand [stænd]	stood [stʊd]	stood [stʊd]	stehen; ertragen
to steal [stiːl]	stole [stəʊl]	stolen ['stəʊlən]	stehlen
to stick in [stɪk‿'ɪn]	stuck in [stʌk‿'ɪn]	stuck in [stʌk‿'ɪn]	einkleben
to swim [swɪm]	swam [swæm]	swum [swʌm]	schwimmen
to take [teɪk]	took [tʊk]	taken ['teɪkən]	(mit)nehmen; dauern
to teach [tiːtʃ]	taught [tɔːt]	taught [tɔːt]	unterrichten; lehren
to tear [teə]	tore [tɔː]	torn [tɔːn]	(zer)reißen
to tell [tel]	told [təʊld]	told [təʊld]	erzählen; sagen
to think [θɪŋk]	thought [θɔːt]	thought [θɔːt]	(nach)denken, glauben
to throw [θrəʊ]	threw [θruː]	thrown [θrəʊn]	werfen
to understand [ˌʌndə'stænd]	understood [ˌʌndə'stʊd]	understood [ˌʌndə'stʊd]	verstehen
to wake up [weɪk‿'ʌp]	woke up [wəʊk‿'ʌp]	woken up [ˌwəʊkən‿'ʌp]	aufwachen
to wear [weə]	wore [wɔː]	worn [wɔːn]	tragen (Kleidung)
to win [wɪn]	won [wʌn]	won [wʌn]	gewinnen
to write [raɪt]	wrote [rəʊt]	written ['rɪtn]	schreiben

Bild- und Textquellen

Bildquellen

Titel Blum-Design & Kommunikation, Hamburg
10 ullstein bild, Berlin
11 ullstein bild/Joker/Eckenroth, Berlin, (o. l.); picture alliance/dpaweb/epa Smith, Frankfurt (o. r.); Derya Gök, Wiesbaden (u. r. & l.)
12 ullstein bild/Underwood, Frankfurt (o.); ullstein bild/ddp, Berlin (mi.); Cinetext Bildarchiv/Columbia, Frankfurt (u.)
13 picture alliance/photoshot, Frankfurt (o.); ullstein bild/Michael/Momentfoto, Berlin (o. mi.); Corbis/Charles Gold, Hamburg (u. mi.); Derya Gök, Wiesbaden (u.)
15 Ch. Walsdorf-Lotz (fish and chips); C. F. Shatwell, Heswall, Merseyside, England (tea and gardening); ullstein bild/KPA, Berlin (cheerleaders); picture alliance/dpa/dpaweb/Icon SMI Rich Kane, Frankfurt (baseball); Derya Gök, Wiesbaden (Hummer); picture alliance/Empics Adam Davy, Frankfurt (football); Harald Thumser, Frankfurt (sandwich); Jutta Eckardt-Scheurig, Wiesbaden (queueing); R. Jonczyk, Wennigsen (chewing gum)
17 Tony Stone, Brad Hitz, München
18 Jens Bolhöfer, Hannover (o. r.); Corbis/Picture Press/Macduff, Hamburg (l.); Corbis/Picture Press/Underwood, Hamburg (u. r.)
20 Photo courtesy of the Wm Wrigley Jr. Company (o.); Advertising Agency, Greece (u.)
22 ullstein bild, Berlin (o.); picture alliance/Picture Press/camera press/ED/N/B (u.)
25 Derya Gök, Wiesbaden
27 ullstein bild/Gerlick, Berlin (o. l.); MEV/Mark Kitz (o. r.); Jens Bolhöfer, Hannover (u. r.); terre des hommes/Theo Dom, Osnabrück (u. l.)
28 Michael Tetzlaff, Mörfelden (A); Bernd Junge, Hannover (B); ullstein bild/Peter Arnold Inc. (C); ullstein bild/Dorn, Berlin (D)
29 Jens Bolhöfer, Hannover (E); Schuster GmbH/Liaison, Oberursel (G); Silvestris/Photopress/Schoefmann, Kastl (H); MEV/Mark Kitz, Augsburg (I)
30 picture alliance/Bildagentur, Frankfurt (l.); MEV/Johann Kaiser, Augsburg (mi.); picture alliance/dpa-Report/Hinrich Bäsemann (r.)
31 ullstein bild/Joker/Ausserhofer, Berlin (o.); mauritius images/Oote Boe, Mittenwald (o. mi. r.); mauritius images/Workbookstock, Mittenwald (mi. l.); picture alliance/dpa (u. mi. r.); mauritius images/Word pictures, Mittenwald (u. l.); mauritius images/age, Mittenwald (u. r.)
32 ullstein bild; Berlin (o.); ullstein bild/DIAGENTUR (u.)
34 ullstein bild/Imagebroker.net/Alexander, Berlin
36 picture alliance/dpa Bildarchiv/Jerzy Dabrowski, Frankfurt
37 Jens Bolhöfer, Hannover
38 ullstein/iT, Berlin (Willis, Bullock); picture alliance/IMAGNO/Austrian Archives, Frankfurt (Einstein); ullstein bild/Camera Press Ltd., Berlin (Heinz); Picture Alliance/dpa/epa Sanchez-Gonzalez (Di Caprio)
39 picture alliance/Düren, Frankfurt (o. l.); Corbis/Leland Bobbé (Li) (o. r.); Alamy/Robert Fried (u.)
40 picture alliance/ZB/dpa Bildarchiv, Frankfurt (u.)
41 terre des hommes/Theo Dom, Osnabrück
43 picture alliance/Bildagentur Huber, Frankfurt (o. l.); MEV/Mark Kitz (o. r.); The Library of Congress, USA (u. r.); ullstein bild/imagebroker.net, Berlin (u. l.)
45 ZEFA/Vaeisaenen, Düsseldorf (o. l.); Schuster GmbH/Liaison, Oberursel (o. r.); Manfred Jung, Bad Vilbel (u. r.); ullstein bild, Berlin (u. l.)
47 picture alliance/Bildagentur Huber/Gräfenhain, Frankfurt (o.); picture alliance/Bildagentur Huber/Picture Finders, Frankfurt (mi.); Corbis/Picture Press/Alan Schein, Hamburg (u.)
48 David Klemm, Frankfurt (o.); ullstein bild/KPA, Berlin (u.)
51 Das Fotoarchiv/D. Eisermann, Essen (o. l.); Das Fotoarchiv/J. Cammack, Essen (o. mi.); Okapia/Bios/R. Schoen, Frankfurt (o. r.); Transglobe Agency/Naarden, Hamburg (mi. l.); Silvestris/Janicek, Kastl (u. mi.); IFA-Bilderteam/Walz, Frankfurt (u. r.); Manfred Jung, Bad Vilbel (u. l.)
52 Silvestris/Photopress/Schoefmann, Kastl (r.); David Klemm, Frankfurt (l.)
53 The Library of Congress, USA (o.); picture alliance/HB Verlag/Olaf Meinhardt, Frankfurt (mi. l.); ullstein bild/Herrmann, Frankfurt (u. l.); picture alliance/dpa/dpaweb/UPI, Frankfurt (mi. r.); Corbis/Bettmann, Düsseldorf (u. r.)
55 Wisconsin Historical Society (o.); Derya Gök, Wiesbaden (l.); Harald Thumser, Frankfurt (r.)
57 Harald Thumser, Frankfurt
61 Interfoto, München (o. l.); ullstein bild/Granger, Berlin (o. r.); dpa, Hamburg (u. r.); CORBIS/Hulton-Deutsch Collection, Düsseldorf (u. l.)
62 ullstein bild/Granger, Berlin
63 Das Fotoarchiv/A. Riedmüller, Essen
67 dpa, Hamburg
68 Corbis/Wolfgang Kaehler, Düsseldorf (l.); Corbis/Philip Gould, Düsseldorf (r.)
69 alamy images/North Wind Picture Archives
71 ullstein bild, Berlin (o. l.); Corbis/Bettmann (o. r.); akg-images, Berlin (u.)
73 Corbis/Bettmann, Düsseldorf (o.); Picture Press, Hamburg (u.)
74 Corbis/Hulton-Deutsch Collection
75 ullstein bild/ullstein-POP-EYE (o.); Annelise Kömür, Mainz (u.)
77 MEV, Augsburg (o. l.); picture alliance/dpa/dpaweb/Bernd Settnik, Frankfurt (o. r.); Pamela Hanus, Hannover (u. r.); Picture Press/Kelly-Mooney Photography, Hamburg (u. l.)
78 ullstein bild/dpa, Berlin (o.); ullstein bild/Rzepka, Berlin (u. l.); ullstein bild/Bergmann, Berlin (u. mi. l.); Corbis/Bettmann, Düsseldorf (u. mi. r.); ullstein bild/Bongarts, Berlin (u. r.)
79 picture alliance/dpa/dpaweb/Icon SMI Rich Kane, Frankfurt (Baseballspieler o.); dpa/T. Yamanaka, Frankfurt (Basketballspieler); ullstein bild/Firo, Berlin (American football-Spieler o.); picture alliance/ASA/Chevodian Philippe, Frankfurt (Surfer); picture alliance/dpa/dpaweb/Bernd Settnik, Frankfurt (Volleyballspieler); Corbis/Picture Press/Sean Aidan, Frankfurt (American football-Spieler u.); ullstein bild/Reuters (Baseballspieler u.)
80 ullstein bild/Bongarts, Berlin (o.); picture alliance/ASA/DPPI Franck Faugers, Frankfurt (u.)
81 dpa/Jeff Haynes (u. l.); dpa/Frankfurt (o); ullstein bild/KPA, Berlin (u.)
84 Patrick Buchenot, Hannover (o.); Pamela Hanus, Hannover (u.)
86 Das Fotoarchiv/T. Sobolik, Essen
88 Cinetext Bildarchiv/Allstar, Frankfurt (m.); Cinetext Bildarchiv/Columbia, Frankfurt (l.); Cinetext Bildarchiv/Buena Vista, Frankfurt (r.)
89 picture alliance/dpa/dpaweb/epa Justin Lane, Frankfurt
93 ullstein bild/Eckel, Berlin (o. l.); Food Archiv/C. P. Fischer (o. r.); ullstein bild/Peter Arnold Inc., Berlin (u. l.); Patrick Buchenot, Hannover (u. r.)
94 mauritius/Rosenfeld, Mittenwald (o. l.); Food Archiv/C. P. Fischer (mi. o.); MEV, Augsburg (o. r.); Manfred Jung, Bad Vilbel (u. l.); Derya Gök, Wiesbaden (u. mi. & r.)
95 picture alliance/dpa Bilderdienste/Ken Liu, Frankfurt (l.); David Klemm, Frankfurt (mi.); picture alliance/dpa/dpa-Report/Gero Breloer, Frankfurt (r.)
99 picture alliance/dpa/Stockfood/Food Photography (l.); Envision/Corbis (o. r.); PPP Studio/Zefa/Corbis
101 ullstein bild/Peter Arnold Inc., Berlin
105 ullstein bild/Eckel, Berlin (o. l.); David Klemm, Frankfurt (o. mi.); Patrick Buchenot, Hannover (o. r.); Alamy Ltd./brt Food, London (u. r.); picture alliance/dpa/Stockfood/Food Photography Eising, Frankfurt (u. mi. l. & mi. r.)
109 Dr. Christian Krug, Hannover (o. l. & r., u. r.); Averil Grieve, Hannover (mi. l. & r.); Gabi Uplawski, Hannover (u. l.)
112 Associated Press/Rich Pedroncelli, Frankfurt
113 Vintage, London (Cover)
115 plus49/M. Desjardins (l.); Jutta Eckardt-Scheurig, Wiesbaden (r.)
118 Picture Press/Dave G. Houser, Hamburg (o.); Thomas A. Kelly (u.)

Textquellen

28 "The kids in school with me", © 1994 by the estate of Langston Hughes.
52, 113 "Oh, play that thing", © Roddy Doyle, 2004.
74 "I have a dream", Martin Luther King, 1963.
114 "The earth on turtle's back", www.rice.edu
115 "How the raven got its black feathers", Cowl MonBeDel, British Columbia www.monbedel.com
116 "Marathon Macho", adapted from Teen Angst? Naaah ... A Quasi-Autobiography by Ned Vizzini, © 2000.used with permission from Free Spirit Publishing Inc., Minneapolis, MN; All rights reserved. 001-800-735-7323; www.freespirit.com
118 "The story of the first Thanksgiving", © Elaine & Don Bolognese. In: The story of Thanksgiving, Scholastic, New York 1991.
120 "improve", PONS Großwörterbuch Englisch-Deutsch/Deutsch-Englisch, Ernst Klett Sprachen, Stuttgart: 2005, S. 478.

Liedquellen

19 "Does your chewing gum lose its flavor on the bedpost overnight?", lyrics and music by Billy Rose, Marty Bloom and Ernest Breuer © 1924 (Renewed 1951) EMI Mills Music Inc., USA worldwide prints rights controlled Warner Bros Inc., USA/IMP ltd. reproduced by permission of International Music Publications Ltd.
44 "New York, New York", © lyrics by F. Ebb and music by J. Kander, 1977.
62 "Return to innocence", © Enigma, 1993.
75 "Mr Cab Driver", © Lenny Kravitz, 1989.

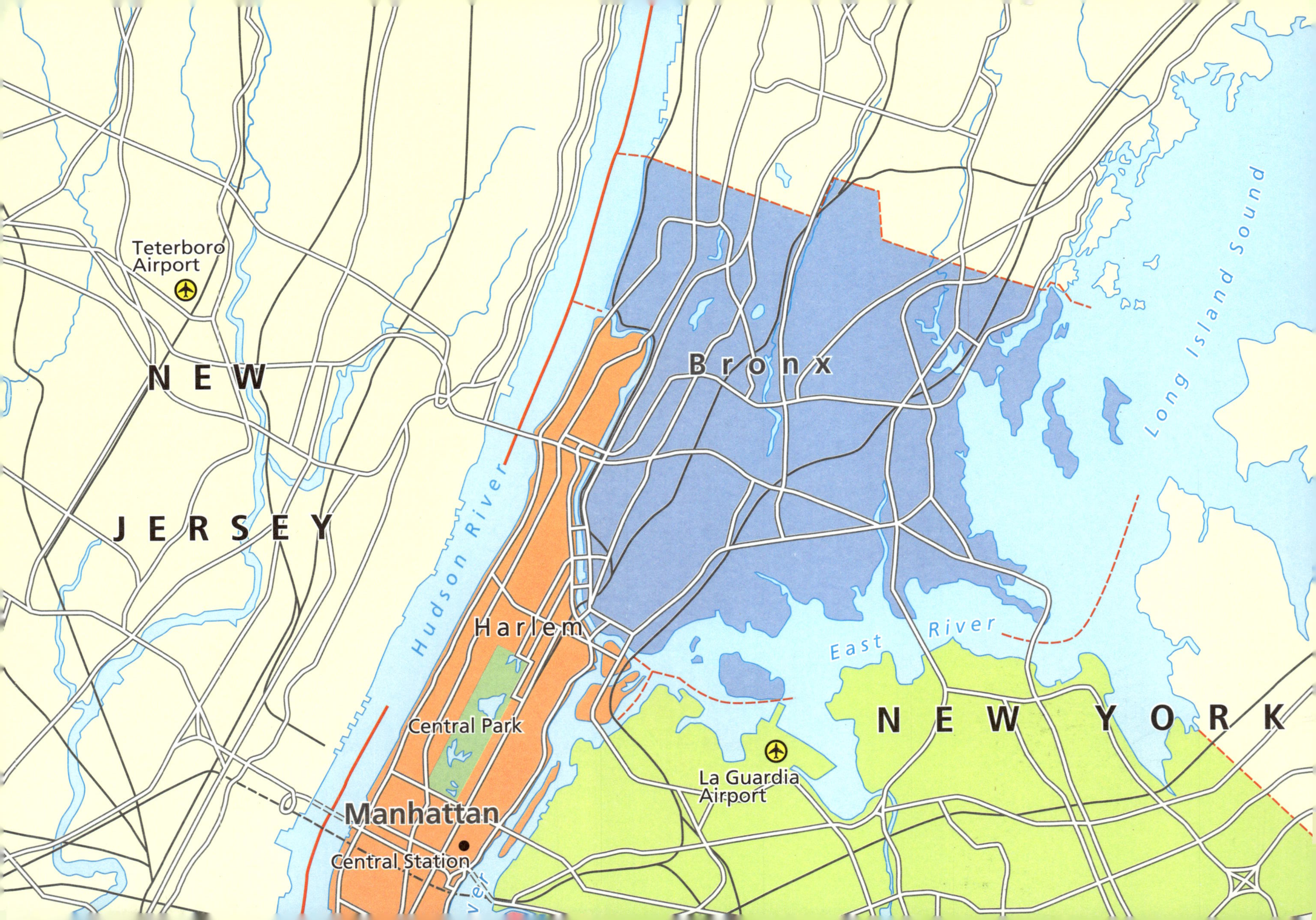

Teterboro Airport
NEW JERSEY
Bronx
Long Island Sound
Hudson River
Harlem
East River
Central Park
NEW YORK
La Guardia Airport
Manhattan
Central Station